The Literary Guide and
Companion to Middle Englan

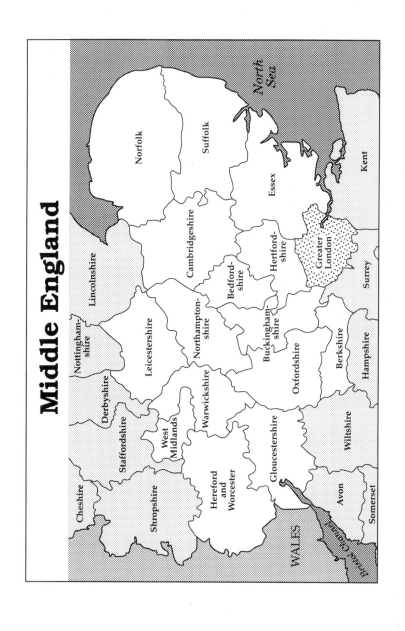

Middle England

The Literary Guide and Companion to Middle England

ROBERT M. COOPER

Ohio University Press

Athens

Ohio University Press books are printed on acid-free paper ⊗

Library of Congress Cataloging-in-Publication Data

Cooper, Robert M.
  The literary guide and companion to middle England / by Robert M.
Cooper.
    p. cm.
  Includes index.
  ISBN 0-8214-1032-6 (cloth). — ISBN 0-8214-1033-4 (paper)
  1. Literary landmarks—England—Guidebooks. 2. Authors, English-
-Homes and haunts—England. 3. English literature—History and
criticism. 4. England in literature. I. Title.
PR109.C68 1992
820.9—dc20   92-13580
                                                CIP

LONDON
NEIGHBORS

I

I never knew how my husband planned to dedicate this book. His last book had been dedicated to me, and when I would ask him about this one, he would just grin and say, "Wait and see." At that time we had only one grandchild whose name, like mine, is Polly. Knowing my husband's delight in wordplay, I had toyed with the idea that this book might have a dedication something like, "To Polly, too." But now we have three grandchildren, and I think their grandfather would like this book dedicated:

TO

POLLY, SAMANTHA, AND WALTER

CONTENTS

II. THE HEART OF ENGLAND

GLOUCESTERSHIRE

HEREFORD AND WORCESTER

III. ESSEX AND EAST ANGLIA

MAPS

FOREWORD

At the time of my husband's death, he had completed all the research and writing of this book. He had not, however, arranged for the maps, done the final reading to check for accuracy of spelling, dates and highway numbers, and he had not completed the indices. I have tried my very best to complete these tasks with the care and precision that would meet his demanding standards of excellence. I hope with all my heart that I have done a job he would be proud of. But if any errors remain, they are mine.

Polly Cooper

PREFACE

In the preface of the first volume in this series, *The Literary Guide and Companion to Southern England*, I wrote:

This book was written for the person who unabashedly loves travel, loves England, and loves English literature. In short, for somebody remarkably like the person I was when I began to plan my first trip to Britain and look for just such a book—in vain.

To prepare the best possible itinerary before I got there, and to best use my time and enrich each moment after my arrival, I wanted answers in particular to six specific questions. But I found no answers.

Since then a number of books on literary England have appeared, some of real value. But each has its own different purpose, and therefore its own format and choice of contents.

And so, my initial questions remain to be answered for Middle England, too:

1. If I go to such-and-such, what else is there of literary interest nearby? Well, while in London you'll probably want to run out to Ayot St. Lawrence to see George Bernard Shaw's wonderfully preserved home. But just down the road and open to view is a place equally rich in literary associations: Hatfield House, the great country manor built by the Earl of Salisbury in the days of James I on the very spot where in 1558 Elizabeth I learned that the death of her sister, Bloody Mary, had transformed her in a twinkling from royal prisoner to queen.

That notable diarist, Samuel Pepys, stopped by Hatfield House in 1661 to have a look, and tried to steal his lordship's dog. And in 1835 a twenty-four-year-old London reporter named Charles Dickens came up to cover a fire that destroyed the manor's west wing—a scene he later put to spectacular use in *Oliver Twist*. And in the 1870s Lewis Carroll, fresh from the triumph of *Alice in Wonderland*, was a regular guest, spinning out similar stories for the children of his host, the Lord Salisbury who was thrice prime minister.

2. What's the most interesting route to take from such-and-such to so-and-so? This can be real serendipity. Suppose, for instance, you are in Stratford-upon-Avon with historic Tewkesbury as your next stop. You can zip down the thirty miles between the two on the A 439 and A 435. Most people do.

But in not much more time, you can take far more pleasant byroads and discover such unexpected delights as the ruins of Hailes Abbey of Chaucer's Pardoner in *The Canterbury Tales* . . . the site of T. S. Eliot's empty, desolate pool in *Burnt Norton* . . . and the little village of Adlestrop, where Jane Austen used to visit her grandfather, and where a momentary glimpse of its railway sign (still there, but now in a bus shelter), moved Edward Thomas to compose a memorable poem.

3. I know the usual things about it, but is there anything else of literary interest connected with this place (this street, this house, this room) I'm in? Sometimes the answer can be most rewarding. Nearly everybody who goes to Windsor Castle hustles from State Apartments to Crown Jewels to Queen Mary's Dolls' House, then rushes back to London in time for tea.

But stretching from the castle is Windsor Great Park, where Shakespeare's Falstaff in *The Merry Wives of Windsor* made his way through the towering oaks to his rendezvous with the wives, only to run into their irate husbands instead. This is the park, too, which Thomas Gray hailed in his "Distant Prospect of Eton College" . . . Alexander Pope rhapsodized in a rare pastoral outburst called "Windsor Forest" . . . and Shelley strolled among those same oaks of Falstaff and sailed his little paper boats on Virginia Water when he lived at the forest's edge in 1815.

4. Once you arrive in a town or the general area of a place, how do you actually find the place itself—say, Burnt Norton? Often it's not easy. The usual descriptions for Burnt Norton don't help much: "One and a half miles north of Chipping Camden." You need to know that after you reach Chipping Camden, you take the Mickleton Road, then turn left into a farm lane as it goes downhill, then go through woods for half a mile. There's no missing the house when you get to it; it's now a school.

5. What is the best way—i.e., the shortest, quickest, most comprehensive way—to cover a town with a number of literary sites? For such, I've included detailed itineraries and, where called for, route maps locating specific stops of interest.

6. Are there any places of literary interest where I can get a meal, a pint of half-and-half, or even stay overnight? Yes, indeed—many! All you have to do is turn to the special section of the index headed "Hotels, Inns, Restaurants, and Pubs" and you'll find them listed town by town.

While you're doing the usual in Oxford, for instance, just a short drive along the Thames brings you to Godstow, where Matthew Arnold's Scholar-Gipsy meandered about after dropping out of school, and where in Tennyson's play *Rosamond* Henry II's mistress found refuge in Godstow's nunnery from the fury of his jealous Queen Eleanor.

At Godstow, right on the river's edge, is the charming old Tudor inn called The Trout, with literary associations of the grandest kind. While they were painting the murals on the walls of Oxford's Debating Hall, for example, Dante Gabriel Rossetti sent his young protegé William Morris up to The Trout to use the innkeeper's daughter as a model. But the girl's mother would hear none of it. Almost before he knew it, Morris was back on the road to Oxford.

And as you sit on The Trout's patio, sipping your drink and watching the peacocks strut about the garden, you can look down at the river flowing by your feet and dream it's a pleasant afternoon in July of 1862, with a little boat gliding by that very spot. Pulling the oars is an Oxford mathematics teacher in straw hat and flannels, entertaining a little girl named Alice by making up, as they go along, a wild, fanciful tale about a rabbit hole filled with characters like a Mad Hatter, a Duchess, and a White Rabbit.

At Bromsgrove near Worcester, you can stay at a delightful hotel called Perry Hall, an ivy-colored mansion that was once the boyhood home of A. E. Housman and his younger brother Laurence, author of *Victoria Regina*. If your room overlooks the garden, you can look down and see a cherry tree with a plaque announcing that it's a gift of Tatsuzo Hijikata of the Japanese Housman Society.

And if you're a Charles Dickens enthusiast, you can practically eat, drink, and sleep your way through England without leaving the company of Dickens and his characters, in places such as The Eight Bells in Hatfield, where Bill Sikes recoiled in horror at his table as he listened to a mountebank-peddler extol a potion wondrous for removing beer-stains, mudstains, blood-stains . . . Blood-stains? Sikes had just come from murdering Nancy.

At Ipswich in Suffolk, there's The Great White Horse Inn, where Mr. Pickwick gets lost in its labyrinthine passageways, wanders into the wrong bedroom as he undresses for the night, and becomes aware of a middle-aged lady in yellow curl papers similarly engaged in bedtime chores.

Bury St. Edmunds has The Angel, one of Dickens's own favorites . . . and Chigwell in Essex has The King's Head, which Dickens, in *Barnaby*

Rudge calls The Maypole . . . and Tewkesbury has The Royal Hop Pole, whose liquid refreshments so enticed Mr. Pickwick and party that after they piled back into their coach following dinner, he and Mr. Allen fell fast asleep for the next thirty miles . . . and at—well, on and on it goes.

Surely no writer ever travelled England as extensively as Charles Dickens, or knew its hostelries so well. But then Dickens loved travel, and England, and literature, too.

I hope you will find this book fun in the best sense of the word—fun to plan your trip with, fun to use at the various stops along the way while you're there, and fun to recollect with after you're back home.

It certainly was fun to write.

ACKNOWLEDGMENTS

The editing, maps and indexing of this book could not have been done without the help and dedicated interest of Charles Wilkinson of the English Department of Rhodes College, Loretta Martin of Memphis State University's Cartographic Services Department, and Bill Short of Rhodes College's Burrow Library. I am deeply indebted to them and express my grateful thanks.

Maps by
The Cartographic Services Laboratory
Memphis State University
Memphis, Tennessee

HERTFORDSHIRE

Hertfordshire

1. Waltham Cross to Baldock

2. Knebworth to the County's End

3. Access or Connecting Routes

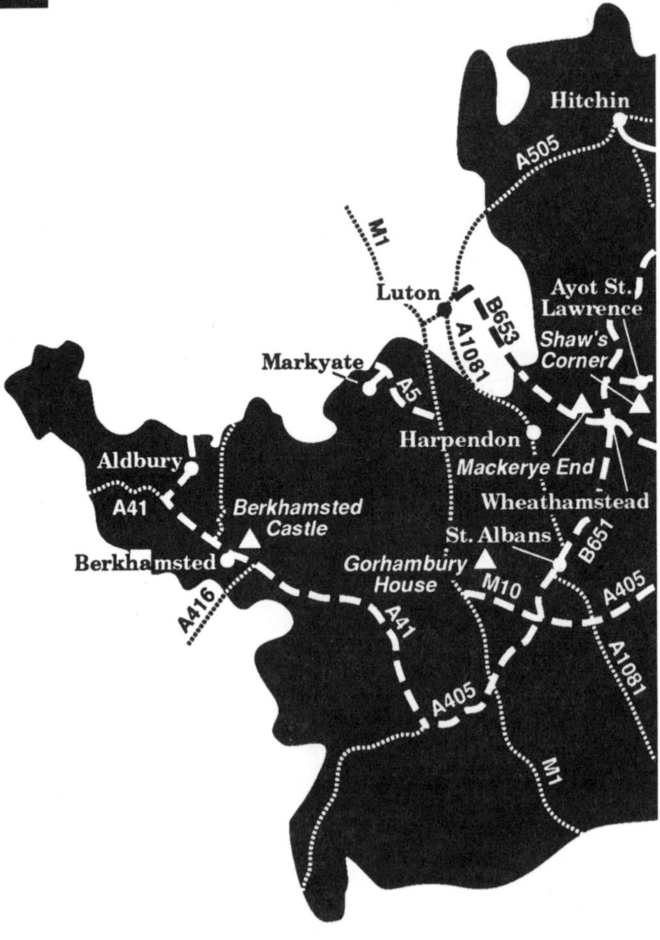

Hitchin

A505

M1

Luton

B653

A1081

Ayot St.
Lawrence

Shaw's
Corner

Markyate

A5

Harpendon

Mackerye End

Aldbury

Wheathamstead

A41

Berkhamsted
Castle

St. Albans

B651

Berkhamsted

Gorhambury
House

A416

M10

A405

A41

A1081

A405

M1

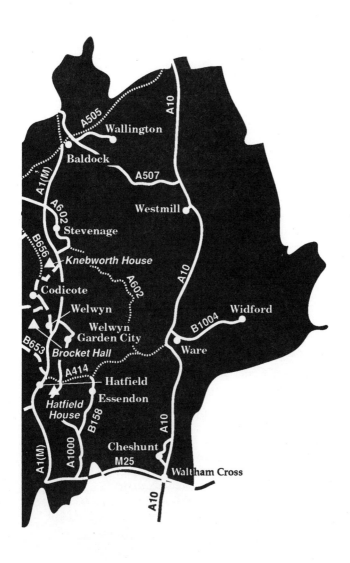

"I cannot see that London has any great advantage over the country, for my part, except the shops and public places. The country is a vast deal pleasanter, is it not, Mr. Bingley?"

"When I am in the country," he replied, " I never wish to leave it; and when I am in town, it is pretty much the same. They have each their advantages, and I can be equally happy in either."

Mrs. Bennet and Mr. Bingley in Jane Austen's *Pride and Prejudice*

"When a man is tired of London, he is tired of life; for there is in London all that life can afford."

Samuel Johnson in Boswell's *Life of Dr. Johnson*

"Those slender ties, that prove as gossamer in the rending atmosphere of a metropolis, bind faster . . . in hearty, homely, loving Hertsfordshire."

Charles Lamb in his "Mackerye End"

Had Mrs. Bennet heard Dr. Johnson, she would have been most annoyed: the "country" she so delighted in was Hertfordshire (HART-ford-sh'r) and Charles Lamb would seem to be on her side. In a sonnet written when he was twenty, he goes even further. Heading for Hertfordshire and recalling the "merrier days" of childhood romps there, he inveighs against London:

I turn my back on thy detested walls,
Proud City!

Not too long after this, however, Lamb was writing a friend, "[I] have cried out with fulness of joy at the multitudiness scenes of life in the crowded streets of dear London." Here Lamb is not only supporting Johnson, but practically echoing him. For when Boswell, confessing no relish for the beauties of Nature, agreed that Greenwich Park might be fine, but "not equal to Fleet Street," Johnson replied promptly, "You are right, Sir." London to Johnson *was* Fleet Street, even as London to Lamb was "the motley Strand crowded with to and fro passengers." Fleet Street, of course, becomes the Strand. They are a single street.

Most likely, if pressed, Lamb would have wound up backing Mr. Bingley, as wouldn't most of us? And therein lies one of the special charms of Hertfordshire. As a London neighbor, it can offer all the magic of the metropolis at its very doorstep. Yet three miles off the A 10 Motorway and the hurtling six-lane traffic that roars in and out of London, one can get lost in the little village where Lamb visited his great aunt Bruton at Mackerye End . . . and searching for the little lane that leads to the shrine of George Bernard Shaw, the traveller can find the countryside so isolated and empty that he begins to despair of even finding a pub for lunch. And, in England, that's empty!

Holding forth in his Gough Square parlor just off Fleet Street, Dr. Johnson liked to boast "there is more learning and science within the circumference of ten miles from where we now sit than in all the rest of the kingdom." Well, in its own right, within a radius of thirty miles from that same parlor—which still exists—Hertfordshire can counter with literary associations that run from Becket to Bunyan, from Bacon to Bulwer-Lytton, and from Lewis Carroll to George Orwell, to say nothing of Shaw.

1. Waltham Cross To Baldock

From the heart of London—the Strand and Fleet Street, say, or the Tower of London—you can get directly into Hertfordshire simply by going north on Kingland Road, which in fact is the A 10 that takes you into Hertfordshire at Waltham Cross, just past Edmonton.

Waltham Cross

Waltham Cross via Edmonton makes a fitting literary entry into Hertford-shire. For on Church Street in Edmonton lived at one time or another both John Keats and Charles Lamb. After the sudden death of Keats's father, in 1804, his mother soon remarried, just as quickly separated, and went to Edmonton to live with her mother on Church Street. There Keats, who had been going to school in nearby Enfield, joined them in 1805.

When his mother died in 1810, Keats was apprenticed to an Edmonton surgeon, but remained with his grandmother until mid-1814.[1] During these

[1] The surgeon also lived on Church Street, at No. 7, and a plaque now marks the place.

years, he discovered the world of literature, did a prose translation of the *Aeneid*, and wrote some less than promising poems, such as "Imitation of Spenser" and "Sonnet to Byron." If they are less than distinguished, however, one should remember that they came between his seventeenth and nineteenth birthdays . . . and that the glorious outburst of 1819—with "Eve of St. Agnes," "Ode to a Nightingale," and the other great odes—was only five years away.

A little west of Keats's grandmother's home was a house called Bay Cottage (now called Lamb Cottage). To it in 1833 Charles Lamb brought his sister Mary for treatment after another in the long series of mental breakdowns that haunted their lives. Lamb died the following year, and is buried in Edmonton churchyard, as is Mary, who died thirteen years later.

The Lambs had lived for six years prior to Edmonton in Enfield, which lies between Edmonton and Waltham Cross, and is—like Edmonton—now part of Greater London.

The "Cross" in Waltham Cross came from Edward I's choosing it as one of the spots to erect a cross to mark the route taken by the procession that brought home to London the body of his queen, Eleanor, after her death in 1290.[2] In a letter written during his Enfield days, Lamb refers to this, and includes a few lines of poetry the cross inspired, with a pun underlining the contrast between Edward's devotion and the beastly treatment George IV gave his queen Caroline, daughter of German Duke Brunswick-Wolfenbüttel, and recently deceased. The pun is a good deal better than the poetry. Lamb writes: "Strolling to Waltham Cross the other day, I hit off these lines. It is one of the crosses which Edward I caused to be built for his wife at every town where her corpse rested between Northamptonshire and London":

> A stately cross each sad spot doth attest
> Whereat the corpse of Eleanor did rest,
> From Harby fetch'd—her spouse so honoured her—
> To sleep with royal dust at Westminster.
> And, if less pompous obsequies were thine
> Duke Brunswick's daughter, princely Caroline,
> Grudge not, great ghost, nor count thy funeral losses:
> Thou in thy life-time hads't thy share of crosses.

Twenty-five years after Lamb's death, Anthony Trollope came to live in Waltham Cross. Trollope is an author who, though not one of England's truly

[2]Waltham Cross still has one of the three crosses that survive. The others are in Geddington and Hardingstone, both in Northamptonshire.

great writers, managed to maintain a level of quality that is remarkable. This is all the more so when one considers that writing was secondary to his full-time job with the postal service.

It was a transfer from assignments in Ireland and the West Indies to the position of Post Office surveyor of England's Eastern Division that enabled him, for the first time in twenty-six years, to establish a real home. His new territory included the counties of Essex, Suffolk, Norfolk, Cambridgeshire, Huntingdonshire, and the major part of Hertfordshire. Since he yearned for the literary world of London, he and his wife chose Hertfordshire as their home base. "In December 1859," he wrote in his autobiography, "I settled myself at a residence about twelve miles from London, in Hertfordshire . . . which was too grandly called Waltham House."

It was grand enough. Comely, capacious, and solidly early Georgian, it had four stories of mellowing brick, plus a walled garden complete with sundial, summer house, and a small pool. From the main body of the house there were two wings. In one he put his hunting dogs (hunting was another of Hertfordshire's attractions), and in the other the postal clerks who worked under him.

It was "a rickety old place requiring much repair and occasionally not as weathertight as it should be," he said. But he loved it, and after the initial lease, bought it. He had joined the old-fashioned aristocracy of the land: he had become a country gentleman at last. Not bad for a man whose mother had once run a department store in Cincinnati, Ohio.[3]

Gentleman or not, Trollope got right to work at both his jobs. His routine was awesome. He was up each morning at five, and a servant brought him coffee. By six he was at his writing desk, scribbling away diligently until nine-thirty sharp, with his watch in front of him to make sure he was writing 250 words each quarter hour to achieve his goal of 2,500 words per day. Promptly at nine-thirty he put down his pen, dressed, ate a hearty breakfast, and began his official day of postal work.

Amazing! Yet not to Trollope. For writing to him was largely a mechanical thing calling for discipline rather than inspiration. Hardly settled into Waltham House, he plunged at once into producing *Framley Parsonage* in serial form for Thackeray's new *Cornhill* magazine. "Fabricating a hodgepodge"

---

[3]She was Frances Trollope, and when the store failed, she returned to England to become a fairly successful novelist herself. Legend has it her young women employees' behavior so shocked the good people of Cincinnati that they invented a word to describe them: "trollops." (Why spoil a good story by pointing out that the *Oxford English Dictionary* shows the word in use as early as 1615, meaning—that's right—"slattern or slut.")

were his words for it, while conceding the "characters are so well-handled the work from the first was popular."

Trollope remains popular, as highly successful television versions of his novels attest, more than a century after his death. And rightly so. Some of his best novels—*Orley Farm* (1862), *The Small House at Allington* (1864), *Can You Forgive Her?* (1864), and *The Last Chronicle of Barset* (1867) among them— were written during his stay at Waltham House. He could justly say: "I feel confident than in amount no other writer contributed so much during that time to English literature."

In addition to all the novels, there were political, critical, social, and sporting articles for "periodicals without number."

To his sorrow, in 1870 Trollope was forced to conclude that he must give up Waltham House, mainly for financial reasons. He had lived a bit lavishly, had given up his postal position, lost money in a futile bid for a seat in parliament, and lost more on costly ventures for his sons. Poor soul! It took two years to sell the house—and he lost another £800 on the sale.

Today no trace of Waltham House remains. It was totally demolished in 1936.

Just beyond Waltham Cross, you run into the M 25, and you can take it west to the A 1 (or M 1) that leads to a host of literary locations in Hertford-shire. Or, you can postpone that a bit and keep going north on the A 10 to Ware and Westmill, with a side jaunt to Widford. All three are worth more than an asterisk.

Ware—Widford—Westmill

Ware   Eight miles above Waltham Cross, Ware today is a town with about fifteen thousand people and a bustling High Street that still has gabled and straight-fronted houses dating from the sixteenth century. Some of them provided the setting that July day in 1553 when poor little Lady Jane Grey, great-granddaughter of Henry VII, learned that she was to be Queen of England (only sixteen, she fainted at the unwelcome news) for a reign that lasted exactly the nine days it took Henry VIII's daughter Mary to supplant her.

An extra fillip in going up to Ware from London is knowing that you are pretty much paralleling the wild runaway route taken by John Gilpin, the redoubtable hero of William Cowper's hilarious poem, "The Diverting History of John Gilpin."

"A linen draper bold," of "famous London town," Gilpin set out from the heart of the city headed for Edmonton. There, at the Bell Inn, he intended to celebrate the anniversary of their wedding day with his spouse of "twice-ten tedious years"—their first holiday in all that time.

On the appointed day his chaise, filled with wife and party, goes on without him, leaving him to follow on a horse he had to borrow from a friend. Just as he is about to mount, however, three customers come into his shop:

> So down he came; for loss of time
> Although it grieved him sore,
> Yet loss of pence, full well he knew
> Would trouble him much more.

Finally, John and his less than cooperative horse go careening off to Edmonton, dogs barking, children screaming, cloak flying in the wind. Wife and friends see his reckless advance from the balcony of the Bell:

> Stop, stop, John Gilpin!—Here's the house—
> They all at once did cry;
> The dinner waits, and we are tired
> Said Gilpin—So am I!

Much good that did:

> But yet his horse was not a whit
> Inclined to tarry there;
> For why?—his owner had a house
> Full ten miles off, at Ware.

If you have a nagging feeling that you've heard of Ware in some other connection equally odd, you're right. It is Sir Toby Belch in Shakespeare's *Twelfth Night*, egging cowardly Sir Andrew Aguecheek to challenge the supposed page Cesario to a duel, however much he must stretch the truth to do so. Sir Toby says:

> [Tell him] as many lies as will lie
> in thy sheet of paper, although the sheet
> were big enough for the bed of Ware in England,
> set 'em down.

The "Great Bed of Ware," as it has been known for centuries, ten feet nine inches square, was originally in an inn in Ware. Reputedly, it could hold four couples at a time—to what end no one says. The bed is also referred to in *Epicoene* (1609), the play by Shakespeare's contemporary Ben Jonson, and in eighteenth-century playwright George Farquhar's *The Recruiting Officer* (1706).

But if you do go on to Ware, don't look for the great bed there. It is now in the Victoria and Albert Museum in London, and looks mighty lumpy.

Widford   Four miles northeast of Ware, on the country road marked B 1004, is the little village of Widford. For Charles Lamb it was a cherished spot as a child, a needed retreat as a man. In a mansion called Blakesware, a mile or so to the east, lived Grandma Mary Field, a favorite among the relatives he said were "sprinkled about in Hertfordshire."

The mansion wasn't hers, but in Lamb's boyhood it might just as well have been. By then Mary Field, for decades housekeeper-companion to the Plumers who owned the place, had been left as caretaker, alone save for a handful of servants.

It was an immense, rambling structure, and had been elegant. After it was pulled down in 1820, Lamb records in one of the *Last Essays of Elia* (1833), "Blakesmoor in H - - - - shire," written in his fifties, of a time when he went some few miles out of his way while journeying northward to view what remained. Could this "mere dust and rubbish" have been that fine old family mansion, he wonders.

Yes, even in his childhood "it was an old deserted place," yet "traces of the splendour of past inmates were everywhere apparent," and "every plank and panel of that house for me had magic in it." His sister Mary, too, made use of her memories of it in her tale, "The Young Mahometan."

Even more important in the youth of Charles Lamb was a lovely girl named Ann Simmons, a year or so younger than he, who lived about a half mile from Blakesware. Charles fell in love with her in 1792, when at seventeen he came to nurse his grandmother, who was dying.

Family opposition (hers, not his) soon broke up the romance, and she went on to marry a John Bartrum. But Lamb never forgot her. She is the "Alice W - - - n" of several essays; "Anne, the mild-eyed maid" of some of his sonnets; and, in part, the "Rosamund" of his short novel, *Rosamund Gray* (1798). Most poignant of all is that heartbreaking little essay, "Dream Children."

Here Lamb—in true life the lonely bachelor forced to devote his years to the care of an unstable sister—imagines that he *has* married Anne (again "Alice" in the essay), and that after her early death their two children, John and young Alice, beg him to tell them some stories about their pretty dead mother. So he describes seven long years of courtship, and tries to explain it all,

When, suddenly turning to Alice, the soul of the first Alice looked out at her eyes with such a reality of re-presentment, that I became in doubt which of them stood there before me, or whose that bright hair was; and while I stood gazing, both the children gradually grew fainter to my view, receding, and still receding, till nothing at last but two mournful features were seen in the uttermost distance, which, without speech, strangely impressed upon me the effects of speech: "We are not of Alice, nor of thee, nor are we children at all. The children of Alice call Bartrum father, We are nothing; less than nothing, and dreams."

Westmill There is yet one more stop the devotee of Charles Lamb will want to make while in the area of Ware before turning westward into other parts of Hertfordshire, and that is Westmill.

Today Westmill—eight miles north of Ware and just off the A 10 to the west—is the kind of little village you want to hug, with some charming old houses and maybe three hundred people in all. Here in the late eighteenth century a Londoner named Francis Field owned a delightful thatched country cottage called Button Snap.

Though he was a shopkeeper, he had, in Lamb's words, "pretensions above his rank." He enjoyed associating with the theatrical world, and claimed to be a close enough friend of Richard Brinsley Sheridan to get free tickets to that dramatist-actor's Drury Lane Theatre.

But his interest to us is that in 1775 he stood as one of the godfathers at Charles Lamb's christening, and when he died left Button Snap to Charles in his will. Lamb lived there from 1812 to 1815, when he sold it for £50. Happily, the cottage not only still exists, but it is now owned by the Charles Lamb Society. It is marked by a plaque saying "Dedicated to Elia's Memory," and you can reach it in Westmill by taking the turn to Cherry Green.

Hatfield House and Hatfield

As noted earlier, when leaving Waltham Cross on the A 10 toward Ware, the traveller crosses the M 25 and can, if he likes, go west on it rather than continuing north. Within six miles the M 25 brings you to the A 1000, which—together with the A 1 that parallels it—will take you to Hatfield House and Hatfield, Stevenage, and Baldock and Wallington. The route is richly rewarding: the literary associations range from Charles Dickens and Lewis Carroll to E. M. Forster, George Orwell, and Samuel Pepys.

Hatfield House   On the morning of August 7, 1661, Pepys was up betimes, a-horseback by four A.M., and on his way out of London on a day's holiday from his duties as clerk of the King's Ships. He records his jaunt in his celebrated *Diary*: "At Hatfield we bayted [i.e. stopped] and walked into the great house through all the courts; and I would fain have stolen a pretty dog that followed me, but I could not, which troubled me."

The great house that Pepys had gone to see was Hatfield House, then fairly new, built in 1610–11 after James I got Robert Cecil, first Earl of Salisbury, to accept it in return for his own manor of Theobald's in Cheshunt, outside Waltham Cross. In Pepys's day it was already a showpiece, and it still is, with a magnificent house, a maze in the gardens, and a great park with "Queen Elizabeth's Oak."

The young daughter of Henry VIII and Anne Boleyn had been confined to the old Hatfield Palace, then in the park, by her half-sister, Queen Mary (yes, the "Bloody" one), and is said to have been standing under this very tree when messengers galloped up to announce that Mary was dead. Thus, in the twinkling of an eye, Elizabeth was transformed from prisoner to monarch.

The Salisburys have long been among England's powerful families, and one of them (the third Marquis of Salisbury and later thrice prime minister) was presiding at Hatfield House when Lewis Carroll came, during the New Year's of 1872–73, to visit and to photograph the Salisbury children. Carroll, who had sought the assignment, admitted that what opened the doors to him was the success of *Alice in Wonderland* (1865).

He was pressed into service as storyteller and noted "the appetite of the party for stories was insatiable." Visits and tales became a pattern for the next few year-end holidays, but in 1875–76 he grew weary of the routine: "I declined to undertake my usual role of storyteller in the morning, and so (I hope) broke the role of always being expected to do it."

This may well have been why several years elapsed before Carroll was there again. In 1878 Lady Salisbury did write him, "Though you have forsworn children's parties, perhaps grave old folks may tempt you." Carroll did return in 1884, and some of his Hatfield House stories found a place in his *Sylvie and Bruno* (1889), but it's hardly his best work.

Hatfield   Immediately west of Hatfield House, on the A 1, is Hatfield itself; in fact, the main entrance to the park is just opposite to the Hatfield railway station. Hatfield retains a touch of the small town, despite a population of over twenty-five thousand. It was a spectacular fire at Hatfield House that brought Charles Dickens to Hatfield, a happier circumstance than he thought at the time.

Only twenty-four and a reporter for London's *Morning Chronicle*, he was ordered one day in December 1835, to cover a fire raging at Hatfield House. He was none too pleased. Not only would this break a date with Kate (Catherine) Hogarth, whom he was ardently courting, but it would delay the next in a series of articles he was writing for the *Evening Chronicle* (published collectively in 1836–37 as *Sketches by Boz*).

In a hasty note to Kate, he complained of having "only 3 hours notice and being previously out of bed until 3 o'Clock." But the fire made a great story. It utterly destroyed the west wing of Hatfield House, and in the bargain killed the aged Marchioness of Salisbury (grandmother of that same third Marquis who later was to entertain Lewis Carroll). Moreover, covering the story was to provide Dickens with two grand scenes for his first real novel, *Oliver Twist* (1837–38).

Toward the end of *Oliver Twist*, the robber Bill Sikes murders his girl Nancy: "Of all bad deeds that, under cover of the darkness, had been committed within wide London's bounds, that was the worst."

Fleeing toward St. Albans, Sikes reaches Hatfield by nine o'clock at night, creeps into a small public house, sits alone in the farthest corner, falls asleep, and is awakened by "an antic fellow, half pedler [sic] and half mountebank," who proceeds to tout his "infallible and invaluable composition for removing all sorts of stain, rust, dirt, mildew, spick, speck, spot" and on and on he goes. Seeing the cowering Sikes, he cries:

"Here is a stain upon the hat of a gentleman in company, that I'll take clean out, before he can order me a pint of ale."

"Hah!" cried Sikes, starting up. "Give that back."

"I'll take it clean out, Sir," replied the man, winking to the company. "Whether it is a wine-stain, fruit-stain, beer-stain, mud-stain, or blood-stain ———" Blood-stain? Sikes bolts, and is gone.

Next comes the fire scene, based on the one at Hatfield House. Hiding in terror in a shed beyond the town, Sikes is drawn outside by the noise of distant shouting, and sees "The apertures, where doors and windows stood an hour ago, disclosed a mass of raging fire; walls rocked and crumbled into the burning well; the molten lead and iron poured down, white hot upon the ground." But for Sikes, there is no escaping his guilt and fear. "Suddenly, he took the desperate resolution of going back to London."

You can, if you like, see both these settings from *Oliver Twist* for yourself—and think of Bill Sikes as you do. The "small public house" he crept into is the Eight Bells, on the bend where Fore Street and Park come together; the tap room where the peddler accosts Sikes still does a brisk business.

And in season, Hatfield House is open to the public most days of the week. From the M 25, it is easily reached by driving about six miles north on the A 1000 and then turning off where it is signposted. In the staterooms of the house itself are tapestries, paintings, and furniture collected over the centuries . . . . and in the garden is the surviving wing of the Royal Palace that held Elizabeth I as a girl, with some of her relics.

Essendon—Welwyn Garden City—Welwyn

Next major literary stop along the A 1 is Stevenage. But first, worth mention in the immediate vicinity of Hatfield are Essendon, Welwyn Garden City, and Welwyn.

Essendon   A village of fewer than one thousand people, Essendon, a few miles east of Hatfield on the B 158, has little to go on about except a superb view of the countryside, an engaging pub (on West End Lane with the appropriate name of the Salisbury Crest), and a church with a Wedgwood basalt font. But to the creator of Peter Rabbit, Beatrix Potter, as a child it meant everything. Her grandmother lived in Essendon and periodic visits to her provided the young Beatrix with almost the only relief from the restrictive, lonely, "unloved birthplace" where she lived with her parents until well into middle age. No wonder she later called Essendon "the place I love best in the world."

Welwyn Garden City   Welwyn (WELL-in) and Welwyn Garden City are not to be confused, especially if you're trying to reach Ayot St. Lawrence and the home of George Bernard Shaw directly from London. Welwyn Garden City's the big one—over forty thousand people—about three miles north of Hatfield on the east side of the A 1. It was created in 1919 by Sir Ebenezer Howard, whose concept of fully planned cities, springing full-blown from their creator's head, anticipated American William J. Levitt and his vaunted Levittowns by fifty years. Sir Ebenezer called his "garden cities."

Welwyn   Welwyn, five miles north of Hatfield and to the west of the A 1, has only eight thousand people, but it *is* the southeast approach to Shaw's home—about which, more later. Edward Young, author of a number of plays and poems, but best known for his lugubrious "Night Thoughts," was rector at Welwyn from 1730 until his death in 1765.

In 1781 Samuel Johnson, who wrote a life of Young that declared him "with all his defects . . . a man of genius and a poet," stopped in Welwyn with Boswell on their way north to Bedfordshire, and how they came to visit the poet's house makes a nice story. Boswell very much wished to see where Young had lived. But neither Boswell nor Johnson knew Young's son, then living there, and Boswell feared that if he suggested they approach the son directly Johnson would forbid it.

So Boswell sneaked off to try it on his own. If his reception there proved unfavorable, he'd say nothing about it; if it proved agreeable, well and good. It was agreeable: "Sir," said the junior Young, "I should think it a great honour to see Dr. Johnson here." And so it came about. Boswell ends his account dryly: "Dr. Johnson luckily made no enquiry how this invitation had arisen."

Stevenage

Stevenage, thirty-two miles from London and twelve miles north of Hatfield via the A 1, is really two towns in one. The old part dates from the seventh century, when it was known as Stithenaece, meaning "strong hatch." The other part, one of the so-called New Towns developed after World War II, is well laid-out and extensive. The seventy thousand persons who inhabit the two sections seem reasonably content with either. Certainly delighted to live there during the latter part of the nineteenth century was E. M. Forster.

An odd thing about Forster, who—like H. G. Wells and T. S. Eliot—is identified by initials rather than Christian name, is that he *should* be known as H. M. Forster. At least his mother intended that he be christened *Henry Morgan Forster* when he was born January 1, 1879. But before the actual ceremony, when the verger asked the baby's name, the nervous father blurted out his own instead, Edward Morgan Forster; and that's the way the child was christened. The parents decided to leave it that way.

Forster's coming to Stevenage wasn't exactly planned either. In fact, the family was in Bournemouth in October of 1880 when his father suddenly died. It was nearly a year later before his mother, after much searching, stumbled upon Rooksnest in Stevenage as a new home for herself and baby.[4]

---

[4]She makes the house's name one word, not two.

It was lonely, she admitted, a mile and a half from the station, "a very old gabled house, and yet perfectly new. It has been rejuvenated, the inside scooped out—everything as pretty and nice as possible—good sanitary arrangements. The rent is £55 with four acres of land." Rooksnest was ample and appealing, with rose red brick covered with vines, and dormer windows in a steep roof that in back reached almost to the lawn. The ground floor, described by Forster at fifteen, was unusual—no fewer than five doors in the hall opened variously to dining room, drawing room, kitchen, porch, and staircase. Yes, staircase. Visitors, not seeing any stairs, wondered how anyone got to the floor above.

Upstairs were three large rooms, and above them three "attics," the central one a box room (i.e., for storing trunks, etc.) with a maids' room on either side, entered only by clambering over a beam on the floor that was eighteen inches high and twelve inches wide. Maids hated it.

Mother and son moved into the house in March of 1883 when young Morgan, as he was called, was four. There began what were undoubtedly the ten happiest years of his life. The boy had every reason to be happy. As an only child he was almost obsessively loved by his widowed mother; his whims indulged, his precocity encouraged. And he was precocious, as this schoolboy reflection of his grandmother's views of "liberated" women suggests:

> Here come the women, out they walk
> In groups of two or three
> To chatter forth their silly talk
> O're filthy cups of tea.

The wrench when, in 1893, the landlord refused to renew the lease and they had to move to Tonbridge in Kent, was considerable for both mother and son. Forster never relinquished the memories of Rooksnest. "The house is my childhood and my safety," he wrote later. "The three attics preserve me." Just how much so is discernible in his novel *Howards End* (1910). (Howard, incidentally, was the name of one of its former owners). In 1946, when Forster was in his sixties and a literary lion, he tried to buy Rooksnest after being ousted from Abinger Hammer in Surrey, but in vain.

Rooksnest still stands on Weston Road in Old Stevenage, near St. Nicholas Church. And if you want to stay in Stevenage at a place with historic connections and not too far off, there's the three-star Cromwell Hotel on the High Street in the old town. It was originally a sixteenth-century farm, later owned by Oliver Cromwell's secretary, and in the years 1640–50 it now and then played host to Cromwell himself.

Baldock—Wallington—Hitchin

Baldock   Samuel Pepys was often at Baldock (six miles above Stevenage on the A 1, population about seven thousand) because his father's place was in Brampton, another nine miles north in Cambridgeshire. Travelling for Pepys, and he was often "a-horseback," was never dull, as a few entries from his *Diary* concerning stops in Baldock—he calls it Baldwick—amusingly illustrate.

The evening of August 6, 1661, for instance, he looks in on his father at Brampton, "who could discern that I had been drinking, which he never did see or hear of before." So after a quick visit to friends, Pepys takes horse for London, but "the ways being very bad, got to Baldwick, and there lay and had a good supper by myself. The landlady being a pretty woman, but durst not take note of her, her husband being by." Instead, he continues ruefully, "I went to see the church, which is a very handsome church."

In September of the same year he is once more at Brampton, "and sad to hear my father and mother wrangle as they used to do in London." So he and a companion "took horse and got early to Baldwick, where there was a fair, and we put in and eat a mouthfull of pork, which they made us pay 14d. for, which vexed us much." Baldock, apparently, had a way of frustrating Pepys. But on another occasion in 1661, by coincidence also at fair time, the one vexed is Mrs. Pepys, "whom," Pepys recorded, "the thought of this day's journey [home to London] do discourage." After admiring the "cheese and other such commodities" at the Baldock fair, nevertheless, he insists on pushing on to Hatfield. But there, his wife "being very weary" and—more to the point, perhaps—lucking upon an empty London-bound coach that offered the irresistible bargain of a half-a-crown fare, he relents and puts her aboard . . . . and then beats her to London: "by and by comes my wife by coach well home, and having got a good fowl ready for supper against her coming, we eat heartily, and so with great content and ease to our own bed, there nothing appearing so to our content as to be at our own home, after being abroad a while." To which any traveller can only say, "Amen."

Wallington   From the spring of 1936 to the middle of 1940, the Baldock post office regularly received letters addressed to a storekeeper named Eric Blair. This would in no way be worthy of noticing except he wasn't really a storekeeper . . . he didn't live in Baldock . . . and to many who wrote him he wasn't Eric Blair.

Storekeeping was only the man's sideline; he was a writer. Where he lived was Wallington, four miles east of Baldock—a village too tiny to have a post office of its own, on a road still too little for maps to number. And to the readers, fairly few in number but discriminating, of *Down and Out in Paris and London* (1933), *Burmese Days* (1934), *A Clergyman's Daughter* (1935), and *Keep the Aspidistra Flying* (1936), the man's name was George Orwell (Blair chose the pen name in 1933, "George" because it had a good English ring to it, "Orwell" for the river in the Suffolk area where he grew up).

Then thirty-two, Orwell rented the cottage in Wallington called The Stores as "rather a pig in the poke," arranged for by friends while he was in Wigan, Lancs, gathering material for *The Road to Wigan Pier* (1937). On April 3 he wrote "I moved in yesterday [and] find myself pretty comfortable . . . so will dig in if the landlord doesn't raise the rent." Not "what you might call luxurious," but good as could be expected for only 7/6 a week so near London. In fact, he said later, "it was bloody awful," but he could afford no better. During winter rains, the kitchen tended to flood, the living room fire smoked, and now and then the cesspool choked up. The garden was in the "most frightful state." On one day alone he dug up twelve boots.

As its name suggested, the cottage had once been the village shop. Orwell decided to reopen it. He didn't expect a profit from a village of fewer than a hundred inhabitants, but he could hardly lose, either, since he had to pay rent in any case. Besides, there were advantages: he could stay open only at stated times, so it wouldn't interfere with his writing . . . and unlike customers he'd known when he'd worked in a London bookstore, "in a grocer's shop people come in to buy something; in a book shop they come in to make a nuisance of themselves."

He would not stock tobacco, however, because "the two pubs here (two for about seventy-five inhabitants!) stock it, and I don't want to make enemies, especially as one pub is next door to me." And, profit or no, by May of that first year he had decided to marry Elaine O'Shaughnessy, a young graduate student he had met in London. Marriage would "never be economically justified" anyway, so he "might as well be unjustified now as later . . . [I] don't see myself ever writing a best seller."

Orwell worked on his writing, too, on *Road to Wigan Pier,* finished that December, and an essay on the shooting of an elephant, though as he wrote the editor of a left-wing magazine, "I doubt there is anything anti-Fascist in the shooting of an elephant."

What was definitely anti-Fascist was the revolt against Franco that broke out in July. Writing and new bride notwithstanding, Orwell had to be a part of it. Before Christmas of that year he left for Spain. He soon became a member of the rebellion's Workers Party Militia, was gravely wounded, and in June 1937 forced to flee to France.

Next month he was back in Wallington, using his wartime experiences to develop his masterful and sensitive *Homage to Catalonia* (1938), and working on some of the essays of *Inside the Whale*. Wallington remained a base for the next several years, though there were excursions elsewhere, Morocco in 1938, for instance, and sporadic visits to his parents' home in Southwold, Suffolk, where he was when he finished *Coming Up for Air* (1939).

But as early as July 1938 his doctor had warned him that his tubercular lungs demanded warmer winters, which meant giving up The Stores. Shortly after the publication of *Inside the Whale* in 1940, Orwell bid Wallington farewell.

Hitchin   Ten miles southwest of Baldock, and within calling distance of each other, lie two of Hertfordshire's, and indeed England's, better-known literary attractions: Knebworth House and Shaw's Corner. To reach them from Baldock, simply head back to the A 1, and go south along it to the Stevenage exit on the A 602. To the west, five miles or so en route, you'll pass Hitchin.

A fair-sized town (thirty thousand), Hitchin has several streets of considerable charm. Among them Tilehouse Street, with a number of half-timbered and Georgian houses, has not one but two literary connections. At No. 35 Tilehouse, a plaque informs you that George Chapman lived there; he may have been born there, too, about 1559. An Elizabethan playwright of some success, Chapman is best remembered today for the translation into English of Homer that inspired Keats's soaring sonnet of discovery, "On First Looking Into Chapman's Homer."

Also on Tilehouse Street is the Baptist church established by John Bunyan in 1674; it still has a chair presented by the author of *Pilgrim's Progress* (1678) when it was under his pastoral care.

Hitchin has its share of Hertfordshire's "sprinkling" of Charles Lamb's kin, too. His maternal great-grandfather, Francis Field, was a gardener there, and kept the Bridewell, or House of Correction, as well. And *his* son, Grandfather Edward Field (husband of Blakesware's Mary Field[5]), was likewise a Hitchin gardener. Both are buried in the local churchyard.

2. Knebworth to the County's End

Knebworth House

When you turn to the west of the A 1 at the Stevenage exit, go up the long driveway in Knebworth Park, and burst upon Knebworth House, your first

[5]See page 12.

reaction may be, "Big!" . . . or even, depending on your taste for the Victorians' version of Gothic, "Monstrous!" It's as if someone, a Hollywood movie maker, perhaps, dissatisfied with a fairly simple fifteenth-century mansion, however large, had decided to demonstrate what Tudor aristocracy *should* have done with their great country homes.

Only the "someones" (plural in this case) were mother and son, the Bulwer-Lyttons, who owned the place for most of the nineteenth century. Mother was Elizabeth Barbara Lytton Bulwer, whose Lytton family (and Knebworth) went back to two years before Columbia discovered America. The son was Edward George Earle Lytton Bulwer-Lytton, first Baron Lytton—better and more simply known as Edward Bulwer-Lytton, author of well over fifty novels, plays, and short stories, among them *Pelham* (1828), *Paul Clifford* (1830), *Eugene Aram* (1832), *The Last Days of Pompeii* (1834), and *Rienzi* (1835).

It took a series of happenstances for Edward to lay his hands on Knebworth House at all. As a third son, he couldn't normally expect to inherit much from his father. But, luckily, Knebworth was his mother's, not his father's, to give. Moreover, both the other sons were already provided for. The oldest would get their father's estate; the second son their grandmother's. This left Knebworth for Edward. Even so, he nearly lost it. His marriage so angered his mother she disavowed him. It took some doing to win her back.

His mother's first intimate experience with Knebworth House had come when, as a sixteen-year-old girl, her father asked her to be mistress of the place in his estranged wife's stead. But the manor depressed her. A huge, two-story quadrangular edifice of yellow brick, it needed six staircases to get to the innumerable upper rooms. It was uncomfortable, cheerless, neglected. Within twelve months, she was back with her mother in London.

When she returned to Knebworth House in 1811—now Mrs. Bulwer-Lytton, having added her old family name after her husband died—she packed young Edward off to school and set about "re-doing" the house, tearing down three of the Tudor wings completely, and bestowing her own blend of Gothic on the fourth.

Sir Edward married an unstable Irish beauty named Rosina Wheeler in 1827, and after his mother cut him off, had to turn to writing for a livelihood, which he did with surprising success. He regained the maternal blessings following his legal separation from Rosina, and finally inherited Knebworth in 1843. He added "Lytton" to his name as his mother had wished, and added what today's promotional brochures kindly call "spectacular high Gothic decoration" to his house.

As visitors in the ensuing years there came, naturally enough, a parade of notable figures—social, literary, and political, for Bulwer-Lytton went on to be a highly visible member of Parliament as a representative from Hertfordshire. One of his literary guests was the poet Swinburne. The invitation took real courage on Bulwer-Lytton's part, for the visit came at the peak of public uproar at Swinburne's newly published *Poems and Ballads* (1866). Lines like

> . . . her sweet white sides
> And bosom carved to kiss

from "A Ballad of Life" seemed incredibly naughty, typical of the "fleshly school of poetry" at its worst.

But the writer most often at Knebworth House was Charles Dickens. The summer of 1850 Bulwer-Lytton invited Dickens, his friend John Forster (the editor, critic, and biographer), and actor William Charles Macready to discuss producing a dramatic festival there.

Warmed by the hospitality at what Macready dubbed "a most finished baronial seat," Dickens leaped at the idea: "It stirs my blood like a trumpet." The resultant performances of Ben Jonson's *Every Man in his Humour* for Bulwer-Lytton's high-toned friends and neighbors, Dickens said, "was a whirl of triumph that fired the whole length and breadth of the county of Hertfordshire." Dickens shone in the role of the boasting, cowardly Bobadill.

Out of this grew a scheme to establish a Guild to aid impecunious writers and artists. Bulwer-Lytton would write a play (it turned out to be an eighteenth-century piece called *Not so Bad as We Seem*), and Dickens and company would perform it. The project reached dizzy heights. The mighty Duke of Devonshire offered "my services, my house and my subscription." The Prince Consort Albert and Queen Victoria agreed to attend.

Even though Bulwer-Lytton's crazy wife—who had made a career out of hectoring him after their separation—threatened to crash the party and throw oranges at the queen, it was a glittering success. There were no oranges. Moreover, Dickens got an unexpected bonus. When at the last moment they needed a volunteer for a bit part, someone suggested a young man named Wilkie Collins. He was to become not only Dickens's life-long friend and sometime collaborator, but also a successful novelist in his own right, still remembered for his *The Woman in White* (1860) and *The Moonstone* (1868).

In 1852, Dickens's wife bore him another son, his seventh, "whom," said the new father wryly, "I cannot afford to receive with perfect cordiality, as on the whole I could have dispensed with him." Even so, he named the baby Edward Bulwer-Lytton Dickens.

June of 1861 saw him again at Knebworth House, where Bulwer-Lytton persuaded him to change the ending of *Great Expectations,* turning the penniless Pip, who had loved not wisely but too well, into a middle-aged sobersides reunited with a now-chastened Estella.

A final joint gala came at Knebworth House in 1865, when Bulwer-Lytton and Dickens celebrated the culmination of their Guild project, the building of three Gothic cottages on a bit of the estate to house their artistic indigents. The cottages still stand, though the enterprise itself proved a failure, and they became far more prosaic almshouses.

Even after Bulwer-Lytton's death in 1873, Knebworth House did not lose its literary coloring. His only son, Edward Robert (later first Earl of Lytton and viceroy to India) inherited not only his father's peerage, but some of his bent for writing as well. Under the pen name "Owen Meredith," he published several volumes of poetry, including a number of more than passable lyrics.

Now open to the public, Knebworth House has its own entrance off the A 1, train service at Knebworth Station, and bus service from London's Victoria Station. Two of the rooms on display are of special interest. The great Banqueting Hall, chiefly Jacobean, is where Dickens staged those theatricals. And in the State Drawing Room, best example of Bulwer-Lytton's "spectacular" Gothic touch, Winston Churchill once set up his painter's easel, pulled out a cigar, and went to work.

There is more available than just the house, however. In the surrounding 250 acres of parkland are such attractions as—brace yourself!—a kiddies' "Adventure Playground" featuring good old "Fort Knebworth," palisades and all . . . the Astroglide, and Konkord Kastle.

If that's a bit more than you can handle, there is a fully licensed bar in connection with restaurants housed in two four hundred-year-old tithe barns.

Ayot St. Lawrence (Shaw's Corner)

There *is* a village called Ayot St. Lawrence, but fewer than 175 people live there. The only reason that it is known world-wide and visitors overrun it in the summer is that until as recently as 1950 George Bernard Shaw lived there. And if he'd had his way, he would still be among that handful of residents. He joined them in the first place because they seemed to have the right view of longevity. A tombstone in the cemetery salutes a Mary Anne South: "Born 1825. Died 1895. Her Time Was Short."

If you are at Knebworth House and want to cover the homes of Bulwer-

Lytton and Shaw in a single day, it's quite feasible. They are only nine miles apart if you leave Knebworth Park by the back exit and follow road signs to Codicote and the B 656 to Welwyn. There a right turn takes you the rest of the way along well-marked but N-A-R-R-O-W lanes.

You can't miss the house. Large letters woven into the iron gate out front proclaim it "Shaw's Corner," the name he gave the place himself after he bought it in 1931.

When they first came there in 1906, the Shaws rented the place as an escape from London, though they maintained their city flat. They could afford to. Charlotte Payne-Townshend was known as the "green-eyed millionairess" when the dramatist had married her eight years earlier. And he was already famous and well-off from the success of such plays as *Arms and the Man* (1894), *Candida* (1897), *Caesar and Cleopatra* (1901), *Man and Superman* (1905), and *Major Barbara* (1905).

It's a two-storey house, unpretentious inside and out, but who would expect more from a residence that had been the village vicarage? (It was called the New Rectory when the Shaws first took it). Their first guest, arriving even as they settled in, was the actor-dramatist-director Granville-Barker on one of what were to be many visits, usually to discuss the staging of a play. In this instance the play was *The Doctor's Dilemma*, which had its premiere in November.

Granville-Barker already knew that Shaw could be an unusual host, to say the least—as a galaxy of guests from the H. G. Wellses, the Sidney Webbs, and Sir Arthur Pinero to Galsworthy, Yeats, and Sean O'Casey discovered, either here or at Shaw's London place.

Among the instructions Granville-Barker came across that first night after his host had retired was: "If Barker decides to play the Pianola before retiring, he is requested to select a quiet piece, and wedge down the soft pedal." When the local squire's wife came calling the first week, seeking the donation of a yearly prize for the village school, Shaw welcomed her with "I am prepared to give a handsome prize to the worst behaved child, for I was at school, and look at me now."

Guests got nothing but vegetarian food unless they gave prior notice that they needed meat. Yet Shaw could be unpredictably gracious, too, even to the extent of a bit of fiction. He was ninety when dignitaries of his native Dublin came from Ireland to present him with the Freedom of the City. Blandly, Shaw asserted that Dublin alone had the right to affirm that he had never disgraced her. This despite confiding to his inamorata Ellen Terry, the actress: "O, a devil of a childhood, Ellen, rich only in dreams, frightful and loveless in realities."

In 1944, the year after his wife died, Shaw's Corner was given to the National Trust. (His ashes and hers are scattered in the garden). House and garden are open five afternoons a week, spring to fall. A visit is a special treat, for even more than Carlyle's London home on Cheyne Row, rivalling Kipling's Bateman's in Sussex, Shaw's Corner gives one an eerie sense of the master's continuing presence.

Inside the hall, Shaw's collection of hats and walking sticks suggest that he has just paused to select one of each after sitting in the basket chair to put on his walking boots. In the study, desk, chair, typewriter, and reference books all look as if momentarily pushed aside for a needed breather before his return to writing.

All about are mementos reflecting his unique personality. There's a photograph of heavyweight champion Gene Tunney, dear friend and most welcome of visitors. Boxing was Shaw's only interest in sport. One drawer of the filing cabinet is labelled "Keys and Contraptions." Two cameras lie atop the bookshelves. There is a photograph of a group acting in an unfinished film by James M. Barrie—among them Barrie himself, G. K. Chesterton, and Shaw—dressed as cowboys.

The drawing room was Mrs. Shaw's, while she lived, but now comes closer than the study to justifying Sir Harold Nicolson's charge that it, "like all Shaw's homes, was a narcissistic art gallery . . . even the doorknocker is an image of himself." (It is, a brass likeness with an inscription "Man and Superman.").

There is a bronze of Shaw in 1926 in the bay window . . . a bust of him by Rodin on the large desk . . . various pictures of him on the walls . . . and, on a small stool, a marble of his hand. Two objects symbolize a pair of his best plays. The chimney piece holds a statuette of Joan of Arc and the Oscar that *Pygmalion* won in 1938 for best screenplay. Next to them is a reminder that Shaw was as much man as superman—a Staffordshire figure of Shakespeare. It's atrocious!

The dining room was perhaps Shaw's favorite room, and fittingly the room in which he died. Meals, especially when he ate alone, could go on and on as he read a book, forgetting to eat. Two hour lunches were not uncommon, punctuated usually by his soaking a bit of bread in his soup and flinging it out the French windows for the birds. He never did wait to watch them fly down to get it. This room abounds with personal items: spectacles, pocket watch, fountain pen and reversible pencil, a membership card for the Cyclists' Touring Club dated 1950. In 1950 Shaw was ninety years old.

Outside the dining room, a long footpath leads to the bottom of the garden and Shaw's writing hut. The hut is just that, a very small (about eight feet wide), rather crude wooden shack. The fixtures inside are equally simple: a homemade flap table extending from the wall as a desk, telephone but no typewriter, wicker chair, wall heater, and a folding stool. It is no way comparable to the Swiss chalets of George Meredith at Box Hill or Dickens at Gads Hill. But it did provide the one thing all three writers needed to produce their masterpieces—privacy.

The narrowness of the lanes immediately adjacent to Shaw's Corner cannot be exaggerated. At times even a single car seems to be scraping the bushes on both sides. In summer, rains can inundate the low spots. In winter, what Shaw wrote one year when his wife was off on a Christmas holiday still obtains: "I am here in Ayot St. Lawrence, snowed up and slushed up in the filthiest manner."

To reach these lanes, Welwyn will serve equally well from north or south off the A 1. From St. Albans to the south or Luton to the north, head for Wheathamstead on the B 651.

Wheathamstead—Mackerye End—Brocket Hall

At Wheathamstead, two miles southwest of Ayot St. Lawrence, you're back in Lamb country. Not one Lamb, but two . . . totally unrelated, totally different. One is the familiar, sweet, self-deprecating clerk and essayist on an excursion to nostalgia and Mackerye End. The other was the titled master of Brocket Hall, married to a femme fatale whose affairs involved two of the nineteenth century's most dashing literary figures, and bordered on the bizarre.

First to Charles Lamb, the self-deprecating one, and Mackerye End.

Mackerye End   "A gentle walk from Wheathamstead," in Lamb's own words, Mackerye End is a restored seventeenth and eighteenth-century house just to the northwest off the Lower Luton Road. "The oldest thing I remember," Lamb wrote, "is Mackerye End; or Mackeral End, as it is spelt, perhaps more properly, in some old maps of Hertfordshire." (Today's maps usually have it "Mackerye.")

Lamb first went there, before 1780, as a very young child to visit his great-aunt Ann Bruton Gladman, who was housekeeper of what was then a farmhouse. He was shepherded by his sister Mary, eleven years older, and it is to her *Mrs. Leicester's School* (1809) one must turn for details of that visit. But the vague memory persisted, and as a grown man of forty and more, Lamb promises at the end of his essay, "My Relations": "In my next, reader, I may perhaps give you an account of my cousin Bridget—if you are not already surfeited with cousins—and take you by the hand, if you are willing to go with us on an excursion which we made a summer or two since, in search of *more cousins—*"

Lamb does take us by the hand, and most pleasantly, in the next essay, "Mackerye End." Both essays are in the first series of *Essays of Elia*, written for the *London Magazine* during the years 1820–23. The pen name "Elia" (pronounced Ellya) was borrowed from an Italian fellow clerk at South Sea House, Lamb said, but was an anagram for "a lie." Elia, of course, was Lamb himself, and "Cousin Bridget" Sister Mary.

"The sight of the old farm house, though every trace of it was effaced from my recollection, affected me with a pleasure which I had not experienced for many a year," he wrote. But he despaired of getting into the house itself: "a difficulty which to me singly would have been insurmountable; for I am terribly shy in making myself known to strangers and out-of-date kinsfolk. Love, stronger than scruple, winged my cousin in without me." In a moment, Bridget-Mary was back to fetch him in, where "the fatted calf was made ready," along with "an appropriate glass of native wine."

Lamb provides his own fitting farewell to Mackerye End. In a letter to a friend, he writes the line "Hail, Mackerye End—" and explains, "This is a fragment of a blank verse poem which I once meditated, but got no further."

Brocket Hall   Brocket Hall is on the other side of Wheathamstead, about three miles to the east, a fine country mansion built in the late eighteenth century. There, only a few years and a few miles from Lamb's sentimental journey to Mackerye End, a woman began a dalliance which, coupled with another affair twenty years earlier, made her the talk of London's loftiest social circles.

One lover was already a titled aristocrat and wildly popular writer when he met her. The other went on to become both, after he escaped her clutches. The first was George Gordon, Lord Byron; the second, Edward Lytton Bulwer, later Bulwer-Lytton, Lord Lytton. The woman was Lady Caroline, wife of William Lamb, liege of Brocket Hall (later to become Lord Melbourne and twice prime minister).

Lady Caroline, whom this Lamb had married in 1805, met Byron when the publication of the first cantos of *Childe Harold's Pilgrimage* (1812) had just made him an overnight celebrity. She pursued him with such intensity that—though he succumbed briefly—he threw her over to marry Annabella Millbanke. She retaliated by writing a novel, *Glenvarron* (1816), which caricatured him, and continued her writing with *Graham Hamilton* (1822) and *Ada Reis, a Tale* (1823).

But Lady Caroline never got over Byron. When word reached Brocket in the spring of 1824 of his death in Greece, she took to her bed with fever. By a fantastic stroke of fortune, her first venture forth—to Brocket's gates—came not only on the very day in July, but at the very moment that the poet's funeral procession was passing on its way to his home in Nottinghamshire.

Devastated anew, Lady Caroline returned to her bed for over a month. Then began affair number two. Four years earlier a lad at nearby Knebworth House, still in his teens, had published in *Ismael* (1820) some verses praising her kindness to a wounded stranger. Now to comfort her she summoned to Brocket, from his Cambridge studies, Edward Bulwer, age twenty-one.

The ensuing seduction was easy. He already idolized Byron—*Ismael* was blatantly Byronic—and he was all too overwhelmed by a woman who had been Byron's mistress. Soon, however, she tired of the boy, and by the following January dismissed him for a new lover. He emerged with scars that never healed.

Incredibly enough, though, Edward Bulwer was not through with either Lady Caroline or Brocket. For now begins the other side of the story of Bulwer's disastrous marriage, touched on earlier in the section on Knebworth House.[6] In 1825, the year her husband obtained a legal separation, Lady Caroline took under her wing a young Irish beauty named Rosina Wheeler. In April 1826, Edward met this same Rosina at a London party. Smitten, he came up to London again and again to woo her, even though it meant running into Lady Caroline repeatedly. By August, most fantastic of all, he had accepted her invitation to come to Brocket to share a holiday with Rosina.

Soon after, Rosina became Mrs. Bulwer. . . Edward's mother disavowed him . . . and he turned to writing all those novels and plays. The marriage itself never saw its tenth anniversary. The stuff of novels? Yes indeed, as Mrs. Humphrey Ward proved in her *The Marriage of William Ashe* (1905).

St. Albans

Easily accessible from both the M 10 and the A 1, St. Albans is no more than seven miles south of Ayot St. Lawrence. Shaw liked to ride there on his

---

[6]See page 22.

bicycle, and once did so after a bout of flu, riding back against a hurricane. The result, he reported hyperbolically, was "collapse, senile decay, childish impotence, and ruin."

The city's history is ancient. Soon after 43 A. D. the Romans crossed its Ver River and built what was for a time their most important settlement in England. They called it Verulamium, meaning "beyond the Ver." The modern name came from a later Roman, a soldier named Alban who in 303 A. D. won the dubious distinction of being England's first Christian martyr. He got his head chopped off for befriending the priest who had converted him.

In 793 King Offa of Mercia made amends of a sort. He established a Benedictine Abbey that grew to great power, and produced in Matthew Paris the best of the medieval chroniclers and historians. What may well have been the boat house or gate of this monastery is now the Fighting Cocks Inn—of which more anon.

In the fourteenth century St. Albans was the scene of two significant battles of the War of the Roses, between the royal houses of Lancaster (they wore red roses) and York (they wore white). The Yorks won the first battle, fought in 1455 near Holywell Hill, moving the Earl of Warwick—in Shakespeare's *Henry VI Part II* at least—to boast

> St Albons battle won by famous York
> Shall be eterniz'd in all age to come.

Short eternity. The Lancasters beat that same Warwick six years later, in a battle fought on Barnard's Heath.

Shakespeare's contemporary, Francis Bacon, author of the first-rate *Essays* (1597) and the *Novum Organum* (1620), knew St. Albans well. He inherited the estate of Gorhambury two miles to its west, and adopted both the city's names when titles fell his way as Lord Chancellor, becoming Baron Verulam in 1618 and Viscount St. Albans in 1621.[7] He is buried in St. Michaels Church. A statue outside shows him in a favorite pose, as the Latin inscription indicates: *sic sedebat*, "this is how he used to sit."

Two writers with unhappy memories of St. Albans were John Bunyan and William Cowper. Bunyan was arrested near there for preaching without a license and imprisoned for twelve years. Cowper's experience was the bitterest of his often clouded life, but he rose above it.

The year was 1763, the place London, and Cowper was thirty-two. Facing

---

[7]Today's Gorhambury dates from 1784, but has some family relics, and the ruins of Bacon's house are in the park.

the dreaded ordeal of an oral exam to win a clerkship in the House of Lords, his mind snapped under the strain. He attempted suicide repeatedly—by drowning, poison, stabbing, hanging— before his brother John bore him off to the "Collegium Insanorum" (i.e. madhouse) in St. Albans. Within five months he was well enough to joke and tell stories, but he stayed another year. Then, as he has recorded, he left for lodgings near Cambridge, where John taught. ". . . having spent more than eighteen months at St. Albans, partly in bondage, and partly in the liberty wherewith Christ has made me free, I took my leave of the place at four in the morning [17 June 1765], and set out for Cambridge." The liberty of Christ found eloquent expression in several of Cowper's famous Olney hymns.

In Dickens's *Oliver Twist*, when Bill Sikes was accosted by that "pedler-mountebanke" in Hatfield, he was bound for St. Albans. The city also figures in *Bleak House* (1852–53). But though that novel's bricklayers and their cottages are real enough, the house of that name that claims to be his original "bleak house" is no such thing.

Dickens made several visits to St. Albans, and one of his favorite stopping places was the White Hart on Holywell Hill, close to where Warwick made that short-lived boast to eternity. The inn is a fine old half-timbered specimen of the fifteenth or early sixteenth century.

Even older is the Fighting Cocks Inn on Abbey Lane mentioned earlier, with cellars that apparently go all the way back to Offa and his abbey. The building is interesting, octagonal in shape and half-timbered, and gets its name as a center for cockfighting from Tudor times until the sport was banned in 1849.

Berkhamsted—Aldbury—Markyate

When William Cowper was confined in St. Albans, he was in an ironic sense coming home. For even more than Charles Lamb, Cowper was Hertfordshire's own. He was born there in Berkhamsted, and as a boy lived in nearby Aldbury and Markyate.

Berkhamsted   Berkhamsted, ten miles due west of St. Albans on the A 41, is a town of fifteen thousand people now. But it was only a village of fifteen hundred when Cowper was born there in 1731. Soft, sunny slopes, beechwood trees, and the Chiltern Hills rising in the background assured Berkhamsted a place among the loveliest spots in Hertfordshire. One of its two principal streets, Castle Street, led to the ruins of the fortress marking the site of the Saxons' submission to William the Conquerer after the Battle of Hastings.

Not much remains of the castle now, save a great earthwork forty-five feet high with a diameter of sixty feet at the top. But it has a glamorous past. It was once under the control of Thomas à Becket, the "blisful martir" of the *Canterbury Tales*, and later, appropriately enough, Chaucer himself lived here. Among its notable former owners are Katharine of Aragon, Anne Boleyn, Jane Seymour, and the future Queen Elizabeth I.

Cowper's father was rector of Berkhamsted parish, and belonged to one of Hertfordshire's leading families. The poet's mother was a descendant of John Donne. For the first five years, Cowper's life was well nigh idyllic. But within a week of giving birth to another son, John, in 1737, his mother died, a blow which contributed heavily to the instability and melancholy that plagued his life.

Fifty years later her memory was as fresh, his grief as keen, as if she had just died. When a cousin sent him a portrait of her, he wrote: "I received it the night before last, and viewed it with a trepidation of nerves and spirits somewhat akin to what I should have felt had the dear original presented herself to my embraces. I kissed it, and hung it where it is the last object that I see at night, and, of course, the first on which I open my eyes in the morning."

From 1737 on, Cowper was mainly away from Berkhamsted at his various schools, but he usually went there for vacations. And even after the death of his father, who married again, he visited his stepmother in 1756. But apparently he was not fond of her. The following year he said a final farewell to the rectory he had so loved: "no man ever quitted his native place with less Regrett than myself."

The rectory was replaced by the one now standing on the same site. The ruins of the castle of Becket, Chaucer, Anne Boleyn and the rest are open the year round.

Aldbury and Markyate   The villages of Aldbury and Markyate are both within walking distance of Berkhamsted—Aldbury three miles northwest on an unmarked road off the A 41, and Markyate six miles northeast, just off the A 5.

Aldbury, strewn about with thatched cottages, is particularly charming. William Cowper stayed there briefly following his mother's death in the care of the Rev. William Davis, a friend of his father's. And from the last decade of the nineteenth century until her death in 1920, the novelist Mrs. Humphrey Ward lived there at The Stocks; her *Marcella* (1894) is woven around a sensational local murder. Among the writers she attracted to Aldbury were Henry James, her young kinsmen Julian and Aldous Huxley, and George Bernard Shaw, who once rented her cottage. She is buried in the village churchyard.

From Aldbury, six-year-old William Cowper was dispatched for two years to a boarding school at Markyate. And frightful years they were. Older bullies quickly reduced the lonely, sensitive child to what one biographer called "a quivering jelly of fear." Half a century thereafter, Cowper struck back at the whole public school system of England in "Tirocinium" (i.e., novitiate), a long poem in heroic couplets published in 1785, with lines like:

> Would you your son should be a sot or dunce,
> Lascivious, headstrong; or all these at once . . .
> . . . .
>
> Train him in public with a mob of boys
> Childish in mischief only, and in noise
> . . . .
>
> In infidelity and lewdness, men.

—   —   —   —   —

And So to Buckinghamshire

The thin finger of land that contains Berkhamsted and Aldbury makes an excellent entry into Buckinghamshire, surrounded as it is on three sides by that county. And Buckinghamshire—with memories of Pope, Gray, and Milton . . . of D. H. Lawrence and Benjamin Disraeli . . . Peacock and Shelley . . . and once again, William Cowper—beckons appealingly.

BUCKINGHAMSHIRE

Buckinghamshire

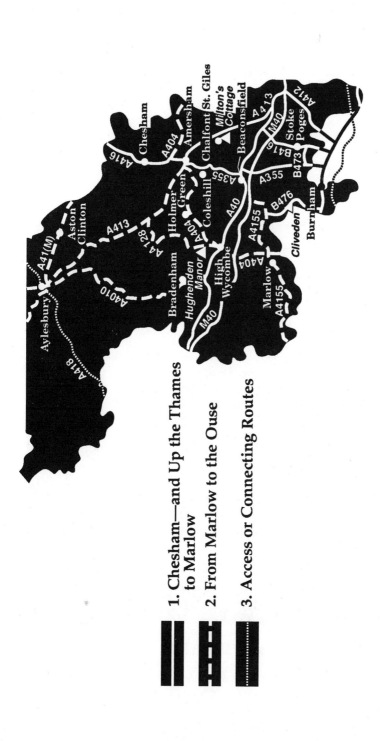

1. Chesham—and Up the Thames to Marlow

2. From Marlow to the Ouse

3. Access or Connecting Routes

Here Ouse, slow winding through a level plain
Of spacious meads with cattle sprinkled o'er,
Conducts the eye along its sinuous course,
Delighted.
>> William Cowper, *The Task*

In its unbroken loveliness this is, perhaps, the sweetest
stretch of the river.
>> Jerome K. Jerome, *Three Men in a Boat*

Miles and long years separate William Cowper, Jerome K. Jerome, and their rivers. When Cowper was bending to his task of writing an epic about an everyday sofa, his monarch, George III, was still puttering around Kew Gardens. When Jerome and his friends turned their little boat upstream, Victoria had been at her royal duties for over fifty years, and it was her son Edward who did the puttering. Cowper's river was the Ouse at Olney, meandering through the heart of middle England; Jerome's the Thames at Cliveden, flowing out of London itself. What binds all this together is Buckinghamshire.

If one could straighten up its highly irregular boundaries, Buckinghamshire would be a rectangle about twenty-five miles wide and fifty miles long, with Olney at the top and Cliveden at the bottom. In between is largely unsullied country. The chief business is still agriculture; the major city, High Wycombe, has sixty-five thousand people at most.

Chained to his London desk as prime minister, Benjamin Disraeli would mourn as the long winters drew to an end, "I want to get back to my woods and watch the burst of spring."

His woods were in Buckinghamshire.

1. Chesham—and up the Thames to Marlow

Chesham—Holmer Green—Coleshill

As noted above, the traveller coming south from Cowper's Berkhamsted can slip into Buckinghamshire easily, taking the A 416 and A 413 to reach the county's first major literary stop, Milton's Cottage at Chalfont St. Giles. Near at hand along the way are Chesham, Holmer Green, and Coleshill.

Chesham   With a population of over twenty thousand, Chesham ranks among Buckinghamshire's larger towns. It is three and a half miles south of Berkhamsted on the A 416 and the Chess river.

D. H. Lawrence came here in August 1914, settling in at The Triangle on Bellington Lane, "a delightful cottage," he said at first, "really buried in the country." But his friend and fellow novelist Compton Mackenzie called it the ugliest cottage he'd ever seen, and buried in nettles. Before long, Lawrence was agreeing, terming The Triangle "this God-forsaken little hole."

While here, Lawrence worked at his book on Thomas Hardy "out of sheer rage" at England's role in World War I, and resumed the writing of his novel, *The Rainbow* (1915). Now and then he would visit Katherine Mansfield, the short story writer, and John Middleton Murry, who lived three miles from him. But The Triangle proved cold and damp that winter, particularly bad for his tubercular lungs. Before long he was in London, vainly fighting a court order that *The Rainbow* be seized and burnt as obscene.

Holmer Green and Coleshill   Three miles below Chesham, at Amersham, the A 404 goes off to the right, with a village on either side, each worth a mention. Just to the highway's west is Holmer Green, and to the east Coleshill.

Holmer Green was the site of a summer cottage belonging to an Italian London family named Polidori. To it in 1829 a married daughter brought her year-old firstborn to await the birth of another child. The firstborn was Gabriel Charles Dante Rossetti, later to become celebrated (and notorious) as the poet-painter Dante Gabriel Rossetti. The secondborn was William Michael Rossetti, critic and editor.

Coleshill, too, owes its brief brush with literary history to an infant. Edmund Waller, the seventeenth-century lyric poet, was born there at the manor house, home of his wealthy Buckinghamshire parents, in 1606.

Chalfont St. Giles

From Amersham, you reach Chalfont St. Giles by following the A 413 south for about three miles and turning right at the signpost into the village.

And to reach Milton's Cottage, you go down the hill and through the village. The cottage, clearly marked, is on the left, just before you come to a large meadow.

Beginning in the final decade of the Commonwealth and continuing into the Restoration, fortune dealt John Milton a series of cruel blows, the last of which brought him to Chalfont St. Giles. A lesser man might well have been crushed by any one of these. Milton refused to bow. Often he responded with a poetic piece of first rank.

In 1652, while serving as Cromwell's Latin Secretary, he became totally blind—and wrote that great sonnet on his blindness ending with the resounding "They also serve who only stand and wait." Then in 1658 came the sudden death of his second wife whom he loved deeply. Again the result was a sonnet of highest order: "Methought I saw my late espoused saint."

When the Commonwealth collapsed and the monarchy was restored in 1660 under Charles II, those prominent in the revolt against his father were in grave peril. For a time Milton feared for his life and went into hiding. He lost his fortune, was arrested and fined, and had the books he'd written in support of the Commonwealth taken up by the public hangman and burned.

He had hardly recovered from all this when the devastating plague of 1665 hit London. With people dying all about him by the thousands, Milton felt forced to flee to safer ground. For help, he turned to a young Quaker named Thomas Ellwood whom he had tutored in Latin: "I was desired by my quondam master, Milton, [wrote Ellwood] to take a house for him in the neighborhood where I dwelt, that he might go out of the city for the safety of himself and his family, the pestilence then growing hot in London. I took a pretty box in Giles Chalfont, a mile from me. . . . "

Pretty it was, but the box was small. A two-story brick building, it is L-shaped, with one angle of the "L" facing the street, the other the garden. Downstairs were parlor, kitchen and the study. Upstairs were the bedrooms; if four, as is claimed, they had to be minuscule. Yet somehow they housed his wife (he had married again in 1663), his three daughters, and a maidservant.[1] Milton himself slept downstairs. The only access to the rooms above was more ladder than staircase.

This cottage witnessed the final stages of one Miltonic masterpiece and the very first inkling of another. Again, Thomas Ellwood furnishes the details. He had come down from Aylesbury, he says, fresh from a prison stint for attending a Quaker funeral: "After some common discourse had passed

---

[1]Some accounts do say only one of the three daughters accompanied him to Chalfont St. Giles.

between us, he called for a manuscript . . . bidding me take it home with me, and read it at my leisure." It was, Ellwood discovered, "that excellent poem which he entitled 'Paradise Lost'."

On his return visit, Ellwood continues, having duly praised the poem, "I pleasantly said to him, Thou hast said much here of 'Paradise Lost,' but what hast thou to say of 'Paradise Found?' He made me no answer, but sat some time in a muse; then broke off that discourse, and fell upon another subject."

Two years were to pass before Milton went seriously to work on *Paradise Regained*, and it wasn't published until 1671. But Milton credited Ellwood with its inception, handing him the manuscript on a later visit to London, and saying "This is owing to you, for you put it into my head by the question you put to me at Chalfont, which before I had not thought of."

At Chalfont, Milton maintained his disciplined schedule, arising at sunrise in the winter, at four in summer, to meditate and, when work was in hand, to compose in his head lines which, at his dictation, his daughters would later put on paper.

But he couldn't have taken to Chalfont many of the books he would have needed for reference, he had no skilled amanuensis to assist him, and the quarters were too confined to provide the quiet and privacy sustained writing demands. When, six to nine months later, with the city "well cleansed and habitable" again, he could quit the cottage for London, Milton must have been more than pleased.

We can thank Queen Victoria's Jubilee for that cottage today. As the gala neared in 1887, inhabitants of the village "unanimously resolved"—according to a plaque now to the left of the entrance—that "Her Majesty Queen Victoria's happy reign might be loyally commemorated in this parish" by buying what had become the country's sole surviving Milton residence. They must have been heartened when the queen herself led off their fundraising campaign with a gift of £20.

The Milton's Cottage Trust still manages the place, keeping it open February through October with the two ground floor rooms on display. You enter through the garden, not the street door.

The kitchen parlor is to the left, and mainly reflects Milton's era, though a number of items are of a later date. (Wife No. Three was a Cheshire girl, and distributed his possessions widely about that county when she returned there after his death in 1674).

The study, where Milton spent most of his daytime hours, is to the right. It now holds a number of treasures, in addition to the inevitable lock of hair, such as first editions of *Paradise Lost* and *Paradise Regained*, two editions of

Eikon Basilike, purported to be the meditations of Charles I before his execution in 1649, and Milton's refutation, *Eikonoklastes* (1649) and his *Defence of the English People* (1651).

Most striking, perhaps, is the collection of translations of *Paradise Lost*, striking in their testimony to the work's lasting and world-wide appeal. Among languages represented are Chinese, Korean, Swedish, Finnish, Romanian, Dutch, Serbo-Croatian, Italian, Hebrew, Spanish, French, and Japanese.

As you leave the cottage, pause to read the verses on the wall to the right, proof enough that literary shrines do indeed inspire memorable poetry from visitors. One Ms. Carasan Davies from South Wales, all of twelve years old, for instance, wrote:

> Peace within the maddening pace
> Of the savage cruelty of human race
> For a hundred years of killing has gone by,
> But the cottage still is standing against the sky. . . .

And an A. J. Ford contributed:

> An ancient thought, a solemn dream,
> Of Milton in his cottage scene,
> A timely sight, a new born mind
> Within it poems of a divine kind. . . .

Mr. Ford was nine. Also nine was Ms. Dawn Bartlett when the garden stirred her to:

> The pink roses
> The apple trees tall
> Little wells, so neat and small.
> The grass so neat, but best of all
> So quiet a garden I now [sic] it is best of all.

Bless her soul.

One final word. If you're in London and want to go directly from there to Milton's Cottage, simply pick up the Uxbridge Road (A 4020) in Kensington and follow it to the M 40, which will take you right to the A 355, southern approach to Chalfont St. Giles.

Beaconsfield—Stoke Poges—Cliveden

In a cluster within seven miles of Chalfont St. Giles are Beaconsfield, Stoke Poges, and Cliveden, all of considerable literary interest.

Beaconsfield   Beaconsfield is a mere three miles southwest of Chalfont St. Giles, on the A 40. If the name Beaconsfield rings a bell at all, it's probably because of Benjamin Disraeli, the Victorian who managed to combine careers as novelist and prime minister with great success: "Oh yes, isn't that the title Disraeli took when he retired—Lord Beaconsfield?"

Well, yes. But it was really the title his wife took when she became a viscountess in 1868. Disraeli remained a commoner for another eight years before he accepted an earldom. Besides, the title Lord Beaconsfield should have gone to another noted writer-statesman nearly a full century before the Disraelis.

Beaconsfield itself is more importantly connected with Edmund Waller, the seventeenth-century Cavalier poet; Edmund Burke, the eighteenth-century defender of the American Revolution; and G. K. Chesterton, the nineteenth-century jack-of-all-genres.

From birth to death, Beaconsfield and the surrounding area were the centers of Edmund Waller's life, save for the few years when one of his several political miscues drove him into exile in France. Soon after his birth in nearby Coleshill in 1606, his family bought Hall Barn in Beaconsfield. He was living there when, still in his teens, he became a member of parliament for Amersham, four miles to the north, and inherited Hall Barn.

Much good his early training in government did him. His hallmark was the political flip-flop, often unseemly, and once nearly fatal. In the long struggle between Charles I and Parliament, he began pro-Parliament. Then (1643) he hatched a pro-King plot and won exile rather than execution only by betraying his co-conspirators. It was while abroad that he wrote his best known poem, "Go, lovely Rose!"

Next (1651) he was pro-Parliament again, back at Hall Barn, and writing "A Panegyric to my Lord Protector." Finally (1660), he was balancing this effusion to Cromwell with "To the King, upon his Majesty's Happy Return." When that majesty, Charles II, asked why the Cromwell poem was so much better than his own, Waller replied urbanely, "Sir, we poets never succeed so well in writing truth as in fiction."

Having survived all these vicissitudes, Waller died at Hall Barn in 1681, and was rather lavishly entombed in the Beaconsfield churchyard.

Buried in that same churchyard is Edmund Burke, Whig spokesman for the last forty years of the eighteenth century. He was also, beyond doubt, one of the century's great prose writers, as *On Conciliation with the Colonies* (1775) and *Reflections on the Revolution in France* (1790) affirm.

As a young man, in fact, Burke had hoped for a career in writing. At twenty-seven he published a political satire called *A Vindication of Natural Society,* and a philosophical treatise called *Sublime and Beautiful*—neither exactly the stuff with which to mend the fortunes of a penniless Irishman. Such income as he had when he bought Gregories in Beaconsfield in 1769 came chiefly from being private secretary to Lord Rockingham, the Whig leader.

It was a bold purchase. The six hundred-acre estate cost £22,000. Even with a legacy from an older brother and a loan from Rockingham, Burke could come up with only a third of that amount. The rest was covered by a mortgage he never managed to pay off.

For Burke was a generous friend and expansive host. Among literary lights who enjoyed his hospitality were George Crabbe, Richard Brinsley Sheridan, David Garrick, Fanny Burney, and above all Dr. Samuel Johnson. Johnson and Burke were the closest of friends, despite their fierce differences over politics. "I can live very well with Burke," Johnson once told Goldsmith. "I love his knowledge, his genius . . . but I would not talk to him of the Rockingham party."

Johnson came to Gregories in 1774 with Henry and Hester Thrale, the younger couple who had practically adopted him, hoping for a long and pleasant stay. He should have come alone. Hester, already fretting at the manor's dust and cobwebs, was further disenchanted on the first day when their host returned from a political errand "much flustered with liquor." Meanwhile Henry, a member of parliament, decided a call for new elections required his immediate presence at home. The visit lasted a total of two days.

Edmund Burke was the writer-statesman who nearly became the first Lord Beaconsfield. George III offered him the title, and the necessary patent was being drawn up when Burke abruptly refused. Crushed by the sudden death of his only son, all he would accept was a pension. "They who ought to have succeeded me have gone before me," he said. "I am torn up by the roots and lie prostrate on the earth."

G. K. Chesterton deserted London for Beaconsfield in 1909, much to the astonishment of friends like Hilaire Belloc and G. B. Shaw. At first the Chestertons rented Overroads on Grove Road, but in the 1920s built their own house across the way.

Chesterton thoroughly enjoyed his new suburban existence, showing off his toy theater with the cardboard figures he had painted himself . . . tossing buns in the air and catching them in his mouth at tea . . . dismissing himself when writing duties called with a cryptic "I must get back to Tommy." Tommy, it turned out, was Thomas Aquinas, subject of a book published in 1933.

"Tommy" or his equivalents often called, for Chesterton was a prodigious producer in a wide range of genres. Among serious poems of the Beaconsfield years, which lasted until his death there in 1936, are "Lepanto" and *The Ballad of the White Horse*, both in 1911. The latter, running to almost a hundred printed pages, was tossed off in less than two weeks. His extensive and perceptive critical studies are well represented by *The Victorian Age in Literature* in 1913, the same year he showed his skill as a dramatist with *Magic*. His highly successful series of Father Brown detective stories began here, too, with *The Innocence of Father Brown* in 1911. And all the while he was turning out light verse that can still bring a timely chuckle:

> Oh Will to Get On that makes everything go—
> O Hustle! O Pep! O Publicity! O!

Both Waller's Hall Barn and Burke's Gregories have been rebuilt, but the little-restored fifteenth-century church where they are buried is much as it was then. Chesterton's Overroads is marked with a plaque, and there is a memorial to him in his church, St. Theresa's.

Stoke Poges   It's a short jaunt from Beaconsfield to Stoke Poges (PO-jez) and what may be the best-known little country churchyard in the world: east along the A 40, then south on the B 416 to where it meets the B 473, perhaps six miles in all.[2]

Thomas Gray and his "Elegy Written in a Country Churchyard" belong to Stoke Poges only because when his father died in 1741, his mother went to live there at West End House (now Stoke Court) with her two sisters. On a visit in 1742, Gray began the poem, but didn't finish it until 1750.

Originally entitled "An Elegy wrote in a Country Church Yard," it was first published anonymously at Gray's request by his friend Horace Walpole. Walpole, remembered now for his pioneer Gothic novel, *The Castle of Otranto* (1764), furnished it with a preface saying "As he cannot but feel some Satisfaction in having pleas'd so many Readers already, I flatter myself he will forgive my communicating that Pleasure to many more."

Many more readers there were! The "Elegy" may be the best-known single poem of the eighteenth century, and as widely quoted as any short piece in the English language. Not that its ideas were new; they were commonplaces of the century. What Gray did was to epitomize Pope's dictum, "what oft was thought, but ne'er so well express'd."

Among those readers was Shelley (a product of nearby Eton, like Gray),

[2]From London, it's twenty-three miles via the Uxbridge Road (A 4020) and the A 412 to Slough, where you pick up B 416 going north.

who often strolled the Stoke Poges churchyard. The "Elegy" finds a counterpart in Shelley's own "A Summer-Evening Churchyard, Lechlade, Gloucester."

The haunting power of Gray's churchyard remains today. Dating in part back to 1086, the church itself is small, built of egg and orange-sized stones, with a V-shaped roof of hewn timbers. Cool, dark, quiet, it invites contemplation. Outside the serenity continues, soothing with its greensward and flowers and weathered tombstones.

Here, side by side, near the church's east wall, lie Gray and his mother. The slab atop the tomb bears his epitaph to her: ". . . the careful mother of many children, one of whom alone had the misfortune to survive her."

Down from the churchyard, a little path leads to a field (now National Trust) with a monument dated 1799, bearing quotations from the poem.

Stoke Poges also inspired two other of Gray's poems, "Ode on a Distant Prospect of Eton College" and "A Long Story." They are strikingly different. The Eton poem—the manuscript is dated "at Stoke, Aug. 1742"—is a sermon, however eloquent, on the vanity of human wishes. Why should those happy little schoolboys yearn to grow up and come to know all the miseries of adulthood: "Where ignorance is bliss, 'tis folly to be wise."

"A Long Story" (1750), on the other hand, is a rollicking "The Owl and the Pussy-Cat" sort of thing, written to flatter the viscountess Cobham and her protege, a Miss Speed. Lady Cobham, presiding at Stoke Poges's Manor House, much admired the "Elegy" and longed to know its author. Miss Speed called on the poet to arrange this, and thus began a warm and lasting friendship.

The poem describes the imaginary first encounter of "The Bard" and "The Peeress." He is eager to speak to her, but struck dumb with awe. Besides, the disapproval of the long-nosed onlookers is evident:

> The ghostly Prudes with hagged face
> Already had condemn'd the sinner
> My Lady rose, and with a grace—
> She smiled, and bid him come to dinner.

It's called a long story, though there are only 144 lines in all. Just before the final quatrains appears the notice: "(Here 500 Stanzas are lost.)" When Dr. Johnson called Thomas Gray "dull in company, dull in his closet, dull everywhere," he couldn't have read "A Long Story."

Cliveden   Cliveden (as in "alive then") is not a town, but an estate, reached from Stoke Poges by going three miles west through Burnham to the

B 476, then north for two miles. And a goodly estate it is: included in its 327 acres are Cliveden House and garden, hanging woods, and Taplow Court Woods. It extends into two counties, Buckinghamshire and Berkshire, and lies on both sides of the Thames.

The beauty of the river at this point has long been famous, as the quotation from Jerome K. Jerome's *Three Men in a Boat* indicated. But over the centuries Cliveden has drawn more dramatic attention as well. In the first half of our century its name became for some almost an epithet, as in "That Cliveden set!" In both the seventeenth and eighteenth centuries it was a synonym for scandalous wealth and even more scandalous conduct.

The American-born Lady Nancy Astor gave Cliveden its not altogether welcome twentieth-century reputation. Married to the second Viscount Astor, she was the first woman to sit in the House of Commons, and kept that body atwitter with her sharp tongue and outspoken views.

It was the second Duke of Buckingham who gave Cliveden its much less savory name in the seventeenth century and later. Oddly enough, he was a politician, too—and a writer.

Buckingham was George Villiers, son of the George Villiers who, as handsome favorite of James I, rose in six short years (1617 to 1623) from obscure younger son of a knight to marquess to earl to first Duke of Buckingham. When this Buckingham fell under an assassin's knife in 1628, his infant son was raised by Charles I as almost his own. The younger Buckingham repaid this by fighting for Charles II during the Civil War, getting himself imprisoned in the Tower in 1658. But he rode high again when Charles II secured the throne in 1660.

There followed for Buckingham a career as remarkable for its shifting political ups and downs as its notorious scandals. Most incredible of the latter had to be that of 1668, involving the Earl of Shrewsbury, Shrewsbury's wife—who was Buckingham's mistress—and Buckingham. Buckingham found Shrewsbury inconvenient, in politics as well as love. So with one quick stroke, he resolved both matters. While Lady Shrewsbury, disguised as a page, held Buckingham's horse for him, he killed her husband in a duel, then cooly took her off to Cliveden with him to celebrate the happy occasion.

Noted for his good looks, astounding wealth, profligate ways, and wit, Buckingham was a patron of writers, too, befriending such authors as Abraham Cowley and William Wycherly. He was a writer of considerable talent himself. His occasional poems and satirical verses were better than amateur, and one play at least, *The Rehearsal* (1672), would have assured him mention in any account of Restoration drama.

Ironically, that play won him literary immortality in a work greater than any of his own. For *The Rehearsal* parodied the fashionable high-flown heroic tragedies of Dryden and his ilk. Dryden got revenge by impaling Buckingham as "Zimri" in his brilliant satirical poem, *Absalom and Achitophel* (1681).

Dryden uses the Biblical story of David and Absalom to attack a plan to force Charles II to accept his illegitimate son, the Duke of Monmouth, as his heir. In the poem, Charles becomes David, Monmouth is Absalom, and Buckingham is Zimri, a counselor embodying all human frailty.

"Stiff in opinions, always in the wrong," goes the devastating portrait of Zimri-Buckingham, and "all for women, painting, riming, drinking."

> In squand'ring wealth was his peculiar art
> Nothing went unrewarded but desert.

In short:

> A man so various that he seemed to be
> Not one, but all mankind's epitome.

Nor was literature done with the Duke of Buckingham. In the next century, Alexander Pope depicts Buckingham's death in a squalid Yorkshire inn, destitute and alone, his fortune dissipated:

> In the worst inn's worst room, with mat half-hung,
> The floors of plaister, and the walls of dung
> ....
> Great Villiers lies—alas! how changed for him,
> That life of pleasure, and that soul of whim!
> Gallant and gay, in Cliveden's proud alcove,
> The bower of wanton Shrewsbury and love.

The nineteenth century remembered Buckingham, too, as a villain in Sir Walter Scott's novel, *Peveral of the Peak* (1823). Scott's portrait of the duke is suitably immoral and dastardly, with the heroine falling into his evil and licentious clutches. But she is—of course!—saved in the nick of time, and all ends well.

The same mansion that embowered Buckingham and his obliging Lady Shrewsbury was still standing in 1740, and saw the first performance of a masque, *Alfred*, written by James Thomson and David Mallet, with music by Thomas Arne. Arne is known today for his delightful music for Shakespeare's "Blow, blow thou winter wind" (*As You Like It*) and "Where the bee sucks" (*The Tempest*).

Alfred is forgotten, however, save for a song tucked casually into its second act. Whenever pride and defiance and courage are called for, Englishmen still rally to

> Rule, Britannia, Brittania rule the waves,
> Britons never, never will be slaves.

Today's Cliveden House is the third to be built on the site, though it rests on a red brick terrace that goes back to 1666. Together with an endowment, in 1942 it was given by the second Viscount Astor to the National Trust, and is let to America's Stanford University and used for overseas courses. But the grounds are open to the public daily from March to the end of December, and two rooms of the house are open weekends during the season.

2. From Marlow to The Ouse

Marlow

Marlow stands on a lovely loop of the Thames, a bit more than three miles northwest of Cliveden. The A 4155 runs right through the town, crossing the river via a suspension bridge that goes back to 1828. Marlow's popularity as a boating and fishing resort is rooted in time, too. In the seventeenth century it attracted no less a fisherman than Izaac Walton, who stayed at a local inn while working on *The Compleat Angler* (1653 and 1655).

Among Marlow's citizens in the nineteenth century was G. P. R. James, an indefatigable and—in his own day, anyway—highly successful writer. The British Museum catalogs sixty-seven of his works, mainly historical romances that unabashedly reflect Sir Walter Scott, but including poems that can charitably be described as undistinguished.

Better at both verse and fiction was Thomas Love Peacock, who came to Marlow in the second decade of the same century, and stayed until 1823. Among the products of these years was *Nightmare Abbey* (1818), an entertaining novel that satirized both Byron and Shelley.

The former was caricatured as Mr. Cypress, a modishly melancholy young man who sings a song parodying *Childe Harold* so cleverly it out-Byrons Byron. Shelley is amiably lampooned as "Scythrop," a creature of high discussions and lofty delusions. Shelley took no offense. On the contrary, when living in Leghorn, Italy, in 1819, he dubbed the small roofed terrace he used as his study "Scythrop's Tower."

Actually, Peacock and Shelley were the best of friends. Even as *Nightmare Abbey* was being written, Shelley was not only living in Marlow himself, but just down the street from Peacock's house at 47 West Street. Shelley had stayed in that house in December of 1816, househunting after the death of his wife Harriet left him free to marry Mary Godwin. From Bath, Mary had written him urgently to find "our little mouse hole to retire to." Within a week Shelley had done so, leasing a place on West Street called Albion House, and asking Peacock to have it put in order while he returned to Bath.

Shelley and Mary were married at the end of December 1816, and by next mid-March were living in Marlow. Albion House was a commodious, rambling two-story building with gabled roof and dormer windows. The room Shelley chose as study was big as a ballroom.

Outwardly, their life was happy, filled with rowing, sailing, and walking excursions, and evening sessions around the new grand piano—still unpaid for. Guests came, too, including Mary's father, William Godwin, the philosopher and writer. The poet-critic-essayist Leigh Hunt came with his wife and four children and stayed for a month. Both Byron and Keats were invited, too, but neither came.

The Shelleys were busy writing, as well. Mary, only twenty, worked at a tale of terror she had begun as a joke, which she had decided to call *Frankenstein.* Shelley labored at the long poem, *Revolt of Islam,* and some twenty-six shorter poems, turning out six thousand lines in all in less than a year.

But beneath all this were grim undercurrents. Two suicides in a little more than a month in the year before still haunted them—that of Mary's half-sister Fanny in October, and of Shelley's first wife Harriet in November. On a walk with Peacock one day, Shelley announced, "There is one thing to which I have decidedly made up my mind. I will take a great glass of ale every night." Peacock laughed, saying it was a good resolution. "Yes," Shelley replied, "but you do not know why I take it. I shall do it to deaden my feelings, for I see that those who drink ale have none." Next day he was explicit: "I was thinking of Harriet."

There were other burdens as well—financial, legal, and literary—crushing in their accumulation. Added to those was Shelley's steadily deteriorating health. By December 1817, doctors warned that Shelley must discontinue writing and move to a warmer climate, or face lingering death from consumption. Albion House, leased so optimistically for a period of twenty-one years only twelve months earlier, must be given up.

By March 1818 they were at Dover, preparing to sail for Italy. Shelley never saw England again.

Shelley's Albion House still stands on West Street, as does Peacock's place. In fact, you can have lunch in the latter. It's now a restaurant, predictably called The Peacock. And you can stay overnight, elegantly, where Izaac Walton did. The Compleat Angler Hotel at Marlow Bridge is four-star, with period furniture, luxuriant gardens, and superb views of the river.

Hughenden Manor

What should be connected with Benjamin Disraeli, Lord Beaconsfield, is not the town of Beaconsfield (discussed earlier), but Hughenden Manor. The estate is five miles almost due north of Marlow, and reached via the A 404 and A 4128.

Hughenden's name comes from "Hitchindene," i.e., valley (dene) of the Hitchin. Before Disraeli bought it, it had a long history almost totally devoid of interest. The fourth Earl of Chesterfield, he of the famous letters, owned it in the eighteenth century, but there is no indication that he let this concern him unduly. To Disraeli, however, it was of paramount importance, both as symbol and physical reality.

Disraeli's father's home, Bradenham House, was almost within eyeshot, and when Hughendon became available in 1845, it seemed just the place to accommodate Disraeli's conviction that the next leader of parliament's Conservatives should be a solid landowner. Disraeli meant to be that leader. He had nothing like the £35,000 the estate would require, an enormous sum then. But political allies advanced him £25,000, and in the summer of 1848 he was able to write his wife, "It is all done, you are the Lady of Hughendon." And by 1849, *he* was the leader of the Conservatives.

The road to this eminence had been tortuous. By the laws of the times, as a Jew he had no right even to be in politics. But his father, after a squabble with its leaders, had left the synagogue and allowed his children to be baptized. So Disraeli was a Jew who wasn't a Jew.

Other obstacles remained, many self-made, for the young Disraeli had an extraordinary flair for failure. At twenty (in 1824) he had quit his training to be a solicitor. At twenty-one he traded his way into heavy debt by gambling on South American stock, and made things worse by trying to organize a new daily paper that failed. At twenty-two he published a lively, witty novel called *Vivian Grey* (1826–27). This did succeed, mainly because a number of characters were all-too-thinly disguised high-placed figures of the day.

At twenty-four he entered Lincoln's Inn for another try at a legal career, but illness and depression made him give that up, too. And with his first fling at politics, the old losing ways were back with a vengeance. From 1832 on, he managed four straight defeats while seeking a seat in parliament before winning the right to represent Maidenstone in 1837. At that, his initial speech in the House of Commons failed. And when the Conservatives came to power in 1841 and he asked for a government post, he got a flat refusal.

Gradually, however, he made his way in politics and lessened his financial burdens with a series of novels: one a love story, *Henrietta Temple* (1837) . . . another, based on the lives of Shelley and Byron, *Venetia* (1837) . . . and a trio of strong political novels, *Coningsby* (1844), *Sybil* (1845), and *Tancred* (1847).

Thus the Disraelis' star was definitely on the rise when they came to Hughendon. What they had bought was essentially an old farmhouse converted in the eighteenth century into a three-storey Georgian manor. Over the next two decades they worked at transforming it into something grander.

To the exterior were added a new parapet with pinnacles, and other "Jacobean" embellishments. The inside was treated to the kind of Gothicizing then in vogue. And the grounds got particular attention: a "German" forest on the hill to the north, a garden in the "Italian" style, a terrace with peacocks, a lake with swans.

Meanwhile Disraeli's political career went on apace. Three stints as Chancellor of the Exchequer (1852, 1858–59, 1866–68) culminated in 1868 with a ten-month term as prime minister. When his government then had to yield to Gladstone's Liberal party, Disraeli asked but one favor of the queen: that she bestow a title on his wife. Victoria did, and Mrs. Disraeli became Viscountess Beaconsfield. Disraeli himself turned back to writing, producing perhaps his best novel, *Lothair* (1870).

The death of his wife in 1872 was devastating. But Disraeli went on. In 1874 he returned to power for the six dazzling years that placed him among Britain's greatest prime ministers. He made his queen "Empress of India," a title she had coveted, and his nation the world's unquestioned imperial power.

Victoria was more than appreciative of his loyalty and devotion. In 1876 she created him Earl of Beaconsfield, and in 1877 did him the almost unprecedented honor of dining informally at Hughenden, accompanied only by her daughter, Princess Beatrice, and one or two attendants.

Disraeli retired to Hughendon when his party lost again to Gladstone and the Liberals in 1880, and finished writing *Endymion* (1880), the novel long laid aside for politics. But without his lady, the manor must have been vastly empty; and death, when it came in April of 1881, welcome. He was buried beside his wife against the east wall of the Hughendon church, as he had wished.[3] Four days later Queen Victoria came herself to lay a wreath upon the grave of her favorite minister. Her further tribute can be seen in the church today: the personal monument "placed," says the inscription, "by his grateful Sovereign and Friend, Victoria R.I."

Hughendon Manor is now owned by the National Trust and open in season five afternoons a week. The rooms on view and their assortment of pictures, furnishings, and furniture are too many and varied to enumerate here. They represent Disraeli the statesman well.

More representative of Disraeli the writer is the study, which he called "my workshop." Especially evocative are the writing table he had made in High Wycombe, its inkstand, the desk he used as a schoolboy, and—a final poignant note—the black-edged paper he habitually used after his wife's death.

Bradenham House—Aylesbury—Aston Clinton—Stowe

Bradenham House   Bradenham House is a fine old seventeenth-century manor in the village of Bradenham, off the A 4010 three miles northwest of Hughendon. Benjamin Disraeli's father Isaac D'Israeli[4], had only recently bought it when his son went there in 1829, at twenty-five, to recuperate from the illness and depression that had led him to abandon studying for the law. Idleness was his chief occupation during this period, but he did stir himself to write his second novel, *The Young Duke* (1830).

Even without Benjamin Disraeli, however, Bradenham House would be worth a word, for Isaac D'Israeli was an author in his own right. Sir Walter Scott and Robert Southey, the poet laureate, were among contemporaries who admired him, and Byron said, "I don't know a living man's books I take up so often—or lay down so reluctantly—as D'Israeli's."

Byron was a warm friend of the elder D'Israeli, who wrote an essay taking Byron's side in the controversy with William Bowle over the value of Alexander Pope's poetry. An engraving of himself that Byron gave D'Israeli now hangs at Hughendon Manor.

Isaac D'Israeli was more than a dilettante writer. Among his works were *Curiosities of Literature* in several volumes, the first of which appeared in 1791, and *Essay on a Literary Character* (1795). Both of these, anecdotal in style,

---

[3]In the same vault, in compliance with her request, was buried Disraeli's eccentric friend, Mrs. Brydges Willyams, who had left him a considerable fortune.

[4]The son dropped the apostrophe early in his career.

have real taste and charm. He also wrote a number of novels, three of which were published in 1797 alone. He died at Bradenham in 1848, the very year his son bought Hughendon.

Aylesbury Ten miles above Bradenham, the A 4010 meets the A 413, and two more miles northwest on the latter takes you to Aylesbury. With a population of well over forty thousand, Aylesbury is one of Buckinghamshire's bigger towns and its county seat. It also had the prison where poor Thomas Ellwood was lodged shortly after finding John Milton that cottage in Chalfont St. Giles. In Queen Elizabeth I's time, it was represented in parliament by John Lyly, playwright and author of *Euphues* (1578 and 1580).

Representing Aylesbury two hundred years later was a man who might well have surpassed Lyly as a literary figure had he applied to writing the zeal he brought to debauchery. He was John Wilkes, politician, publisher and profligate—and subject of one of the best vignettes in Boswell's *Life of Samuel Johnson.*

Schooled at Hertford and tutored at Aylesbury, at twenty Wilkes married an Aylesbury heiress half again his age: "a sacrifice," he confessed, "to Plutus, not Venus." He went on to buy the Aylesbury seat in parliament (an under-the-table deal that cost £7,000!) and, abetted by the satiric poet Charles Churchill, published a weekly political periodical. Called *The North Briton,* the magazine's outrageous attacks on the king and his Tory favorites gained Wilkes expulsion from parliament, and exile abroad. Nothing daunted, he returned to England four years later, and wound up not only being re-elected to parliament (this time for Middlesex), but lord mayor of London as well.

Matching the sheer audacity of the man was his cutting wit. After a voter refused him support, saying he'd rather vote for the Devil, Wilkes replied, "And if your friend is not running ———?" When Lord Sandwich (yes, *the* sandwich man) predicted Wilkes would die either on the gallows or from a venereal disease, his response was classic: "That depends, my lord, on whether I embrace your principles or your mistress."

Even in so lax an age as his, Wilkes's morals were shocking. He and Churchill were both members of the Hellfire Club, which met regularly in the ruins of Medmenham Abbey outside Marlow to stage obscene orgies. That Dr. Johnson, of all people, should sit down to dinner with such a man defies belief. Yet Boswell, as he recounts with great relish, managed to arrange exactly that.

Invited to a dinner party for Wilkes, Boswell yielded to "an irresistible wish" and asked the host, a Mr. Dilly, to invite Johnson, too. "What, with

Mr. Wilkes? Not for the world," said Mr. Dilly. "If you'll let me negotiate for you," Boswell replied, "I will be answerable that all shall go well."

Boswell explains his strategy: "Notwithstanding the high veneration which I entertained for Dr. Johnson, I was sensible that he was sometimes a little actuated by the spirit of contradiction." So he conveyed the invitation, but only after Johnson had accepted did he add, "Provided, Sir, I suppose, that the company which he is to have, is agreeable to you."

Johnson bristled: "What do you mean, Sir? Do you think that I am so ignorant of the world that I am to prescribe to a gentleman what company he is to have at his table?"

Boswell: "Perhaps he may have some of what he calls his patriotick friends with him."

Johnson: "Well Sir, and what then? What care I for his *patriotick friends?* Poh!"

Boswell: "I should not be surprised to find John Wilkes there."

Johnson: "And if John Wilkes *should* be there, what's that to *me*, Sir?"

Nevertheless, when they actually entered Mr. Dilly's drawing room and Johnson learned that the gentleman in lace was Mr. Wilkes, he withdrew to a window seat and picked up a book to read, or at least pretend to read, until "the cheering sound of 'Dinner is upon the table' dissolved his reverie."

Boswell's recital of what ensued is delicious:

> Mr. Wilkes placed himself next to Dr. Johnson, and behaved to him with so much attention and politeness, that he gained upon him insensibly. No man eat more heartily than Johnson, or loved better what was nice and delicate. Mr. Wilkes was very assiduous in helping him to some fine veal. "Pray give me leave, Sir;—It is better here—a little of the brown—some fat, Sir—a little of the stuffing—some gravy—let me have the pleasure of giving you some butter—allow me to recommend a squeeze of this orange;—or the lemon, perhaps may have more zest."

> "Sir, Sir, I am obliged to you, Sir," cried Dr. Johnson, bowing and turning his head to him with a look for some time of "surly virtue," but, in a short while, of complacency.

Flourishing in the days of both Lyly and Wilkes was Aylesbury's King's Head Inn—and it's still flourishing, rated two-star. You'll find it pleasant for either a meal or an overnight stay, and its history is fascinating. For the royal touch, there's Henry VIII, who is supposed to have stayed there while courting Anne Boleyn. (Her father was lord of the manor of Aylesbury). And for a matching bit of democracy, Oliver Cromwell received the official thanks of parliament here in 1651—for defeating the Royalists.

The inn still has the bedroom where Cromwell slept, with a listening hole that allowed him to hear everything that was being said in the hall below. The King's Head courtyard is still cobbled and the ancient wooden entrance gates still stand.

Aston Clinton   Evelyn Waugh's first published novel was *Decline and Fall* (1928), a boisterous and in no way unbiased satire on preparatory schools. If there is more of Dickens in the style than Waugh would have liked to confess, there is perhaps more of Aston Clinton in the content than the village would willingly admit.

Waugh taught at Aston Clinton—four miles east of Aylesbury on the A 41—from the fall of 1925 to the spring of 1927 and began the book while there. But Waugh had already taught at a school in North Wales and perhaps his fictional school is based on it, also. In any case, it was the Welsh school master who visited him in Aston Clinton on whom the character Captain Grimes in the novel is based.

Stowe   A visit to Bath in Avon makes you feel that it was deliberately laid out to present eighteenth-century architecture at its best. A visit to the great estate called Stowe makes you feel the same way about that century's landscaping.

Reached from Aylesbury by going seventeen miles northwest along the A 413 to Buckingham, then another two miles on a side road off the A 422, Stowe is at once a testament to the age's magnificence and its good taste, and abounds with literary associations. Sir Richard Temple (later Lord Cobham), the owner who in 1710 began turning a seventeenth-century mansion into an Augustan showpiece, belonged to London's Kit-Cat Club. Author-members of that club, so named because its mutton pies were called "kit-cats," included Addison, Steele, Garth, Congreve, and Vanbrugh.

William Congreve and Sir John Vanbrugh were directly connected with Stowe, as were James Thomson, Alexander Pope, and Horace Walpole. Vanbrugh was one of the designers of the elaborate buildings and gardens with which Temple surrounded his house. Another was William Kent, whom Walpole called "the father of modern gardening."

Among Kent's contributions were the Temple of Ancient Virtue, the Temple of British Worthies (with busts of Bacon, Shakespeare, Locke, Milton, and others), and an odd monument on an island in the middle of a man-made lake—an obelisk topped by a monkey. The monkey was Congreve, a favorite summer guest. To open up vistas, Kent replaced hedges with ha-ha's, sunken barriers so cunningly hidden that when you came to one you said, "ha HA! So *there* you are!"

Vanbrugh, both playwright and architect, brought to his work for Temple the same kind of broad strokes he had given comedies like *The Relapse* (1697), *The Provok'd Wife* (1697), and *The Confederacy* (1705). The Lake Pavilion, Rodondo, and Bourbon Tower at Stowe are his.

Thomson and Pope both left lasting poetic records of their approval of the results of Kent's and Vanbrugh's efforts—and Temple's money. Wrote Thomson in "The Autumn" section of *The Seasons* (1716–30), illustrated by Kent:

> Oh! Lead me to the wide extended walks,
> The fair majestic paradise of Stowe!

Pope used Temple and Stowe in his *Moral Essays* (1731–35) to lecture on the proper use of riches:

> Still follow Sense, of every Art the Soul,
> Parts answ'ring parts shall slide into a whole,
> . . . .
> Nature shall join you; Time shall make it grow
> A work to wonder at—perhaps a STOWE.

By the end of the eighteenth century, Stowe had practically passed into the language as a cliché for elegance, as in this anecdote from William Cowper about his servant Sam: "I said to Sam, "Sam, build me a shed in the garden with anything you can find, and make it rude and rough like one of those at Eartham." "Yes, sir," says Sam, and straightway laying his noddle and the carpenter's noddle together, has built me a thing fit for Stow [sic] Gardens. Is not this vexatious?"

Olney and Weston Underwood

Last of the literary stops in Buckinghamshire for those going north are Olney and Weston Underwood, within three miles of Northamptonshire to the north and west, and Bedfordshire to the north and east. Olney is on the A 509, and Weston Underwood is an easy walk away to the southwest. Both Weston Underwood and Olney are on the River Ouse. (That's "OWN-y" on the OOZE."). To get to them from Stowe (twenty-five miles in all), take the A 422 through Milton Keynes, then the A 509 north to Olney.

Were it not for a former slave trader and his friend, an eccentric fancier of hares, the world would never have heard of Weston Underwood. And Olney's fame would largely be limited to a pancake race.

Not to low-rate that race, mind you. It's widely known. Every Shrove Tuesday eager ladies line up at the market place, then race wildly down to the church, flipping and catching the pancakes in their skillets three times en route. The victor's reward: a prayer book and a kiss from the sexton.

The contributions of the one-time slave trader and his friend to Olney's fame? Well, how about "How Sweet the Name of Jesus?" and "Amazing Grace?" and "There is a Fountain Filled with Blood?" and "God Moves in a Mysterious Way?"

Olney   Curate of this pleasant little market town in 1767 was the Reverend John Newton, a man with a curious background. Impressed aboard a man-of-war as a youth, he worked his way up to master of slave-trading ships. By age thirty he was tide-surveyor at Liverpool and studying Greek and Hebrew. In 1764 he accepted the post at Olney.

In 1767 a friend asked him to run down to Huntingdon in Cambridgeshire to comfort a Mrs. Mary Unwin, whose husband—a fellow minister—had died in an accident. Newton went, met Mrs. Unwin and her boarder, a shy and rather troubled bachelor named William Cowper, and persuaded them to return with him to Olney. To the Unwins Cowper had been almost as a son, though at thirty-four he was just seven years younger than Mary Unwin.

At first Cowper and Mrs. Unwin lodged with Newton, but in February 1768 they took over a house on the marketplace called Orchard Side. Here Cowper lived for the next ten years, and here he wrote the pieces that raised him from obscurity to a ranking place in English literature.

The house today looks much as it did when they moved in: large, three storeys high, in patterned brick, with the clean, simple lines that mark Georgian architecture. Though it looks like a single house, actually it was two, the left side being for the servants. Beyond the yard out back stretched the sixty-foot garden so beloved by the poet and celebrated in *The Task*, separated from the vicarage garden by an orchard—whence the name, Orchard Side.

Even here, however, Cowper remained prey to the fits of depression that so dogged his life, and in 1771 as a palliative, Newton suggested that together they write a series of hymns. Thus came about "How Sweet the Name of Jesus" and "Amazing Grace" among the 281 contributed by Newton, and "There is a Fountain Filled with Blood," "God Moves in a Mysterious Way," and "OH! for a Closer Walk with God" among the sixty-seven of Cowper's.

Assisting Cowper's recovery were his hobbies: gardening, carpentering, and most of all attending to his three pets, Puss, Tiney, and Bess, who were to become celebrities through his writings. As he explained in a delightful essay published in 1784, "Not withstanding the two feminine appelations, I must inform you that they were all males." They had distinct personalities. "Bess . . . was a hare of great humour and drollery." And while "Puss might be said to be perfectly tame . . . not so Tiney; upon him the kindest treatment had not the least effect." Cowper's poem, "Epitaph on a Hare," bears this out:

> Old Tiney, surliest of his kind,
>   Who, nurs'd with tender care,
> And to domestic bounds confin'd,
>   Was still a wild Jack-hare.

Two events furthered his recovery and poetic progress. In 1789 Newton took a post in London; with his removal Cowper's religious fervor mellowed and broadened. And in 1781 he became friendly with a Lady Austen, who was visiting at nearby Clifton Reynes. It was she who told him the story of John Gilpin and his runaway horse, which Cowper turned into a ballad overnight and published anonymously in 1782. It was Lady Austen, too, who in 1783 playfully assigned him the duty of writing an epic upon the sofa in his parlor. The result, Cooper's most impressive and best-known work, was *The Task*, six books of mock-Miltonic blank verse with warm and winning details of his placid rural life. Who else in all poetry ever celebrated a dung heap with:

> The stable yield a stercoraceous heap.

With *The Task* Cowper reached his pinnacle. Among its host of admirers was Robert Burns, who kept it with him to while away time "in a lonely room or in a brew house," and despite "a few scraps of Calvinistic divinity" exclaimed, "Is not 'The Task' a glorious poem?"

From then on it was pretty much all down hill for Cowper. In 1786, his cousin, Lady Hesketh, who had temporarily become a tenant of Olney vicarage, was so concerned about him she advocated a change of residence, and rented him a house in Weston Underwood called Weston Lodge. When he left Olney in November, his career was essentially over.

Orchard Side is now the Cowper and Newton Museum, open Easter through October, and thoroughly worth a visit. You can park right outside the door in the marketplace except—you guessed it—on market day (Thursdays).

The front door opens on to the hall, with its porthole for Puss, Tiney, and Bess to parade into kitchen and parlor. To the left is the parlor itself, a small room chock-a-block with items like Cowper's writing table (really a chest of drawers), fly table, greatcoat and cane, the waistcoat in which he died, and not only a lock of his hair but a lock of his wig as well. And of course, the sofa. Actually, it looks more like a lounge chair, with a cane headrest on chains so that it can be lowered.

Stairs from the parlor lead to the John Newton Room, with mementos of him, and above that is the Mary Unwin Room, with souvenirs of her and Lady Austen. Adjacent is Cowper's bedroom, where he often wrote. In the stairwell is a painting of his dog, entitled "Beau with a Water Lily," after the poem he wrote on that subject. The top floor is devoted to the history of Olney.

Caution: the notice on the first landing means it when it says, "These stairs are very steep and narrow. Do not attempt to go down them unless you are very agile."

The grounds of Orchard Side must be seen, too. The yard immediately back of the house has the tiny "Viper Barn," on the spot were Cowper killed the snake commemorated in his "The Colubriad," and now housing the pew from his church.[5] And beyond that is the garden, with the little hut he called variously his "Sulking Room" or the "Verse Manufactury." One aches that such surroundings could not give him more lasting serenity.

Weston Underwood   Lady Hesketh's choice of Weston Underwood as a change of scene for Cowper would seem ideal. He called the village "one of the prettiest I know." It's no distance at all from Olney down the Ouse, and had been one of his favorite walks from Orchard Side.

Weston Lodge, which he and Mrs. Unwin moved into on November 15, 1789, was commodious and comfortable. Though it was in the middle of the village, an abundant orchard gave them the feeling of being surrounded by a wood. Out back was the garden where his man Sam built the intended "rough and rude" little shack on so grand a scale.

Weston Underwood did furnish him with some bright moments. He worked on a translation of Homer, and wrote a number of poems, including the one on his pet, Beau, and another after receiving the picture of his long dead mother. He even attempted to edit Milton's works.

But the sad downward slide continued, accelerated by the misfortunes of

[5]The Memorial Chapel of the church has a window honoring Newton, Cowper—and the hares.

Mrs. Unwin. Hardly had they moved into the lodge when her only son died. Then in 1791 she suffered a stroke. By 1792 her health, both physical and mental, was deteriorating so drastically that at times Cowper's melancholy approached imbecility. The lines addressed to her in "To Mary," written in 1793, are heartbreaking:

> Thy spirits have a fainter flow,
> I see thee daily weaker grow—
> 'Twas my distress that brought thee low,
>   My Mary!

Finally in 1795 his devoted young cousin, John Johnson, insisted they come with him to Norfolk. It was supposed to be just a visit, but something in Cowper suggested otherwise. He wrote on the window shutter of his bedroom:

> Farewell, dear scenes for ever closed to me;
> Oh, for what sorrows must I now exchange ye!

You can see that shutter on the wall of Cowper's bedroom in Olney today. For the words proved all too prophetic. Though he lived another five years, he never returned to Buckinghamshire.

BERKSHIRE

Berkshire

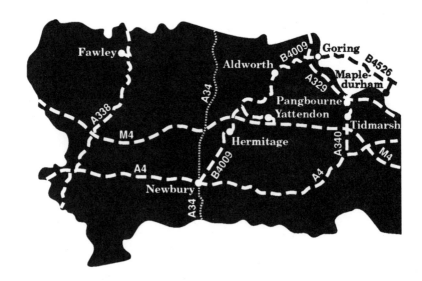

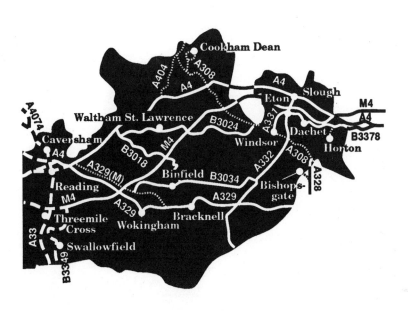

Legend:
1. Berkshire East
2. Berkshire West
3. Access or Connecting Routes

Ye distant spires, ye antique towers,
That crown the watry glade,
Where grateful Science still adores
Her HENRY's holy shade;
And ye, that from the stately brow
Of WINDSOR's heights th'expanse below
Of grove, of lawn, of mead survey,
Whose turf, whose shade, whose flowers among
Wanders the hoary Thames along
His silver-winding way.

> Thomas Gray, "On a Distant Prospect of Eton
> College"

Ask the veriest newcomer to England to name its greatest surviving castle, its best-known boys' school, and its most famous river and he'll probably have no trouble at all coming up with Windsor Castle, Eton, and the Thames. The opening lines of Gray's poem, just quoted, have all three. And so does Berkshire (BARK-sh'r). The spires of grateful Science still rise over Eton; the Castle still graces Windsor's stately brow; and the Thames winds on, hoarier by 250 years.

Berkshire is also the county where Milton wrote his first poems of any consequence . . . where Oscar Wilde went to jail . . . and where Pope, Swift, John Gay, and Dr. Arbuthnot (originator of the nickname, John Bull) spent a bibulous afternoon collaborating on a ballad hailing an innkeeper's daughter.

It's a long, thin county, Berkshire, about forty-five miles wide and fifteen high. Elias Ashmole, the seventeenth-century antiquary, thought it looked like a lute. His contemporary, Thomas Fuller, author of *The Worthies of England* (1662), thought it looked like a slipper. The more prosaic modern may see it as a crudely drawn dumbbell, with its county town of Reading at the handgrip in the center. At the south, its border runs all along the top of Hampshire; at the north all along the bottom of Oxfordshire.

Berkshire is indeed a London neighbor. Its eastern tip actually touches the western edge of Greater London. If you like, you can leave your West End hotel after breakfast, run over and see both Windsor and Eton, and be back by tea time.

Windsor and Eton provide an ideal entry into Berkshire for an extended tour of the county, too.

1. Berkshire East

Horton—Windsor—and Eton

The easiest way to Windsor and Eton from the heart of London is to pick up the M 4 where it begins just west of Hammersmith, and keep on it until you come to Exit 5. If you *do* just want to dash over to them for the day, however, both busses and trains run there regularly, and you'd be a lot better off to use one or the other and leave your automobile in the carpark. In either case, you'll be passing above John Milton's Horton.

Horton   The little village of Horton offers almost nothing to remind you of Milton any more, but it was of paramount importance in his development. If you want to give it a quick look, it's off the B 3378, a bit south of Exit 5.

Milton's father, a prosperous scrivener (a kind of private banker) retired to his country home in Horton in 1632, and was quickly joined by his son, the new recipient of an M. A. from Cambridge. Only twenty-four, but already convinced he was divinely ordained to be a great poet, and free at last of academic "saw-thistles and brambles," Milton began at once the preparation for that awesome task, as described in his *Second Defense of the English People* (1654): "On my father's estate, where I had determined to pass the remainder of my days, I enjoyed an interval of uninterrupted leisure, which I entirely devoted to the perusal of Latin and Greek authors."

In college he had shown some signs of promise with poems like "On Christ's Nativity," (1629), written when he was twenty-one, "On Shakespeare" (1630), and "L'Allegro" and "Il Penseroso," both in 1631. But as he makes clear in the first-rate "Sonnet VII," written either just before or just after he came to Horton, he was unhappy that by his twenty-third birthday he had yet to produce the ripened fruit of a major work:

> How soon hath Time the subtle thief of youth,
> Stolen on his wing my three and twentieth year!
> My hasting days fly on with full career,
> But my late spring no bud or blossom show'th.

The years at Horton did yield the masque, *Comus* (1634), and the notable elegy "Lycidas" (1637) before he left in 1638 for a grand tour of the continent. Time, however, abetted by long and devoted service to the cause of Cromwell and the Commonwealth, was to prove the thief not only of Milton's youth, but of middle age as well. He was fifty-nine when *Paradise Lost* was printed in 1667.

Milton's Horton retreat is long gone, but the parish church does have a window in his honor, and his mother is buried under a flat blue stone in the chancel.

Windsor   From Exit 5 on the M 4, you get to Windsor by driving through Dachet and straight along the A 331 (it becomes King Edward VIII Avenue) to the Windsor railway station. Were it not for Windsor Castle, the town would be only an unprepossessing community of something over thirty thousand persons, with a basic pattern of Victorian brick buildings, a sprinkling of Georgian, and a couple of cobbled streets to give the occasional visitor a suggestion of antiquity.

But, you see, there is that castle, its grey battlements looming right up the hill from the station. And with the castle come not only centuries and centuries of fabulous background—historical and literary alike—but the teeming tourists as well.

The name, originally "Wyndeshour," comes from that silver-winding Thames in the quotation from Gray's Eton poem: "Wynde" for winding, and "shour" for shore, or bank. The Romans held it in their day. The Saxon Edward the Confessor had a royal residence three miles down the river in what is now "Old Windsor." But it was William the Conqueror who, after 1066, built the Norman stronghold that is the core of today's castle. Various later monarchs added their touches—Henry III, Edward III, Edward IV, Henry VIII . . . on through George IV and even Victoria, though her hand is evident inside rather than out.

In turn, the castle left its mark upon the monarchs, often for the worse. One June day in 1215, King John left the castle to pop down to Runnymede and sign that bothersome Magna Carta. In the early part of the fifteenth century, James I of Scotland was a prisoner there. So was Charles I more than two hundred years later. In January of 1649 he left it a captive, and in February he came back a corpse, beheaded by Parliament.

Among others buried there are Henry VIII, Lady Jane Seymour (also beheaded), George III, George IV, William IV, Edward VII, and George V. In the royal bedrooms, Edward III and Henry VI were born, and in the chapel Victoria wept at the sudden death of her beloved Albert. For the next forty years she was to be the "Widow at Windsor," as in Rudyard Kipling's poem of the same name:

> "Ave you 'eard o' the Widow at Windsor
> With a hairy gold crown on 'er 'ead?
> She 'as ships on the foam—she 'as millions at 'ome,
> An' she pays us poor beggars in red.

Windsor Castle remains a royal residence. When Victoria's great-great-granddaughter chooses to stop by, the State Apartments are closed to the public. Victoria's grandson, George V, even changed the ruling family's name to Windsor (from Albert's Saxe-Coburg-Gotha) when he renounced all things German during World War I.

The castle's literary connections go all the way back to the first major works in what may be considered the English (as opposed to Anglo-Saxon) language. For Chaucer lived there off and on in Winchester Tower, while he was in charge of all royal residences as Master of the Royal Works from 1389 to 1391. During these years he was working on the General Prologue and earlier sections of *The Canterbury Tales*. In the *Romaunt of the Rose* (about 1370), Windsor is slyly used to enhance a character's social status. He's a "bacheler," fair and tall, but alas Chaucer can say ("sey") no more about him except that he was ("All hadde he be") the son of the lord of Windsor:

> I can not telle you what he highte [was called],
> But fair he was and of good highte [height],
> All hadde he be, I sey no more,
> The lordis sone of Wyndesore.

In 1423 Windsor even produced a poet who was himself royal. While imprisoned there, James I of Scotland wrote "The King's Quair" (the King's quire or book) about a kingly prisoner who is smitten by a beautiful lady seen strolling in the garden beneath his castle window. In real life the woman was Lady Jane Beaumont, allied to the ruling house of Lancaster, and James married her. The Victorian poet-painter Dante Gabriel Rossetti quotes from "The King's Quair" in his own *The King's Tragedy* (1881), which elaborates on James's misfortunes.

Another monarch who linked Windsor Castle with literature was Elizabeth I—not once, but twice. She was there in 1563 with her private tutor, Roger Ascham, and a dinner-table debate about the best methods of teaching provided the impetus for Ascham's outstanding *The Scholemaster* (1570). And Elizabeth is credited with moving Shakespeare to write *The Merry Wives of Windsor* (about 1600) to satisfy her desire to see Falstaff in love.

Windsor, the castle, and especially the St. George's Chapel and its Knights of the Garter, are all central to the play, which may well have had its first performance at Windsor Castle itself in connection with the Garter Feast for installment of new knights. One character in the play is the Keeper of The Garter, Windsor's leading inn in Shakespeare's day, and typical of the many references to Knights of the Garter is Mistress Quickly's request to the "fairies" to

> Search Windsor Castle, elves, within and out
> Strew good luck, ouphes[imps], on every sacred room
> . . . .
> Each fair installment, coat, and several crest,
> With loyal blazon [coat of arms] evermore be blest!

The Garter was still in business when Samuel Pepys made one of his visits to Windsor in 1666. In his *Diary* he gives a colorful account:

> So took coach and to Windsor, to the Garter, and thither sent for Dr. Childe [chapel organist]; who come to us, and carried us to St. George's Chappell; and there placed us among the knights' stalls (and pretty the observation that no man, but a woman may sit in a knights' place, where any brass-plates are set); and hither come cushions to us, and a young singing-boy to bring us a copy of the anthem to be sung. And here, for our sakes, had this anthem and the great service sung extraordinary, only to entertain us. It is a noble place indeed, and a good Quire of voices . . . After prayers, we to see the plate of the chappell, and the robes of the knights, and a man to shew us the banners of several knights in being, which hang up over the Stalls. Was shown where the late king [Charles I] is buried, and King Henry the Eighth, and my Lady [Jane] Seymour. This being done, to the King's house, and to observe the neatness and contrivance of the house and gates; it is the most romantique castle that is in the world.

Two poets who anticipated Gray's tribute to the magnificence of a distant view of Windsor and the Thames were Sir John Denham in the seventeenth century, and Alexander Pope in the eighteenth. Denham's "Cooper's Hill" (1642) exclaims in all-too-controlled iambic pentameter on the vista from that promontory in Surrey, seven miles away—of Windsor Castle, with its "crown of such majestic towers," and of the Thames:

> Oh, could I flow like thee, and make thy stream
> My great example, as it is my theme!

Though deep, yet clear, though gentle, yet not dull,
Strong without rage, without o'erflowing full.

Pope obviously found Denham more Olympian than we. In "Windsor Forest" (1713), he dubs him "lofty Denham," and begs his friend Grenville to emulate Denham:

To paint anew the flowery sylvan scenes
To crown the forests with immortal greens,
Make Windsor-hills in lofty numbers rise,
And lift her turrets nearer to the skies.

The eighteenth-century authoress, Fanny Burney, like Chaucer, saw royal service at Windsor Castle. George III's Queen Charlotte appointed the novelist her Second Keeper of the Robes, but Ms. Burney in no way liked it. And who can blame her? A celebrity after the publication of *Evalina* (1778), she found herself attending to the queen's toilet and caring for her lap dog and snuff box. Worst of all, Fanny confided to her *Diary* (1842–46), was putting up with her superior, Mrs. Schwellenberg, a "peevish old person of uncertain temper and impaired health, swaddled in the buckram of back-stairs etiquette." In 1791, after six years of this, Fanny was more than grateful to be allowed to resign with a pension of £100 a year.

The precincts of the castle are open year round, the hours varying with sunset. State Apartments and St. George's Chapel, however, as mentioned, are closed when the Queen is in residence. When she is there, the Royal Standard flies from atop the Round Tower. Otherwise, it's the Union Jack, and you're in luck. In summer, though, the crowds can be enormous and the lines long, so be prepared to wait.

The view from the top of the Round Tower (reached by 122 steps!) is superb. Fifteen counties and that ever-winding river unfurl before you. The State Apartments and Queen Mary's Dolls' House next door—both to the east of the Tower—are also "musts" for most visitors. The apartments are satisfactorily lavish and huge, though one wonders, as at all such grand mansions, where the poor residents go to be comfortable.

The Dolls' House, presented to George V's queen as a gift, is remarkable, let the sophisticates scoff as they will. Four floors of rooms are reproduced in miniature so meticulously that the Dolls' House even has its own doll's house—and the gnat-sized electric iron actually works.

St. George's Chapel in the lower ward near the Henry VIII Gateway entrance gives you an almost overpowering sense of England's great past. Here in the chapel choir are the stalls of the knights of England's oldest and most illustrious order, with their historic insignia, swords, helmets, and banners. In their tombs sleep the long line of royal dead enumerated earlier.

Outside the castle grounds proper are Home Park, immediately adjoining on the north and east; and Windsor Great Park, stretching on and on to the south. Within Home Park is the mausoleum where Victoria and Albert are buried.

Windsor Great Park is the setting for the climax to *Merry Wives of Windsor,* where Falstaff, buck's head and all, enters for his final attempt at assignation, beset upon by the supposed fairies, egged on by Mistress Quickly:

> Pinch him, and burn him, and turn him about
> Till candles and starlight and moonshine be out.

From the bottom of the park you'll get the greatest view of all. There, across three miles of green lawn, colorful gardens, and great trees rise those towering Norman turrets in all their awesome majesty. Involuntarily you'll find yourself exclaiming, "Now that's what a castle ought to be!"

*****

Back in town, two old inns of historic interest still wait to serve you. The present building of The Castle on the High Street was built as a coach house in George III's day, and boasted among its fixtures the bed of Nell Gwynn, mistress to Charles II. She lived on Church Street, handy should His Majesty need solace.

And on Thames Street is the Old House Hotel, built in 1676 by that period's foremost architect, Sir Christopher Wren, when he was Comptroller of the Works at Windsor Castle.

Eton   From Windsor, Eton is quite literally a stroll. At the foot of the castle, you simply go down Thames Street, cross the bridge, and you're on Eton's High Street. And there, directly ahead, is Eton College. (If you're coming straight from the M 4, take Exit 6 south). During term the school is open to the public 2–5 P.M. only, but holiday hours are more generous.

Don't let that word "College" fool you. It's used in the medieval sense of a community of clergy living together for a common purpose. Henry VI founded it as a school for boys in 1440, his original endowment of the "College of the Blessed Mary of Eton" providing for a provost, ten "sad priests," four lay clerks, six choristers, and twenty-five poor men. The boys, at least, have been properly grateful to Henry. Ever since his murder in 1471, they have gone up to the Tower of London on his birthday to place a red rose on the very spot where he died.

Eton itself is a charming little village, and old. Some of the shops on its one main street date back to the fifteenth century; and with their sagging, rough-hewn timbers and five-foot high doorways, they look it.

As products of England's most prestigious school for five and a half centuries, Eton's sons have contributed lavishly to literature. To list them would be lengthy: "A" is for Anstey, Christopher; "B" is for Bridges, Robert; "C" is Connolly, Cyril . . . and so on through Fielding and the Fletchers (père et fils) down to "W" is for Waller, Walpole; and Whyte-Melville, George John. But why bother?

Exciting as it might be to learn that Christopher Anstey was the author of *New Bath Guide* (1766), the anapestic saga of the Blunderheads at Bath, by the time one reaches Whyte-Melville the desire to know that he was called "the laureate of fox hunting" for novels like *Santanella* (1872) and *Katerfelto* (1875) may be minimal. Instead, mention of a few of the more colorful Etonian writers may suffice. Like Nicholas Udall, for instance.

Udall can be called the father of British comic drama. His rollicking *Ralph Roister Doister* (about 1553), though following classic Roman form, was the first comedy in English with truly native figures and life. He was headmaster of Eton from 1534 to 1541, and famous for flogging the boys whether they needed it or not.

One of his students was Thomas Tusser, author of the vastly popular *Five Hundredth pointes of good Husbandrie* (1557, 1561, etc.) which ran through many editions. In it he describes how he left St. Paul's ("Poules") School in London to go to Eton ("Aeton") and became the unhappy recipient of Udall's "mercy:"

> From Poules I went to Aeton, sent
> To learn strait wais the Latin phraise;
> Where fifty-three stripes given to me at once I had;
> For fawt but small, or none at all;
> It came to pass thus beat I was;
> See, Udall, see the mercie of thee to me, poor lad.

Some accounts have it that Udall wrote *Ralph Roister Doister* for his Eton boys to act, but this can hardly be. The play dates from 1553 or 1554, and in 1541 Udall had confessed to a bit of mischief with one of his wards, and been fired and sent to jail.

When it came to flogging, Udall's predecessor, a man named Cox, seems to have set an example hard to equal. In his *Scholemaster,* Ascham calls Cox "the best scholemaster and greatest beater of our time." It was, in fact, such brutality that in 1563 provoked the dinner debate at Windsor Castle that in turn led to Ascham's most famous work.

One of the diners had reported "strange news; that divers scholars of Eaton be run away from the schole for fear of beating," and deplored such methods of correction. When during the argument that ensued Ascham also denounced flogging, he was asked to produce a guide to "the right order of teaching." *The Boke of the Scholemaster* was the result.

By the time of Shelley and Swinburne in the nineteenth century, Eton's whipping had become renowned in a day when a teacher's cane was standard equipment. Even Dr. John Keate, Shelley's headmaster and basically well-meaning and kind, was known to say, "Blessed are the pure in heart. If you are not pure in heart, I'll flog you."

There is no record that he ever flogged Shelley, however. Shelley's miseries stemmed from the traditional bullying of bigger boys and his own vulnerable but determinedly rebellious nature. He set fires to trees with a burning glass, refused to join in games, defied authority, and once stabbed a young tormenter in the hand with a fork. No wonder they called him "Mad Shelley."

He found refuge in crossing over the bridge to Windsor especially to visit eccentric old Dr. James Lind, physician to the royal household, and listen to wild tales of his youth in East India. Reflections of Dr. Lind would emerge later in the old philosopher of Shelley's *Laon and Cythna*, renamed *The Revolt of Islam* (1818) and the prince's preceptor in the fragment, *Prince Athanase*.

Another escape was in writing. When Shelley left Eton for Oxford in 1810, though he was only eighteen, he had already written a surprising amount, including *Zastrozzi*, *Original Poetry by Victor and Cazire* (Victor was Shelley, Casire his oldest sister, Elizabeth), "The Wandering Jew," and *St. Irryne*. They were all wild—and terrible.

Swinburne came to Eton in 1849, nearly thirty years after Shelley left. Like Shelley, who was his hero, Swinburne was only twelve when he entered. And *his* often strange behavior earned *him* the nickname "Mad Swinburne." The title was not undeserved. Even so early an enthusiast of Swinburne's poetry as John Ruskin was to allow, "he is a demoniac youth."

Swinburne's appearance supported this. His was an absurdly small body and an incongruously large head topped by an unruly shock of flaming red hair. He was fair game for mockery. Although at Eton his talents were already manifest, his years there failed to produce even such abortive buds as Shelley's. Worse, for Swinburne, the whipping block was a much too real and frequent experience, surfacing later in sexual preferences that were, to put it mildly, bizarre.

None of this, however, shows in the hollow if stately verse of his "Eton: an Ode" (1891), written after the passionate flame that was the true Swinburne had long burned out.

From time immemorial youngsters have, like Shakespeare's "whining schoolboy," gone "unwillingly to school," especially if they were unusually sensitive and bright—and outsiders. So it was with Eton even unto the twentieth century, and so it was with George Orwell and Cyril Connolly.

They came to Eton together in 1918 on scholarships from St. Cyprian's School in Eastbourne, as bright and sensitive outcasts—as they had been there. And at Eton they continued the discontent they had shared so enthusiastically as friends at St. Cyprian's. In *The Enemies of Progress* (1938), Connolly deplores the way a boy's experiences at such schools so dominate his after-life that he is frozen in a kind of "permanent adolescence," preventing development into full maturity.

Orwell's assessment of Eton is even harsher: "I did not work there, and I don't feel that Eton has been much of a formative influence on my life." To be sure, Orwell had no use for the whole English system of private education. Defending his grim picture of society in *Nineteen Eighty-Four*, he said, "the only English parallel for the nightmare of totalitarianism was the experience of a misfit boy in an English boarding school." By way of caveat, however, note Orwell's word "misfit." That he was. He was only the son of a civil servant in India. Shelley was heir to a baronetcy. Swinburne's father was an admiral, his mother the daughter of an earl.

"Fine . . . mellow . . . stately" are the usual adjectives applied to Eton's ancient red brick buildings, and justly so. Mainly they are built around two interconnected courts or quadrangles. Most interesting are those in the larger of the two, with the "School Yard" in the center, statue of Henry VI and all.

On the north side of the yard is the Lower School, on the west the Upper School, on the south the Chapel, and on the east the impressive Lupton Tower, dating from 1517. Beyond are the cloisters and, beyond them, stretching toward the river, the famous playing fields and the Poets' Walk, named for Thomas Gray. Over fifteen thousand names of former Etonians are carved on the panelling of classrooms and staircases of the Upper School—and the older ones (including Shelley's) carved by the boys themselves. Later ones have been done professionally as a sort of running record of the school's alumni.

The Chapel was begun in 1441, but touches were added here and there in each century since, including, unfortunately, the twentieth. Inside are some notable tombs and brasses, fifteenth-century frescoes, and ancient wall paintings discovered in the 1920s.

Best known of Eton's features are the playing fields, largely because of the Duke of Wellington's statement, "The battle of Waterloo was won on the playing fields of Eton." In his essay, "England Your England," George Orwell may scoff: "Probably the battle of Waterloo *was* won on the playing-fields of Eton, but the opening battles of all subsequent wars have been lost there."

Maybe so. But in the colonnade below the Upper School a bronze frieze bears the inscription "FOR KING AND COUNTY, IN MEMORIAM, 1914–1919," and the names of her 1,175 sons who died for England in the great war.

View that, if you can, without a lump in your throat.

Slough and Bishopsgate

In the close vicinity of Eton and Windsor are Bishopsgate and Slough (as in "how"). The former sleeps on still, tiny and secluded and happy to be so. But in the last fifty years, the latter has exploded into so sizeable a symbol of industrial growth it stirred the poet laureate to wrath.

In the nineteenth century, both were deliberately sought out for their privacy—Slough by the most popular novelist of his day, Bishopsgate by a poet not yet twenty-three who had already written the poem that was to make him loathsome to the Victorian guardians of propriety.

Slough   Only three miles north of Windsor by way of the A 332, which becomes its High Street, Slough destroyed its rural tranquility in the 1940s by adding some 850 factories almost overnight, moving the poet laureate, Sir John Betjeman to cry:

> Come, friendly bombs, and fall on Slough
> It isn't fit for humans now.

But in 1867, Slough was secluded enough for a Charles Tringham to slip into and out without notice. For the first six months of that year he came nearly every week end to be with his "Nelly," who lived in Elizabeth Cottage on the High Street. Gossip had it the woman was pregnant. For added secrecy, he came via a footpath across a neighboring estate from the Dachet station rather than Slough itself.

Charles Tringham was Charles Dickens. Nelly was Ellen Ternan, a former actress and his long-time mistress. Years later, his daughter Kate said that Dickens and Ellen did indeed have a child that died in infancy.

Slough has two other literary ties, both tenuous. Buried in the parish churchyard is the "watcher of the skies" of Keats's "On First Looking Into Chapman's Homer," Sir William Herschel, the astronomer who discovered Uranus. And now assimilated by Slough is the village of Langley. Milton used to stroll there from Horton to use the village church library.

Bishopsgate   Bishopsgate is three miles south of Windsor, a little west of the A 328 and practically in Windsor Great Park. The nineteenth-century poet who fled there for sanctuary was Percy Bysshe Shelley. The cottage he and Mary Wollstonecraft Godwin moved into in August of 1815 was down a hidden lane near the park's Rhododendron Walk.

As always, troubles had descended on the poet from all sides. Relations with his estranged wife, Harriet, had turned bitter and threatening. Creditors hounded him. He had to hide from bailiffs to avoid arrest. His health was wretched. And both Harriet and Mary were pregnant. Shelley's Bishopsgate cottage, low-roofed and unpretentious, provided a refuge he badly needed.

For diversion, he and Mary rambled amidst the ancient oaks of the park, floated paper boats in nearby Virginia Water, and took country walks, sometimes to see friends in Bracknell, six miles to the west. Thomas Love Peacock came down often from his home in Marlow. Once with Peacock and Charles Clairmont, Mary's stepbrother, they took a ten-day boating holiday up the Thames through Reading and Oxford all the way past Lechlade to within eleven miles of the stream's source. Shelley wrote a friend:

> The exercise and dissipation of mind . . . produced so favourable an effect on my health that my habitual dejection and irritability have almost deserted me, and I can devote six hours in the day to study without difficulty. I have been engaged lately in the commencement of several literary plans which, if my present temper of mind endures, I shall probably complete in the winter.

Most important of these plans was *Alastor,* into which Shelley poured newly matured intellectual and philosophical powers, and a love of beauty that included, in part, impressions of the Thames and Windsor Forest. Today the poem is seen as proof that before his twenty-fourth birthday he had become the equal of any poet then living. But contemporary criticism was harsh. One review, citing his "sublime obscurity," suggested that next time he furnish his readers, "if he has any," with a glossary and explanatory notes.

Not strangely, there grew in Shelley the desire for "hiding myself and Mary from that contempt which we so unjustly endure." By early May 1816, they had given up Bishopsgate for Paris and a tour of the continent.

Cookham Dean and Waltham St. Lawrence— Bracknell—Binfield—and Wokingham

The M 4, which brings you into Berkshire in the first place, slashes all the way across the county before bustling on to Wiltshire and Avon. Half way along, at Exit 11, you'll pass Reading, giving you a chance to murmur, "Oh yes, Oscar Wilde," as you whiz by.

Before Reading, however, you'll be skirting a number of places of literary interest, and it won't hurt a bit to be aware of them at least. And who knows? You may even be persuaded to abandon the dubious delights of the motorway to see one or two.

Anyway, north of the M 4 between Slough and Reading are Cookham Dean and Waltham St. Lawrence, (both off the A 4); south of it are Bracknell, Binfield, and Wokingham (all on or near the A 329).

Cookham Dean   The little village of Cookham Dean is Kenneth Grahame country, and that suggests at once the Mole and the river that "chattered on to him, a babbling procession of the best stories in the world, sent from the heart of the earth to be told at last to the insatiable sea." And the Thames does lie immediately to the north.

After his mother died in 1864, Grahame lived here with his grandmother for a while at The Mount. He returned in 1906 as a man of forty-seven and Secretary of the Bank of England. He, his wife, and young son Alistair settled in for the next four years at a place called Mayfair. Alistair soon went off to school, and it was in letters to him that Grahame wrote the stories that developed into *The Wind in the Willows*, published in 1908. Alistair was "Mouse."

The book was hardly an instant success. But it did have an impressive pair of supporters: Theodore Roosevelt, then president of the United States, and A. A. Milne. Roosevelt wrote to Grahame from the White House, "I have read it and reread it, and have come to accept the characters as old friends." Milne said he was "almost offensively" its champion, and turned it into a hit play called *Toad of Toad Hall*. *The Wind in the Willows* went on to become second in sales only to *Alice in Wonderland*.

Waltham St. Lawrence   Waltham St. Lawrence is tiny, too. Six miles southwest of Cookham Dean, it's on the B 3024 just below the A 4. John Newbery—friend of such eighteenth-century notables as Samuel Johnson, Christopher Smart, Tobias Smollett, and Oliver Goldsmith—was born there, went to its village school, and after a successful career in London, was buried there. He deserves his modest niche in literary history on several counts.

As a bookseller, he originated the publishing of children's books, at least on any considerable scale. Goldsmith's *Vicar of Wakefield* credits him with writing a number of these stories himself. Newbery is in fact a character in that novel, dashing about collecting material for "The Travels of Tommy Trip" when he comes upon the vicar. He is depicted as good-natured, red-faced, and altogether likeable: ". . . the philanthropic bookseller in St. Paul's churchyard who has written so many little books for children: he called himself their friend, but he was the friend of all mankind."

In the novel, he lends the vicar enough money to go on his way in pursuit of his daughter Olivia. In real life, Newbery lent money to Goldsmith, Smart, and Dr. Johnson. In addition, we owe him thanks for helping to make Johnson's *The Idler* possible. He was one of the publisher friends who expressly set up *The Universal Chronicle* magazine as a vehicle for those essays.

Bracknell   Nine miles southwest of Windsor on the A 329, Bracknell today boasts a population of over fifty thousand, having been selected for development after World War I as one of what were called "New Towns." Between 1813 and 1816, however, it often furnished Shelley a pleasantly bucolic hideaway in those everlasting flights from creditors and their bailiffs.

The poet and his wife Harriet were there for some months from mid-July of 1813 on, for instance, at High Elm House. They had come to be near their friends, Mrs. Boinville and her young married daughter, who had recently moved from London. (Mrs. Boinville, Shelley thought, was "a most admirable specimen of a human being.")

A hiatus intervened, occasioned no doubt by those same relentless bailiffs. But after intervals at Ambleside, Edinburgh, London, and Windsor, they were back in Bracknell again. And even during the Windsor stay, Shelley often used the bedroom Mrs. Boinville had set aside for him, for he and Harriet had begun to grow apart. In 1814 their pattern was similarly peripatetic: a furnished place in Bracknell, or Shelley in his Boinville bedroom while Harriet visited in London, or Harriet in Bath and Shelley in London.

Even during the 1815–16 sojourn in Bishopsgate, when Harriet had left Shelley and Mary Godwin had replaced her, the ties to Bracknell continued. Shelley had only one more year before he was to quit England completely. But one memory of Bracknell he never forgot—the pond on the heath just outside town. Here, he said, was the best place he had ever found for launching paper boats.

Binfield   Binfield was to Alexander Pope on the order of Milton's Horton, but its rewards came much more rapidly. The village is two miles north of Bracknell, on the B 3034. If you're coming directly from Waltham St. Lawrence, simply take the B 3018 south.

Pope came to Binfield in 1700 as a boy of twelve, to what he called

> . . . . my paternal cell
> A little house, with trees a-row
> And like its master very low.

(To explain that two-fold "very low": his father was only a linen dealer, and the house was far more humble than the much revised and enlarged "Pope's Manor" of today). For the next sixteen years Pope stuck doggedly to a self-imposed regimen of study, weighted heavily toward the Latin classics and Milton and Dryden.

The rewards arrived with amazing promptness. In his "Epistle to Dr. Arbuthnot" (1735), Pope explains how skill in poetry ("numbers") came to him spontaneously, almost before he could talk:

> As yet a child, nor yet a fool to fame
> lisped in numbers, for the numbers came.

The fruits of Binfield bear this out:

Pastorals, 1709—age 21
"An Essay on Criticism," 1711—age 23
"Messiah" and "The Rape of the Lock", 1712—age 24
"Windsor Forest," 1713—age 25
Volume I of translation of *The Iliad*, 1715—age 27.

"An Essay on Criticism" dazzled the intellectual elite of London with the maturity of thought, the learning and elegance of language from one so young. The translation of *The Iliad* (and later *The Odyssey*) made him a wealthy man, enabling him in 1716 to quit Binfield for London, and in 1719 to acquire that estate outside of London that has stamped him ever since as the "Wasp of Twickenham."

Wokingham   Wokingham, three miles west of Bracknell on the A 329, is also associated with Pope. At its Old Rose Inne one rainy afternoon in 1726, he and three other of the century's sharpest wits—Jonathan Swift, John Gay, and Dr. Arbuthnot—tossed off, along with a few pints, a ballad composed as they drank to honor their waitress, Molly Mog.

Molly was the pretty daughter of the innkeeper, and being courted by the young squire of the neighboring village of Arborfield. The last stanza of their poem was prophetic:

> When she smiles on each guest like her liquor
> Then jealousy sets me agog,
> To be sure, she's a bit for the Vicar
> And so I shall lose Molly Mog.

Though she lived to be seventy, Molly never married.

You can toss a pint or two at Ye Olde Rose Inne yourself, if you like. It's still there at the Wokingham Market Place, and though the outside is mostly Georgian with Victorian and more recent additions, great stone fireplaces and oak beams survive inside to testify to its fifteenth-century origin.

2. Berkshire West

Reading

Reading is big: nearly 140,000 people. Reading is an important transportation center, both by rail and by car. The A 4 cuts right through it; the M 4 is only a mile to the south (Exit 11). Reading is a county town and a university town. Its museum of English rural life is noteworthy, and at one time its Norman abbey was the third greatest in all England.

But literature has often given Reading a bad press. In *The Merry Wives of Windsor* Shakespeare depicts the innkeepers of Reading as dupes of the three "cozen [cheating] Germans" who descend upon Windsor. To many, Reading is known only as the grim setting of Oscar Wilde's *The Ballad of Reading Gaol* (1898):

> In Reading gaol by Reading town
> There is a pit of shame,
> And in it lies a wretched man
> Eaten by teeth of flame,
> In a burning winding-sheet he lies
> And his grave has got no name.

Thomas Hardy's use of Reading in *Jude the Obscure* (1896)—he calls it "Aldbrickham"—leaves a bad taste in the mouth, too. To a tawdry "third-rate inn near the station" Jude brings his "mere female animal" Arabella for a furtive ten-hour rendezvous. Incongruously enough, he blunders into that same hotel only a month later with the more appealing Sue Bridehead, with equally depressing effect.

In *Three Men in a Boat*, Jerome K. Jerome says "one does not linger in the neighborhood of Reading."

But Reading has deserved better. Certainly Henry I thought so. He not only built the great abbey there in 1121, but chose to be buried in it. And about one hundred years later the abbey demonstrated its culture by producing one of the earliest as well as the loveliest of English lyrics:

> Sumer is icumen in,
> Lhude sing cuccu!

It was written by one of the Reading monks as a canon, a religious song for several voices.

Samuel Pepys found no fault with Reading, either, on his visit in 1668: ". . . and in the evening betimes come to Reading and there heard my wife read more of "Mustapha," and then to supper, and then I walk about the town, which is a very great one, I think bigger than Salsbury: a river runs through it, in the seven branches, and unite in one, and runs into the Thames half-a-mile off."

In the late eighteenth century Reading boasted a school good enough to have drawn as pupils Jane Austen and her older sister Cassandra, and Mary Russell Mitford. Mary was nine when her family came to Reading in 1797. When the lottery ticket her father bought for her tenth birthday won first prize of £20,000, they moved first into a sizeable house at 39 London Road (now marked with a plaque), and then into a rather grand place called Bertram House that Dr. Mitford built outside town.[1]

---

[1]For details of what happened to the rest of the money, see p. 84.

Mary went on to become the author of a number of highly successful works, among them a rather idealized novel of Reading, *Belford Regis* (1835). What remains to be seen today of the literary reflections of Reading's past—good and bad—is curiously enough all centered about what is left of Henry I's old abbey on Forbury Road. The abbey was virtually obliterated in the Great Rebellion, so only scanty ruins survive. But in the flint walls of its former chapter house there is a tablet bearing the musical notes of the canon, "Sumer is icumen in."

In rooms over the gateway of the ruins was the school the Austen girls and Mary Mitford attended, run by Mrs. Latournelle, a French emigré. And Oscar Wilde's jail (since rebuilt), where he served two years at hard labor following his conviction for homosexuality, adjoined those same ruins. Incidentally, though Wilde did write *De Profundis* (1905) while in prison, *The Ballad of Reading Gaol* was not written there, but in Berneval during those last forlorn years of exile in France.

The inn of Jude's unfortunate trysts with Arabell and Sue is still in business on King Street, but happily is now a two-star hotel, The George.

Caversham and Mapledurham,
Three Mile Cross and Swallowfield

Close about Reading are: to the north, Caversham and Mapledurham; and to the south, Three Mile Cross and Swallowfield. Caversham provided pleasure for James I's Queen Anne, Mapledurham for Alexander Pope. For Mary Russell Mitford, Three Mile Cross meant three decades of grinding effort, and Swallowfield a final five years of release and serenity.

Caversham   When they get to Reading, modern guide books are apt to say reassuringly, "Across the River Thames is the pleasant residential district of Caversham." (It's off the A 4074) James I's Danish wife Anne found it pleasant, too. She came to visit Baron William Knollys in 1613 and to see a masque written by Thomas Campion, best remembered today for his lilting "There is a garden in her face."

Anne got so carried away she jumped up and personally led the dancing that followed. The occasion did Knollys' career no harm, either. James soon made him Viscount Wallingford, and ultimately Earl Banbury.

Mapledurham   Mapledurham, four miles northwest of Reading off the B 4526, is another of those captivating Thames-side villages. Strictly speaking, it's in Oxfordshire, but is so much a part of the Reading area it might best be discussed here.

In the grand Tudor manor called Mapledurham House lived the Blount sisters, Mary and Martha, long-time friends of Pope, and he thoroughly enjoyed his visits there in both 1713 and 1714. His poem to Martha, "Epistle to Miss Blount, on her leaving the Town [London], after the Coronation" is a sprightly spoof of her day at Mapledurham:

> She went for Op'ra, park, assembly, play,
> To morning-walks, and pray'rs three hours a day;
> Or o'er cold coffee, trifle with the spoon,
> Count the slow clock, and dine exact at noon;
> . . . .
> Up to her godly garret after sev'n
> There starve and pray, for that's the way to heav'n.

Mapledurham House is open to the public from Easter Sunday through September, weekends and Bank Holiday afternoons.

Three Mile Cross   Three Mile Cross is only four miles south of Reading on the A 33. But for Mary Russell Mitford it was another world, thanks to her father.

Dr. George Mitford had to be one of the dearest, warmest, sweetest, lovingest, and most thoroughly exasperating and irresponsible human beings who ever lived. Before he bought that lottery ticket in 1797 for Mary's tenth birthday, his lavish living and high-stake gambling had already run through his wife's fortune of £50,000. By 1820, he had done away with Mary's £20,000 lottery prize, too. This meant abandoning Reading and their grand Bertram House for Three Mile Cross. Their new home was a humble laborer's cottage, Mary's new life a never-ending struggle to earn money, which her father dissipated faster than she could make it with her writing.

She had already shown real gifts for spontaneous humor, wit, warmth, and freshness in the sketches of rural life that began to appear in *The Lady's Magazine* in 1819. They were to be published in five volumes between 1824 and 1832 as *Our Village*, with Three Mile Cross and its vicinity furnishing most of the material.

There followed a number of plays, novels, and other books. But though her success was considerable, her life of servitude to an infirm mother and wastrel father was wretched. She said she'd rather be a washerwoman than a writer. She had "tasted as bitterly . . . of anxiety, of fear and hope," she wrote a friend, as any woman could. Even so, *Our Village* was dedicated to that "most cherished friend . . . beloved and venerable"—her father.

Finally fortune turned kind. In 1837 friends secured her a Civil List pension; and when Dr. Mitford died in 1842, they paid off all his debts. She was a free woman, at peace with herself and the world, when she left the cottage in Three Mile Cross to move to Swallowfield.

Her little house still stands, called somewhat too grandly The Mitford.

Swallowfield   When Mary Russell Mitford moved to Swallowfield from Three Mile Cross, she didn't have far to go: only two miles down the road that today is the B 3349. Here she spent her last four years, publishing in 1852 *Recollections of a Literary Life*, especially interesting today for the sketches of some of her contemporaries.

She died in 1855, and was buried amid the yew trees she had described so charmingly in *Our Village*. Yes, there's a house there still "where the roads meet" (her words)—but so changed Mary would never recognize it as hers.

Pangbourne and Tidmarsh

Also no distance at all out of Reading are Pangbourne and Tidmarsh, Pangbourne six miles to the north at the junction of the A 329 and the A 340, and Tidmarsh one mile south of Pangbourne on the A 340. Both are the kind of small English riverside village that makes the word "lovely" almost redundant.

Pangbourne   Pangbourne—the "bourne" (end or limit) of the Pang—is where the little stream called the Pang enters the Thames. Tennyson and Jerome K. Jerome both chose it as a pleasant stop-over: Tennyson in real life on his honeymoon in 1850, Jerome for his trio in *Three Men in a Boat* (they stayed the night at the Swan Hotel).

More importantly, Pangbourne shares not only the Thames with Cookham Dean, but shares Kenneth Grahame as well. After the shattering death of his son Alistair, for whom *The Wind in the Willows* was written, Grahame found peace at Pangbourne's Church Cottage, where he lived from 1924 until his death there in 1932. Moreover, his illustrator, E. H. Shepard, drew inspiration for his drawings from this stretch of the Thames, so Pangbourne can claim a share of Mole, Rat, and Mr. Toad, too.

Church Cottage remains in private hands. Grahame was buried initially in the local churchyard, but later his body was interred in Oxford's Holywell cemetery, as he had wished.

Tidmarsh   On the Pang river at Tidmarsh in the days of World War I was a wooden watermill with a house at one end—a large house, with three reception rooms, six bedrooms, garden and orchard, one and a half acres in all. To it in 1917 came the thirty-five-year-old Lytton Strachey with his twenty-two-year-old friend Carrington. That they would attempt domesticity together is hard to believe. The difference in age was the least of it. Strachey was an avowed homosexual, and Carrington, you see, was a woman. Not just a woman, either, but a woman who hated being a woman (hence the "Carrington" rather than Dora Carrington), and hated being treated as such by men. In fact their first meeting, in 1915 at Virginia Woolf's house in Asheham, nearly ended in mayham.

On some weird impulse, as they walked together on the Downs, Strachey had suddenly kissed her—maybe because she looked so like a boy. She retaliated by creeping into his bedroom next day at dawn, armed with large shears to cut off his "horrid beard." Instead, the gentle, near-hypnotic sweetness of his look as he opened his eyes undid her.

Thereafter she devoted herself to him. She found the Tidmarsh Mill House, as it was called. She furnished it and ran it. She provided the orderliness and discipline he needed to complete the series of biographical essays he was then working on.

And so it was Carrington more than anyone else who turned him from a self-admitted failure to an overnight literary sensation. For the biographical essays were published on May 9, 1918, as *Eminent Victorians,* and made Strachey at once rich and famous. Hitherto obscure, he had finally matched his fellow founders of the Bloomsbury Group in both achievement and public recognitions.

He went on to write the equally triumphant *Queen Victoria* (1921), dedicated to Virginia Woolf, and *Books and Characters* (1922). Meanwhile Carrington babied him and accommodated the visitors, from the Woolfs and Maynard Keynes to E.M. Forster and D.H. Lawrence, who came to Mill House.

At last, however, its dampness proved too much for Strachey, and he moved on to Ham, in Wiltshire. Carrington went with him, of course. What in the world would he have done without her? No one thought to ask, what would she do without him? When Strachey died in 1932, Carrington took her own life.

Aldworth—Yattendon—and Hermitage—
Newbury and Fawley

A scant seven miles northwest of Pangbourne is Goring. Besides being a likeable little village in itself, attractively set in the gap between the Chilterns and the Berkshire Downs, Goring is an excellent take-off spot for a final look at Berkshire's literary points of interest.

At Goring you can pick up the B 4009, strung along which, heading south, are Aldworth (with Tennyson and Laurence Binyon), Yattendon (Robert Bridges), Hermitage (D. H. Lawrence and Richard Aldington), and Newbury (Thomas Hardy). To the northwest of Newbury, for the last stop of all, is Fawley (and Hardy again).

Aldworth   Right on the B 4009, Aldworth sits at the top of the steep road overlooking the Thames and Goring, six miles off to the northeast. If the name sounds familiar to Tennyson buffs, it should. Aldworth was his wife Emily's family home, and they named their house at Haslemere, Surrey, after it.

Aldworth's other claim to literary notice, Laurence Binyon, is buried there. Though for forty years he was an official at the British Museum in London, he found time to write a considerable body of poetry, some of it quite good (e.g., "For the Fallen," 1914), as well as plays and some important books on art.

Yattendon   Yattendon is six miles directly south of Aldworth on a side road off the B 4009. The poet Dr. Robert Bridges came to live at the Manor House there in 1882 to be with his mother, after a severe illness persuaded him to give up the practice of medicine for full-time writing and the simple pleasures of rural life, such as playing his harpsichord and leading the Yattendon village choir.

Before he left Yattenden in 1904, he produced quantities of poems, and eight plays. They won him perhaps more acclaim than he deserved, and led to the poet laureateship. But in his simple poem, "Fortunatus Nimium," Bridges's self-appraisal is modest:

> I have lain in the sun
> I have toiled as I might
> I have thought as I would
> And now it is night.

Hermitage   Hermitage is also directly on the B 4009, just where it ducks under the M 4. D. H. Lawrence took over Chapel Farm Cottage there in December of 1917, but found it "cold and comfortless." Worse, the owner reclaimed it in February, "so I suppose we are to camp out like babes in the wood, and ask the robins to cover us with warm leaves." He left by April, but was back the following spring for another brief interlude.

These days were hardly his most productive. In fiction, he was between the crushing reception of *The Rainbow* (1915) which the authorities had burned, and the perhaps overpraise of *Women in Love* (1920), which was yet to come.

He did make a start on *Aaron's Rod* (1922), but found the going slow. Oddly enough, for most people now think of him only as a novelist, some of his best work at Hermitage may well have been in preparing for the American edition of his *New Poems* (1918), with its pacesetting preface and his essays on American classics.

Richard Aldington, the poet, novelist, and controversial biographer, came to Hermitage after World War I ended to live in a cottage outside town. He was a friend of Lawrence's then, but later in *Portrait of a Genius, But . . .* (1950) his treatment of the man was far less kind than the evaluation of his work.

Aldington himself had insisted on joining the army as a private, and was mustered out a shattered victim of shell-shock, and penniless. The primary purpose of his stay in Hermitage was convalescence. The best of the poetry that had placed him as an Imagist—along with Ezra Pound, Amy Lowell, and "H. D." (Hilda Doolittle, whom he married)—was behind him. His *Images of War* and *Images of Desire* had just been published.

But he continued to write poetry and critical essays, and toward the end of his eight years in Hermitage began working toward a career as a novelist for which he is best known today. *Death of a Hero*, the first novel, was published in 1929, and remains a bitter, moving commentary on the war that had served him so badly.

One thing Aldington kept was a sustaining love of England. In the midst of war, far from home and stuck with the menial, bone-tiring task of transferring bales of hay from barge to truck to train, he could write: "Heart of me, heart of me, be not sick and faint though fingers and arms and head ache; you bear the gifts of the glittering meadows of England. Here are bundles from Somerset, from Wales, from Hereford, Worcester, Gloucester—names we must love, scented with summer peace."

Newbury   At Newbury, about eight miles down from Hermitage, the B 4009 ends. Newbury is the "Kennetbridge" of Hardy's *Jude the Obscure*, where poor Jude goes to seek solace of the composer of the hymn, "The Foot of the Cross." Surely, thought Jude, "if there were any person in the world to choose as a confidant, this composer would be the one." But alas, the composer discovers Jude is poor, and their dialogue ends abruptly.

Fawley   With Fawley, just west of the A 338, one is ready to say goodbye to Berkshire. The border of Oxfordshire is only two miles to the north, that of Wiltshire seven to the West. Fawley, like Newbury, in short, is at the northernmost edge of Thomas Hardy's fictional "Wessex." Hardy's grandmother came from Fawley, and in *Jude the Obscure* is "Marygreen," where the boy Jude (his last name is Fawley!) lives with his Aunt Drusilla.

Hardy didn't like what progress had done to the village:

> Many of the thatched and dormered dwelling-houses had been pulled down. . . . Above all, the original church, hump-backed, wood-turreted, and quaintly hipped, had been taken down. In place of it a tall new building of German-Gothic design, unfamiliar to English eyes, had been erected on a new piece of ground by a certain obliterator of historic records who had run down from London and back in a day.

But then, Hardy himself had been an architect who specialized in *restoring* old churches.

OXFORDSHIRE

Oxfordshire

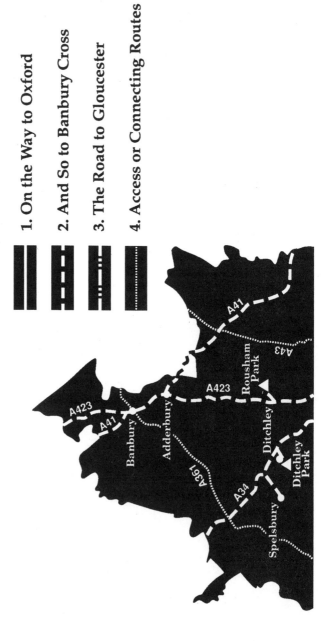

1. On the Way to Oxford

2. And So to Banbury Cross

3. The Road to Gloucester

4. Access or Connecting Routes

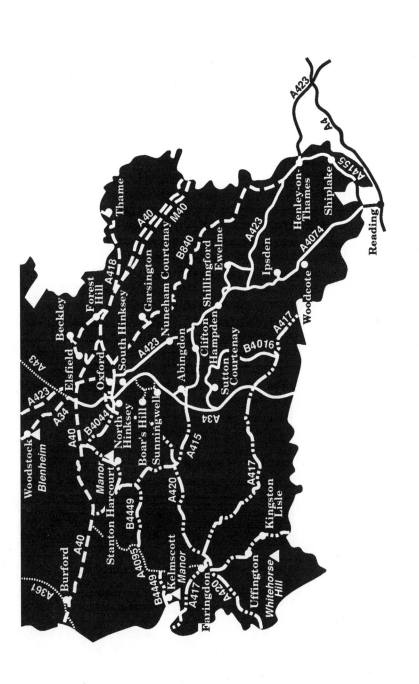

The cumulative labours of Vanbrugh and "Capability Brown" have
succeeded at Blenheim in setting an Italian palace in an English park
without apparent incongruity.

Sir Winston Churchill, *Lord Randolph Churchill*

Beautiful city! So venerable, so lovely, so unravaged by the fierce
intellectual life of our century, so serene! . . . who will deny that
Oxford, by her ineffable charm, keeps ever calling us nearer to the true
goal of all of us, to the ideal, to perfection?

Matthew Arnold, *Preface to Essays in Criticism*

The country between Oxford and Blenheim is not particularly
interesting, being almost level, or undulating very slightly; nor is
Oxfordshire, agriculturally, a rich part of England.

Nathaniel Hawthorne, *Our Old Home*

Hawthorne's lordly dismissal of Oxfordshire other than Blenheim and Oxford has been echoed often. Even in our century a popular guide book of the
1920s was equally offhand: "not one of the picturesque counties." How
unfair.

Yes, Blenheim and Oxford are to be seen. But there is so much more of
Oxfordshire. It is forty-five miles from bottom to top, thirty-five miles from
east to west. And within these boundaries are some lovely spots.

At the bottom, along the Berkshire border between Goring-on-the-
Thames and Henley-on-Thames, the river of Matthew Arnold's "Scholar-
Gipsy" runs sparkling as ever. Nearby, too, are the charming Chilterns,
beginning their run northeastward through Buckinghamshire and beyond.

And running along most of the county's western border with Gloucestershire are the glorious Cotswolds, among whose tawny-stoned villages none is
more delightful than Oxfordshire's Burford. As for Arnold's encomium about
Oxford: yes, the city is still "so venerable, so lovely"—in parts. But "so
serene?" Stand outside today's Randolph Hotel trying to cross the street
against the high noon traffic, and you'll soon yearn for a bit of that Cotswold
calm.

1. On the Way to Oxford

Henley-on-Thames and Shiplake

Oxfordshire has located its literary sites well. First, they are heavily concentrated in the southeastern quarter of the county, roughly between Henley-on-Thames and Oxford. Second, those in this area are still reached with reasonable ease from a single highway, the A 423, which directly links those two cities. And third, Henley-on-Thames itself, along with neighboring Shiplake, is an excellent place to start your tour.

If you are in London, the A 4 will deliver you right to Henley and the A 423. Should you happen to be in the Reading section of Berkshire, it's even easier: simply slip across the Reading bridge, pick up the A 4155, and Shiplake and Henley are just down the road.

Henley-on-Thames   Some literary legends, if they are to live, are best left unquestioned. Like the "actual" Old Curiosity Shop of Dickens on Portsmouth Street in London, for instance. Or the "genuine" Round Table of King Arthur in Winchester's Castle. Or the rooms in Henley-on-Thames's Red Lion Hotel where Dr. Johnson and Boswell stayed in 1776, and the poet William Shenstone scratched some verse on a window pane in 1750.

The trouble with the Old Curiosity Shop is that had she lived, Little Nell would have been a grandmother before the place ever opened its doors for business. And Arthur's table is made from a tree that wasn't cut down until eight hundred years after his death.

Henley's Red Lion Hotel? Although Boswell mentions no hotel by name, most guide books still rely on his account in the *Life of Johnson* to verify his visit, as follows:

1. Bound for Birmingham, he and Johnson leave Oxford on Thursday morning, March 21, 1776 . . . visit Blenheim . . . have mid-day dinner on the road . . . stop for tea at Stratford-upon-Avon . . . then push on with twenty-four miles to go.

2. But it's been a long day in their post chaise, so a bit short of Birmingham, they put in for the night.

3. "On Friday, March 22," Boswell continues, "having set out early from Henley, where we had lain the preceding night, we arrived at Birmingham about nine o'clock, and, after breakfast, went to call on his old schoolfellow Mr. Hector."

The trouble is, Henley-on-Thames and its Red Lion are *eighty miles from Birmingham*, which means:

1. Though almost within sight of their destination Thursday evening, they turned around and went not only all the way back to Oxford, where they had started the day, but another twenty-four miles as well—just to spend the night.

2. Then (fresh as daisies no doubt), Friday morning they're up betimes and make Birmingham for breakfast. Eighty miles before breakfast? In a post chaise?

What's awry? Legend makers. They picked the wrong Henley. For there *is* a Henley right out of Stratford and only fifteen miles from Birmingham. It's called Henley-in-Arden, and it's got to be Boswell's Henley. It would seem that Oxfordshire's Henley would have to give up Shenstone, too. For Boswell indicates that their Henley inn is also Shenstone's:

> We happened to lie this night at the inn
> at Henley, where Shenstone wrote these
> lines—
>> Whoe'er has travell'd life's dull round,
>> Where'er his stages may have been,
>> May sigh to think he still has found
>> The warmest welcome at an inn.

Happily, however, the Red Lion Hotel has an authentic name-dropping past for all that: Charles I was a guest both in 1632 and 1642 . . . the first Duke of Marlborough kept a room there for journeying between London and Blenheim . . . George III stopped over often . . . his son, the Prince Regent is said to have eaten fourteen of its renowned mutton chops at a sitting . . . and the Duke of Wellington tarried there after Waterloo.

You'll find it a pleasant place to stay, too, especially if you're there for the famous Henley Regatta. The hotel overlooks the course.

And Henley-on-Thames does have an unchallengeable literary tie. In 1907, Richard Blair settled his family there while he went back to complete his Civil Service duties in India. After his retirement in 1912, they lived for a while in Shiplake, but in 1915 returned to Henley at No. 36 Mark's Road. The Blairs' son Eric, of course, grew up to become George Orwell.

Shiplake In addition to George Orwell, Shiplake has connections with Tennyson and Swinburne. By coincidence, the same Georgian house— Holmwood at Binsfield Heath—involved both poets. Tennyson married Emily Sellwood in Shiplake on June 13, 1850, and Emily stayed at Holmwood before the wedding. They were in Shiplake because of its vicar, Drummond Rawnsley. He was married to Emily's cousin and performed the ceremony. He had also been instrumental in persuading Emily's parents to abandon their long-time opposition to the match because of Tennyson's suspect piety and lack of income.

In Memoriam had just come out, giving promise of financial success. And who knows, maybe such lines as

> There lives more faith in honest doubt
> Believe me, than in half the creeds.

helped remove the religious objections as well.

Anyway, though the wedding cake was not ready, and Emily had neither white dress nor gloves, and Tennyson forgot the ring, all ended well. Said Tennyson: "The peace of God came into my life before the altar when I wedded her."

Swinburne's association with Holmwood was hardly as happy. It was his parents' home from 1865 to 1879, and they all too often carted him off there to dry out from his drunken bouts in London. He was there in 1879 when Theodore Watts-Dunton came on a mission as astonishing as its outcome.

Watts-Dunton was a solicitor by profession, but had written commendable literary criticism and was to write one novel, *Aylwin* (1897) of some merit. He was also a devoted and understanding friend of Swinburne's. His mission was no less than to lure the poet to the confines of a house in Putney, a London suburb, and there isolate him from the temptations of flesh and wine.

Incredibly, the plan succeeded. Swinburne moved to Putney that fall. More incredibly, Watts-Dunton whittled Swinburne down to a single bottle of beer a day and a program of healthful strolls on the heath in the morning and writing reams of inoffensive poetry and prose in the afternoon. And, most incredibly of all, Swinburne stayed there until April 10, 1909. That was the day he died . . . seemingly content.

Ipsden—Woodcote—and Ewelme,
Shillingford and Nuneham Courtenay

Ten miles or so northwest of Henley-on-Thames the A 423 meets and absorbs the A 4074 coming up from Reading. Just off the A 4074 are Ipsden, three miles before the two roads meet, and Woodcote, two miles below Ipsden.

Two miles above this same junction are Ewelme, on a side road to the east, Shillingford, and Nuneham Courtenay.

Ipsden   Charles Reade was born in the manor house of Ipsden in 1814. Although he is remembered today for his novels, particularly *The Cloister and the Hearth* (1861), he began his writing career as a dramatist, and he asked that his tombstone put that first in a listing of his achievements.

Woodcote   Edward Bulwer (later Bulwer-Lytton) came to Woodcote in 1827 after his ill-advised marriage to Rosina Wheeler and the consequent falling out with his mother.[1] Though the maternal allowance had been cut off and his own resources were slender, he rented a handsome country house with extensive grounds, gardens and stables.

Somehow, he managed to stick it out until 1829, when his mother renewed his subsidy and he was able to rejoin the elite of London society. Product of the Woodcote years was his novel *Pelham*, published in 1828.

Ewelme   Ewelme is one of those pretty little Chiltern Hills villages overlooked by detractors of Oxfordshire. Chaucer is supposed to have visited Ewelme to see his granddaughter Alice, whose father, Thomas Chaucer, is generally accepted as the poet's son.

At any rate, the Ewelme church has the tombs of Thomas and his wife, as well as that of Alice. Alice was the Duchess of Suffolk, and the figure on her tomb is especially interesting. On her left arm she wears the Order of the Garter—one of only three effigies of ladies thus decorated known to exist.

Jerome K. Jerome is buried in the churchyard. He came to live at Gould's Grove, an old farmhouse east of town, soon after the publication of two of his most popular books, *Idle Thoughts of an Idle Fellow* and *Three Men in a Boat*, both in 1889.

Among fellow authors who came to Ewelme to visit Jerome were H. G. Wells, Israel Zangwill, W. W. Jacobs, and Eden Phillpotts. Wells everybody knows. Zangwill wrote now-forgotten novels like *Children of the Ghetto* (1892) and *Ghetto Tragedies* (1893). Jacobs was a prolific writer of short stories, including the classic "The Monkey's Paw." And Phillpotts was the man who said he limited his life to an endless flood of novels and plays because "I am not robust, and I detest society in any shape or form."

[1]For the bizarre story of this match, see pp. 22 and 29.

Shillingford   Minchen's Cottage on the Warborough Road was the home of William Butler Yeats for some months in 1921, after he let his Oxford house for the summer to save money. While at Shillingford, Yeats was occupied with *The Player Queen* and *Seven Poems and a Fragment,* both published in 1922.

Nuneham Courtenay   Nuneham Courtenay is an example of what happened to several eighteenth-century villages that experienced well-nigh instantaneous obliteration and rebirth elsewhere for offending the eye of its lordly owner. To improve the view from his stately home, the lord would simply have every single building torn down and its inhabitants carted off to new homes at a less obtrusive location.

A brief stop at Nuneham Courtenay today—it's right on the A 423 five miles above Shillingford—to see the paired cottages marching down each side of the main street will show you that the results weren't always unpleasant.

That was pretty much the verdict of William Whitehead, England's poet laureate from 1757 to 1785 and the kind of writer now dismissed with "his earlier works were not without worth." In a poem with the no-nonsense title of "The Removal of the Village at Nuneham Courtenay," Whitehead reassures us that the housewives thus uprooted were

> Well pleased to house their little train
> In happier mansions warm and dry.

And though "mansions" may be a bit much, you get the idea that he generally approved.

In his "Deserted Village" (1770), Oliver Goldsmith takes quite the opposite view of similar upheavals:

> Sweet smiling village, loveliest of the lawn
> Thy sports are fled and all thy charms withdrawn;
> Amidst thy bowers the tyrant's hand is seen
> And desolation saddens all thy green.

There are even those who still stoutly insist that Nuneham Courtenay is the one, true, and only "Sweet Auburn" of that poem.

Never mind that in his dedication Goldsmith expressly states that it is "the depopulation of the country I inveigh against." Since its dispossessed were provided a whole new village, Nuneham Courtenay can hardly claim to have been depopulated. Never mind also that if the poem is to be taken literally, the village with its "seats of my youth" would have to be in Ireland, since that's where Goldsmith grew up. Ignore, too, the fact that there are as many English "originals" of Auburn as there are of legendary Camelot. Back to the real Nuneham Courtenay and its real uprooter. He was the first Earl of Harcourt and the date was 1765. His landscaper was that same Capability Brown who did Stowe. But the gardens were laid out by the Earl's friend, William Mason, like Whitehead, a poet who earned less than thunderous applause even in his own day.

In 1744, Mason had brought forth an elegy, "Musaeus," in the manner (if hardly the style) of Milton's "Lycidas." But he may be forgiven: he was only nineteen at the time. Two pseudo-classic plays that followed are another matter. One of these, *Charactacus* (1759), Horace Walpole described as "laboured, uninteresting, and no more resembling the manners of Britons than of Japanese." And he was Mason's friend!

However, Thomas Gray liked Mason; corrected his shaky syntax; called him "Skroddles;" and made him his literary executor. So maybe William Mason was a pleasant fellow for all that.

Two literary visitors to Earl Harcourt's re-embellished estate, Nuneham Park, had sharply different impressions of it. Novelist Fanny Burney, when she came there in 1786 with George III and Queen Charlotte (she was the queen's "Second Keeper of the Robes") found the place "half-new, half-old, half-comfortable, half-forlorn." The American writer, Nathaniel Hawthorne, thought house and grounds "as perfect as anything earthly can be,— utterly and entirely finished." Of course, Hawthorne did come seventy years after Fanny.

Nuneham Park is still privately owned, so cannot be visited. But it is part of the National Gardens Scheme, and open to NGS members on the day designated in the guide book.

Clifton Hampden—Sutton Courtenay—
Abingdon—Sunningwell—and Boar's Hill

On the way up the A 423 from Shillingford, a mile or so before reaching Nuneham Courtenay, you may or may not notice a road running off to the west labelled A 415 and signposted for Abingdon. You might want to go back to it after Nuneham Courtenay for a short detour. Your reward will be four bits of pleasant serendipity:

1. a fourteenth-century inn noted for Jerome K. Jerome and gargantuan breakfasts (Clifton Hampden);

2. the simple churchyard grave of one of the twentieth century's best known iconoclasts (Sutton Courtenay);

3. the town that indirectly caused Oscar Wilde to volunteer for road-building (Abingdon); and

4. the thirteenth-century church tower Roger Bacon used for astronomical experiments (Sunningwell).

From Sunningwell, too, you'll be able to reach Oxford in no time, passing en route Boar's Hill, home of two twentieth-century poets laureate.

Clifton Hampden   The Barley Mow Inn in Clifton Hampden is mentioned in Jerome K. Jerome's *Three Men in a Boat,* and has bedrooms named for the characters. Jerome even wrote some of the book while staying there himself, though most of it was done in the more prosaic precincts of his Chelsea flat in London.

The inn is a picture-book timber and thatch building dating from 1350, with beamed ceilings low enough to challenge guests of even modest height. Standing on the south bank of the Thames, it offers visitors a great view of the river, and—at least at last report—that "gargantuan breakfast."

The poet laureate John Masefield lived from 1939 until his death in 1967 at the Borcote Brook House in Clifton Hampden. His major work was long over when he came—he was sixty-one then—but he did oversee the publishing of his *Collected Poems* (1946) while there, and wrote the autobiographical *So Long to Learn* (1952).

Clifton Hampden is on the A 415, two miles west of the A 423.

Sutton Courtenay   Three miles southwest of Clifton Hampden on the B 4016, Sutton Courtenay is another Oxfordshire village that well deserves the word "picturesque." In the cemetery of its interesting old (twelfth to fourteenth century) All Saints Church is the grave of George Orwell. His burial there was hardly a routine affair

Before his death in London in 1950, Orwell had expressed the wish to be buried in a churchyard. But this wasn't easily done for a man who had no regular religious affiliation, refused to go to church, and had begun his essay "What I Believe" with "I do not believe in Belief." The influence of friends managed it somehow, however, and there he lies in Sutton Courtenay. The stone that marks his grave is suitably simple.

Perhaps so determined a foe of the establishment would have been abashed to know he would share his final resting place with a prime minister and lord, Herbert Henry Asquith, first Earl of Oxford and Asquith. But maybe not. The Earl was responsible for abolishing the veto power of the House of Lords.

Abingdon   Abingdon, off the A 34 two miles northwest of Sutton Courtenay, was the town that indirectly brought about Oscar Wilde's stint as a roadbuilder. In 1870 John Ruskin became Oxford's first professor of art, and soon took lodgings at Abingdon's Crown and Thistle Inn. His trips to the university, seven miles away, took him through North Hinksey, where carts and farm vehicles were destroying the village green because there was no road for them.

Ruskin determined to build one, and recruited a number of his undergraduates to help him. Among them was Oscar Wilde. If the thought of the future high priest of the aesthetic cult, with or without a lily in his hand, breaking stones seems ridiculous, so apparently was the road that resulted. Ruskin himself called it "about the worst in the three kingdoms." But laugh as we will at Ruskin and his odd notions, we must admit that when he saw that something needed doing, he gave it a try.

Sunningwell   Sunningwell is three miles above Abingdon, a bit to the west of the A 34 and within hailing distance of Oxford. Roger Bacon studied at the university in the early part of the thirteenth century, and returned there about 1250 to teach, study, and write.

Today he is often called the father of English philosophy. In his own day he was more often thought of as a practitioner of black magic who manufactured brass heads that talked, and the authorities kept a close eye on him.

Actually, he seems to have been a practical fellow. He invented spectacles and worked at the basic principles of the telescope. His interest in science led him to Sunningwell and its church tower, which he found just the place for various experiments in astronomy.

Today the church's west porch has a model showing how the building looked in the thirteenth century, with Bacon himself in friar's robe clutching his astrolabe. The porch, too, added in 1550, is interesting. Its seven-sided design is unique.

Boar's Hill   Barely out of Sunningwell, west off the A 34 and only two and a half miles from Oxford, Boar's Hill was the home of a pair of poets laureate who between them held the post for more than half of the twentieth century: Robert Bridges and John Masefield.

Bridges got there first, in 1907, and lived there at Chilswell House until his death in 1930. He was widely touted as a poet in his own day. Yeats said "no living man" could equal his emotional purity and rhythmical delicacy. A. E. Housman called Bridges's collection, *Shorter Poems* (1890), perhaps the most perfectly sustained "single volume of English verse."

But Cyril Connolly was perhaps more accurate when he said Bridges was "unblessed by any heavenly visitation." After being named poet laureate in 1913, Bridges quickly became known as "the silent laureate." Even his most heralded work, *The Testament of Beauty*, which was written at Boar's Hill—in 1929 at age eighty-four—is far more often mentioned today than read.

Masefield lived at Hill Crest in Boar's Hill from 1919 until 1933, and it was there that he received news in 1930 that he had succeeded Robert Bridges as poet laureate, a position he was to hold for the next thirty-seven years. His best poetry came before the Boar's Hill days, too, though he did write some good novels while there, such as *Sard Harker* (1924) and *Odtaa* (1926). Hill Crest still survives, with a new name: Masefield House.

Oxford

Having reached Boar's Hill on the A 34, or Nuneham Courtenay on the A 423, it's time now to take whichever of the two you are on straight into Oxford, and make that your headquarters while visiting whatever literary sites in the city and vicinity you have time and inclination for. They are many.

The same two highways will also serve those coming down from the north, the A 34 from Stratford-upon-Avon and Woodstock, the A 423 from Bambury. And from London, Oxford is the easiest of trips. It's right up the M 40 by car, there's fast and frequent rail service from Paddington, and direct motorway coach express (every half hour!) from Victoria.

However you get there, it's best from the beginning to realize that Oxford is just too much (so is Cambridge, but that's another story for another page). We think of Oxford as a university town, but Oxford was old long before there was a university. As early as 720–740 A.D., a good five hundred years before the endowment of its first college, a local saint, St. Frideswide, had founded a nunnery there. Traces of her original church survive today near her shrine in the Christ Church chapel, which now doubles as Oxford Cathedral.

In 912, Oxford shared with London responsibility for securing the Thames valley for Saxon Kings. The *Anglo-Saxon Chronicle* for that date records that Edward the Elder, son of Alfred the Great, "held Lundenbyrg (London) and Oxnaford and all the lands that were obedient thereto." The

Old English "Oxnaford," i.e., a crossing for oxen, became the medieval Latin "Oxonia," hence the abbreviation "Oxon." for both city and county.

And for all Matthew Arnold's poem about "that sweet city with her dreaming spires"—an almost obligatory quotation on current promotional pieces—today's Oxford is big (over one hundred thousand) and for the unprepared, shockingly modern, thanks to carmaker William Morris and the huge plant he built there.

Nevertheless, Oxford does remain primarily a university town. Even here, though, it's still too much. The "university" is actually twenty-eight separate colleges. Many of them, if you came upon them singly in some other town, could take up a full day of your time—each most pleasantly.

The history these colleges share overwhelms one. The words Nathaniel Hawthorne wrote in *Our Old Home* (1863) about his visit still apply:

> I take leave of Oxford without even an attempt to describe it,—there being no literary faculty, attainable or conceivable by me, which can avail to put it adequately, or even tolerably, upon paper. It must remain its own sole expression; and those whose sad fortune it may be never to behold it have no better resource than to dream about gray, weather-stained, ivy-grown edifices, wrought with quiet Gothic ornament, and standing around grassy quadrangles, where cloistered walks have echoed to the quiet footsteps of twenty generations.

It stuns one to realize that the university was old before Chaucer ever listed among its graduates,

> A clerk ther was of Oxenford also,
> That unto logyk hadde he long ygo.

The first such "clerks," and a ragged lot they were, came from the Sorbonne in Paris early in the twelfth century. They met haphazardly with their students in the streets, in taverns, in fields, anywhere. "Colleges" as such weren't established until the middle of the thirteenth century.

University and Merton Colleges vie for being first. University's alleged tie with Alfred the Great is the stuff dreams are made on; it was endowed in 1249. Merton, established in 1264, has the oldest statues, the oldest quad, and the oldest library, however, so generally wins the nod.

A list of writers who were Oxford graduates would go on and on. Indeed, just the dropouts who never made it to graduation would be the envy of most other schools: how about Sir Philip Sidney, Thomas Otway, William Wycherly, Thomas De Quincey, Edward Gibbon, and Walter Savage Landor, among others, for starters? And John Donne, Samuel Johnson, Shelley, and Swinburne?

Their reasons for dropping out were varied. Often, as with Johnson, it was lack of money. For Donne and Gibbon it was religion—both were Roman Catholic in a day when a public pledge to the Church of England was required. And for Landor, Shelley, and Swinburne it was the college decree. Landor was suspended for firing a gun at the window of a student he didn't like, and Shelley was expelled for writing his *The Necessity of Atheism* (1811). For his general wild behavior, Swinburne was told, "Leave on your own, or else————." He left.

The dropouts reacted variously, too. Gibbon lashed back: "I spent 14 months at Magdalen College; they proved the 14 months the most idle of my whole life." And when Landor was given a chance to return, he refused.

But Johnson always loved his old school. He accepted an honorary degree from it in 1776 (thus the "Dr." Johnson) and defended Oxford when Boswell censured its expelling of six young Methodists:

Said Boswell, "I am told they were good beings."

Johnson: "Sir, I believe they might be good beings; but they are not fit to be in the university of Oxford. A cow is a very good animal in the field; but we turn her out of the garden."

On his boat trip up the Thames with Peacock and others in 1815, Shelley made a point of stopping at Oxford to show them the Bodleian Library, Clarendon Press, a number of quadrangles, and even the first-floor living quarters at University College from which he had been exiled.

It would be absurd to attempt to discuss all the literary works in which Oxford appears or is referred to. Except, perhaps, to say that it certainly seems to have brought out the worst in poets. Those celebrated "dreamy spires" lines of Matthew Arnold are no great shakes, but there are worse. Consider, for example, Gerard Manley Hopkins's "Duns Scotus's Oxford":

> Towery city and branchy between towers;
> Cuckoo-echoing, bell-swarmed, lark-charmed,
>   rook-racked, river-rounded;

or Lionel Johnson's "Oxford Nights":

> Till the gray morning slowly creep
> Upward, and rouse the birds from sleep:
> Till *Oxford* bells the silence break,
> And find me happier, for your sake.

or Hilaire Belloc's "To the Balliol Men Still in Africa":

> Balliol made me, Balliol fed me,
> Whatever I had she gave me again,
> And the best of Balliol loved me and led me,
> God be with you Balliol men.

And in an untitled sonnet, William Wordsworth, a Cambridge man at that, was guilty of:

> Yet, O ye spires of Oxford! domes and towers!
> Gardens and groves! your presence overpowers
> The soberness of reason. . . .

Yes, in so many ways—including bad poetry—Oxford is too much. Remember that when you plan to go there. These bits of advice may help.

First, prepare yourself. Establish a set of priorities of what *you* want to see, and adjust the list to the amount of time *you* have to spend. You can't see the Bodleian and the Sheldonian Theatre and the Radcliffe Camera and the Ashmolean and the Museum of Oxford and Blackwell's Bookshop and twenty-eight colleges all in one day, or even several. In short, be selective.

And check the days and hours that places are open. Some are open all day, some afternoons only. Sunday hours often differ from weekdays, and in-term from vacations.

Second, before you get to your personal priority list, try to get an overall sense of the city. The seventy-five minute minibus tours are excellent for this. The two-hour walking tours are fine, too, but cover less ground and can be exhausting. Which suggests, don't wear yourself out. (Another way of saying, don't try to do too much: be selective).

Best of all is to give Oxford all the time you can. There are plenty of hotels and guest houses to put you up, especially the latter during vacations. There's a free accommodations service (the Tourist Information Centre on St. Aldates Street will tell you how to get there), but reservations in advance are always safest.

A number of hotels and pubs can provide an extra fillip of historic or literary interest. One such is the Bear Inn on Alfred Street near Christ Church. Built in the thirteenth century, it's been a favorite of students and their tutors ever since. Another is The Mitre on "The High" (High Street). You can drink wine stored in cellars that go back to the university's earliest days. Students made the Mitre their bastion during the endless battles between town and gown.

Then there's the Lamb and the Flag off St. Giles Street near St. John's. Oxford is the "Christminster" of Hardy's *Jude the Obscure*, and the Lamb and the Flag was where Jude, roaring drunk, is called on to "rehearse the Articles of the Creed, in the Latin tongue, for the edification of the company, including those shady ladies, Bower o'Bliss and Freckles."

By way of contrast, The Randolph on Beaumont Street only goes back to 1866, but rates four stars and can drop some formidable names. Edward, Prince of Wales, suggested Oxford needed such a place in 1863. The Randolph Gallery of the Ashmolean across the street provided its name, and Max Beerbohm's novel *Zuleika Dobson* (1911) furnished the theme for the murals painted when the ballroom was enlarged.

Max Reinhart stayed there while producing *A Midsummer Night's Dream*, and Henry James, who treats of Oxford in works like "A Passionate Pilgrim" (1875) and *Portraits of Places* (1883), stopped by. It's been the Oxford base for royalty from Bulgaria's Czar Ferdinand to Egypt's Farouk, and for prime ministers from Lloyd George to Clement Atlee.

Finally, if you like the macabre, there's the Golden Cross on Cornmarket Street. Here Oxford's three famous martyrs, Bishops Latimer and Ridley in 1555 and Archbishop Cranmer in 1556, were guests (if that's the right word) before their trials for heresy. You can step around the corner to the place on Broad Street opposite Balliol, marked by a cross in the pavement, where the three were burnt at the stake.

You'll also be standing on the very spot that Hardy has Jude thoughtlessly pick for Sue Bridehead to meet him for the first time. It gave her the creeps.

The Oxford Fringe

Close in to Oxford lies an assortment of literary scenes. Some are worth a bare mention, some a sentence or two more, and some of them rate special attention. You'll find practically all of them on any large scale map of Oxford and its outskirts (e.g., the A–Z "Street Plan of Oxford," scaled 4½″ = one mile).

The Arnold Group Tying this group together are the Matthew Arnold poems "The Scholar-Gipsy" and "Thyrsis." The former tells the legend of the Oxford student, forced by poverty to drop out, who roams the countryside for centuries learning the gipsy's secret of life. "Thyrsis," the elegy for Arnold's classmate Arthur Clough, then harks back to this scholar's quest and follows his footsteps as Arnold seeks the "single elm-tree bright" that symbolized for him and Clough their own youthful faith. The poem's climax is moving:

> Roam on! The light we sought is shining still
> Dost thou ask proof? Our tree yet crowns the hill,
> Our Scholar travels yet the loved hill-side.

Most of the places named in these poems are within a three mile arc, west and southwest of mid-town Oxford, but they're not always easy to get to today. Leaving Oxford from near the Randolph Hotel, Botley Road runs westward into the A 34. *North* and *South Hinksey* are both off the A 34 to the south. They appear in both poems, and Arnold's words in "Thyrsis" can serve as a warning not to expect too much of any of these spots now: "In the two Hinkseys nothing keeps the same." (Yes, it was *North* Hinksey that provoked Ruskin's quixotic road building).[2]

West, off the A 34 and roughly parallel to the Hinkseys, are "the arm, green-muffled" Cumnor Hills and "fir-topped" *Hurst*, where shepherds glimpse the scholar "in hat of antique shape." South of them are *Bagley Wood*, and the climactic track by *Childsworth Farm*,

> Past the high wood, to where the elm-tree crowns
> The hill behind whose ridge the sunset flames.

Two pedantic notes: Childsworth Farm is now called Chilswell Farm, and a mansion in Cumnor was the scene of a sensational sixteenth-century murder that Sir Walter Scott used in a novel he first called *Cumnor Hall*. His publisher got him to change it to *Kenilworth* (1821).

The River Group   As the crow flies, from the start of this brief river tour at Oxford's Folly Bridge to its end at Godstow is only three miles. For humans, however, it's a bit more. You can zig and zag your way by car, or follow the windings of the river—it's called both Isis and the Thames for this stretch— by boat or on foot along the towpath.

Folly Bridge   Folly Bridge is right off Christ Church Meadow, and gets its name from that wonderful English word for a large, extravagant, ostentatious, and usually useless structure: a "folly." Oxford's stood right here.

Folly Bridge was the landing place for the old time upriver steamers from London. Shelley stopped here for his nostalgic return to his alma mater in 1815. Keats, during his visit of 1817, launched his boat here for his river explorations. And Lewis Carroll took off from here one afternoon for an outing that was to make literary history. (More about this in a minute.)

[2]See page 102.

The present bridge dates from 1827. Its forerunner had a stone gatehouse that Roger Bacon used in the thirteenth century as a study. In the seventeenth century, Robert Burton, author of *The Anatomy of Melancholy* (1621) found the bridge therapeutic. A dour individual, he took his melancholy seriously. Usually nothing could make him laugh. But occasionally he would amble down from his rooms at Christ Church to listen to the barge men yelling and cursing each other. Whereupon, according to ancient record, "he would set his Hands to his Sides and laugh most profusely."

Osney Less than a mile up the river from the bridge, just below Botley Road, is Osney, which figures in Chaucer's naughty "Miller's Tale." While the Oxford carpenter, John, is there on one of his frequent trips, "Clerk Nicholas" and John's young wife work out their plans to cuckold him.

Binsey It's another mile upstream to Binsey, a village Gerard Manley Hopkins loved to stroll to when a student at Balliol in the 1860s. When he learned in 1879 that his beloved copse of trees had been cut down, he wrote an angry poem entitled "Binsey Poplars." Typically overcondensed in style, it yet gives a graphic picture of

> meadow and river and wind-wandering
> weed-winding bank.

Oxonians and visitors alike have long favored The Perch, a Binsey inn. Patrons of the past have included Dylan Thomas, Louis MacNeice, and that self-taught short-story writer and poet, A. E. Coppard, who worked as an accountant in Oxford from 1907 to 1919.

Godstow Last of these literary ties along the river is Godstow, a mile northwest of Binsey and immediately before the Thames-Isis flows under the A 34.

At Godstow Lock are the ruins of the nunnery where "Fair Rosamond" was educated and later buried. Rosamond became mistress to Henry II about 1174. According to medieval historian Ranulf Higden, Henry hid her away at Woodstock in "a house of wonderful working" with a labyrinthine entrance so cunning "no man or woman might come to her but he was instructed by the king." Even so, Henry's Queen Eleanor managed to slip through somehow with a bit of poison, and "so dealt with her that she lived not long after."

Rosamond and her story have provided grist for any number of writers, among them Thomas Deloney, Samuel Daniel, and Michael Drayton. Addison wrote an opera about her, *Rosamond* (1701), and Tennyson a play, *Becket* (1884). Tennyson, however, has Becket rescue Rosamond and ship her off, alive, to Godstow's nunnery.

Matthew Arnold has his scholar-gipsy turn up in this area, too, above Godstow Bridge,

> "Where black-wing'd swallows haunt the glittering
> Thames."

But by all odds Godstow's greatest claim to literary fame came from a boat-trip made by a lecturer at Christ Church the afternoon of July 4, 1862. For this teacher, known to the world for his weighty works on mathematics, lived a secret life.

Ordinarily he was Charles Lutwidge Dodgson and wore the somber black clothes and top hat of a clergyman. But this day, as he and a friend set forth from Folly Bridge with the three small daughters of the college dean for an upriver row, he wore white flannel trousers and a white straw hat, and was (though the girls knew it not) Lewis Carroll.

As they rowed up to Godstow Bridge, he spun out impromptu a fanciful tale to keep his young charges entertained. By the time they were back at Folly Bridge, *Alice in Wonderland* was essentially complete.

Should you find yourself at Godstow, try the Trout Inn, an attractive Tudor house with riverside setting and peacocks strutting in the garden. As you sit and sip on the terrace, you can imagine Carroll and Alice gliding past below you. You'll like it. So did Aldous Huxley and A.P. Herbert, the humorist and writer of musical comedies.

The poet William Morris's visit there, however, left him more than a bit crestfallen. In 1857, Dante Gabriel Rossetti had assembled a group of happy-go-lucky volunteers—Morris (nicknamed Topsy) and Algernon Swinburne among them—to paint scenes from *Morte d'Arthur* on the walls of Oxford's Debating Hall. But Morris had trouble with both the head and body of Iseult. Rossetti suggested he use a model, a Miss Lipscombe, whose father kept the Trout. But when Morris reached the inn, the model's mother would have none of it, and dispatched him right back to Oxford. There, on his bedroom door, he found a tribute from Rossetti:

> Poor Topsy has gone
> To make a sketch of Miss Lipscombe,
> But he can't draw the head,
> And don't know where the hips come.

2. And So To Banbury Cross

If you want a central base for exploring in and about Oxford, but don't want fighting that city's traffic as daily fare, there's a first-rate (three star) hotel at Thame, only a dozen miles to the east. Not only do Thame and this hotel have literary interest of their own, but so do three little villages between them and Oxford. The three are Elsfield, Beckley and Forest Hill. All three are adjacent to the A 40, which also connects with the road to Thame, the A 418.

Elsfield—Beckley—and Forest Hill

Elsfield Practically a suburb of Oxford on its northern edge, Elsfield was the home of two good novelists, R. D. Blackmore and John Buchan. Blackmore was born in the Oxfordshire village of Longworth, but came as an infant to live at the Elsfield vicarage with his aunt and uncle following his mother's death. Blackmore's best known work is *Lorna Doone* (1869), set in the West Country. Elsfield, however, figures in his *Cripps the Carrier* (1877), and the hero's house, now Cripps Cottage, is located in neighboring Beckley.

John Buchan lived at Elsfield's manor house from 1919 to 1935, when he was made Governor General of Canada and raised to the peerage. When he chose his new title, he used the village name: Baron Tweedsmuir of Elsfield. *The Thirty-Nine Steps* (1915), perhaps the most famous of his novels, was written earlier, but among those of his Elsfield days are *Midwinter* (1923), *Dancing Floor* (1926), *The Blanket of the Dark* (1931), and *Gap in the Curtain* (1932), as well as works on Sir Walter Scott, Julius Caesar, and Oliver Cromwell.

Beckley Beckley is two miles further along the Elsfield road. Small, quiet and charming, it attracted both Aldous Huxley and Evelyn Waugh. As Oxford students—Huxley at Balliol, Waugh at Hertford—they knew the area well.

Huxley modeled the three-towered house in *Crome Yellow* (1921) on Beckley Park, which has an interesting history. The house is mid-sixteenth century, has three moats, and the manor was mentioned in the will of Alfred the Great.

Waugh was a devotee of Beckley's Abingdon Arms pub, staying there while writing the latter part of his biography of D. G. Rossetti, published in 1928, and returning with his bride that same year for his honeymoon. The Abingdon Arms still thrives, with fresh salmon a special treat.

Forest Hill   Like Elsfield, Forest Hill almost touches Oxford. It was here that John Milton, in 1642, at age thirty-four, unfortunately found seventeen-year-old Mary Powell living at the manor house. Within a month he married her and took her off to London. Within six weeks she was back in Forest Hill, not to return to Milton for another three years.

The marriage was probably doomed from the start, but at least it gave rise to Milton's famous (in his own time, infamous) tracts on divorce, a subject that hitherto had somehow escaped his attention. Fictional treatments of this marital mismatch include *Mistress Mary Powell* (1851) by the Victorian novelist Anne Manning, and *Wife to Mr. Milton* (1943) by Robert Graves.

Thame

Thame (as in SAME if you lisped), a pleasant market town of over six thousand people, is notable for its unusually wide main street, Georgian and half-timbered houses, a grammar school dating from 1575, and an old coaching inn an eccentric of the 1920s made famous for its cuisine and distinguished clientele. Thame is a mere twelve miles from Oxford, forty-five from London itself. The A 418, which runs right through Thame, connects directly with the main thoroughfare linking Oxford and London, the M (A) 40.

One product of that ancient grammar school was John Hampden, born in Thame in 1594. A cousin of Oliver Cromwell, Hampden was an early opponent of Charles I and won the signal if dubious honor of having His Majesty try to arrest him personally. Hampden got himself mortally wounded in the Civil War, and died and is buried in Thame.

Two other old Thame school boys were Anthony Wood and John Fell. Wood (he later decided "à Wood" had more class) attended in the late 1630s and became a leading antiquarian and historian. Among his works, chiefly valuable now as source material, were histories of both Oxford and its university, and a biographical dictionary of its writers and bishops.

John Fell, a pupil earlier in that same decade, is as famous an unknown as they come. For he is *the* "Fell" of

> I do not love thee, Doctor Fell.
> The reason why I cannot tell;

> But this alone I know full well,
> I do not love thee, Doctor Fell.

written by a disgruntled Oxford student named Thomas Brown.

Who remembers today that Dr. Fell was both a renowned Dean of Christ Church and Bishop of Oxford? Or that he translated Thomas à Wood into Latin and was a major developer of the Oxford Press? Or that he was responsible for Christ Church's tower and its "Great Tom" bell, which nightly heralds the closing of the college gates with 101 mighty strokes?

But it could be worse. Suppose Tom Brown had *liked* him, and had written

> I sure do like you, Doctor Fell,
> In fact I like you very well.
> Just why I do I cannot tell,
> But still, I like you Doctor Fell.

Who then would have heard of Dr. Fell today? Or, for that matter, Tom Brown?

A twentieth-century resident of Thame for some months was William Butler Yeats, who came there in 1921, the year his *Plays for Dancers* appeared. The place where he lived and where his son was born, Cuttlebrook House at 42 High Street, is now a shop.

On Cornmarket Street in the very heart of Thame is that celebrated old hotel, called the Spread Eagle. Charles II is supposed to have stayed there, and French prisoners got something less than royal treatment in its cellars during the Napoleonic Wars.

But what made its reputation was its purchase in the 1920s by a John Fothergill, an individualist to say the least. His designedly haughty ways quickly got rid of the inn's basic constituency of local farmers and commercial travellers. Not for him the ordinary, as he said in describing his cooking: ". . . . of English things we have daily, from three bakers, three different kinds of bread made from flours that I have forced upon them, besides the breads we bake ourselves; cheese from East Harptree, salt from Malden, (sic) mustard from Leighton Buzzard, sausages, after a search all over England, from Glenthorne in Thame. . . ."

Fothergill's demanding standards and superb cuisine speedily enticed an illustrious parade of artists, writers, political figures, and Oxford luminaries that continues to this day. Even the signpost outside the hotel, a magnificent thing of wrought iron, has its touch of distinction. Though the ironwork itself dates from the early nineteenth century, the original art of the sign was done by "Carrington" (Dora Carrington Partridge), Lytton Strachey's friend-of-friends.[3]

She and Strachey were among a number of members of that gifted circle of writers and artists known as the Bloomsbury Group who were attracted to the Spread Eagle in Fothergill's day. D. H. Lawrence based his story "None of That" on Carrington, and she was the Mary Bracegirdle of Aldous Huxley's *Crome Yellow*.

Garsington

The jewel of Garsington, a tiny village on a side road off the B 840 four miles southeast of Oxford, is its lovely little manor house. Great old yew trees frame a Tudor building of much architectural interest. Fishponds and a columbarium, a flower parterre and an Italian garden make it a mecca on the rare occasions when the grounds are open to members of the National Gardens Scheme.

Garsington Manor was all that in 1915, too, when it was bought by a prominent London couple, Lady Ottoline and Philip Morrell. For the next decade and more it was a literary showcase rivalling anything in London. Even a partial list of writers entertained there between 1915 and 1927 would run through most of the alphabet: Auden and Arlen, Brooks, Day-Lewis, Forster, Huxley, Lawrence, MacNeice and Mansfield and Murry, Russell, Sassoon and Strachey, the Woolfs, and Yeats.

Though she fluttered about, as E. M. Forster put it, "in elaborate floating dresses of all colours of the rainbow," Lady Ottoline was an aristocrat and quite capable of being imperial. Lytton Strachey thought of her as being Queen Victoria; D. H. Lawrence as Queen Elizabeth. She delighted in supporting young writers and artists doing battle with the more stodgy members of her own class.

Before World War I, at her Bedford Square place in London, it was the Bloomsbury Group, Virginia and Leonard Woolf, Lytton Strachey, Maynard Keynes, and the rest. During the war it was incendiary pacifists like D. H. Lawrence and Bertram Russell. And after the war it was a still younger coterie, this time Oxford-nurtured, known as "The Gang": W. H. Auden, Louis MacNeice, C. Day-Lewis.

Worldly and patrician yet bohemian and eccentric, keen-eyed and tart-

[3]Their story is on p. 86.

tongued yet humane and generous, Lady Ottoline was the stuff of fiction herself, as Aldous Huxley and D. H. Lawrence were quick to realize. Huxley, one of the first to visit Garsington Manor while a student at Oxford, found her "a quite incredible creature" and captured the "always interesting people" and "very good talk" in his *Crome Yellow*.

Lawrence called on those same lively exchanges that Garsington Manor fostered for the dialog of *Women in Love* (1920), and included a telling sketch of Lady Ottoline as Hermione Riddice. There is also a touching picture of the manor itself, which he calls Breadalby: "So much beauty and pathos of old things passing away . . . it is England—my God, it breaks my soul—their England, these shafted windows, the elm trees, the blue distance. . . ."

Lady Ottoline deliberately set up these scintillating discussions by juxtaposing her guests one against another. There were times when she let them choose their partners, as when she offered E. M. Forster the choice of T. S. Eliot or Wyndham Lewis as a fellow guest. Curiously enough (or so it seems to us now), he chose Lewis. They got on "amicably," according to Forster's account, and fled off together when a company of thirty others, mainly "undulating boys from Oxford," descended on them for tea.

For the most part, however, Lady Ottoline did the choosing herself, her favorite mixer, apparently, being D. H. Lawrence. Early in 1915, for instance, she decided that Forster ought to get to know Lawrence, then her newest discovery. So she seated them together at lunch, and was gratified that they were so drawn to each other. Lawrence invited Forster for a three-day stay with him at Greatham in Sussex.

The gratification was short-lived. Before the three days were up, Lawrence was vehemently attacking Forster and his work, and Forster stormed back to London. Undaunted, Lady Ottoline brought them together again at Garsington. But though they "reconciled," they were never again really close.

Her efforts, also in 1915, to couple Lawrence and Bertram Russell proved even more disastrous, as Russell recounts in his *Portraits from Memory* (1951). "Our acquaintance," he says, "was brief and hectic, lasting altogether about a year." Since both he and Lawrence were anti-war and "full of rebellion," Russell assumed that they were kindred souls, but "we discovered that we differed from each other more than either differed from the Kaiser."

Lawrence charged that the lectures that Russell was giving at Cambridge actually went along with the bourgeois rather than abandoning them: "What's the good of sticking in the damned ship [he wrote Russell] haranguing the merchant pilgrims in their own language? Why don't you drop overboard?"

Even so, Russell reports with a chuckle, Lawrence had the cheek in a subsequent letter to write: "Oh, and I want to ask you, when you make your will, do leave me enough to live on. I want you to live forever. But I want you to make me in some part your heir."

As it turned out, Russell had reason to chuckle. He was then forty-three, Lawrence thirty. But he outlived Lawrence by forty years.

It is good to know that Garsington Manor, so lovely and so steeped in literary history, is still coddled by its private owners. And that if you are a member of the National Gardens Scheme and can time it right, you can get in to see the gardens and grounds. Lady Ottoline and Philip Morrell laid out those gardens themselves.

Woodstock and Blenheim

Woodstock, eight miles north of Oxford on the A 34, has one of England's most famous national shrines. But its historical and literary ties are centuries older than the eighteenth-century palace that today's visitors flock to see.

It was at Woodstock that Henry II, in 1174, built that labyrinthine hideaway in a vain attempt to shield Fair Rosamond from his vengeful Queen Eleanor.[4] Queen Elizabeth I came to Woodstock in 1575 to see a play especially written for her by George Gascoigne, *The Queen Majestie's Entertainment at Woodstock*. And in 1651 a disguised Charles II hid in the old royal lodge there to escape Oliver Cromwell, as told in Sir Walter Scott's *Woodstock* (1826).

Still, it *is* that eighteenth-century palace, Blenheim, that now draws visitors to Woodstock by the tens of thousands every year. They come because it is one of the greatest of stately homes, and because it was the birthplace of Sir Winston Churchill.

Were it neither, however, it would have unique interest. The man for whom it was built, as well as the edifice itself, aroused the passions and activated the pens of most of the major writers of the eighteenth century. Addison, Steele, Swift, Pope, Congreve, John Gay, Nicholas Rowe, Matthew Prior, and Henry Fielding were among literary leaders who praised or condemned the first master of Blenheim.

He had begun life in 1650 as plain Jack Churchill, the son, interestingly

[4] p. 109.

enough, of a Sir Winston Churchill. Before his death in 1722, he had become the first Duke of Marlborough, deified, villified, and deified again.

Young Churchill's rise was meteoric by any measure. At fifteen he was page of honor to the Duke of York (his sister was the Duke's mistress). At twenty-two he was a captain in an English army fighting for France's Louise XIV. At twenty-three he had saved the life of the Duke of Monmouth, and Louis had made him a colonel.

At twenty-five and back in England, he became the secret lover of the Duchess of Cleveland, mistress to no less than Charles II himself. One evening when His Majesty had the bad judgment to arrive for a rendezvous at the very moment when Jack was already engaging that lady's attention, Churchill skipped out of her bedroom window, underwear in hand.

Even when, age twenty-eight, he married Sarah Jennings, a beauty but hardly the heiress he'd had in mind, his upward climb continued. Sarah, it turned out, was the dearest friend of Princess Anne, whose daddy was soon to be James II. Sarah was a great conniver to boot. Backstage politicking with James's successor, William III (the William of William and Mary) won her husband a title and the name by which he is now known to history: Earl of Marlborough.

When Anne herself came to the throne in 1702, she topped even this. In quick succession, Churchill was appointed commander-in-chief of the army, sent off to the continent to fight the French and Bavarians, and raised from Earl to Duke of Marlborough. After he broke the enemy's back at a little Bavarian village called Blenheim, all England was his.

Writers vied to pay him homage: Addison in "The Campaign:"

> Calm and serene he drives the furious blast;
> And, pleas'd the almighty's orders to perform,
> Rides in the whirlwind and directs the storm.

Prior in "Ode to the Queen:"

> Great thanks, oh Captain great in arms, receive
> From thy triumphant country's public voice:
> Thy country greater thanks can only give
> To Anne, to her who made those arms her choice.

and Swift in *Jack Frenchman's Lamentation* (Almanza was a great French victory):

> From this dream of success,
> They'll awaken we guess,

> At the sound of great Marlborough's drums;
> They may think if they will,
> Of Almanza still
> But 'tis Blenheim whenever he comes.

The Queen made him a prince of the empire, and gave him the manor of Woodstock. £240,000 of public money was allotted to build a prodigious palace there, to be called Blenheim to honor him and his victory forever. Architect-playwright Sir John Vanbrugh—creator of Castle Howard and author of *The Relapse* and *The Provok'd Wife*—designed the building. Capability Brown did the landscaping.

But for a public idol, "forever" can be a mighty short time. Soon enemies were attacking his policies and charging him with pocketing military funds. The Queen, bedevilled by Sarah Churchill's ever-shriller tongue, came to agree. On the last day of 1711, Marlborough was stripped of all authority. People cried "Stop thief! Stop!" at him on the streets. Even the building of Blenheim was slowed.

Some few remained loyal. Vanbrugh called his unfinished structure "a monument of ingratitude." Steele wrote, "After a few turbulent years it will be said of us, the rest of mankind, 'they were;' it will be to the end of time said 'Marlborough is.'"

But the denunciations were numerous and acrid. Swift now wrote in *Journal to Stella:* "I confess my belief that he has not one good quality in the world beside that of a general, and even that I have heard denied by several great officers."

Marlborough went into voluntary exile abroad. With the ascension of George III in 1714 he enjoyed a brief return to glory. George's first act was to rename Marlborough commander-in-chief.

But the attacks never really stopped. Alexander Pope was particularly relentless, even after the duke's death in 1722. Pope wrote to the Bishop of Rochester: "At the time of the Duke of Marlborough's funeral, I intend to lie at the Deanery, and moralize one evening with you on the vanity of human glory."

Ten years later, in *Essay on Man* he was writing:

> Oh infamous for plundered provinces,
> Oh wealth ill-fated! Which no act of fame
> E'er taught to shine, or sanctified from shame.

Some were kinder, including Pope's friend John Gay in "Epistle to her Grace, Duchess of Marlborough":

The affliction burdens not your heart alone;
When Marlborough died, a nation gave a groan.
Where'ere men talk of war and martial fame
They'll mention Marlborough's and Caesar's name.

Blenheim Palace had not gone unscathed, either. Swift called it Vanbrugh's "hallowed quarry, whose proportions—and discomfort—are collosal." Pope wrote a friend, "I never saw so great a thing with so much littleness in it. I think the architect built it entirely in compliance to the taste of its owner; for it is the most inhospitable thing imaginable. . . . In a word, the whole is a most expensive absurdity."

But the novelist Henry Fielding thought otherwise. In *Journey from this World to the Next* (1743), he compared its "general splendor" favorably to that of Louis XIV's palace. And when they visited it together in 1776, Boswell remarked to Dr. Johnson: "You and I, Sir, have, I think, seen together the extremes of what can be seen in Britain—the wild, rough island of Mull, and Blenheim Park."

In a letter to his fellow essayist William Hazlitt, Charles Lamb said in 1810 that he had enjoyed his visit to Blenheim with his sister Mary, but regretted that they had been unable to see its great collection of paintings: "The pictures are all Titians, Jupiter and Ledas, Mars and Venuses, etc., all naked pictures, which may be the reason they don't show them to females."

Nathaniel Hawthorne saw it while he was U. S. Consul at Liverpool, 1853 to 1860. He grumbled at the entrance fee. You had to buy a ticket for six at ten shillings, even if you came alone. And attendants popped up everywhere. All, he said, "expect fees on their own private account,—their noble master pocketing the ten shillings." But he was struck by the landscaping magic of Capability Brown: "Art has effected such wonderful things that the uninstructed visitor would never guess that nearly the whole scene was but the embodied thought of the human mind. A skilful painter hardly does more for his blank sheet of canvas than the Landscape-gardener, the planter, the arranger of trees, has done for the monotonous surface of Blenheim."

The approach to Blenheim is a heart-stopper today. You turn off the A 34, enter the more than two thousand acres of parkland, and suddenly across Brown's large artificial lake and the bridge—there it is, the palace!

Inside, room follows room in a vast array. Two are particularly notable: the "Long Library" with ten thousand volumes, at 183 feet the longest such in England. And the bedroom where Sir Winston Churchill was born, with an exhibition of Churchilliana.

Guided tours take about an hour. Or you can wander around on your own, a whole day if you wish. There is ample provision for nourishment—a restaurant, a buffet, and a cafeteria—and there's afternoon tea as well.

If you still haven't had enough of the palace, you can stay in Woodstock overnight at the same old coaching inn adjacent to the palace where Hawthorne stopped. First licensed in 1232, it's now the Bear Hotel (three-star) on Park Street. Hawthorne knew it as the Black Bear, "an ancient inn, large and respectable, with balustraded staircases, intricate passages and corridors, and queer old pictures and engravings."

You may want to take a second look at those parklands, too. For when Woodstock Manor still belonged to the crown, they saw the dramatic last days of yet another literary figure, the scandalous but titled poet, John Wilmot, Earl of Rochester.

Rochester Country: Ditchley Park and Spelsbury, Burford and Adderbury

The date was July 20, 1680. The place was the High Lodge at Woodstock Manor. There in a low and bare little room, with one window in front and a smaller one behind, the suddenly penitent Earl of Rochester lay dying.[5] To his bedside he had called Bishop Gilbert Burnet that he might confess of his sins. Though the earl was only thirty-three, the recital took four days. And little wonder. In an age when libertinism was the rule and a rake sat on the throne, Rochester had managed to outshine them all. The bishop must have done a good job. Two days later his lordship died, "without a convulsion or so much as a groan," wrote Burnet in *Life and Death of the right honourable John Wilmot Earl of Rochester* (1680),

If you've never heard of Rochester, there's no need to hang your head. He could well be dubbed the "Poet who Wasn't." Verses like "Love and Life" show a witty cynicism matching John Donne's, and "A Satire Against Mankind" has an epigrammatic bite worthy of John Dryden, but this output is almost too slim to be reckoned with.

His ways, outrageous beyond belief, consumed his talent as well as his body. He came to the court of Charles II in 1664 at age seventeen, where his charm, good looks, and audacity speedily made him a royal favorite. He and the aptly named "Merry Monarch" became the best of friends. They played jokes together, they wenched together, and drank together. How they did

[5]The description is Nathaniel Hawthorne's.

drink! Rochester once boasted that he had been drunk "by his own count five years on end."

The pranks that amused His Majesty were endless. Once Rochester set himself up on Tower Hill in London as a quack doctor. Another time he took over as tavern keeper, and seduced the wives of his customers. Said the king, "Thou art the happiest fellow in my dominion . . . I [do] envy thee thy impudence."

But the gamut could not last. When Charles made him Keeper of Woodstock Park in 1674, Rochester, still only twenty-seven, had in fact gone full circle. He was back in his own country. Aside from the court, the scenes of the main events of his life were all within a twelve-mile radius of Woodstock: Ditchley Park and Spelsbury, Burford and Oxford and Adderbury.

Ditchley Park and Spelsbury   Ditchley Park and Spelsbury embrace the beginning and the end of Rochester's brief life. Ditchley is six miles above Woodstock, off the A 34. Spelsbury is two miles west of Ditchley.

Rochester was born in 1647 at Ditchley Park, the country home of the Lees. His mother's first husband had been a Lee, a family with strong Cavalier ties. Old Sir Henry and his son Albert, who helped Charles II escape from Cromwell in Scott's *Woodstock*, were Lees.

There is a Ditchley Park still, and it is open to the public for a fortnight beginning the last week in July. It is not the "low antient timber house" described by John Evelyn in his *Diary*, however, but a replacement built in 1722.

At Spelsbury is the church with the family vault in which Rochester was buried after his death at Woodstock in 1680. In the church are memorials to various Lees.

Burford   As a boy, Rochester prepared for Oxford at the grammar school of Burford, a pretty little village on the A 40 that serves as a gateway to Gloucestershire and the Cotswolds. Today's school is mainly Victorian, but a touch or two of the Tudor original remain.

At Oxford, he attended Wadham College from 1660 to 1661. He left, age fourteen, with an M. A. degree—which no doubt says more about the school than the student. The lad was not unappreciative. He gave the college a set of four silver tankards, which it still has.

Adderbury   Among a number of fine old homes in Adderbury, twelve miles north of Woodstock on the A 41, is Adderbury House, which Rochester inherited in 1658 along with his title. Here he brought his bride, Elizabeth

Malet, in 1667. Typically, however, his had been no simple man-meets-and-marries-girl affair. In 1665, apparently, he had kidnapped her. At least the authorities said he had, and he spent several unpleasant days in the Tower of London before he managed to pull the strings that set him free. Alexander Pope visited Adderbury House in 1739, but found little inspiration from sleeping on Rochester and Elizabeth's nuptial couch. Says a verse dashed off before he left:

> With no poetick ardors fired
> I press the bed where *Wilmot* lay;
> That here he lov'd, or here expired
> Begets no numbers [i.e. poetry] grave or gay.

Maybe it's just as well Pope's muse remained unstirred. He and Rochester were hardly kindred souls. But one must mourn the loss of the poet that might have been, the Rochester who stole down to his sleeping monarch's door one night and wrote upon it:

> Here lies our sovereign lord the King
> Whose word no man relies on;
> He never says a foolish thing,
> Nor ever does a wise one.

Adderbury House is now a home for the elderly, but you can get in to see it if you arrange things in advance with the warden.

Rousham Park and Banbury

Close by Adderbury are a country house with important memorabilia of Pope, Swift, Horace Walpole, and Gay that few have heard of; and a town that has been on the lips of English-speaking children since the sixteenth century. The house is Rousham Park, off the A 423 seven miles south of Adderbury. The town is Banbury, the Banbury of "Ride a cock-horse to Banbury Cross" and the Banbury cakes. It's on the A 41, four miles to the north.

Rousham Park   Rousham Park has attracted travellers for well over two hundred years. The house is seventeenth-century, the grounds, laid out by William Kent, eighteenth. A mediocre painter, Kent made amends as architect of such notable London landmarks as the House Guards building and Devonshire House. Rousham Park proves he was an equally impressive landscaper. Horace Walpole deemed it elegant enough for a Roman emperor. Pope, a great friend of the owners, called its ponds and waterfalls "the prettiest that I ever saw."

The grounds are open to the public today all year round, the house during the spring and summer. Among its treasures are an autographed copy of Pope's *Works* (1735), and letters of Swift and Gay, as well as Pope.

Banbury   Today's Banbury Cross is an upstart replacement (1858) for the one the Puritans knocked down in 1602. And the town is far bigger than you'd like—over thirty thousand. A cock-horse could get bowled over by the traffic, and the fine lady on her white steed would be baffled by the one-way streets.

Some spoilsports even say the lady wasn't all that fine, but only a local girl chosen for the annual May Day procession. Oh well, you can still buy those Banbury cakes, and at a seventeenth-century cake shop.

3. The Road To Gloucester

From Oxford to the county line and Gloucestershire is less than twenty miles. Along or slightly off of the A 420 that takes you there are a number of tempting stops. Like Stanton Harcourt and the ruins of the tower where Pope translated the *Iliad*. And Uffington, with both the 375-foot figure of a horse (described in *Tom Brown's Schooldays*) and the knoll where St. George (perhaps) killed that dragon. And Kelmscott, where William Morris shared both house and wife with Dante Gabriel Rossetti.

Topographically, the country gets more interesting, too.

Stanton Harcourt

Five miles west of Oxford and the A 420, in Stanton Harcourt, are what's left of an old Tudor mansion: a gatehouse, the kitchen, and a tower. The interesting thing is that the place was already partly in ruins when Pope stayed there in 1718 translating the *Iliad*. (If you want to see the ruins, they're on the B 4449 via B 4044. They have been open to the public at times, but better check the current status.)

The guest of Lord Harcourt, a patron of writers, Pope worked in the top room of the tower. He was much amused by his housing. The huge kitchen, he insisted, was staffed by witches with Satan as the head cook. On entering the drawing room, "you are convinced by a flight of birds about your ears & a cloud of dust in your eyes, that 'tis the Pigeon-house."

During his stay, two local lovers had the misfortune to he struck dead by lightning while perched on a haystack. On the bright side, Pope wrote friends, there was "no mark or blemish on the Bodies; except the left Eyebrow of Sarah a little sing'd and a small Spot between her Breasts."

Through Pope, the pair won a touch of immortality. John Gay spread Pope's account widely. Goldsmith borrowed from Gay in *The Vicar of Wakefield*. Thackeray used it in his lecture on Prior, Gay, and Pope. Pope himself wrote an epitaph for their tombstone, which his sharp-tongued sometime friend, Lady Mary Wortley Montagu, promptly mocked. Maybe, said she, the lightning bolt was a blessing:

> Who knows if 'twas not kindly done?
> For had they seen the next year's sun,
> A beaten wife and cuckold swain
> Had jointly cursed the marriage chain.

In *Our Old Home*, Hawthorne quotes Pope's letters, and describes his tower room: ". . . a chamber, not large, though occupying the whole area of the tower, and lighted by a window on each side. . . . The room once contained a record by himself, scratched with a diamond on one of the window-panes [saying] he had here finished the fifth book of the "Iliad" on such a day."

Stanton Harcourt has two other literary ties. The playwright John Marston, contemporary of Shakespeare, was ordained deacon here in 1609. And near the church is the house (now Wesley Cottage) where those hymn-writing brothers, John and Charles Wesley, stayed when visiting.

Uffington

Tom Brown's Schooldays (1857) is one of those books, like *Pilgrim's Progress* or *Uncle Tom's Cabin*, that most people have heard of but never read. Uffington, sixteen miles southwest of Oxford on a side road off the A 420, is where both Tom Brown and his creator, Thomas Hughes, were born. (Hughes in 1822).

Grandson of the village vicar, Hughes describes both Uffington and its area, especially Whitehorse Hill to the south in the novel. On Whitehorse Hill, 856 feet high, are Uffington Castle, an eight-acre earthwork, "a magnificent Roman camp, and make no mistake;" Dragon's Hill Knoll, supposed site of St. George's triumph; and along the ridge a timeless dolmen (crude stone burial chamber) named Wayland Smith's Cave, whose legend Scott used in *Kenilworth*.

Dominating Whitehorse Hill is that horse—all 375 feet of him, cut into the turf of the chalk downs. He's probably the work of early Britons, and not, as popular myth has it, a memento of Alfred the Great's victory over the Danes in 871. Hughes also features the horse in *The Scouring of White Horse* (1859), a tapestry of Uffington legends.

Just southeast of Uffington is Kingston Lisle, where Hughes's grandmother lived after the vicar's death. She was a great favorite of novelist William Harrison Ainsworth. He visited her often, worked on both *Jack Sheppard* (1839) and *Guy Fawkes* (1841) while there, and dedicated the latter to Mrs. Hughes.

You can enter the grounds of the White Horse and Uffington Castle if you want to. Both are open most days of the year.

Faringdon

Faringdon is five miles north of the White Horse, at the junction of the A 420 and the A 417. Its stone-built houses give it character and its eighteenth-century Market Hall provide an historic focal point. It also has the last Folly tower of any consequence built in England. But its greatest claim for attention is the poet laureate born there in 1745. In a century that listed such household words as William Whitehead and Laurence Eusden among his more immediate predecessors, Henry James Pye was the consummate nobody.

Pye's masterpiece was a treatise on the duties of a justice of the peace out of season. It's in prose, at that! Nevertheless, laureate from 1790 to 1813, Pye was the first to get a regular salary (£27) instead of an annual cask of wine. And the home he built in 1780, Faringdon House, remains a showcase. Its resident ghost, a headless fellow who stalks the park seeking a stepmother who had him done in, appears in Richard Harris Barham's *Ingoldsby Legends* (1840).

In that same park is the Folly Tower, built by Lord (Gerald Hugh Tyrwhitt-Wilson) Berners, author of *The Camel* (1936) and *Far From the Madding War* (1941). At last report, the park was open to members of the NGS for a couple of days toward the end of March.

Kelmscott Manor

Early in 1871, William Morris began "looking for a house for the wife and kids." In May he found it at Kelmscott, five miles above Faringdon just off the B 4449. Kelmscott Manor, he said, was "a heaven on earth." He took a second look with his wife Jane and his friend Dante Gabriel Rossetti, the poet-painter. Rossetti had mentioned their sharing a place. By July 6 they had signed their joint tenancy, Morris had ensconced Jane and their two girls at Kelmscott, and was off to explore Iceland and its sagas.

If that sounds odd, it was, especially since Rossetti had both known and loved Jane longer than Morris had. When they were in Oxford in 1857 painting murals on the walls of the Union Debating Hall, Rossetti stumbled upon a dark-haired beauty named Jane Burden. He had her pose for him, and they fell in love. But he was already engaged to a young model named Elizabeth Siddal. So he persuaded Morris to marry Janey. Or so rumors said.

Indisputably Morris, a great shaggy bear of a man too self-effacing for his own good, did marry Jane in 1859. Indisputably, too, he loved her deeply, as proved by the portrait of her in his poem, "Praise of My Lady" (1858).

By the time of Kelmscott, both Morris and Rossetti were established figures. Morris had already published *Defence of Guenevere, and Other Poems* (1858), *Life and Death of Jason* (1867), and *Earthly Paradise* (1868–70), and won acclaim as artist, decorator, stained-glass designer, and manufacturer of furniture. (The Morris chair was his).

Rossetti, long known only as a painter, had recently arrived as a poet too, but at bitter cost. He had finally married Miss Siddal in 1860. Two years later she lay dead of an overdose of laudanum. Overcome, Rossetti had buried with her the only manuscript of several of his best poems. In 1869, readying his first collection of verse for the press, he made the anguished decision to retrieve those poems from her coffin.

The publication (*Poems*, 1870) was a great success, netting Rossetti £300 in less than a month. Since some of the poems were a bit sultry for Victorian tastes, he had feared the critics. But most were kind, among them Swinburne and Morris. Still, Rossetti was a troubled man, pursued by the memory of his wife's ravaged grave and fearful that hostile critics might yet appear. Thus Kelmscott Manor (and Janey) provided a haven he sorely needed.

"The loveliest 'haunt of ancient peace that can be imagined," he wrote in an early letter to his mother, "purely Elizabethan in character." But as Rossetti himself suspected, it was neither Elizabethan nor, technically speaking, a manor. It was simply a seventeenth-century mansion with two full storeys and gabled upper floor, topped by stone slates, "the most lovely covering a roof can have," as Morris said.

July through September of 1871, when Rossetti finally left Kelmscott for London, may have been the happiest period of his life. While Morris, as Rossetti jokingly put it, was "up to his navel in ice," Rossetti painted in the morning, took riverside walks with Janey in the afternoon, and read to her at night.

The river rambles produced poetry as well: "Rose Mary," "Sunset Wings," "The Cloud Confines," and about thirty sonnets that were to appear later in his *House of Life* (1881). A number of the sonnets are actually love poems to Janey, despairing in tone, though he disguised them before publication by such transparent devices as changing the color of his beloved's hair.

In September, Rossetti left Kelmscott. Janey had gone off somewhere, and his final days were lonely and forlorn, as he indicates in his bleak sonnet "Without Her":

> What of her glass without her? The blank gray
> There where the pool is blind to the moon's face.

and the even more revealing question:

> . . . . Her pillowed place
> Without her?

Rossetti came back to Kelmscott in September 1872, for what turned out to be an almost unbroken stay of two years. He was more in need of succor than ever. The much-feared attacks on his poetry had materialized, climaxed by a vicious piece entitled "The Fleshly School of Poetry." His health and nerves already undermined, Rossetti had broken down and attempted suicide.

Now, as his letters indicated, all at first went swimmingly. "Here I am, as well as ever I was in my life," said one. "The place is perfect Paradise," said another. He painted, with Janey as model, and wrote some poetry, mainly sonnets. He romped with the children, whom he adored. When Morris himself was there, which was seldom, the strange menage got on well.

But as the months passed, everything began to fall apart. More and more, Janey was away and he was alone. Old afflictions returned: insomnia, fought with deadly doses of whiskey and drugs, resulting in hallucinations that he was a victim of a universal conspiracy.

The inevitable, devastating finale came in July 1874. Janey and Morris were away together, perhaps deliberately to escape him. (Janey later revealed she thought him mad). Walking along the river with his aide, George Hake, one morning Rossetti fancied a trio of local fishermen had insulted him as he passed. He turned on the unsuspecting strangers so fiercely Hake had to rush to separate them. Word spread in the neighborhood; soon staying there became impossible. By the end of the month, Rossetti quit Kelmscott forever.

Morris never lost his love of Kelmscott. He kept it as his country home for the rest of his life, and was buried in the village churchyard. When he bought a home in Hammersmith to be his London center of operations, he called it Kelmscott House. The famous printing shop he set up in 1890 was called Kelmscott Press. Kelmscott Manor is the house of both his essay, "Gossip About an Old House on the Upper Thames" and "the old house to which the people of this story went," he says in his Utopian romance, *News from Nowhere*. He even has a charming little piece, "For the Bed at Kelmscott," in which the bed itself murmurs, ". . . . kind and dear / Is the old house here."

Kelmscott is now owned by the Society of Antiquaries, and in past years has been open to the public the first Wednesday of each month, April to September, but better check before you go.

With Kelmscott you've reached the very western edge of Oxfordshire, and are ready for the heart of England. Just over the border, Lechlade and Gloucester are calling.

THE HEART
OF ENGLAND

GLOUCESTERSHIRE

Gloucestershire

 1. To Gloucestershire: Along the A417

----- 2. Cheltenham and the North

.... 3. Access or Connecting Routes

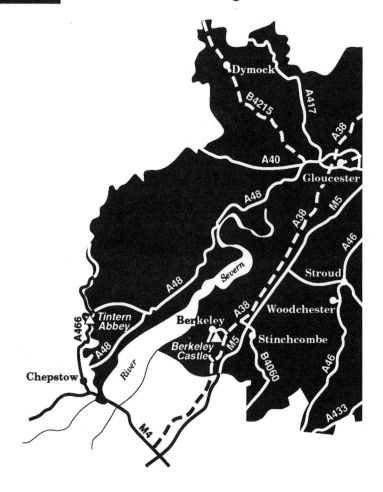

Dr. Foster went to Gloucester
In a shower of rain;
He stepped in a puddle up to his middle;
And never went there again.

> Nursery Rhyme

BOLINGBROKE: How far is it, my lord, to Berkeley now?
NORTHUMBERLAND: Believe me, noble lord,
I am a stranger here in Gloucestershire.
These high wild hills and rough uneven ways
Draws out our miles, and makes them wearisome,
And yet your fair discourse hath been as sugar,
Making the hard way sweet and delectable.

> William Shakespeare, *Richard II*

It's such a pity that poor bedraggled Dr. Foster never went back. Gloucestershire (GLOSS-ter-sh'r) offers such an infinite variety of things to see. Most visited, perhaps, are those "high wild hills" of Northumberland in *Richard II*, for they are the glorious Cotswolds.

But Gloucestershire also has within its forty-five by thirty-five-mile area the two major rivers of England, the Thames and the Severn. *And* the Wye, as lovely a stream as any celebrated in poetry. *And* two of England's six Avon rivers, one of the two being indeed Shakespeare's Avon. (More about those rivers later).

In addition, there are the beautiful old Forest of Dean, the picturesque Severn Vale, and the great Severn Estuary with a "bore" (high tidal flood) so powerful it pushes the sea's salt water almost to the middle of the county.

There's an old saying, "Sure as God is in Gloucester. . . ," referring to its abundance of wealthy abbeys and churches.[1] Among these are the historic abbey at Tewkesbury and the splendid cathedral at Gloucester.

[1]In his "Verses on the Death of Dr. Swift," Swift uses this saying to attack Thomas Woolston, who had been imprisoned for questioning Christ's miraculous powers:

> He shows, as sure as God's in Gloucester
> That Jesus was a grand imposter;
> That all his miracles were cheats
> Performed as jugglers do their 'feats.

Gloucestershire's literary sites include Dymock, Cheltenham, Gloucester, Tewkesbury, Woodchester, Berkeley Castle and Lechlade. And just two steps over its western border into Wales is Tintern Abbey.

1. To Gloucester: Along the A 417

A handy entry to Gloucestershire is the A 417, which cuts into the county at Lechlade just beyond Kelmscott Manor. From Lechlade, the A 417 can take you all the way to Gloucester, if you like, with various stops en route. And, for the rest of Gloucestershire, you couldn't have a better central base than Gloucester or its neighbor, Cheltenham.

Lechlade

In the vicinity of Lechlade (LECK-lade) the Thames begins to grow as several streams flowing off the eastern slopes of the Cotswolds converge, providing in the process a bit of Gloucestershire's southeastern borders with Oxfordshire, Berkshire, and Wiltshire.

On their boat trip up the Thames from Bishopsgate in 1815, Shelley, Thomas Love Peacock, and their friends were halted three miles above Lechlade by shallow water and thick water-weeds. Before returning home, they spent two days at a Lechlade inn.

Shelley had felt ill on the way up, but "three mutton-chops, well-peppered" worked wonders, according to Peacock, and nearing Lechlade Shelley "rowed vigourously, was cheerful, merry, overflowing with animal spirits."

At Lechlade, Shelley wrote a rather good poem, too, "A Summer-Evening Churchyard, Lechlade, Gloucestershire," reflecting the peace he found in this little village:

> Thus solemnized and softened, death is mild
> And terrorless as this serenest night."

Fifty years later, Dante Gabriel Rossetti walked to Lechlade frequently with Janey Morris from Kelmscott Manor, after he and William Morris leased that house in 1871. He liked Lechlade, singling it out in a letter to his mother: "The nearest town, Lechlade, (three miles off) is a most beautiful old town." He remembered Shelley and his visit, too: "I have not told you what beautiful old churches there are here. [There is] a famous one at Lechlade, in the churchyard of which Shelley wrote one of his poems." Rossetti was right about the Lechlade church. It's worth a look, especially the fine priest door and the tower with its distinctive, oddly marked buttresses. If you want to stay overnight in Lechlade, you can stop at Shelley's place, the New Inn, which, in fact, dates back to the eighteenth century.

Fairford—Bibury—and Cirencester

From Lechlade, the A 417 goes almost due west to Cirencester, "the Capitol of the Cotswolds." Before Cirencester come Fairford and Bibury, both utterly delightful.

Fairford   Four miles out of Lechlade, Fairford is right on the A 417, and right on the Coln River, too, one of those streams that feed the Thames.

In this truly charming village, John Keble was born in 1792, son of the rector. Keble's fame today comes mainly from his co-authorship of The Oxford Movement's *Tract for the Times* (1833–41). But millions are familiar with other of his writings, perhaps without even knowing his name. For he was a prodigious and fantastically popular writer of sacred verse which, interestingly enough, he hadn't really wanted to publish.

In 1823, at age thirty-one, he had left his tutorial post at Oxford to return to Fairford as assistant to his father and curate for one or two small churches in the area. He continued to work at polishing and revising what he envisaged as a lifetime project.

The enterprise was monumental: a separate poem for every Sunday of the year, and for every Saint's Day and Festival of the Church of England. None of this, he vowed, would be published until after his death when, as he put it, he was "fairly out of the way."

But his father's repeated requests to see his son's work in print before his own death ultimately won out. The poems, entitled *The Christian Year* (1827), were an outstanding success. By 1872 they had run through an incredible 158 editions. The verses have never been out of print, and many were set to music. Sunday after Sunday in churches everywhere, millions still sing the likes of "Sun of My Soul, Thou Saviour Dear" and "God, the Lord, a King Remaineth."

Bibury   Above Fairford, four miles northwest on the A 433, Bibury (BY-bury) is a village that makes "enchanting" seem an understatement, especially the Arlington Row of seventeenth-century stone houses. It's well worth the seeing anyway, but Alexander Pope and William Morris provide a literary excuse for a slight detour off the A 417, should you need one.

Wrote Pope to Jonathan Swift after they'd gone there in 1726 when visiting Cirencester:

> I shall never more think of . . . the
> woods of Ciceter [sic] or the more
> pleasing prospect of Byberry [sic] but
> your Idea must be join'd with 'em.

And William Morris, whose country home was only seven miles away, called it "the most beautiful village in England."

Cirencester   Cirencester, a town of over fifteen thousand, is an important highway junction. The A 417, 419, 429, 433, and 435 all meet there. It is also on the Churn River, another of Gloucestershire's contributors to the Thames. It has a magnificent fifteenth-century parish church that is one of England's largest: 180 feet long, with a tower 134 feet high. And it has a name whose pronunciation even the natives have been known to argue about.

To Shakespeare it was Ci-ces-ter (SISS-sess-ter). Here's Bolingbroke speaking in *Richard II*:

> Kind Uncle York, the latest news we hear
> Is that the rebels have consum'd with fire
> Our town of Cicester in Gloucestershire.

To Pope, as in that Bibury letter to Swift, it was CI-ce-ter (SIGH-seh-ter.)

And to most modern gazetteers, it is either SIREN-sess-ter (like the sirens in the *Odyssey*) or SISS-i-ter. You'll come close to what's the most current today with SIREN-sess-ter, though Shakespeare's version can still be heard.

Cirencester was the country seat of one of the eighteenth century's notable literary patrons, the first Earl of Bathurst. Among those who visited him there, either at his original Oakley House or its even grander replacement, Cirencester Park, were John Gay, Jonathan Swift, Alexander Pope, Matthew Prior, and Laurence Sterne. Pope was there often. On one visit, in 1718, he brought Gay. On another, in 1726, Swift came along, and they had to be housed by one of Bathurst's tenant farmers. Gay loved his visit, and plunged into a swarm of magnificent but wholly imaginary landscaping projects. Swift merely grumbled at having to walk several miles to dinner.

Bathurst figures twice in Pope's *Moral Essays*. Epistle III is dedicated to Bathurst, and Epistle IV hails his lordship's taste in gardening.

> Who then shall grace, or who improve the Soil?
> Who plants like BATHURST or who builds like BOYLE?

No one can fault Pope's approving Bathurst's landscaping ideas, however. The poet had supplied some of them himself.

Cirencester Park is on the west side of town, off Tetbury Road, and you can visit it any time you like. It's open daily, year round. But be warned in advance: it's three thousand acres in all—and cars are not allowed.

Sapperton—Woodchester—Stinchcombe, Berkeley Castle and Tintern Abbey

Almost in a straight line running from Cirencester to Gloucestershire's border with Wales are five villages worth a word. The one of major importance, indeed, is actually in Wales.

Westward from Cirencester come in turn Sapperton, where John Masefield lived; Woodchester, beloved by Housman; Stinchcombe, for a while Evelyn Waugh's home; Berkeley Castle, steeped in history; and Tintern (the one in Wales) with its fabled abbey.

Sapperton   You reach Sapperton, five miles west of Cirencester, by picking up the A 419 off Tetbury Road below Cirencester Park. John Masefield, poet laureate from 1930 until his death in 1967, left his home in Clifton Hampden, Oxfordshire, for several years during World War II to live at Sapperton's Pinbury Park. In his sixties, he manfully continued to churn out the paeons on christenings, deaths, and national events expected of a laureate—all suitably undistinguished. He did, however, also publish his *Land Workers* (1942) and *Collected Poems* (1946) while there.

Woodchester   The easiest way to Woodchester is the A 419 into Stroud, then south two miles on the A 46. An appealing little village of grey stone houses at the edge of the Cotswolds, it furnished A.E. Housman, often indrawn and lonely, with precious moments of companionship and warmth.

His paternal grandfather was rector of Woodchester, and Housman and his mother visited there regularly. He was especially fond of Mrs. Edward Wise, wife of a cloth mill owner and his godmother. As a boy of twelve, he stayed with the Wises during his mother's final illness. Thereafter, their solid old mansion became a second home. It was Mrs. Wise who helped him through his difficult teenage religious doubts, reflected later in the delicately balanced "Easter Hymn."

Even when misfortune forced Mrs. Wise to move to a house too small for a spare bedroom, the poet continued until the day of her death in 1892 to return to Woodchester for the security and love she offered.

Stinchcombe   In the early 1920s, a well-born but impoverished Oxford student had a dream: He would not only write about grand country homes; one day he would own one. For Evelyn Waugh that day came in 1937. His novels since graduation—*Decline and Fall* (1928), *Vile Bodies* (1930), *Black Mischief* (1932), and *A Handful of Dust* (1934)—provided the money. Stinchcombe, eleven miles southwest of Stroud on the B 4060, provided the place.

It was so lovely to play squire there at Piers Court, as the estate was called, while comfortably savaging the bourgeois who made it all possible. The more biting Waugh's attacks, the more they bought his books: *Put out the Flags* (1942), *Brideshead Revisited* (1945), *The Loved One* (1948), *Men at Arms* (1952), *Love Among the Ruins* (1953), *Officers and Gentlemen* (1955), and *The Ordeal of Gilbert Pinfold* (1957).

Such success, however, is precisely what put an end to Waugh's Stinchcombe stay. With so much money now, Piers Court was a bit, well, outgrown. "Perhaps," said his favorite daughter, "we could keep a horse."

And so they did. The time was 1957. The place Combe Florey in Somerset. It had, Waugh reported, "great possibilities."

Berkeley Castle   The village of Berkeley and its castle are three miles west of Stinchcombe. In *Richard II,* Bolingbroke and Northumberland are on their way to Berkeley when they talk about those "high wild hills." But the most sensational event in the castle's long history—it goes back before 1100—was the murder of Edward II by his queen, Isabella, and her paramour Mortimer. They'd locked the king up in the tower and their original plan was rather considerate: simply to let him starve to death.

But when Edward proved less than cooperative about dying, the lovers took things into their hands. Or, more accurately, the hands of a pair of minions named Matrevis and Gurney, and their accomplice Lightborn.

Many historians are vague about exactly what happened next, usually mumbling something about "they murdered the king in an agonizing, but allegedly undetectable fashion." Not so Christopher Marlowe's play, *Edward II* (1593), in a scene satisfactorily forthright and gruesome:

Lightborn enters the king's tower chamber, and when Edward asks why he has come, answers, "To rid thee of thy life." Lightborn calls for Matrevis and Gurney, they come, and the king speaks:

> K.Edw: I am too weak and feeble to resist—
> Assist me, sweet God, and receive my soul!
> Light [to the others]:   Run for the table.
>   [*Matrevis brings in a table. King Edward is mur-*
>   *dered by holding him down on the bed with the table,*
>   *and stamping on it.*]
> Light: So, lay the table down, and stamp on it, But not too hard, lest
>   you bruise his body.
> Mat: I fear me that this cry will raise the town, And therefore let us
>   take horse and away.
> Light: Tell me, sirs, was it not bravely done?
> Gur: Excellent well: take this for thy reward.
>   [*Stabs Lightborn who dies*]

The ruins of Berkeley Castle are worth a look. Enough of the domestic buildings remain to give some idea of how people lived in Edward's day. And above the external staircase approaching the keep is the room where he is said to have been murdered.

The castle is open every afternoon of the week except Monday, from the first day of April until the last day of September.

Tintern Abbey   Tintern is in Wales, yes. But who could come this far into Gloucestershire and fail to go on to Tintern Abbey? Here Wordsworth wrote one of his greatest poems, and Tennyson finished a memorable section of *In Memoriam*. And here the ordinary traveller, literature to one side, finds a beauty and a majesty that strike awe.

Only twenty miles separate Tintern from Gloucester. In fact, Tintern is only nine miles from Berkeley Castle. Getting from Castle to Abbey, however, is another matter: twenty-three miles in all. You've got to go down to the M 5, take it to its junction with the M 4, follow the M 4 across the Severn Bridge to Chepstow in Wales, and thence north for five miles on the A 466.

Cistercian monks founded the Abbey on a watermeadow of the Wye in 1131, and completed their church in 1287. The heavy hand of Henry VIII's Dissolution fell in 1540. Today, the Abbey's roof is gone, but somehow the clerestory and much of its delicate tracery survive.

All about the ruins lies the setting so vividly described by Wordsworth in "Tintern Abbey," his major contribution to the joint collection of poems he and Coleridge called *Lyrical Ballads* (1798).[2] It was composed entirely in his head during the twenty-one mile walk from above the Abbey back to Bristol. At a friend's house there, Wordsworth said, he set it down: "Not a line of it was altered, and not any part of it was written down till I reached Bristol."

In essence, the poem compares the "dizzy raptures" of his "thoughtless youth" five years earlier, when he had first seen the Abbey, with the "sober pleasure" it brought now, and the "still, sad music of humanity."

He captures the beauty of the place powerfully:

> . . . again I hear
> These waters, rolling from their mountain-springs,
> With a soft inland murmur.—Once again
> Do I behold these steep and lofty cliffs,
> That on a wild secluded scene impress
> Thoughts of more deep seclusion; and connect
> The landscape with the quiet of the sky.

In July of 1836, Alfred Tennyson came to Tintern Abbey. Haunting him was the recent, sudden loss of his dearest friend, Arthur Hallam, dead at twenty-two and buried just twenty miles away at Cleveden on the banks of the Severn. Tennyson had noticed how the Severn's tidal sea-water, pushing up twice daily from the Bristol Channel, engulfed and silenced the Wye as they met near Chepstow.

Out of this Tennyson wove a striking image for his elegy to Hallam, *In Memoriam*, depicting how grief can overwhelm one's very power to express it. As the Severn stills the Wye, he wrote, so his own overbrimming sorrow drowns his song. But then, just as the tide flows back down and the Wye again is vocal, so too Tennyson's "deeper anguish" ebbs, and he "can speak a little."

The precision of the point to point comparison is remarkable.

> There twice a day the Severn fills;
>   The salt sea-water passes by,
>   And hushes half the bubbling Wye,
> And makes a silence in the hills.
>
> The Wye is hush'd not moved along,
>   And hush'd my deepest grief of all,
>   When filled with tears that cannot fall
> I brim with sorrow drowning song.

---

[2] The formal title of the poem is an abomination: "Lines Composed a Few Miles Above Tintern Abbey on Revisiting the Banks of the Wye During a Tour, July 13, 1798."

> The tide flows down, the wave again
> Is vocal in its wooded walls,
> My deeper anguish also falls,
> And I can speak a little then.

In the same vein, Tintern Abbey also inspired Tennyson's famous "Tears, Idle Tears," for such is the power of the place. In the nearly two hundred years since Wordsworth's poem, the Abbey has fulfilled for multitudes who gazed upon it the poet's hope:

> That in this moment there is life and food
> For future years.

The Abbey is open daily except Christmas.

Gloucester

From Tintern Abbey, Gloucester is an easy drive over a little back road to the A 48, and then straight up the A 48 to the A 40 and into town—a total of twenty miles. The city's greatest asset, as a base for exploring the rest of Gloucestershire, is its central location. The seven major highways that lead into it provide accessibility to every corner of the county.

In the past, Gloucester has had its champions. Edward A. Freeman, the eminent Victorian historian, declared that "in the reign of Rufus almost everything that happened at all, somehow contrived to happen at Gloucester." And King John—he of the Magna Carta—said he loved Gloucester better than London.

But Nathaniel Hawthorne, who visited in 1856, observed, "It is a large town, and has a good deal of liveliness and bustle, in a provincial way." This is still true, but need not be taken as derogatory. It's simply that Gloucester isn't cosmopolitan, but sensible, workaday, and heavily industrial. It is a thriving commercial port, too, served by the Severn, whose five-to-six-foot tidal crest in spring rolls all the way up from the Estuary at Bristol.

Gloucester's lack of pretension makes all the more striking the fact that it has one of the most beautiful cathedrals in all England. The cloisters have been called "unsurpassed" by those who make cloisters a career. The spectacular East Window, dubbed "the glory of Gloucester," seventy-eight feet high, is the largest in the world. And two of its tombs are outstanding—those of Robert Curthose and Edward II.

Poor Curthose. Eldest son and heir to William the Conquerer, he got pushed aside by his younger brother Henry in 1106, and locked up until he died twenty years later. But Henry made amends of a sort, with a grand tomb right in front of the cathedral altar.

If the fate of Edward II was even more luckless, his tomb is even more splendid. Murdered so barbarously at Berkeley Castle in 1327, Edward was hardly to be confused with a saint.[3] Even so, his son Edward III somehow achieved the minor miracle of transforming him into a martyr, and making his tomb a shrine rivalling that of Becket down there in Canterbury.

There's one more memorial American visitors may want to see. On the western corner of the transept, it honors John Stafford Smith. Those who find the range of "The Star Spangled Banner" hard to handle can blame Mr. Smith. He composed the tune long before young Francis Scott Key ever got around to the words.

Gloucester's literary heritage, alas, scarcely matches the grandeur of its cathedral. It's almost wholly of the "true, but . . . ." order, as in: "John Taylor, the "water poet," was born in Gloucester in 1580. He wasn't much of a poet, true; but he was a friend of Ben Jonson's. . . ."

In fact, Taylor *was* a friend of Jonson's, and an amusing fellow to boot. A Gloucester-trained waterman, he transferred his trade to London, where his antics kept the Jacobeans chuckling. On one occasion, he sailed up the Thames to Queensboro in a paper boat, with fish tied to canes as oars.

Another time, learning that Jonson planned a holiday trip to Scotland afoot, Taylor announced that he would do the same thing, but without a penny in his pocket. When he caught up with the playwright in Leith, Jonson, amused, offered Taylor twenty-two shillings. Taylor took the money—for a drink when he got back home, he said.

Other of Gloucester's "true, but's" are: George Whitefield, born there in 1714, was author of only a fairly routine hymnbook, true; but his fiery sermons shook up Methodists throughout Great Britain at home, and in the colonies from Georgia to Massachusetts, where he died and was buried in 1770.

Robert Raikes was born in Gloucester in 1735. He was only a run-of-the-mill writer for the *Gloucester Journal* (which he owned), true; but he was the inventor of Sunday Schools, opening the first one in St. Catherine Street at what is now Raikes House.

William Lisle Bowles, a visitor to Gloucester in 1835, was only a so-so

---

[3] For all the scandalous details, see Christopher Marlowe's play, *Edward II* and pages 139–40 above.

poet, true; but his *Fourteen Sonnets* (1789) revived the sonnet as a poetic form, and his views on Pope provoked Byron into some memorable satire. What's more, Bowles wrote a sonnet "On Hearing *The Messiah* Performed in Gloucester Cathedral."

Elizabeth Barrett was a visitor the summers of 1821 and 1822, true: but she was just a little girl of fifteen then, called "Ba," and known only to her family.

Finally, there is W. E. Henley, a good deal above the "true; but." Born in Gloucester in 1849, he was gifted as an editor, playwright and poet. "Invictus" ("Out of the night that covers me. . . .") is his. He was a great friend of Robert Louis Stevenson, and is supposed to have served for the model of Long John Silver.

Three small buildings in Gloucester also deserve mention—a house and two inns. The house, in College Court and now an antique shop, was where the hero lived in Beatrix Potter's *The Tailor of Gloucester* (1903). The inns are The Bell in Southgate and The New Inn in Northgate.

In fiction, The Bell was where Tom Jones and Partridge put up when their wanderings took them to Gloucester. In real life, George Whitefield was born there—his father was the landlord—and at age fifteen helped as a tapster before going off to Oxford.

The New Inn owes its existence to that tomb of Edward II. By the fifteenth century it had become so popular that a far-sighted monk built the inn to accommodate the pilgrims. One of the building's interesting features is an open gallery off the upper floor, on which Lady Jane Grey was proclaimed queen in 1553 for her pathetic nine-day reign.

That same gallery functioned in Tudor days as a balcony for audiences to view shows put on below by travelling companies of actors.

You can't miss the spot where the actors stood, should you stop by for a farewell toast as you leave Gloucester. To enter the inn, you have to pass through an archway into the very courtyard that was their stage.

2. Cheltenham and the North

Cheltenham

Cheltenham (CHELT-num), or Cheltenham Spa as it is called often enough, is only eight miles northeast of Gloucester, which it rivals as a center for investigating Gloucestershire. Its hotels are more numerous, more varied, and several are more elegant than anything Gloucester can offer. And though the cities are nearly of a size—both nearing one hundred thousand people—Cheltenham provides an air of genteel quiet in contrast to Gloucester's hustle and bustle. The A 40, which goes through the heart of Cheltenham, touches virtually every major highway in the county at one place or another in its windings from eastern boundary to west.

The city's lures are many. The highest point in the Cotswolds, at 1,100 feet, is only four miles off at Cleeve Cloud. Cheltenham's graceful Regency architecture adds its special charm. Annual festivals of all kinds—from literary to musical, even to cricket—proliferate. And still operating, though their heyday is past, are the mineral springs that added "Spa" to the original name.

Cheltenham owes those springs, and therefore much of its prosperity, to a flock of pigeons. Rather noisomely described as "sulphated and alkaline-saline mineral waters," the springs were discovered one day in 1716 when a farmer saw the birds pecking at grains of salt around a pool in his field. He began to bottle and sell the water. Physicians wrote treatises about its restorative powers. In 1788, his shrewd son-in-law put the family into business in a big way by building a pump room.

But it was the visit of George III and his family in 1788 that made the spa fashionable. The novelist Fanny Burney, then still Second Keeper of the Robes to George's Queen Charlotte, accompanied them and records their stay in her *Diary* (1842–46).

The list of other notables, literary and otherwise, associated with Cheltenham is long. Dr. Johnson and the composer George Handel were there in the eighteenth century before Miss Burney. Both stayed at the Plough, the same hotel that Byron, Disraeli, and the Duke of Wellington all stayed at a century later. William Cobbett, that self-educated and controversial jack-of-all-writings also visited Cheltenham in the nineteenth century. He was there shortly before 1830 while on a tour to gather material supporting his views on agricultural reform. His comments on the places he visited were published in a book, still pungent and entertaining, called *Rural Rides* (1830).

Among residents of Cheltenham that same century were the poet James Elroy Flecker and the actor William Charles Macready, and Sydney Dobell lived in the adjacent village of Charlton Kings from 1848 to 1853. Author of such poems as *The Roman* (1850) and *Balder* (1854), Dobell's powers of invention were not unlimited. The best he could come up with by way of a pseudonym was Sidney Yendys.

Macready, a leading Victorian actor, got himself both a new wife and a new home in Cheltenham in 1860. Among the newlyweds' first houseguests was Charles Dickens. Dickens was back again the next year on a dramatic reading tour. Macready was so moved by the novelist's performance that he met his friend afterwards, so Dickens reported, with "the tears running down his face."

Cheltenham's good schools account not only for Flecker's being there, but for Margaret Kennedy and C. Day-Lewis as well. Flecker grew up there from the age of two, when his father became headmaster of Dean Close School. Best known for the poems in *The Golden Journey to Samarkand* (1913), he showed great promise as a playwright, too, with *Hassam*, published posthumously. He died of tuberculosis in Switzerland at thirty, but was buried in Cheltenham.

Margaret Kennedy came to Cheltenham as a student, Cecil Day-Lewis as a teacher. After attending the well-known Cheltenham Ladies College just before World War I, Miss Kennedy went on to fame as the author of *The Constant Nymph* (1924) and *The Fool of the Family* (1930).

C. Day-Lewis became English master at Cheltenham College, a ranking public school for boys, in 1930, and lived at Box Cottage in Charlton Kings until 1938. A poet of real distinction, he wrote *The Magnetic Mountain* (1933) and many of the verses in *Collected Poems, 1929–36* (1938) while there. It was there, too, that as "Nicholas Blake" he began writing detective stories like *A Question of Proof* (1935).

In addition to the above, Cheltenham also played host in the nineteenth century to a trio of writers whose achievements and fame surpassed them all: Gordon, Lord Byron; Alfred, Lord Tennyson; and Elizabeth Barrett (Browning).

As a schoolboy at Harrow, Byron came to Cheltenham with his mother on several summer holidays. Especially memorable was a trip to the nearby Malvern Hills in 1801. Homesick for the Highlands, he said they were the only things he'd seen in England that reminded him "even in miniature, of a mountain." His account, written later, betrays the sensitivity he took such pains to hide: "After I returned to Cheltenham, I used to watch them every afternoon, at sunset, with a sensation I cannot describe. This was boyish enough; but I was then only thirteen years of age, and it was the holidays."

Far closer to his dashing public image was the Byron who returned to Cheltenham at twenty-four, in August of 1812. *Childe Harold* had just made him the sensation of London society, hounded by highborn young ladies determined to marry him.

So he fled to Cheltenham, staying first at The Plough Hotel, then at his friend Lord Holland's house. He went partly to take the waters (for kidney trouble), and partly to frolic with some London friends who came with him. But by September they had gone and, he confessed, he relished the delight of doing nothing: "I am quite alone, go out very little, and enjoy in its fullest extend the *dolce far niente.*"

Being Byron, however, he wasn't quite that alone. Somewhere in Cheltenham he had found himself a sultry Spanish songstress. She was black-eyed, had "not very white skin," and spoke no English. But she did have one great attraction—she was safely married.

For Tennyson, Cheltenham was his nearest approach to a home base for sixteen years. In 1837, at twenty-eight, he left the rectory in Somersby where he was born. In 1853, he and his wife settled down on the Isle of Wight. In between, his life was largely nomadic.

He had first visited Cheltenham in 1822 with his father, the Reverend George Tennyson. Waiting to greet them were George's brother Charles and sister Elizabeth. All three elder Tennysons came for the waters. George and Charles had drinking problems; Elizabeth had rheumatism.

Cheltenham then had yet to shake off a reputation for being vulgar, dull, full of spouse-hunters, male and female, and overrun with foreigners. Elizabeth's husband complained there were so many "mahogany faces" he thought himself in India.

Nevertheless, Alfred returned to the spa in 1831, this time with his sister Emily, whose own health had deteriorated sadly while watching their father dwindle into death that February. Their grandfather, a rather mean-spirited man, paid their way, but made their mother repay him out of her allowance. While at Cheltenham, Alfred and Emily enjoyed a visit from Arthur Hallam, his best friend and her fiancé (and later to be the subject of Tennyson's *In Memoriam*). But Hallam's presence had to be kept secret. His father had forbidden Arthur to see Emily until Hallam was twenty-one.

In 1843 Mrs. Tennyson herself was back in Cheltenham to stay. After her husband's death, she had held on to the Somersby rectory another six years. When they finally had to surrender it, the family had flitted from Epping Forest near London to Tunbridge Wells and Boxley in Kent. But near the end of 1843 she gave up the too-expensive home in Boxley for "a nasty house in Bellevue Place, Cheltenham," later moving to No. 10 St. James's Square.

Alfred was thirty-four then, and desperately in need of roots. Despite the recent publication of his collected work, *Poems* (1842), he was despondent, though the two volumes contained some of the best verse he was ever to write: "Morte d'Arthur," "Ulysses," "Break, Break, Break," and "Locksley Hall."

There in Cheltenham on the last day of 1843, he was spotted by Elizabeth

Barrett, an established poet herself. (Her poem, "Lady Geraldine's Court-ship," whose compliment to Robert Browning brought them together, was two years off.)

Elizabeth had known Cheltenham even before the Tennysons did, for her grandmother came to live there when Elizabeth was twelve, and the girl visited her often.

Miss Barrett's account of sighting Tennyson was graphic, but unknow-ingly misleading: "Tennyson is dancing the polka, and smoking cloud upon cloud at Cheltenham."

Actually, as soon as his family was fairly settled in Bellevue Place, he was at nearby Prestbury taking the water cure for acute melancholia. He re-peated the process in 1847 after unkind reviews of *The Princess*.

In fact, he was never to completely overcome these bouts of mental depression. Until his marriage in 1850, he remained restless and rootless. Even when he returned to his mother and Cheltenham, he stayed aloof for the most part, reading amidst his perpetual clouds of tobacco smoke in his study at the top of the St. James's Square house, but talking into the night when visitors came, and taking solitary walks by way of diversion. Once he did propose to take a balloon flight from the city's fashionable Montpelier Gardens, but nothing ever came of it.

Something like serenity ("the peace of God," he called it) came to Tennyson only after his long-delayed marriage to Emily Sellwood. They had planned to share a larger house in Cheltenham with his mother. When the time came, however, Emily was pregnant and they wisely decided not to do so.

By the fall of 1853, the Cheltenham saga was over for all the Tennysons. Alfred and Emily had settled on the Isle of Wight, and his mother had given up St. James's Square for London.

As stated earlier, should you chose Cheltenham as your Gloucestershire headquarters, there is a wide selection of hotels available, among them The Plough that housed Dr. Johnson, Byron, Handel, and Disraeli—on High Street and rated two-star. The grandly restored Pittville Pump Room is on view, too. And remember, you can still try those mineral waters—but you don't have to.

Tewkesbury

Tewkesbury, a town of ten thousand, consists largely of three main streets that form a rough "T," and a network of byways and alleys. The top of the T

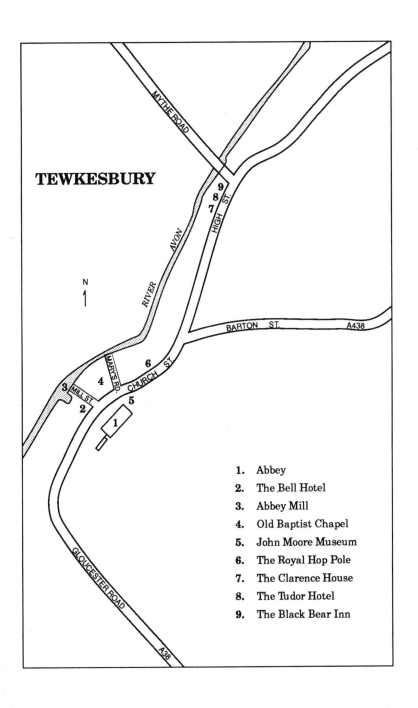

TEWKESBURY

1. Abbey
2. The Bell Hotel
3. Abbey Mill
4. Old Baptist Chapel
5. John Moore Museum
6. The Royal Hop Pole
7. The Clarence House
8. The Tudor Hotel
9. The Black Bear Inn

is made by the A 38, which enters from the south as the Gloucester Road, becomes in succession Church Street and The High Street, and exits as Mythe Road, heading for Worcester. The leg of the T is the A 438 coming west from Evesham, known in town as Barton Street.

Two words suffice for Tewkesbury: See it! Or maybe four words: See it in May! Viewed through great iron gates and framed by cherry blossoms, Tewkesbury Abbey is as beautiful and moving a sight as any England can provide.

Tewkesbury was missed by the Industrial Revolution of the eighteenth century and slighted by the railway barons of the nineteenth. Thank God! Yes, there is that shopping precinct anomaly down near the bridge and some industrialization on the fringes. But once safely past these, you are in the Tewkesbury that stretches back, in fact and fiction, to a time that's almost dateless.

Surrounding you as you stand facing the Abbey is the early twentieth-century "Elmbury" of John Moore's "Brensham Trilogy" (*Portrait of Elmbury*, 1945; *Brensham Village*, 1946; *The Blue Field*, 1948), and the nineteenth-century "Nortonbury" of Mrs. (Dinah Mulock) Craik's *John Halifax, Gentleman* (1887). It's the Tewkesbury where the eighteenth-century George III came to climb a hill, the seventeenth-century Charles II to hide in an attic, and the fifteenth-century Edward of Lancaster to be murdered. But Tewkesbury is older than that. Two improbably named Saxon brothers, Oddo and Doddo, built their stronghold there in the eighth century; a chap called Theoc named it in the seventh: Theocsbury.

The very air of Tewkesbury breathes antiquity. In his *Tour through the Whole Island of Great Britain* (1724–27), Daniel Defoe calls Tewkesbury "a quiet, trading, drunken town." The number of pubs and inns that survive from his day, and before, suggest that he was probably right. Tewkesbury houses bespeak their age, too—low ceilinged and labyrinthine inside, timbered with overhanging eaves outside. The eaves did double duty, protecting both the walls of the building and the wares of their shopkeeper proprietors displayed outside.

The row of Abbey Cottages along Church Street, originally twenty-three shops of this sort, was built by monks forty years before Columbus decided to go off and find America. Their careful renovation in 1970, which won a British Tourist Award, was typical of Tewkesbury.

A similar need a hundred years earlier produced momentous results. On March 5, 1877, the poet William Morris dropped the London newspaper he was reading, picked up his pen, and wrote *The Atheneum*: "My eye just now caught the word "restoration" in the morning paper, and, on looking closer, I saw that this time it is nothing less than the Minster of Tewkesbury that is to be destroyed by Sir Gilbert Scott. . . ." Castigating the "barbarism" which the modern architect, parson, and squire called "restoration," Morris concludes: "What I wish for is that an association should be set on foot . . . to protect against all "restoration" that means more than keeping out wind and weather. . . ."

On March 22, 1877, England's Society for the Protection of Ancient Buildings held its first meeting.

Tewkesbury is blessed by location, too. On the south and east are the Cotswolds, on the northwest the Malvern Hills. The view from Mythe Tute Hill enticed George III and Queen Charlotte to get down on hands and knees to clamber to the top when they came from Cheltenham in 1788.[4] The Severn River and Shakespeare's Avon meet in Tewkesbury, adding to their loveliness.

In a direct line, Stratford-upon-Avon is only twenty-five miles away. Surely Shakespeare was drawing upon personal knowledge when in *Henry IV, Part II*, after Doll Tearsheet says Poins has a "good wit," he has Falstaff reply:

> He a good wit? Hang him, baboon! His wit's
> As thick as Tewkesbury mustard.

Tewkesbury mustard in Shakespeare's day was famous, so pungent that people said of a wry-faced fellow, "He looks as if he lived on Tewkesbury mustard balls." In *Worthies of England* (1662), Thomas Fuller, going on about mustard, says: "The best in England (to take no longer compass) is made in Tewkesbury. It is very wholesome for the clearing of the head, moderately taken; and I believe very few have ever surfeited thereof."

At No. 13 on Barton Street there's a building once known as the Mustard House. On the floor of its upper storey mustard seed was laid out to dry before being made into oval balls and shipped throughout the kingdom.

Center of all that is Tewkesbury, of course, is its Abbey. (1) Its dimensions are as impressive as those of several well-known cathedrals. It is 312 feet long, compared to Rochester's 305 feet and Wells's 383. And its tower is 148 feet high—Rochester's 156, Wells's 165. Only a priory when William the Conquerer's Matilda took it over late in the eleventh century, it was consecrated an abbey in 1121 and speedily proved that God was indeed in Gloucester. By 1509, when Henry VIII was crowned, the Abbey consisted of

---

[4]The name Mythe Tute Hill is a classic in redundancy. "Mythe" *means* hill—and so does "tute."

two hundred men and boys, and controlled twenty-one parsonages and twenty-seven vicarages in a dozen counties. It even escaped the ravages of Henry's Dissolution. The townsfolk simply bought Henry off by paying £453 for the church, based on the value of the metal in the lead roof and twelve great bells of the tower.

Thirty-eight years before Henry, town and abbey had witnessed a pivotal battle in the Wars of the Roses. For two decades two branches of the Plantagenets, the Yorks (they of the white roses) and the Lancasters (they of the red) had fought for England's throne. As 1470 began, the Yorks seemingly had won, with the Lancaster's Henry VI imprisoned and their own Edward IV as king. But Henry's queen, Margaret, refused to give up, and by year's end had even driven Edward into exile.

Soon, however, the Yorks were back. On May 4, 1471, Edward and his brothers—George, Duke of Clarence, and Richard, Duke of Gloucester— caught up with Margaret at Tewkesbury. At the end of the day, Margaret had been routed, her troops slaughtered in "Bloody Meadow," south of the Abbey. Her eighteen-year-old son, Edward, Prince of Wales, lay dead.

Of the conflicting accounts of just how the youth died, Shakespeare's is easily the most dramatic. In *Henry VI, Part III*, the victorious Yorks summon the prince before them to recant. Instead, young Lancaster denounces the trio for usurping his father's throne, and adds a personal insult for each: Edward for his licentious ways, Clarence for his earlier disloyalty to Edward, Richard for his grotesque hunchback:

> Lascivious Edward, then thou perjured George,
> And thou misshapen Dick, I tell ye all
> I am your better, traitors as ye are
> And thou usurps't my father's right and mine.

Whereupon with cool ferocity, the brothers draw their daggers and take turns hacking him to death.

In *Richard III*, Shakespeare depicts the retribution that ensued: King Edward dead at forty-one, victim of a dissolute life; Clarence murdered by his brother Gloucester; and Gloucester himself, now Richard III, vainly crying "a horse, a horse" before he falls at Bosworth Field.

Today, both Clarence and young Lancaster lie at rest together in Tewkesbury's Abbey. Clarence's vault, under an iron grating, is behind the altar screen. The young prince is buried directly under the center of the tower, the spot marked by a brass plate on the floor. A translation of its original Latin inscription reads: "Here lies Edward Prince of Wales, cruelly slain while still a youth, on May 4, 1471. Alas the fury of men. Thou art the soul [sic] light of thy mother, and the last hope of the flock."

Every year during the week of May 4, the date of his death, a vase of red roses (the Lancaster flower) appears there on the floor—tribute, incredibly enough, from the Richard III Society. One more reason to be in Tewkesbury in May.

Three other stops of literary interest while in the Abbey are the Lady Chapel of the south transept, the choir, and the Chapel of St. Margaret of Scotland. In the Lady Chapel is a tablet commemorating Mrs. Craik for *John Halifax, Gentleman*. St. Margaret's Chapel honors the wife of Malcolm, son of the Duncan so foully murdered by Macbeth. And on the south side of the choir is "Milton's Organ."

For so huge an object, that organ certainly got around. Built in 1610, it was originally installed at Magdalen College, Oxford. Then, in 1654, Oliver Cromwell kited it off to Hampton Court, where it got its Miltonic aura. The reasoning goes thus: Milton was a skillful organist. Milton was Cromwell's Latin Secretary. So Milton must have been at Hampton Court when the organ arrived—and of course had to give the instrument a turn or two. Ergo: Milton's Organ.

Anyway, after the Restoration in 1660, the organ was returned to Oxford. In 1727 the Abbey bought it, and there it sits in the choir today.

Leaving the Abbey to explore the town is like strolling through history and literature. Practically across from the Abbey gates is The Bell Hotel, (2) reaching all the way back to Elizabethan times, and perhaps earlier. Now rated three-star, it remains as it has been for for centuries, a haven for pilgrims to the Abbey.

In fiction, it was the home of Abel Fletcher in Mrs. Craik's novel, and she is supposed to have written some of the book at The Bell. It's a handsome, three-gabled building, with overhanging eaves. At a bar inside, there are exposed seventeenth-century wall drawings.

Behind The Bell, up Mill Street, (3) is the Abbey Mill, with foundations as old as 1190, the year the monks began using the Avon's flow to grind their grain. Mrs. Craik used it as her "Abel Fletcher's Mill," now the name of a restaurant it houses.

Also on Church Street, opposite those Abbey Cottages, is the Old Baptist Chapel, (4) one of England's first. Its deed is dated 1623, and its panelled pulpit and some of its furnishings survive from the seventeenth century.

Number 41 of the Abbey Cottages is the John Moore Museum, (5) depicting the countryside and the life he wrote about. (Open daily in season, except Sunday and Monday).

A bit further down Church Street is yet another still-thriving hotel with literary associations: The Royal Hop Pole. (6) In *Pickwick Papers*, Charles Dickens has Mr. Pickwick and party stop there for dinner, with liberal liquid embellishments: " . . . there was more bottled ale, with some Madeira and some port besides, and here the case bottle was replenished for the fourth time. Under the influence of these combined stimulants, Mr. Pickwick and Mr. Ben Allen fell fast asleep for 30 miles." Like The Bell, The Royal Hop Pole is rated three-star.

After Church Street changes its name to The High Street, there come in quick succession three buildings of interest: The Clarence House; (7) The Tudor House Hotel; (8) and The Black Bear Inn (9).

The Clarence House, though much altered in the seventeenth century, has roots in the fifteenth. It's supposed to be where the Duke of Clarence planned the Yorks' strategy before the Battle of Tewkesbury. But if so, he must have been quick about it. At 5:00 P.M. the night before, the Yorkists were in Cheltenham eight miles away, still panting from having covered thirty-one miles in twenty-four hours.

The Tudor House Hotel, a timber-framed building of the seventeenth and eighteenth centuries, has double literary ties. John Moore lived there as a boy, and Mrs. Craik made it the home of her heroine, Ursula March. As if that weren't enough background, it was also the Court of Justice in the days of James I, and Charles II is said to have hidden in its attic after losing the Battle of Worcester.

Finally, at the end of High Street, just at the turn into Mythe Road and the A 38, is The Black Bear Inn, redolent of the past. The oldest inn in Gloucestershire, it has served the public ever since 1308. Its rambling timber-framed structure and mullion windows provide a fitting last touch of Tewkesbury, a town you won't soon forget.

Hailes and Burnt Norton—
Adlestrop and Dymock

From The Black Bear Inn, you could almost toss a stone into the next county, Hereford and Worcester, it's that near. Before yielding to the latter, however, Gloucestershire offers as final treats some abbey ruins and Chaucer, a fireswept mansion and T. S. Eliot, a town nameplate and Edward Thomas, and a cluster of cottages with a cluster of poets. The places involved are Hailes, Burnt Norton, Adlestrop, and Dymock.

Hailes Ten miles east of Tewkesbury, off the A 46 near the village of Didbrook, are the ruins of Hailes Abbey, once possessor of not less than a phial of the actual blood of Christ. So widely known was this relic that it became a common cussword.

Chaucer has fun with this in "The Pardoner's Tale" when he has the Pardoner, that paragon of hypocrites, working on his fourth or fifth ale, brazenly preach against cursing. God, avows the Pardoner, deems "swerying" even more abominable than murder. What kind of swearing? Well, oaths like

> "By Goddes precious herte," and "By his nayles,"
> And "By the blood of Crist that is in Hayles."

Now owned by The National Trust, the ruins are open to the public. So is a museum that has bosses, tiles, and other relics of the Abbey. Not, however, that phial.

Burnt Norton   Another ten miles up the A 46, outside the very pleasant village of Chipping Campden, is an old country mansion called Burnt Norton. Fire ravaged it in the eighteenth century—hence its name—but it was later rebuilt.

When T. S. Eliot visited it in the 1930s, however, it was abandoned, its desolate garden a symbol of the timeless emptiness he expressed in the first of his *Four Quartets*, which he entitled "Burnt Norton" (1936). Momentarily, he says, there may be brightness, a suggestion of reality, but all is illusion, as in the garden.

> So we moved . . . in a formal pattern
> Along the empty alley, into the box circle,
> To look down into the drained pool.
> Dry the pool, dry concrete, brown edged,
> And the pool was filled with water out of sunlight . . .
> . . . .
> Then a cloud passed, and the pool was empty.

Today Burnt Norton is a school, and the house is not open to the public. But through NGS the grounds are, for one weekend in June and another in August.

Adlestrop   This little place (pronounced ADD'l-strop) is twenty miles east of Tewkesbury off the A 436. A visitor early in the nineteenth century was Jane Austen, whose grandfather was the rector. Of much more interest, however, is the fact that Adlestrop is the subject of a poem—and a good one—based solely on its railway sign. A train pulls into the station. A passenger gets a hurried glimpse of the sign. The train pulls out. That's all there is to it.

But to Edward Thomas, the most commonplace event could be rich in poetry. His "Adlestrop" is proof:

> Yes, I remember Adlestrop—
> The name, because one afternoon
> Of heat the express-train drew up there
> Unwontedly. It was late June.
> The steam hissed. Someone cleared his throat.
> No one left and no one came
> On the bare platform. What I saw
> Was Adlestrop—only the name.
>
> . . . .
>
> And for that minute a blackbird sang
> Close by, and round him, mistier,
> Farther and farther, all the birds
> Of Oxfordshire and Gloucestershire.

You can still see that sign, but things have changed a bit. You'll have to go to the bus shelter.

Dymock   Dymock (DIM-muck), eleven miles west of Tewkesbury on the B 4215, is a tiny place, but it is famous for four things: its daffodils . . . the house where Alexander Pope's exemplary "Man of Ross" was born . . . the official challenger to the monarchs of Britain . . . and, most importantly of all, the beginning of an important poetic movement just prior to World War I, which included the very man who wrote "Adlestrop."

Because of Dymock, northwest Gloucestershire is often called "The Daffodil County," and there's even a strain called "Little Dymock." Pope's man of Ross was John Kyrle, born in Dymock's White House in 1634 and used by the poet in his *Moral Essays* to show how a wealthy man should use his riches.[5] And the Dymock family (who gave the village its name) since 1377 has held the office of King's Champion, charged with challenging claimants to the throne at their coronation.

That poetic movement started in 1911, when Lascelles Abercrombie at thirty came to live at The Gallows in Ryton, outside Dymock. He was joined by Rupert Brooke (age twenty-six) and John Drinkwater (age thirty-one) in

[5]See pages 167–68.

1913, the same year Wilfred Gibson moved into the Old Nail Shop a mile or two away at Greenway Cross.

Known today as the Georgian Poets, they were drawn together by a common interest in showing the extraordinary that they saw in ordinary things, and by a desire for a simpler, more natural mode of expression. They found vehicles for their poems in *New Numbers* magazine, published from Ryton, and the *Georgian Anthology* originated by Brooke, which established their collective name.

But of more lasting importance than any of these, and with certainly more impact on each other, were a pair who settled in their midst in 1914: Edward Thomas and Robert Frost. Frost rented Little Iddens, a laborer's cottage in the hamlet of Leadington. Thomas moved into a neighboring house called Old Fields. Quickly the two became fast friends.

They had much in common. No longer young—Frost was thirty-eight, Thomas thirty-six—both had worked long and hard without any great success. An American, Frost toiled at mill working, reporting, teaching, and farming while writing poetry his countrymen almost totally ignored. In desperation, he had chucked it all in 1912 to try again in England. Thomas had written nearly thirty volumes of prose on everything from topography and nature to biography and literary criticism while living mainly hand-to-mouth.

Rambling the fields about Dymock, it all came together for them both. In the natural, the nonrhetorical and direct, the things of everyday life, they had a common creed. And each gave the other the encouragement and faith so sorely needed. Thomas's enthusiastic review of his friend's first collection of poems, *North of Boston* (1914), published in England, may be said to have launched Frost's career as a major American poet. As well it might: the book included such gems as "Mending Wall" and "The Death of the Hired Man."

In turn, Frost practically bullied Thomas into applying himself steadily and seriously to the writing of poetry. Typically, the diffident Thomas took refuge in a pseudonym, "Edward Eastaway," and was able to prepare a thin volume of only sixty-four poems before he shipped off to France in 1915, where he died in battle.

Frost loved to tease Thomas about his indecisiveness, and later said the latter's mooning about "what-might-have-been's" had inspired "The Road Not Taken." But thanks to Frost, Thomas had, after all, found the right road. Slim though his total output was—no more than 135 poems in all—his works have outlasted those of many a more popular contemporary. And his reputation continues to grow.

With Dymock you have reached the end of Gloucestershire. But, unlike Doctor Foster, you'll probably come back again. Or, at least, want to.

HEREFORD AND WORCESTER

Hereford and Worcester

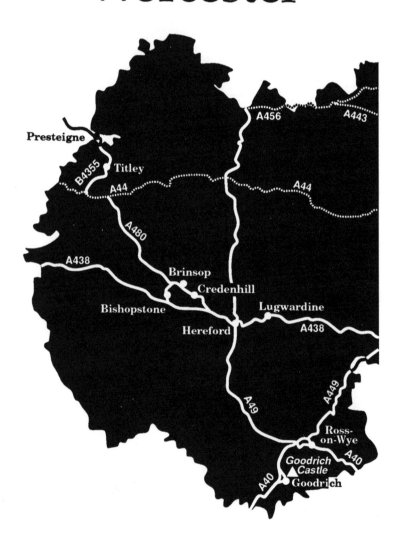

1. The Hereford Half

2. The Worcestershire That Was

3. Access or Connecting Routes

In summertime on Bredon
   The bells they sound so clear;
Round both the shires they ring them
   In steeples far and near,
   A happy noise to hear.

Here of a Sunday morning
   My love and I would lie,
And see the coloured counties,
   And hear the larks so high
   About us in the sky.
                A. E. Housman, "Bredon Hill"

Who travels Worcester county,
   Takes any place that comes,
When April tosses bounty
   To the cherries and the plums.
                John Drinkwater, "Mamble"

"Herefordshire farmers live rich, Monmouthshire farmers die rich."
                An Old Saying

When in "Bredon Hill" Housman wrote "both shires," there were indeed two counties involved. One was called Worcestershire, and stretched from its eastern boundary with Warwickshire, just below Stratford-upon-Avon, as far west as Great Malvern. The other was Herefordshire, from Great Malvern to the Welsh border. But now, after the 1974 government restructuring that knocked a number of venerable county lines askew, the two are one: Hereford (as in the first two syllables of (HER-e-[tic]) *and* Worcester (WOO-ster)—without the "shires."

Many a native of each half wishes this weren't so. And no mere official fiat will convince the visitor that they are now, thanks to the blessings of bureaucracy, actually one and the same. The voices that you hear don't sound the same. The towns and their houses don't look the same. And the people don't live the same.

The Hereford half is mainly agricultural, and splendidly so, with cattle and cornfields, hopyards and orchards. Thomas Fuller in *The Worthies of England* called it "a continued orchard of apple-trees, whereof much cider is made." The farmers of Hereford prosper and unabashedly enjoy their prosperity. They do live rich. Unlike their Monmouth neighbors in Wales, they know you can't take it with you.

The Worcester section on the other hand, though it has its share of farmland, is much more varied. In its center are those Malvern Hills that so enchanted the young Byron. And toward the top, Kidderminster and its sprawl to the north grow ever closer to the ominous shadow of Birmingham.

Even in their literary offerings, the differences are marked. Worcester's portion is decidedly superior, both in quantity and quality. Most important among those in what was old Herefordshire are a pair on its old eastern edge, Ledbury and Ross-on-Wye. A literary tour of today's Hereford and Worcester may well begin with them.

1. The Hereford Half

Ledbury and Hope End,
Ross-on-Wye and Goodrich Castle

There couldn't be easier entries into Hereford and Worcester than Ledbury and Ross-on-Wye. From Dymock and Gloucestershire, you simply go straight north up the B 4216, and in four miles there you are at Ledbury and the A 449. From Ledbury, the A 449 then takes you to Ross-on-Wye, gateway to all the western (Hereford) half of the county.

Also at Ross-on-Wye is the A 40. Coming as it does all the way from London, the A 40 serves Buckinghamshire, Oxfordshire, and Gloucestershire before it reaches Ross-on-Wye. And thanks to its junction with the M 5 to the southwest, it serves Avon, Somerset, and all the West Country similarly.

What's more, you couldn't ask for a pleasanter introduction to Hereford and Worcester than Ledbury and Ross-on-Wye.

Ledbury Ledbury is a little town (under four thousand) with some striking buildings. There's an enormous church with a foundation put down before the Norman Conquest and a massive eighteenth-century tower. The arcaded Market Hall, built in 1633, seems to float in the air, still supported by its original sixteen pillars of Spanish chestnut. And black and white half-timbered buildings abound, including two picture-book inns—one has no fewer than five gables!—old enough to have served Shakespeare if he passed that way.

In William Langland, Ledbury may have a poet who can challenge Chaucer as the first important writer of Middle English, if . . . If, that is, he wrote *Piers Plowman* (about 1360) . . . and if his name *was* William Langland . . . and if he *was* born in Ledbury.

A dream-allegory that survives in three versions, varying in length from 2,500 to 7,300 lines, the poem itself supplies about all that is known of its author. Though Cleobury Mortimer in Shropshire insists he was born there, the evidence does seem to favor Ledbury.

First, as to the poet's name. At one point the poem's narrator says, "I have lived long in the land; Long Will men call me." Ergo, Long . . . land, Will. And there is still a large field outside Ledbury called "Longland."

Also supporting Ledbury is the poet's description of where and when the hero has his dream: "On a May morning on a Malvern hillside."

Langland to one side, there is no denying that Ledbury did produce a real, genuine, true-blue poet laureate. John Masefield was born there June 1, 1878, and grew up in a big, comfortable Victorian house called The Knapp. And though he ran off to sea at thirteen, he loved the town. "Pleasant to the sight," he recalled fondly in his autobiography, *Grace Before Ploughing*, with "fair and half-timbered houses."

The tales he heard told as a boy and the sights he saw as he wandered about Ledbury and the Malvern Hills are warmly reflected in *The Everlasting Mercy* (1911), *The Widow in the Bye Street* (1912), and *Reynard the Fox* (1919).

Masefield never forgot Ledbury's great church, either, or its "golden vane surveying half the shire." The vane of St. Michael and All Angels, as the church is called, sits atop a 127-foot detached tower erected in 1727. When its nearly three hundred-year-old peal of bells needed restoration, Masefield contributed profits from several of his books to its fund.

The church has other literary associations, too. In the fourteenth century, during the reign of Edward II, a devout young lady named Catherine Audley was told in a vision to establish a refuge for the poor at a place where she would hear church bells ringing of their own accord. Worn out with searching for this place, she had lain down one night by Ledbury Church when suddenly its bells began chiming with never a human being at hand.

William Wordsworth tells the tale in one of those less than immortal sonnets he was quite capable of turning out from time to time, called "St. Catherine of Ledbury" (1835):

When human touch (as monkish books attest)
Nor was applied nor could be, Ledbury bells
Broke forth in concert flung adown the dells,
And upward, high as Malvern's cloudy crest. . . .
. . . .
Warned in a dream, the Wanderer long had sought
A home that by such miracle of sound
Must be revealed . . .
And there, a saintly Anchoress, she dwelt
Till she exchanged for heaven that happy ground.

In the north chapel of this church is a rather melodramatic memorial to
Edward Moulton Barrett, Elizabeth Barrett Browning's brother, and in its
yard is the grave of Jacob Tonson, one of the eighteenth century's foremost
publishers. He owned the copyright of *Paradise Lost,* and published many
works by Dryden and Addison, as well as a *Miscellany* (from 1684 to 1708) that
included poems by Swift, Pope, and Ambrose Philips. Pope in his *Dunciad*
(1743) calls him "left-legged Jacob," but treats him gently.

Up the way a bit is Church Lane, with its literary touch. Here, amid a
wealth of black and white houses, is the fifteenth-century grammar school
attended by Thomas Traherne, seventeenth-century writer of first-rate
poetry and prose.

For an overnight stay in Ledbury, you have those two famous old inns.
Oldest and largest is the three-star Feathers on High Street. Built in 1560
and with seventeenth-century additions, its four storeys—half-timbered
black and white topped by those five gables—have to be seen to be
believed.

Almost as old but much more modest is Ye Olde Talbot on New Street. It,
too, is gabled and half-timbered, and carries an original date of 1596. It only
has a few rooms, two of which are said to have things that go bump in the
night. But in the oak-panelled dining room with its handsome Jacobean
mantlepiece, they can still show you two bullet holes made when the
Cavaliers of Prince Rupert and the Roundheads of Cromwell had at it
following the Battle of Ledbury.

Hope End   During the first quarter of the nineteenth century, the biggest, most flamboyant estate in the vicinity of Ledbury was Hope End, not
quite two miles northeast of town. The house, set amidst five hundred acres
of park and forest, had minarets and domes, twenty bedrooms, and mahogany doors inlaid with pearl and stained glass. The stables were a wonder

to behold. While she was still a young princess, Victoria herself had come to take a look at it all.

Since 1809, its owner was Edward Barrett Moulton-Barrett. Born plain Moulton, he had added that second Barrett as a gesture to his maternal grandmother, whose legacy of Jamaican plantations had made such grandeur possible. He came to Hope End with three children. By the time he left twenty-three years later, there were eleven—so many he simply called his seventh and eighth sons Septimus and Octavius.

His favorite was daughter Elizabeth, whom he called Ba. His firstborn, she was three when they arrived. A strange man, Mr. Moulton-Barrett. Stern, almost tyrannical as husband and father, even maniacal when crossed, he could be loving and indulgent when things went his way. Elizabeth was as much companion as daughter to him, and he rewarded her in a most un-Victorian way: he let her take Greek and Latin from her brothers' tutor, unheard of for a mere girl.

But even from her baby days, the Elizabeth Barrett who became the century's best known woman poet was no "mere" child, male or female. Almost before she could talk, she was writing verses, hiding them from grown-ups under the mattress of her crib. As she laughingly confided to Robert Browning years later: "At nine years old I wrote what I called an "epic"—and at ten various tragedies, French and English, which we used to act in the nursery."

At above twelve, the epic resurfaced as *The Battle of Maldon* in four books—"Pope's Homer done over again," she joked, "or rather undone." Her father had fifty copies of it privately printed in 1820. On the title page, perhaps to provide these youthful efforts with suitably professional company, were printed several verses by Mark Akenside and Byron.

The very next year at fifteen, though she had recently sustained a fall from her pony that left her a lifelong invalid, Elizabeth achieved real publication: Thomas Campbell's *New Monthly Magazine* accepted two of her poems.

Elizabeth adored Hope End and the view of the Malvern Hills. "Beautiful, beautiful hills, they are!" she said. And the house was "a paradise." Both are recalled warmly in poems like "Hector in the Garden," "The Lost Bower," "The Deserted Garden," and *Aurora Leigh*.

When his Jamaican plantations went awry in 1832, her father had to sell the estate and move to Sidmouth in Devon. Elizabeth wept as she watched the auctioning off of all she held dear: "Our old serene green stillness was trodden under foot."

The house as she knew it is no more. But Mr. Edward Barrett Moulton-

Barrett might yet rejoice. For his beloved stables remain, minarets, crescent moons and all.

Ross-on-Wye   Ross-on-Wye, a town of 7,500 or more, twelve miles southwest of Ledbury on the A 40, is charmingly situated on a spit of land rising above the river. ("Ros" means a spit of land in Welsh.) Its chief literary association—like that of Porlock in Somerset—stems from a shadowy figure usually referred to only as "the man" rather than as a particular, identifiable individual.

The Porlock man was, of course, that mysterious stranger who appeared out of the dark one night, shattered Coleridge's vision of Kubla Khan forever, and vanished, still nameless and unknown. The "man of Ross" on the other hand—Alexander Pope's model of generosity and good works in *The Moral Essays*—is completely identifiable, both by name and deed.

His name was John Kyrle, his deeds legion. Born in Dymock, he came to Ross as a child, attended Ross grammar school, and after graduating from Oxford, returned to make beneficence a career. He donated the town waterworks, its Prospect Gardens, and a causeway to the Wilton Bridge. He provided medicine for the sick, apprenticeships for orphans, and dowries for penniless maidens. He gave the fourteenth-century Church of St. Mary a new steeple and great tenor bell.

Pope, who could tick off kings in a couplet, devotes over fifty lines to listing these good deeds, one by one, and more:

> Who taught that heaven-directed spire to rise?
> "The MAN of Ross," each lisping babe replies.
> Behold the Market-place with poor o'er spread;
> The MAN of Ross divides the weekly bread;
> He feeds yon Alms-house, neat, but void of state
> Where Age and Want sit smiling at the gate.

Most amazing, the poem suggests, was the limited income which supported all this:

> Of Debts and Taxes, Wife and Children clear
> This man possest—five hundred pounds a year.

The visitor to Ross-on-Wye can still see much of what Kyrle wrought for his town: the causeway; the sixteenth-century almshouse near the church; the church itself, where he lies buried; the gardens, with a gateway dedicated to him; and the Market Hall where he fed the poor. And Kyrle's big half-timbered house in the Market Square still stands, now housing two shops.

Pope wasn't the only poet to salute this good man. After his death, Kyrle's home became The King's Arms Inn. On a trip to Wales in 1794, Coleridge stayed there and composed "Lines Written at the King's Arm, Ross," beginning:

> Here dwelt the MAN of Ross! Oh Traveller, hear!
> Departed Merit claims a reverent tear.
> Friend to the friendless, to the sick man health
> With generous joy he view'd his modest wealth.

Kyrle's house is no longer an inn, but for an overnight stay with literary interest, Ross offers the three-star Royal Hotel at Palace Pound ("Royal" because both Queen Victoria and Queen [then Princess] Mary were among its guests).

Charles Dickens and his friend John Forster spent a night there in 1867 arguing about the novelist's going to America for a lecture tour. Forster was vehemently opposed to it, but Dickens went anyway—and made a fortune.

Goodrich Castle   Three miles southwest of Ross-on-Wye, outside the town of Goodrich, are the ruins of a twelfth-century castle, rated "splendid" by those who dote on such things. William Wordsworth was a doter, and the result was his moving little poem, "We are Seven."

"The Little girl who is the heroine," he explains in a note, "I met within the area of Goodrich Castle in the year 1793." Asked about brothers and sisters, the child says they are seven in all, though

> Two of us in the church-yard lie,
> My sister and my brother.

Repeatedly, the poet tries to make her realize that if two of them are dead, then they are only five, not seven.

No, says she. Often she goes to knit by their graves, or sing a song to them, or take her little bowl of porridge to eat her supper there. The child has the final word, though the poet persists:

> "But they are dead; those two are dead!
> Their spirits are in heaven!"
> 'Twas throwing words away; for still
> The little Maid would have her will,
> And said, "Nay, we are seven!"

Wordsworth didn't get around to writing this poem until 1798, when he and Coleridge were readying *Lyrical Ballads*. Interestingly enough, he tells us, he wrote the last line of the last stanza first, and it was Coleridge, not he, who wrote the first stanza.

Goodrich Castle is now open to the public daily the year round, the hours varying with the season.

Hereford

With about fifty thousand people, Hereford, fifteen miles northwest of Ross-on-Wye on the A 49, is Hereford and Worcester's third largest city. It is an ancient town, the seat of a bishop since 672, and about the year 1200 boasted two writers of importance: Giraldus de Barri (or Cambrensis) author of saints' lives, histories, and topographical works; and Walter Map (or Mapes), a witty satirist.

Still in the north choir aisle of the old Norman cathedral is the great Mappa Mundi, the "mappemound" of Chaucer's *Canterbury Tales*. It's a typical medieval map of the world, worked on vellum about 1300 A.D., with Jerusalem at the center and Paradise at the top.

Since then, Hereford's contributions to literature have been peripheral at best. Sir Thomas Coningsby, who founded Hereford's Coningsby Hospital in 1614, was the model for Ben Jonson's ridiculous Puntarvolo in *Everyman out of His Humor* (1599). Thomas Traherne, writer of religious prose and verse, was born in Hereford (in 1637), as were Nell Gwynne (1650) and David Garrick (1717). And that's about it.

For music lovers, however, Hereford is something else. It is one of the three cities of the "Three Choirs Festival," and thus every third year plays host to one of England's most venerable musical events.[1] The festival dates from the days of Handel, whose "Messiah" is still a standard offering.

More recent composers given a boost by the festival's performances include Vaughan Williams, Gustav Holst, William Walton, and Benjamin Britten. And a young Edward Elgar played second fiddle (actually) in the orchestra.

Credenhill and Lugwardine

On the outskirts of Hereford are Credenhill and Lugwardine. Both, like Hereford, are closely associated with Thomas Traherne. Despite being born

[1]The other two cities are Worcester and Gloucester.

in 1637, Traherne had to wait until the twentieth century for significant publication and recognition. And it took a good deal of luck, even then.

When in 1897 some seventeenth-century manuscripts of verse and prose turned up on a London bookstall, the poems were thought to be by Traherne's contemporary, Henry Vaughan. But a shrewd bookseller established them as Traherne's and published them, simply called *Poems*, in 1903. The prose, *Centuries of Meditation*, appeared in 1908. In 1910, following the discovery of another manuscript at the British Museum, came *Poems of Felicitation*.

Credenhill   Traherne was made rector of this village, northwest of Hereford on the A 480, in 1657, but did not live there until 1661. From then until 1669 when he left for London, moreover, he was studying at Oxford much of the time.

But a number of his works were done at Credenhill, and a passage in *Centuries of Meditation* shows why:

> When I came into the country, and being seated among silent trees and Meads and Hills, had all my Time in my own Hands, I resolved to Spend it all . . . in Search of Happiness, and to Satiate that burning Thirst which Nature had enkindled in me . . . In which I was so resolute, that I chose rather to live upon 10 pounds a yeer, and feed upon Bread and Water."

Sad, isn't it, that such dedication won so little recognition in its own day.

Lugwardine   As Credenhill gives us the "how" of Traherne's poetry, so Lugwardine, a hamlet a mile or so to Hereford's east on the A 438, provides an example of the "what."

The poet's father, a shoemaker, had originally lived in Lugwardine before moving to Hereford. Traherne's poem "To the Same Purpose" makes use of precisely this removal from village to town, but as seen by a little boy.

Here is the very heart of Traherne's poetry, what one critic has called "the memory of seeing God in childhood," based on some commonplace phenomenon of nature. In this poem, it is the sight of the self-same moon the child had seen only the night before far away in Lugwardine (a whole mile!) now miraculously shining in Hereford.

The setting and circumstance are beguiling. It is the boy's first night in his new home, and

> . . . . going to the Door
> To do some little thing

He must not do within
   With Wonder cries
   As in the Skies
He saw the Moon.   O yonder is the Moon
   Newly come to Town,
That shin'd at Lugwardin but yesternight,
   Where I enjoy'd the self-same Light
As if it had e'vn twenty thousand Faces
   It shines at once in many Places.

Perhaps Traherne was a lucky man after all. He never did outgrow such wonder and awe.

Brinsop and Bishopstone

Brinsop and Bishopstone are both northwest of Hereford beyond Credenhill, and both are off the A 480, Brinsop a bit to its north about four miles out, and Bishopstone to its south, six miles out. Both are associated with William Wordsworth.

The poet's brother-in-law, Thomas Hutchinson, lived at Brinsop Court, a rather grand mansion that goes back to the fourteenth century. The Wordsworths stayed there now and then, and William would busy himself planting trees and laying out the garden.

But the real gardener was not impressed, neither at having a distinguished poet as an amateur assistant nor by the result of his handiwork: "Ah, that Mister Wordsworth, he were one to go moonin' about the lanes."

On some visits Wordsworth also wrote sonnets about his experiences, as he often felt compelled to do. His effusion to Ledbury's St. Catherine, for instance, was composed at Brinsop. So was "Roman Antiquities Discovered at Bishopstone, Herefordshire," his reaction to a recent excavation that turned up artifacts from the village's ancient Roman past.

While archeologists pored over these relics for grubby little scientific data, says Wordsworth scornfully, poets (like Mr. Wordsworth, maybe?) caught fire, and saw instead visions of "myrtle crowned" Romans in "festal glee," warring emperors like Trajan, and Romulus and Remus being suckled by that maternal wolf of theirs: "While poring Antiquarians search the ground Upturned, with curious pains, and Bard, a Seer, Takes fire. . . ."

Titley

Titley offers a brief but amusing final touch to a literary tour of Western Hereford and Worcester. For here in 1812, almost to the very border of Wales, the swaggering, all-conquering Gordon Lord Byron fled in near panic to escape the clutches of a determined and decidedly amorous young woman.

The woman was Lady Caroline Lamb, wife of a prominent social and political figure, whose overardent attentions had already forced Byron, in August of that same year, to quit London for Cheltenham in Gloucestershire.[2] Now, in October, he retreated even further, to the country estate of Lord and Lady Oxford outside Titley (on today's B 4355), just three miles south of Presteigne in Wales.

Both lord and lady deserve an individual word. He was Edward Harley, fifth Earl of Oxford, a title long connected with literature. The first Earl had collected a great private library of books and manuscripts, many of them priceless. The second Earl had added to it and given his name to the *Harleian Miscellany* (1744–46), a selection of pieces from the library edited in part by Samuel Johnson.

The collection of the Lady Oxford who was Byron's hostess was more mundane, but considerably more titillating. She collected lovers—and in the process, babies too, a brood of beautiful children of uncertain, but obviously varied, paternity. Inevitably, London high society called them the Harleian miscellany.

Byron's stay with the Oxfords extended, off and on, into the spring of 1813, and apparently included the renting of a house they owned in nearby Kinsham.

Although Lady Oxford was forty, she was still a highly attractive woman, and Byron was—well, Byron. Soon he was writing a friend: "A woman is only grateful for her *first* and *last* conquest. The first of poor dear Lady [Oxford's] was achieved before I entered this world of care, but the *last* I do flatter myself was reserved for me, and a *bonne bouche* it was."

By April of 1813, Byron was hinting to intimates that there might be an addition to Lady Oxford's Harleian miscellany—his own. Fortunately, however, the alarm was a false one.

When Byron left Titley, he fired off a resounding final shot at his other lady, the Lady Caroline. Answering her embittered letter the poet brushes aside her threats of revenge and continues: "nor have I now to learn that an

[2]For further details of their story, see pp. 28–29.

incensed woman is a dangerous enemy. . . . You say you will 'ruin me.'
I thank you, but I have already done that for myself."

2. The Worcestershire That Was

Although the eastern part of Hereford and Worcester, the one-time Worcestershire part, has only one third of the new county's area, it has well over half its population and a majority of its important literary sites.

Ledbury, which served as the gateway to the Herefordshire section, can serve for this one, too, with two highways taking the traveller almost anywhere he wants to go. One is the A 449 running through Great Malvern and Worcester all the way north to Kidderminster and the border with West Midlands and Birmingham. The other is the A 38, which can be picked up either at Worcester or southeast of Great Malvern near Upton-upon-Severn.

The Malverns

Actually, though "Great Malvern" is often used as a generic term for all, there are six Malverns strung out along the compact but lovely little range known as The Malvern Hills. Those hills, plus springs of wondrously pure water, combined to produce a resort and health spa that rivalled any in England and, in the nineteenth century particularly, drew an astounding assortment of writers.

The hills, only eight and a half miles in length and varying from half a mile to a mile in width, rise to their highest at Worcestershire Beacon. From its 1,395 foot top you can see fourteen counties; the cathedrals of Hereford, Worcester, and Gloucester; and the abbeys of Tewkesbury, Evesham, Deerhurst, and Great Malvern itself.

The waters were known and enjoyed locally in the days of Chaucer and his Herefordshire contemporary, William Langland. But it was a Dr. John Wall who launched their commercial success with his *Experiments and Observations on the Malvern Waters* (1757).

Early in the next century, William IV's Queen Adelaide and William's successor-to-be, Princess Victoria, bestowed the requisite royal stamps of approval, giving the waters a celebrity they have never lost. Even today over a million bottles a year are sold throughout the world. Never heard of a brand called "Malvern Water?" How about "Schweppes?"

The A 449 out of Ledbury serves all the Malverns. Nearest, four miles out of Ledbury and due east of Elizabeth Barrett's Hope End, is Little Malvern. At the top of its Herefordshire Beacon is an Iron Age fort begun about 300 B. C. Another two miles along the A 449 comes Malvern Wells, whose Holywell spring is one of the largest.

Next, seven and a half miles north of Ledbury is Great Malvern, the metropolis of the group with over thirty-two thousand people. The Georgian and Victorian buildings of old Great Malvern and its environs must battle the onspreading new housing developments and their train, but the old Priory Church is a gem. Founded a mere twenty years after the first William did his conquering at Hastings in 1066, its fifteenth-century stained glass is matched only by that of York Cathedral.

Adjacent West and North Malverns have served chiefly as the city's residential area. And Malvern Link, its northern suburb, served another way: it got its name because that was where extra horses were linked to arriving stage coaches to help pull them up the steep hill into town.

The writers attracted to the Malverns over the past two centuries and more came for all sorts of reasons, but certainly the famed water cure drew many. Among these were Wordsworth, Tennyson, Sydney Dobell, Charles Dickens, Bulwer-Lytton, and Henry James—all of whom apparently ignored the jingle that went

> Malvern Water, said Dr. Wall
> Is famed for containing nothing at all.

But then, Charles Darwin and Florence Nightingale also drank the waters, and they might be thought knowledgeable about things medical.

The cure was not for the faint of heart. In addition to following a rather loathsome diet and drinking gallons of water, patients suffered cold water douches, wrapping in wet sheets, and endless running up and down the steep, steep hills.

Dickens observed these poor souls with wry amusement while his wife was convalescing there in 1851: "O Heaven, to meet the cold waterers (as I did this morning when I went out for a showerbath) dashing down the hills, with severe expressions on their countenances, like men doing matches and not exactly winning."

Even so, Alfred Tennyson was there several times, once to repeat the treatment he'd already undergone at Prestbury in Gloucestershire, and again in 1852, when he left his pregnant wife at the rectory with a friend while he went off on a fruitless househunting tour.

Though the hills were torture to most who came for the cure, they were a joy to those who came to The Malverns for them alone. To the seventeenth-century diariest John Evelyn they were another Alps, to the boy Byron a possible substitute for the Highlands, and for Shakespearean actress Fanny Kemble the Alban Hills of Rome.

A dour Thomas Carlyle found as much pleasure as he was capable of in trekking about with Sydney Dobell, leaving his wife Jane to "dawdle about on the backs of donkeys," as she acidly put it, amid the "everlasting smell of roast meat." Happier hikers were John Masefield and particularly Harold Nicolson, who gleefully reported in a 1940 article, "I have seen Wystan Auden playing upon the Malvern Hills."

Learning, of all things, brought a few to Malvern. That William Langland was a fourteenth-century student at The Priory is a legend. That novelist Michael Arlen (*The Green Hat*, 1924, etc.) and C. S. Lewis, author of *The Screwtape Letters* (1942), were twentieth-century students at Malvern College for Boys is a fact.

For several years beginning in 1828, Elizabeth Barrett also studied at Great Malvern, but in a highly unusual way. She would ride over on her pony from her father's great estate at Hope End to read the Greek classics with a blind scholar named Hugh Stuart Boyd, often staying with him and his wife a week or more at a time.

Many writers found inspiration or background material for work while at Malvern. Charles Dickens based his farce, *Mr. Nightingale's Diary* (written in collaboration with Mark Lemon), on it. And in *Barchester Towers*, Anthony Trollope takes Mr. Tinkler and Olivia Proudie to Malvern on their less than grand honeymoon.

During their visit together in 1875, Algernon Swinburne and his Greek professor from Oxford, the renowned Benjamin Jowett, both put the time to good use. Jowett worked on his great translation of Thucydides' *History of the Peloponnesian War.* Swinburne, hoping to duplicate his first great success, a play in the Greek style called *Atalanta in Calydon* (1865), began *Erectheus.* He described it to a friend as ". . . a companion poem to 'Atalanta' which I hope will turn out a more perfect original example of Greek tragedy than that was . . . Jowett approves my scheme highly, and helped me with some valuable hints from the classical or scholarly point of view."

On a four-day holiday among the Malvern Hills, Tennyson's great friend, Arthur Hallam, along with future prime minister, William Gladstone—both then were students at Oxford—made arrangements for a Cambridge vs. Oxford debate on the relative merits of Shelley and Byron. Shelley, of course, was Oxford's man.

At Malvern, too, John Ruskin sketched and Edward Elgar often composed while roaming the hills. Elgar based his cantata, *Caractacus* on that Iron Age fort at Little Malvern, and is buried at St. Wulfstan's Church at Malvern Wells.

Nor is this list of Malvern celebrities finished. Daniel Defoe came to wonder that the natives didn't mine more gold (there wasn't all that much) . . . Thomas Gray to read Goldsmith's *Deserted Village* for the first time (he liked it) . . . M. R. James, writer of detective stories, to get The Priory's stained glass renovated (he was a noted medievalist, too). . . and Cecil Day-Lewis because he couldn't help it (he was one year old when his father became rector of that same Priory Church).

Jenny Lind, world famous as the Swedish Nightingale, spent her last years at Wynd's Point behind the Little Malvern priory, gave her final recital in Great Malvern's Cecilia Hall, and is buried in The Wilton Road cemetery. Her home survives and, through the NGS, its gardens with their abundant laurel, a maze, and splendid vistas are open to the public at selected times.

Through the NGS, also, you can see the grounds of Madresfield Court, two and a half miles northeast of Great Malvern between the A 449 and the B 4211. Evelyn Waugh was a frequent visitor here, and it has some claim to being the model for the mansion in *Brideshead Revisited*.

Clearly, the Malverns have a multitude of literary attractions for today's visitors. A particular treat awaits you in May when Great Malvern stages its Shaw-Elgar Festival, begun in 1929 with the premiere of *The Apple Cart* starring Cedric Hardwicke and Edith Evans. Every year since then the festival has featured the plays of Shaw, and added more recently the music of Edward Elgar.

The Malverns can offer you a number of fine hotels for your stay, but in May especially you'd better book in advance. Those hotels can get mighty full—and those steep streets mighty crowded.

Upton-upon-Severn and Bredon Hill

From the Malverns, you can reach the A 38 at Worcester by going eight miles straight up the A 449. Or from Little Malvern, you can go six miles east along the A 4104 and get the A 38 in the neighborhood of Upton-upon-Severn and Bredon Hill. Lovers of A. E. Housman will identify the latter immediately. And though, to readers of Henry Fielding's *Tom Jones*, the name Upton-upon-Severn may ring no bell, surely the mention of Tom's rescue of the near-naked Mrs. Waters and the subsequent battle royal with the innkeeper will.

Upton-upon-Severn   In one of the wildest episodes in Fielding's novel, Tom hears a woman screaming, dashes off to the rescue, and drives away the dastardly Northerton, who has torn off most of the woman's clothing. Directed by the Man of the Hill, Tom takes her to Upton and "that inn which in their eyes presented the fairest in that street."

What follows is pure mayhem. Aroused by the lady's most unladylike condition, the innkeeper's wife comes at Tom with a broom. The innkeeper joins the fray at his wife's side, then Partridge and the half-clothed woman pitch in to help Tom, and are in turn set upon by the chambermaid. Only the timely arrival of a coach (it happens to be Sophia Western's) prevents mass slaughter.

Today's Upton is a pleasant little place on the A 4104 just before it meets up with the A 38. The scene of Tom's epic battle described by Fielding as "a house of exceeding good repute, whither Irish ladies of strict virtue, and many northern lasses of the same predicament, were accustomed to resort in their way to Bath," still survives on the High Street.

Called The White Lion, it is a restored sixteenth-century building with a stuccoed front and the figure of a lion over the porch holding a ball under its paw. Small but friendly, it lives up to its two-star rating and maintains the tradition of a long-gone proprietor whose epitaph read:

> Here lies the landlord of the Lion,
> Who died in lively hopes of Zion;
> His son keeps on the business still,
> Resign'd unto the heavenly will.

Bredon Hill   Bredon (BREE-don) just east of the M 5 is a proud little village, and rightly so. Its site above the Avon River is splendid, its thatched black-and-white cottages exemplary, and its roster of old established families honorable.

Among survivors of its treasured past are a grand eighteenth-century Manor House, an historic Elizabethan rectory, the enormous fourteenth-century stone Tithe Barn, and two old inns—the seventeenth-century Royal Oak and the sixteenth-century Fox and Hounds.

The hill made so familiar by Housman's poem "Bredon Hill" in *A Shropshire Lad* (1896)—though it's not in Shropshire at all—is another of those places that want to make sure you realize you're on a hill. Since "Bre" and "don" mean hill, too, the name comes out Hill-Hill-Hill.

Anyway, the view from its top, three miles to the northwest of the town, is all that the poem suggests:

> Here of a Sunday morning
> My love and I would be
> And see the coloured counties
> And hear the larks so high
> About us in the sky.

Indeed, the coloured counties were actually five in Housman's day: Gloucestershire, Oxfordshire, Warwickshire, Herefordshire, and Worcestershire itself.

To this day, folks around about look for the hilltop to signal their weather. As some unknown poet, lesser but more earthy than Housman, sternly warned:

> When Bredon Hill puts on its hat
> Men of Vale, beware of that.

Worcester

Worcester, eight miles above Great Malvern where the A 449 and A 38 briefly meet, is Hereford and Worcester's biggest city, with eighty thousand or so people. The city's name has undergone several changes since its original Saxon jawbreaker, Weogornaceaster. Now even Americans who stutter on Cirencester and go all to pieces with Magdalen can pronounce it. But this may be because Royal Worcester china is famous in the United States, and Worcestershire sauce practically a household word.

The sauce was invented by two Worcester men, a Mr. Lee and a Mr. Perrins, in 1830, and should you wonder if it is still made there, just stand in the vicinity of Midland Road. If the breeze is right, you'll wonder no more. As for the famous blue and white china, it originated with the same Dr. John Wall who first promoted the mineral waters of Malvern.

Not exactly household words, however, are Worcester's literary lights. It has Shakespeare's marriage license, but not Shakespeare . . . two women novelists, neither of them a Brontë or a George Eliot . . . and a seventeenth-century satirist, but hardly John Dryden.

Even the royalty buried in its cathedral are less than illustrious. King John would rank with George II, say, if he hadn't been brow-beaten into signing the Magna Carta. And Prince Arthur, Henry VII's eldest son, is remembered only because his death at sixteen made possible a Henry VIII.

The Shakespeare marriage license is in Worcester because the city's former St. Helen's Church now houses the county's ecclesiastical and secular archives, and it was the Bishop of Worcester who authorized the playwright's nuptials:

William Shagspere and Anne Hathwey of
Stratford 28 Nov 25 Eliz.

The date was November 28, 1582, the twenty-fifth year of Elizabeth's reign.

Worcester's seventeenth-century satirist was Samuel Butler, who was born nearby in Strensham and got his early—and only—schooling at Worcester's King's School. He was too poor to go to university. And he stayed poor all his life. His one major work, the three-part poem *Hudibras* (1663–64–78), was a smashing success—but only after his death. As his epitaph in Westminster Abbey says:

The Poets Fate is here in emblem shown:
He asked for Bread and he received a Stone.

Worcester's women novelists are Martha Sherwood and Mrs. Henry Wood, both memorialized in the cathedral. Mrs. Sherwood's books for youngsters were widely popular in the first half of the nineteenth-century; one, *The History of the Fairchild Family* (1818-47), has been reprinted often.

Mrs. Wood was the daughter of a Worcester glovemaker. Few now, perhaps, would readily identify her by name. Yet one of her works remains to this day the paradigm of Victorian melodrama. She wrote *East Lynne* (1861).

Worcester also has more or less tenuous connections with William Wordsworth and Francis Brett Young. Wordsworth wrote "A Gravestone upon the Floor in the Cloisters of Worcester Cathedral" (1829). The sonnet is about some unknown sinner who chose to have neither name nor date inscribed on the stone, but only the single word "Miserrimus," and ordered the stone placed on the floor,

That every foot might fall with heavier tread,
Trampling upon his vileness.

Francis Brett Young was born in Halesowen near Birmingham and lived for a number of years in Hereford and Worcester at Fladbury, outside Evesham. He used the Worcester area as a setting in a number of novels, and when he died in 1954, his ashes were interred in Worcester Cathedral.

If you're all that interested in Worcestershire Sauce or the Worcester china, both factories will give you a tour if you make arrangements in advance.

And if you like music, as one of the Three Choirs Festival cities, Worcester presents that great event once every three years. Edward Elgar, whose father had a music shop on Worcester's High Street, played in the festival orchestra early in his career, and his music is a festival staple. Moreover, four miles to the northwest of Worcester is Broadheath, where he was born in 1857. His birthplace is now an Elgar Museum, with a good collection of his scores, photographs, and mementoes.

Abberley and Ribbesford— Hagley—and Ipsley

The final literary stop in Hereford and Worcester, in the county's northeast corner in and about Bromsgrove, is Housman territory. But first Abberley and Ribbesford, Hagley and Ipsley—all within fourteen miles of Bromsgrove—need mention.

Abberley and Ribbesford are both off the A 451, Abberley fourteen miles to the west, and Ribbesford eleven. Hagley and Ipsley are actually in what is now the Bromsgrove District—Hagley eight miles northwest of the town of Bromsgrove, and Ipsley seven miles northeast (outside the town of Wythall but not marked on the map).

Abberley   The lodge at Abberley was once the home of William Walsh, late seventeenth and early eighteenth-century patron of literature. Addison, Dryden, and Pope were among his friends, and all apparently visited him there. As one "whose early voice you taught to sing," Pope was especially grateful to Walsh, praising him in *An Essay on Criticism* as poetry's "judge and friend," with "the clearest head, and the sincerest heart." In "Epistle to Dr. Arbuthnot," Pope says he first published his poems because "Walsh would tell me I could write."

Walsh tried his own hand at both drama and poetry. But the play, *Squire Trelooby* (1704), was: a) only a translation of a play by Molière . . . b) done in collaboration with seasoned playwrights William Congreve and John Vanbrugh . . . and c) published anonymously at that. Walsh's poems fared little better. The best known one, "The Despairing Lover" hardly refutes Dr. Johnson's verdict: "He seldom rises higher than to be pretty."

Ribbesford   In the year 1630 or thereabouts, the church of little Ribbesford scored a coup unique in literary history, with a service involving three of the country's leading poets. George Herbert preached the sermon, Henry Vaughan read the lesson, and John Milton played the organ. Or so, at least, say the local mythmakers.

It is true that the owner of Ribbesford's manor house then was George Herbert's brother, Sir Henry Herbert, of literary interest himself. He was Master of Revels, censor and supervisor of drama, for both Charles I (until the Puritans closed the playhouses in 1642), and after the Restoration, Charles II.

As such, Sir Henry oversaw a tumultuous transition in the English theater. Under Charles I, plays like John Ford's *'Tis Pity She's a Whore* (1633) were sometimes sensational and decadent. But in the reign of Charles II, William Wycherley's *The Country Wife* (1672) and its kin brought drama to the nadir of coarseness and indecency.

What's more, after the Restoration, Henry Herbert's office witnessed the first appearance ever of women actors in England. Even Shakespeare's Juliet and Rosalind—yes, and Lady Macbeth—had all been played by young males. And now real live female forms were parading about a British stage. Shocking!

One wonders what Sir Henry thought of it all.

Hagley   Hagley is as far north and east in Hereford and Worcester as you can get. Stourbridge, only a couple of miles northwest of Hagley, is in West Midlands.

Hagley Park was the family seat of the Lytteltons, and in the middle decades of the eighteenth century George Lyttelton, first Baron Lyttelton, made it a major literary center. To it came novelists Henry Fielding and Horace Walpole, poets William Shenstone and James Thomson, and that giant of things literary, Samuel Johnson.

George Lyttelton was a man of considerable talent and in an offhand way wrote much, including the commendable *Dialogues of the Dead* (1760). His support for writers of the age was ready and generous.

He and Henry Fielding had been best friends at Eton, and in later life Fielding stopped by Hagley now and then. *Tom Jones* (1749), Fielding's masterpiece, was dedicated to Lyttelton.

Horace Walpole was also an Etonian, but ten years younger. When he came to Hagley in 1753, Lord Lyttelton hadn't yet begun the great house rebuilding that resulted in today's mansion, but the vast landscaping project was well along, and Walpole was so carried away he said, "I quite forgot my favorite Thames."

William Shenstone, whose own family place was nearby in Halestone, visited Lyttelton often, and had helped lay out the gardens that so impressed Walpole. On one of those visits, in 1743, Shenstone met James Thomson for the first time.

Thomson and his poetry were much beholden to Lyttelton. The nobleman not only offered the hospitality of Hagley Hall while Thomson revised the "Spring" section of *The Seasons*, but made helpful suggestions that the poet used. Moreover, Lyttelton was instrumental in Thomson's obtaining a pension. "Spring" pays tribute to

> . . . the sacred feelings of thy heart,
> Thy heart inform'd by reason's purer ray,
> O Lyttelton, the friend!

Samuel Johnson's friendship with George Lyttelton went back a long way. Both then sixteen, they first came together at Hagley Hall in 1725 when George was home on vacation from Eton and Johnson was staying with his cousin, Cornelius Ford, a mile away at Pedmore.

Since the Fords and Lyttelton were friendly, young Johnson, uncouth and rough-hewn though he was, was kindly received by the Lytteltons, who provided him with a glimpse of a world of wit and manners and sophistication he never knew existed.

The story that in 1774 Johnson returned to Hagley Hall and was coldly treated still pops up now and then, but stems from mistaken identity. Johnson did visit the Lytteltons with his friends, Henry and Hester Thrale in 1774. But the visit was to Little Hagley, not Hagley Hall. And the Lytteltons were George's uncle and aunt, the William Henry Lytteltons. The visitors were treated badly, however. Mrs. Thrale was forced to play cards, which she hated, and Johnson had his candle carted off while he was still reading.

The house that George Lyttelton built in the 1750s was an elaborate edifice, with all sorts of extravagances inside and landscaping that went on and on outside, including an obelisk on a hill, a Greek temple, and a sham castle. Horace Walpole said that Hagley Park's new grounds were directly inspired by Milton's description of the Garden of Eden. But, if so, where in *Paradise Lost* do you find a Greek temple and a sham castle? Thomson's description of the terrain in "Spring" overpowers anything Eden can offer, too:

> With woods o'er hung, and shagg'd with mossy rocks
> Whence on each hand the gushing waters play,
> And down the rough cascade white-dashing fall

and on and on, through "solemn oaks" and "swelling mounts" and "twisted roots" that seemingly go on forever.

After Oxford, A. E. went on to ten years as a civil servant in London, followed by a brilliant career as professor of classics at the University of London and Cambridge. But he never forgot the scenes of his youth, especially the strolls up Worms Ash Lane and the view westward to those hills:

> The weathercock at sunset
> Would lose the slanted ray,
> And I would climb the beacon
> That looked to Wales away
> And saw the last of day.
>
> *Last Poems,* XXXIX (1922)

A special treat for the literary traveller is to sip, sup, or sleep someplace and sense the presence of a favorite author hovering about. To nurse an ale at The Fox Inn in Felpham, for instance, and look out into the yard where William Blake deposited the drunken soldier he'd accosted in his garden. Or stand at the bar of The Swan in Grasmere where Sir Walter Scott, when he visited Wordsworth, had to come daily if he wanted his whiskey because his host allowed nothing stronger than water in the house. Or sleep beneath the roof of Farringford on the Isle of Wight—the roof on which Alfred Lord Tennyson clambered to fly kites with his sons Hallam and Lionel.

Bromsgrove offers you just such a treat. Perry Hall is now a hotel, and a fine three-star one at that. Inside, after you pass through the handsome oak door, you come upon the oak panelling and fireplace of the Housman's living quarters. A period stairway on the right leads upward to where they slept.

Outside there's a patio to sit on and a garden to gaze at as you sip your drink and await your lunch. If it's spring and the cherry trees are in bloom, it's heaven.

And should you think for one moment that Housman's fame is on the wane—though how could you?—pop out of your chair, go to that little tree at the left of the patio, and read the plaque:

THIS CHERRY TREE WAS PLANTED ON
6th DAY OF APRIL 1976
IN MEMORY OF A.E. HOUSMAN
BY TATSUZO HIJIKATA OF
THE JAPANESE HOUSMAN SOCIETY

What a memory to take with you as you leave Hereford and Worcester!

WARWICKSHIRE
AND WEST MIDLANDS

Warwickshire
and
West Midlands

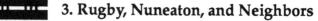	1. Waltham Cross to Baldock
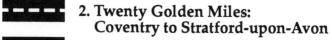	2. Twenty Golden Miles: Coventry to Stratford-upon-Avon
	3. Rugby, Nuneaton, and Neighbors
	4. Access or Connecting Routes

I'm a Warwickshire man. Don't talk to me of Dartmoor or Snowdon or the Thames or the Lakes.

Rupert Brooke

Mr. William Shakespeare was borne at Stratford upon Avon in the county of Warwick. His father was a butcher, and I have been told heretofore by some of the neighbors, that when he was a boy he exercised his father's trade, but when he killed a calfe he would doe it in a high style and make a speech.

John Aubrey, *Brief Lives*

Bremischam [Birmingham] . . . a great part of the towne is mayntayned by smithes, who have their yren out of Staffordshire and Warwikshire, and their sea-coale out of Staffordshire.

John Leland, *The Laboryouse Journey and Searche of Johan Laylande*

For the section on Hereford and Worcester, it made sense to treat that county as if it were still two counties, as was the case for centuries. Warwickshire and West Midlands invite doing just the opposite.

Today's maps show that Warwickshire and West Midlands are indeed two separate and distinct counties. West Midlands is mainly Birmingham, say the maps, with Coventry and a few spots here and there thrown in as a sort of consolation prize. Warwickshire (WAR-ick-sh'r) is Warwick and Rugby, Leamington Spa and Nuneaton, and Stratford-upon-Avon.

But never mind the maps. Both convenience and history suggest you treat them all as one. Leland clearly included Birmingham in his "Warwickshire" of 1546. Coventry was in Aubrey's "county of Warwick" when he gossiped about the young Shakespeare in 1692. And almost all of what is now West Midlands would have been included by Rupert Brooke when he proclaimed himself a "Warwickshire man" in 1912.

Ironically, until England's revamping of counties and county lines in 1971, the literary-minded tended to think of the whole area as indisputably one county, but three "countries": "Shakespeare Country," "George Eliot Country,"—and Birmingham.

Today's two counties—combined they are approximately the size of Gloucestershire—are a peculiarly gerrymandered pair. Warwickshire now surrounds West Midlands on both the south and east. In fact, to go in a straight line from a number of places in the southwest of Warwickshire— Stratford-upon-Avon, say, or Warwick—to others in the northeast like Nuneaton, you have to go through West Midlands.

And so, logistically and practically, when exploring the two counties, it's best to treat them as one. Actually, if you want to see all the area's literary sites for yourself, you will save much time, money, and wear and tear by choosing one central city as headquarters, and fanning out to all the others from there.

Coventry, for instance, though those maps insist that it is in West Midlands while most of your stops will be in Warwickshire, would be ideal. It's superbly central. Birmingham is only eighteen miles away; Nuneaton, nine; Warwick, ten; Stratford-upon-Avon, nineteen; Rugby, twelve. Coventry offers an abundance of hotels of every sort, from modest to truly elegant, and amenities of every kind. And it has a rich literary heritage of its own.

In addition to all this, Birmingham and Coventry together, linked by the M 6, provide the greatest network of M-Ways in England outside of London. From Bromsgrove and Hereford and Worcester and all the southwest, there's the M 5. From the Lake District and the northwest, the M 6. From York Country and the northeast, the M 1. And from London itself and the southeast, again the M 1.

With Coventry as a base, the whole area divides nicely into three compact tours:

1) Birmingham and its environs, which can be done en route to Coventry if you're coming up from Bromsgrove and the southwest;

2) the Coventry to Stratford-upon-Avon region;

3) and Rugby, Nuneaton, and their neighbors.

1. Birmingham and Environs

Halesowen and Stourbridge

The name Samuel Johnson immediately brings to mind London and his famous dictum: "When a man is tired of London, he is tired of life." But Birmingham has considerable claim to being part of "Johnson Country," too.

His mother was born and grew up in King's Norton, now a suburb of Birmingham, and his parents were married in the nearby village of Packwood, where his father had land. Johnson himself grew up in Lichfield only nineteen miles away, and walked the thirty-eight mile round trip between there and Birmingham too many times to mention. He stayed with friends in Birmingham often, both as a youth and later; he lived there once for over a year; and he met his future wife there.

Johnson also had close connections with Stourbridge, just fourteen miles from Birmingham, as well. He had many relatives in and around Stourbridge whom he visited, once for a period of nine months. He finished his pre-college education at the Stourbridge Grammar School, and became enamoured, briefly but futilely, of a young Stourbridge woman.

If Johnson never tired of London, he never forgot Birmingham. In his *Life of Johnson*, Boswell tells of once coming upon his friend in his old age and finding him utterly absorbed by the book he was reading. The book was a history of Birmingham.

With that great network of highways at hand, Birmingham is easily reached. From Coventry and the east, take the A 45; from the north, the M 5; from the south, the M 6; and from the northeast or southwest, the A 38, which runs right through the city.

Stourbridge is west of Birmingham, off the A 458. Between the two on that same road (nine miles out of Birmingham) is Halesowen, home of the poet William Shenstone.

Halesowen   When William Shenstone was born here in 1714 at the Leasowes, his family's estate, Halesowen was a part of Shropshire ("Salops"), hence the term "Salopian" often applied to him. Neither house nor grounds were especially elaborate until the poet inherited them in 1745. Then, moved by an urge to rival the great rebuilding and landscaping program of his neighbor Lord Lyttleton at Hagley Park just over the hill in Worcestershire, Shenstone embarked on a similar project.

But he limited himself to landscaping, according to Sam Johnson: "His house was mean, and he did not improve it; his care was his grounds." Johnson acknowledged that his efforts to "diversify his surfaces, to entangle his walks, and to wind his waters" aroused "the envy of the great and the admiration of the skilful."

Nevertheless, Johnson said sardonically, the poet spent so much money that his groves were inhabited by far more bill collectors than the romantic fauns and fairies he'd planned for. Others, too, found amusement in what Shenstone achieved. When Lord Lyttelton's guests seemed a bit bored, he'd take them over the hill for a peek at the Leasowes and brighten their whole day.

Shenstone's dream has dwindled today into a golf course and park. He lies buried at the Halesowen parish church, where his memorial urn shares space with a tablet commemorating the birth and baptism of the poet and novelist, Francis Brett Young, in 1884.

Stourbridge   Now a sizeable industrial town, Stourbridge was to Samuel Johnson, a country boy from Lichfield, a whole new world of wonder.

In October of 1725, he had come to stay for a week or two with his cousin Cornelius Ford at the Ford's nearby estate at Pedmore. The cousins couldn't have been more unlike. Cornelius, age thirty-one, was brilliant, charming, a man of sophistication and social grace. Johnson, sixteen, was awkward, oversized, almost distressingly rustic in manners and speech.

Yet the two rapidly became the closest of friends. "Neely," as Johnson came to call him, recognized the boy's obvious genius, introduced him to Stourbridge high society, and even polished his manners and speech somewhat. Johnson never did become a model for social behavior, but he did learn that *superior* was not "shuperior," nor *once* "woonce."

Almost imperceptibly, the visit went on. The days stretched into weeks, and then months. This, it turned out, made necessary the greatest of all Neely's services, one absolutely crucial to Johnson's career. For he had lingered far past the reopening of school back home. When he returned to Lichfield in June, the headmaster refused him readmission. Too poor to send their son elsewhere, Johnson's parents were distraught. Cousin Cornelius and the Stourbridge relatives stepped in. By the end of July, Johnson was a student at Stourbridge Grammar School.

Johnson was later to say that he learned "a great deal from the master but nothing in his school." His dealings with that master, however, a John Wentworth, were not easy:

> [he] was a very able man, but an idle man, and to me very severe; but I cannot blame him much. I was then a big boy; he saw I did not reverence him; and that he should get no honour by me. I had brought enough with me to carry me through; and all I should get at his school would be ascribed to my own labour, or to my former master. Yet, he taught me a great deal.

Even so, Wentworth encouraged Johnson's attempt at poetry, and saved the manuscripts. They survive to this day, proof that at seventeen Johnson's talents were already remarkable.

During these schooldays, Johnson had one of his earliest experiences with the other sex. He met and was quite smitten with a young Quaker woman of nineteen named Olivia Lloyd, the daughter of a wealthy Birmingham ironmaster.[1] Nothing, naturally, came of it. But apparently Johnson never forgot her. Years afterward he told Boswell about her and confessed that he had written her love poems.

The Stourbridge School, as Johnson knew it, vanished long ago. King Edward VI School today stands on the same site off Lower High Street, but little of the older building survives.

Stourbridge, incidentally, just missed being more widely known to the poetic world. One lovely poem in Housman's *A Shropshire Lad* begins:

> 'Tis time, I think, by Wenlock town
> The golden broom should blow;
> The hawthorne sprinkled up and down
> Should charge the land with snow.

What Housman originally wrote was:

> 'Tis time, I think, by *Stourbridge* town . . . .

For Housman wasn't really a Shropshire lad at all. He grew up in Bromsgrove, nine miles from Stourbridge.

Birmingham

Birmingham is Britain's second biggest city, and tends to deal in superlatives. It has more miles of waterway than Venice, and seven thousand acres of park. Its Central Museum and Art Gallery has a finer assembly of Pre-Raphaelite paintings than London's Tate, and its Central Library a greater collection of Shakespearean books and documents than the British Museum.

It calls itself the Convention City of Britain, and it may well be. The £130 million National Exhibition Centre to its east sits amidst two acres, has nine meeting halls, and draws two million visitors annually.

All this came from a cluster of huts among thick trees which, about the year 500 A.D., called itself Beorma-ing-ham: the "ham" (home), of the "Beorma" (leader), of the "ing" (tribe).

By 1400 A. D. it had become the third wealthiest town in Warwickshire.

[1] Olivia's nephew was the Sampson Lloyd who founded Lloyd's of London.

When John Leland wrote in 1538 of its "smithes" with their "yren" and "sea-coale," it had fifteen hundred people, two hundred houses, and a Main Street. By 1900 it was manufacturer for the world, making almost anything that could be made of metal, from a screw to a steam engine, and from jewelry to guns. (In the American Civil War of the 1860's, it sent over eight hundred thousand guns to the United States.)

But the price of this prosperity came high, and was by no means widely shared by its citizens, as writers from Dickens to Louis MacNeice have been quick to point out. In 1836, in *Pickwick Papers,* Dickens describes "the dingy hue of every object visible, the murky atmosphere, the paths of cinders and brick-dust, the deep red glow of furnace fires in the distance, the volumes of dense smoke issuing heavily forth from high toppling chimneys, blackening and obscuring everything around."

Nor were things any better one hundred years later when George Orwell, en route to Wigan in Lancaster, walked through Birmingham and into adjoining Wolverhampton, to which the blight had spread: "[I] wandered about the slummy parts of Wolverhampton a while . . . Wolverhampton seems a frightful place. Everywhere vistas of mean little houses still enveloped in drifting smoke, though this was Sunday."

In his poem "Birmingham" (1935), Louis MacNeice bleakly depicts the toll these great metal-working plants exacted. The inner city may glitter with its "proud glass of shops," he says,

> But beyond this centre the slumward vista thins
>> like a diagram:
> There, unvisited, are Vulcan's forges who don't
>> care a tinker's damn
>
> . . . .
>
> [There in] the west the factory chimneys on
>> sullen sentry will all night wait
> To call, in the harsh morning, sleep-stupid faces
>> through the daily gate.

Little wonder, then, that great industrial cities like this produce almost everything in abundance except writers. The authors associated with Birmingham are not natives; almost all are on their way to and from elsewhere.

Samuel Johnson's first recorded visit to Birmingham was in 1719, when as a boy of nine he came with his six-year-old brother Nathaniel on a two-week holiday from school. "Why such boys were sent to trouble other houses," he would say later, "I cannot tell."

The relatives they stayed with were an odd lot. One uncle was "a very mean and vulgar man, drunk every night." Another uncle had a hypochondriac wife whose drug bill was so huge the apothecary wanted them arrested for debt. And an aunt, "a good-natured, coarse woman," once confided to Johnson that when he was a baby, she "would not have picked such a poor creature up in the street."

Johnson's longest stay in Birmingham came under most distressing circumstances. In 1729, poverty forced him to leave Oxford and return to his home in Lichfield. There followed a long period of melancholy bordering on helplessness. Often he would force himself to walk the thirty-eight miles from Lichfield to Birmingham and back, just to be doing something.

Most times he would stop by to see Edmund Hector, his closest chum at Lichfield Grammar School and now beginning practice in Birmingham as a surgeon. It was Hector who, in the fall of 1732, persuaded Johnson to come share his apartment for awhile. Johnson was to live in Birmingham for the next thirteen months—months that were to shape his life profoundly.

For the first six months he remained at Hector's, and even managed to write some articles for a newspaper owned by Hector's landlord. And after he moved to a room of his own, Hector coaxed him into translating a seventeenth-century priest's account of a tour of Abyssinia. Published in 1735, it was Johnson's first book.

But the most important event of these thirteen months was his developing friendship with the Porters. Both were almost twice the age of the twenty-four-year-old Johnson. Henry Porter, a wool-draper, was forty-two; his wife Elizabeth was forty-four. But their hospitality and warmth meant much to poor Johnson, and they became attached to each other.

In February of 1734, Johnson finally went back to Lichfield. Soon, however, Henry Porter fell mortally ill, and during his final days Johnson was with him almost constantly. When Porter died in September, Johnson was equally attentive to the widow. Perhaps she encouraged him. Perhaps it was only mutual need. In any event, despite the disparities between them, the bond grew.

The disparities were great. She was now forty-five, he twenty-five. She had a bit of money (£600); he was penniless. She had been long married and had a daughter of eighteen and two younger sons. He was utterly without any real experience with women.

Nevertheless, on July 9, 1735, the two were married in St. Werburgh's Church in Derby. Johnson's intimate friend and one-time pupil, the actor David Garrick, would one day relish describing Mrs. Porter as "very fat, with a bosom of more than ordinary protuberance, with swelled cheeks, of a florid red produced by thick painting."

Another devoted, later-life friend, Mrs. Thrale, however, contradicts Garrick: "The picture I found of her at Lichfield was very pretty." What matters is what Johnson said: "It was a love match upon both sides."

In the nineteenth century, the Birmingham visits of Charles Dickens and Washington Irving produced material for their books. Dickens used the impressions of Birmingham gained as a young London reporter for an episode in *Pickwick Papers*. He has Mr. Pickwick arrive on Birmingham's Easy Row to present Nathaniel Winkle's plea for his father's help: "[There,] in a quiet substantial-looking street, stood an old red-brick house, with three steps before the door, and a brass upon it, bearing, in fat Roman capitals, the words 'Mr. Winkle.' The steps were very white, and the bricks were very red, and the house was very clean."

And the mission, of course, was very disastrous, helped not at all by Pickwick's being accompanied by Mr. Benjamin Allen and Mr. Bob Sawyer, both more than a little hung over from all that imbibing they'd done at Tewkesbury.

Irving, already a successful writer in America, went to Liverpool in 1815 to try to salvage a business he co-owned with his brother. When it failed, he turned to writing again to recoup, and succeeded with his *Sketch Book* (1819–20), written under the pseudonym Geoffrey Crayon, Gent., and containing both "Rip Van Winkle" and "The Legend of Sleepy Hollow." From Liverpool he had gone to Birmingham to stay with his brother-in-law on Calthorpe Road in Edgbaston. Out of this came another collection of stories and sketches called *Bracebridge Hall* (1822).

The original for Bracebridge Hall was Aston Hall. A fine Jacobean mansion in a park two and a half miles north of Birmingham's city center, the Hall is now a museum and well worth a visit. The building looks much as it did when completed in 1635, with a grand balustraded staircase, old fireplaces and gallery, and a kitchen with cooking equipment of the day.

The rooms' furnishings are seventeenth and eighteenth-century, and in one—of all things—is the original panelling from the Old Square House where Dr. Johnson used to visit his friend Edmund Hector.

If you do go to Aston, by the way, you might want to stop by the Victorian Bartons Arms Pub there. It's long been a favorite of performers at the Aston Hippodrome, so while you enjoy your drink or meal, you can revel in the ghosts of Caruso, Gracie Fields, Laurel and Hardy, and Charlie Chaplin hovering about you.

One nineteenth-century visitor to Birmingham who came and stayed was John Henry, Cardinal Newman. Converted to Roman Catholicism in 1846, he went to Birmingham as an Oratorian—an association of secular priests—to establish the first Oratory in England, on the Hagley Road. There he lived, in seclusion and service, for the rest of his life. And there he wrote that superb justification of his religious beliefs, *Apologia pro Vita sua* (1864). When he died in 1890, he was buried in a tiny cemetery in nearby Rednal, outside the chapel he had built for the Oratory fathers.

The school he established at the Oratory brought two other writers-to-be to Birmingham. The poet Gerard Manley Hopkins, himself converted to Catholicism by Newman, taught there for six months in 1868, but was most unhappy: "I must say [he wrote a friend] I am very anxious to get away from this place. I have become very weak in health and do not seem to recover myself here or am likely to do so. Teaching is very burdensome, especially when you have much of it: I have. [But] the boys are very nice indeed." A pupil at that same school in the late 1880s was that most prolific of writers, Hilaire Belloc.

Other writers who came to Birmingham for various reasons and lengths of time were Conan Doyle, Sax Rohmer, J.R.R. Tolkein, W. H. Auden, and Louis MacNeice.

Doyle, who arrived as a grown man after his invention of Sherlock Holmes transformed him from a doctor into a world-renowned author, lived for a time at 71 Aston Road. Sax Rohmer, creator of the malevolent Fu Manchu, lived as a child at Ladywood; and Tolkein, who wrote *The Hobbit* (1937) and the *Lord of the Rings* trilogy (1954–55), was educated at King Edward School in King's Norton.

Auden came to Birmingham from York as a boy, and was brought up there. MacNeice came as a freshly graduated Oxonian to teach classics at Birmingham University from 1930 to 1936. It was sheer coincidence that Auden had been MacNeice's fellow student and closest friend at Oxford, where together they had spearheaded a group of gifted but rambunctious undergraduates known as "The Gang."

Given the Gang's leftish leanings, it is not surprising that MacNeice should have been so harsh on the Birmingham industrial barons who

> . . . endeavour to find God and score one over
> the neighbor
> By climbing tentatively upward on jerry-built
> beauty and sweated labour.

But perhaps if MacNeice had written his "Birmingham" after World War II rather than before he might have written a poem with more emphasis on that other Birmingham—the Birmingham whose citizens faced with courage and remarkable energy the devastation of that war, and in the process swept away much of the ugliness the centuries had wrought.

And, who knows? Maybe one day some other young man will visit Birmingham for a while, and write just such a poem.

2. *Twenty Golden Miles: Coventry to Stratford-Upon-Avon*

Coventry

Many highways converge at Coventry. They include the A 444, the A 423, the A 46, and the A 427. In Saxon times, Coventry went by the name of Cofa's Tree, though nobody seems sure who Cofa was, or why his tree was so special. Ever since, the town has managed to get itself talked about, adding not only to our literature but to our language.

In the eleventh century, for instance, there was that matter of Lady Godiva and her ride on horseback. Five hundred years later somebody embellished an already good story by appending the detail of Peeping Tom. Beginning with the sixteenth-century cloth made in Coventry was good ("true blue"); but by the seventeenth-century people "sent" to Coventry were bad. And in the twentieth century "to coventrate" gained currency as a verb for Hitler's barbarity at its worst.

On a single night in November 1940, Nazi bombing leveled forty acres of Coventry's center, left only thirty of one thousand buildings unscathed, and—after the heroic rebuilding that followed—produced a Coventry of startling contrasts. The visitor to Coventry today might well take to heart what George Eliot's young Doctor Lydgate says in *Middlemarch* (1871–72). Her provincial manufacturing town called Middlemarch was the Coventry of the nineteenth century, but the words seem equally worth heeding now, though in a new sense: "I have made up my mind to take Middlemarch as it comes, and shall be much obliged if the town will take me in the same way. I have certainly found some charms in it which are much greater than I had expected."

Gone is the picturesque little town visited and described in George Eliot's own day by the American novelist Nathaniel Hawthorne: "Getting into the interior the the town . . . you find the streets very crooked, and some of them very narrow. I saw one place where it seemed possible to shake hands from one jutting storied old house to another."

Instead, there are a spanking new, much debated cathedral; the resolutely modern Upper Precinct shopping place with its dedicatory stone of Phoenix rising from the flames; and the landscaped Broadgate recreational area dominated by an all-too-twentieth-century statue of Lady Godiva.

Although this Godiva is a bit on the chunky side, there is no gainsaying the lady's right to her position of prominence. For she and her husband Leofric created Coventry. The Godiva of legend was a woman who kept nagging her spouse about the nasty taxes he levied on the people of Coventry. Finally he said, joking perhaps, he would remit them—but only if she'd ride naked through the town. So she did just that, covered only by the tresses of her long hair, after first asking everyone to be nice enough to stay indoors and not peek. And nobody did, except for a young tailor named Tom, who was struck blind on the spot for being so naughty.

Landor's "Imaginary Conversations" and Tennyson's "Lady Godiva," which is quoted on the Broadgate statue, are only two of the poems, stories, plays, even operas that have kept the legend alive. Paintings, too, have proliferated, including a version at Coventry's St. Michael's Hall that made the innocent New England eyes of Nathaniel Hawthorne pop: "a picture of the Countess Godiva on horse-back, in which the artist had been so niggardly of that illustrious lady's hair, that, if she had no ampler garniture, there was certainly much need for the good people of Coventry to shut their eyes."

The good people of Coventry aren't about to let you forget that story, either. Streets, businesses, and buildings with the names of Leofric and Godiva abound, including the elegant (four-star) Hotel Leofric in Broadgate. And if you'll stand in front of the arch over Hertford Street on the hour, you can watch the figures of Lady Godiva and Tom act out their story on the clock.

Just how true that story is, is probably beside the point. There is no written account of it earlier than two hundred years after it is supposed to have happened, when a thirteen-century chronicler recorded it. And, as indicated, no one even heard of the peeper named Tom until the sixteenth century. Besides, Leofric seems to have been much too decent a fellow to have been so beastly to his wife. For there really were a Leofric and a Godiva (or Godgyfu).

Leofric was the Earl of Mercia, whose realm included Cheshire, Staffordshire, and Shropshire, and whose main residence was in Chester. But apparently he was especially fond of Coventry. He and Lady Godiva founded a Benedictine monastery there in 1043, and lavished land and treasure upon it.

Leofric was a good businessman, too. He encouraged the development of local arts and trade. In particular, he gave the monks sheep, thus beginning the wool industry that was to make Coventry prosperous for the next five hundred years.

Through Lady Godiva, the Manor of Coventry passed to the Crown. One Lord of the Manor was Edward III's son, Edward the Black Prince. The gateway of his house still stands by the Registry Office. And it was this prince's son, Richard, whom Shakespeare shows in *Richard II* ordering Bolingbroke and the Duke of Norfolk to resolve their quarrel by hand-to-hand combat:

> At Coventry, upon St. Lambert's Day.
> There shall your swords and lances arbitrate
> The swelling difference of your settled hate.

The members of the crafts that Leofric started went on to form guilds and become the real powers of the city, especially those associated with the making and fashioning of cloth. Their impeccably dyed goods made "true as Coventry blue" a standard throughout Europe. Coventry's Puritanism became equally well known. During Cromwell's rebellion, captured Royalists were sometimes dispatched there for safekeeping. Though the citizens humanely allowed their prisoners on the street to stretch their legs, no one would speak a word to them. No wonder being sent to Coventry was no fun.

These same tradesmen contributed to the foundations of English drama in the Middle Ages, when crude presentations of Biblical stories called "miracles" were staged by the guilds of various towns. Of only four collections or "cycles" of such plays still in existence, one came from Coventry.[2] And the depiction of the Nativity from the Annunciation to the flight into Egypt put on by Coventry's Shearmen and Tailors is one of the best of them all.

Coventry's paramount literary association, of course, is with George Eliot. As Mary Anne Evans, she was born in 1819 at Astley, only a few miles to the northwest. When thirteen, she went to Coventry to attend Miss Franklin's School for Girls at 29 Warwick Road. Here she was taught to drop her countrified Midlands speech for the well-modulated, ladylike tones and somewhat high-flown diction of Miss Rebecca Franklin herself. She also learned French. In her school notebook, plain old Mary Anne became, in suitably florid script, "Marianne."

That same notebook contains a deliciously romantic sample of her first

---

[2]The others are from Chester, York, and Wakefield.

attempt at fiction, a handsome young hero who leans on a bridge over the River Wye at Chepstow, and "seemed as he gazed on the beautiful prospect before him to unbend the stern rigidity of his fine features, and a tear started to his eye."

But the rigors of Calvinism that Mary Anne heard Miss Franklin's father preach on Sundays at the Cow Lane Baptist Chapel sank deep, too. Thus may have developed the earnest didactic streak that marks her novels, the "passionate, ideal nature" she ascribes to the wide-eyed Theresa in *Middlemarch*.

She was back in Coventry at age twenty-one, when her father retired in 1841 to a large detached house called Bird Grove set back from Foleshill Road (now the site of George Eliot Road). She lived there for the next eight years, scandalizing Coventry society by her associations with Charles Bray, that notorious, free-thinking ribbonmaker who lived at Rosehill on Radford Road. And through him she met and impressed a visiting American writer named Ralph Waldo Emerson, whose views weren't all that orthodox either.

She also wrote reviews and essays for the *Coventry Herald*, but anonymously (her pseudonym wouldn't come until 1857). She tried her hand at a chapter or two of a novel about rural Staffordshire, but put it aside as "deficient in dramatic power both of construction and narrative." Even so, it was to prove the impetus for her career. Years later, when she showed it to George Henry Lewes, the man she lived with and ultimately married, he said simply, "Try and write a story." She did write a story, *Amos Barton*, and so was born "George Eliot."

Two twentieth-century writers with Coventry connections are George Orwell and E. M. Forster. Orwell began his walking tour for *The Road to Wigan Pier* at Coventry, arriving there by train one evening in January 1936. It was well into the night before he found lodgings—"very lousy," he said, and enhanced not at all by a "half-witted servant girl with a huge body, tiny head, and rolls of fat at the back of her neck." Early as he could next morning, he bounced out of bed and embarked on the hike to Birmingham, barely waiting for the breakfast part of his B & B.

In 1953, a London couple named John and Mary Buckingham moved to Coventry, and as a result, the city became almost a second home to E. M. Forster. He had been practically a father to the Buckinghams in London, and this he continued after their move. He helped them buy their house in the Coventry suburbs, maintained his own room there, and visited often. It was, he said, "very nice," if you didn't look out the window. The garden "forecast an allotment in hell."

In all, the arrangement lasted until his death seventeen years later, though the going got sticky toward the end. Forster became an increasingly difficult guest. Among his annoying habits were littering his bedroom floor with his clothes, and sticking his fingers in his ears while he made faces at the television set. Sometimes he would prolong his stay almost beyond endurance. But the devotion of Mary Buckingham never wavered. So long as Forster lived, she declared, her house would be his home.

It was there that they brought him in May of 1970, following a stroke in his Cambridge flat. And it was in her house, holding Mary's hand, that he fell asleep the night of June 7, and died.

Today's visitor to Coventry cannot expect to see much of its literary past still standing. The Nazis took care of that in 1940. But as Doctor Lydgate said, Coventry does have its charms.

The eighteen miles of the A 46 that wind between Coventry and Stratford-upon-Avon are highly rewarding. Not only do they link George Eliot country to the land of Shakespeare, but they pass a pair of castles rich in historical fact and fiction, and towns that involve writers ranging from Ben Jonson and Michael Drayton to Samuel Johnson and Sir Walter Scott, Charles Dickens, John Masefield, and T. S. Eliot.

Kenilworth Castle

Mention of Kenilworth immediately makes you think of that romantic fictional castle created by Sir Walter Scott in his novel, *Kenilworth* (1821). But there was and is a real Kenilworth Castle, steeped in tales of intrigue and derring-do that go back to centuries before Scott was born. Kenilworth, a considerable town of over twenty thousand people, is barely six miles below Coventry, and its castle perches above a bend in the A 452 at the northwest edge.

Begun by a retainer of Henry I about 1120, the fortress was extensively added to by later owners, especially the fourteenth-century John of Gaunt, Chaucer's patron, and the sixteenth-century Robert Dudley, Earl of Leicester, favorite of Queen Elizabeth. By 1600, Kenilworth ranked as one of England's most redoubtable castles, notable for its great size (over seven acres) and the extent of its water defenses. The walls of its keep were up to seventeen feet thick; the protective lake, formed by damming two streams, covered more than one hundred acres.

Scott was by no means the first to turn its history to literary use. The castle is the "Killingworth" of Christopher Marlowe's play *Edward II*, where that unhappy monarch was imprisoned by his "unnatural queen" and her lover Mortimer. The Earl of Leicester (not Elizabeth's friend, but a fourteenth-century forbear) urges the king to

> Be patient, good my lord, cease to lament
> Imagine Killingworth Castle were your court
> And that you lay for pleasure here a space. . . .

But Edward will hear none of it—and with good reason. Within months he is forced to resign the throne to his son, taken off to Berkeley Castle in Gloucestershire, and brutally murdered.[3]

The castle proved happier for Edward's descendant Henry V, providing Shakespeare with a rollicking scene for his play *Henry V*. The French Dolphin (Dauphin) taunts young Henry for his playboy past by sending him a barrel of tennis balls as more befitting his character than waging war with France. Says Henry amiably:

> We are glad the Dolphin is so pleasant with us. . . .
> When we have match'd our rackets to these balls,
> We will in France, by God's grace, play a set
> Shall strike his father's crown into the hazard.

Which, of course, Henry does, smashing the French king's army at Agincourt, and marrying his daughter to boot.

During the reign of Elizabeth I, Kenilworth was the seat of one of England's great powers, for the queen was devoted to its owner, the Earl of Leicester. She stayed there as his guest on at least four occasions, at "excessive cost." The lavishness of her host's entertainment is attested by the masque, *The Princely Pleasures of Kenelworth [sic] Castle* (1576) by the contemporary poet and playwright George Gascoigne, and vividly described by Scott. Another guest of the earl's, and no doubt less costly, was his celebrated nephew Sir Philip Sidney, no mean poet himself.

Leicester's secret marriage to Amy Robsart and his efforts to keep this from Elizabeth form the basis of Scott's *Kenilworth*, and the castle is the scene of its climactic events. While the queen is visiting there, Leicester orders Amy to appear, posing as the wife of his henchman Varney. Instead, she

[3]For details see pp. 139–40.

arrives secretly to seek recognition as Leicester's countess. Suspicious and jealous, Elizabeth finally forces Leicester to acknowledge the marriage— too late for Amy, alas. By then Varney has dragged her back to her Oxford hideaway and done her in.

Leicester's title became extinct at his death in 1588. By a nice happenstance, however, another nephew, Robert Sidney—Sir Philip's younger brother—became a protegé of Elizabeth's successor, James I. James revived the title and gave it to Robert. Kenilworth's spectacular dramatic entertainments continued, too. Ben Jonson's extravaganza, *The Masque of the Owls*, was performed there in 1624.

Later in the seventeenth century, Cromwell's forces took over Kenilworth and destroyed much of it, but spared the Great Hall built by Gaunt and the Gatehouse modernized by Elizabeth Leicester.

In the nineteenth century, Scott's novel made the castle a major tourist attraction. During her days at Coventry, George Eliot loved to show it off to visitors. Charles Dickens loved it, too. In *Dombey and Son*, he has Dombey take a holiday in Leamington, including "a stroll among the haunted ruins of Kenilworth."

The American journeyman writer, Elbert Hubbard—remembered now if at all for his *Message to Garcia* (1899)—made a point of stopping at the "quaint and curious little inn, just across from the castle entrance," and taking the very room Scott had occupied as he wrote the first chapter of *Kenilworth*. In one of his *Little Travels*, Hubbard waxes embarrassingly cute about the castle itself: "I dreamed of playing 'I-spy' through Kenilworth with Shakespeare, Walter Scott, Mary Ann Evans, and a youth I used to know in boyhood by the name of Bill Hursey. . . . Finally Shakespeare was 'it,' but he got mad and refused to play."

At last report, Scott's (and Hubbard's) hotel, The King's Arms, was still in business, and still offering you Scott's room with its "big canopy affair" of a bed. And the castle, now owned by the government, is open to the public all year round.

Warwick

Since the town of Warwick and its castle are but five miles southwest of Kenilworth, both can be seen in a day if you're stout of heart and fleet of foot—and don't care all that much about castles anyway. For Warwick Castle particularly has much to see.

Indeed, castle-collectors of the highest calibre sing its praises. Sir Walter

Scott called it "the noblest sight in England." American novelist Nathaniel Hawthorne went on and on about the "gray magnificence of Warwick Castle." And Ruth McKenney, author of *My Sister Eileen*, whose *Here's England* remains, after nearly forty years, one of the most readable (and reliable) of travel books, declares it "the best all-around castle in my experience." To Charles Dickens's "Cousin Feenex" in *Dombey and Son* it's appeal never dims: "He has been to Warwick Castle fifty times," says Mrs. Skewton, "if he has been there once; yet if he came to Leamington tomorrow—I wish he would, dear Angel!—he would make his fifty-second visit next day."

The town of Warwick (WAR-rick, of course) is of great antiquity. Hawthorne remarks on a "huge mass of rock" in the western part of town "penetrated by a vaulted passage, which may as well have been one of King Cymbeline's original gateways." He repeats the legend that Warwick was founded by Cymbeline "in the year ONE of the Christian era," and muses about Shakespeare's play *Cymbeline:* ". . . perhaps it was in the landscape now under our eyes that Posthumus wandered with the King's daughter, the sweet, chaste, faithful, and courageous Imogen."

The name Warwick comes from the Anglo-Saxon Waerincwic— "waerinc" (village), by the "wic" (dam)—and more likely Alfred the Great's daughter Ethelfleda, rather than Cymbeline, was its founder in the tenth century. A great fire in 1694 wiped out over 450 buildings and left hundreds homeless, but also offered a chance to build a new town that remains one of the Midlands' most attractive.

Georgian architecture abounds, naturally, but is blended with gabled and timber-framed buildings that survived the flames. Especially worth the visiting are Lord Leycester (sic) Hospital, established for Elizabeth's needy war veterans by her beloved Leicester in 1571, and St. Mary's Church. Much of St. Mary's had to be rebuilt after the fire, but the florid fifteenth-century Beauchamp Chapel still stands, with the grandiose tomb of Richard Beauchamp, Earl of Warwick, who died in 1439.

This is the de Beauchamp of George Bernard Shaw's play, *Saint Joan*, the English nobleman who lets the French burn Joan at the stake, though he murmurs, "I am sorry for the girl. I hate these severities."

To the north of the church choir is the tomb of Sir Philip Sidney's friend Sir Fulke Greville, poet, author of two tragedies and the *Life of Sidney* (1652). By the church entrance is a bust of Walter Savage Landor. The house where Landor was born in 1775, another survivor of the great fire, can still be seen, too, near the foot of Castle Hill.

There was some sort of fortification on that hill as far back as Ethelfleda's time, and William the Conquerer's Henry de Newburgh erected a keep there in the eleventh century. But the greater part of the masonry for which the castle is famous was the work of Thomas Beauchamp, Earl of Warwick, who died in 1369.

Few of his successors were able to resist an urge to add their own embellishments. In consequence, today's edifice is a melange of Norman, Medieval, Tudor, Jacobean, Renaissance, Georgian, and Regency. Fulke Greville, who took over the place in 1604, spent the then prodigious sum of £20,000 on his additions. His descendant Francis Greville's innovations aroused the wrath of poet Thomas Gray, who wrote his friend Dr. Wharton: "He has sash'd the great Appartment, that's to be sure [by putting] certain whim-whams withinside the glass [and has] scooped out a little Burrow in the massy walls of the place for his little self & his children." Gray continues with a snort: "What in short can a Lord do now a days that is lost in a great solitary Castle, but skulk about, & get into the first hole he finds, as a Rat would do in like case." And Francis's son got so carried away with his own projects that he was forced into bankruptcy.

Warwick Castle, in fact, was anything but a good luck charm for many of its masters. The Thomas Beauchamp who built all that masonry rather foolishly picked the wrong side in a revolt against Richard II and wound up in the Tower of London. He did get one slight consolation: the place where he was kept has been known ever since as the Beauchamp Tower.

Richard Neville, the "King-maker" of Shakespeare's Henry VI plays, who gained the title in 1449 through marriage, tried to do better during the Wars of the Roses by picking *both* sides, first the Yorks, then the Lancasters—and was a two-time loser. After he helped Edward of York supplant Lancastrian Henry VI as king, the Yorks snubbed him. So he went over to the Lancastrians, and the Yorks finished him off at the Battle of Barnet in 1471.

Neville's daughter Anne, young widow of Henry's heir, fared no better. As Shakespeare shows in *Richard III*, Richard talks her into marrying him to enhance his plot to succeed his eldest brother, Edward IV. That accomplished, Anne, not so mysteriously, turns up dead.

Unhappily for them, the next two Earls of Warwick also fell afoul of Richard. For they happened to be Richard's middle brother Clarence, and Clarence's son Edward, both closer than Richard in line of succession. So Clarence winds up starring in one of the most bizarre murders of all time. Richard has him drowned in a barrel of wine. As for Edward, only eight years old but now Earl of Warwick nonetheless, Richard tucks him away in the Tower.

After slaying Richard at Bosworth Field in 1485, Henry Richmond (Henry VII) inherits both the throne and the problem of what to do with young Edward. Henry, whose claim to the throne was even shakier than Richard's, thinks it over carefully for fourteen years before he comes to the obvious decision: Edward Plantagenet, Earl of Warwick, age twenty-five, is beheaded.

In the next two centuries, other possessors of Warwick Castle came to untimely ends. One sixteenth-century earl was John Dudley, who continued his forerunners' predilection for choosing the wrong side by backing Lady Jane Grey's abortive nine-day reign. He died on the block in 1554.

The castle jinx caught up with Sidney's chum, Sir Fulke Greville, in the seventeenth century. It not only cost him that £20,000, but in 1628 he was stabbed to death by a faithful old servant who somehow got the idea that he had been slighted in Greville's will. Sir Fulke's spectre still haunts the castle. One of the turrets bears a double name: the Ghost—or Watergate—Tower.

For all this, the castle continues as a family home, as it has been for a longer unbroken period than almost any other in the kingdom. It has become a thriving business, too, open to the public every day of the year except Christmas, and served by a special open-top bus tour that links Stratford, Warwick, and Kenilworth.

On view are priceless paintings, furniture, and *objets d'art*, as well as a gallimaufry of mementoes. Among these are the death mask of Oliver Cromwell, the camp-kettle of Warwick the Kingmaker, and a tiny suit of armor, fashioned for a young Warwick who probably didn't find much use for it: he never made it to his fourth birthday. There's also the very sword, we're told, with which an early Warwick saved England by slaying the Danish giant Colbrand, immortalized in an interminable fourteenth-century verse romance entitled *Guy of Warwick*.

Even Madame Tussaud's is there, but brace yourself. Twenty-nine wax figures fill twelve whole rooms, depicting "A Royal Weekend Party 1898," including Miss Clara Butt and Signor Paoli Tussi singing their hearts out to a group of elegant guests.

Maybe you'd better not plan to do Kenilworth and Warwick in a single day after all.

Leamington Spa

Leamington's full, resounding name is Royal Leamington Spa. *Royal* because when young Princess Victoria first visited it in 1830, she was so pleased she officially granted it that title soon after she became queen in 1837. *Leamington* because it is on the Leam River, a tributary of the Avon described by the Elizabethan poet, Michael Drayton, as "high complexioned Leam," and by Nathaniel Hawthorne as "greenish goose-puddly," and "the laziest river in the world." *Spa* because in Victoria's day salty underground springs made Leamington and its Pump Room one of England's most fashionable health resorts. Renovated in 1925, the Pump Room still draws over fifty thousand people a year seeking relief for various rheumatic aches and pains.

Warwick and Leamington are practically one city, lying only two miles apart and joined by the A 445. With forty-five thousand or more people, Leamington (LEM-ing-ton) is double the size of its neighbor, and especially about the north bank of the river has a decidedly late Georgian-Regency look to it.

Aside from those underground waters and its genteel air, Leamington's chief attraction may well be its proximity to more heralded tourist lures. Kenilworth and Warwick Castles are literally right down the road, of course. Stratford-upon-Avon, Rugby, and Coventry are within fifteen miles or less.

Indeed, both Hawthorne and Charles Dickens made Leamington their headquarters for tours of the region. It is at Leamington that Dombey's friend Major Bagstock introduces him to Mrs. Skewton and her daughter Edith, who later becomes the second Mrs. Dombey.

Hawthorne's Clarendon Hotel, rated by him "by far the most splendid hotel I have yet seen in England" finally succumbed to age a few years ago, but Dickens's Regent Hotel, a big, white Regency building on The Parade survives, with a fascinating history of its own.

In the early nineteenth century a man with the enchanting name of Bertie Bertie Greatheed had a butler and housekeeper called John Williams and Sarah Denby. He encouraged them to marry and, with his blessings, open the Williams Hotel in 1819, then the largest in Europe. Within weeks the place so impressed the Prince Regent, son of George III, that he allowed them to rename it The Regent and to bear his arms and crest. Victoria's visit as princess reaffirmed this royal stamp of approval. Even if she did come equipped with her own bed, she could hardly be faulted. It was the first public building she had ever slept in.

Today there's a "Heritage Board" in the Regent's entrance lobby with the names of seventy of the celebrities who have stayed there during the nearly two hundred years of its life. It's fun to stand in front of the board and see how many of these names you can identify.

The likes of Charles Abbott, Charles Blondin, and Henry "Napper"

Tandy may well stump you. (Abbott was the first son of a hairdresser to become Chief Justice of England. Blondin crossed Niagara Falls on a tight rope three times. In World War I Tandy almost single-handedly captured thirty-seven members of the German army, including a corporal named Adolf Hitler.)

You'll have better luck with William Gladstone, Robert Peel, the Duke of Wellington, Winston Churchill, and Anthony Eden—prime ministers all— and the American president, Ulysses S. Grant. A miscellany that might provide a mixed challenge is the Earl of Elgin, Empress Eugénie, Henry Morton Stanley, and the Earl of Cardigan. Elgin is the one who managed to get those "marbles" moved from the Parthenon in Athens to The British Museum in London. Eugénie was the wife of Napoleon III and briefly a patron of the American writer Ambrose Bierce. Stanley correctly presumed he had found Dr. Livingstone in Africa. And Cardigan's recklessness at Balaclava was immortalized by Tennyson in "The Charge of the Light Brigade."

You'll revel in the large roster of stage people: Sarah Bernhardt, Sarah Siddons, Jenny Lind, Clara Butt, William Charles Macready, Ramon Navarro, Douglas Fairbanks, Sr., and Margaret Lockwood.

Writers who graced The Regent will provide no problem either. Charles Dickens stayed there on several of his reading tours. The American satirist Artemus Ward and poet Henry Wadsworth Longfellow came with their families. John Ruskin arrived for six weeks to drink the waters and recover from "over work" as a student at Oxford. He whiled away the time by writing his delightful "King of the Golden River" (1851).

Backed by such credentials, The Regent goes right on living up to its three-star billing, and serving the hearty English meals that earned one of these luminaries a notable dressing down. The hotel's cuisine, apparently, tempted Ruskin beyond his forbearance. One day his physician unexpectedly burst into his rooms and found him munching away at strictly forbidden fare.

"Sir," said the doctor, "you may trifle with your health, but not with my reputation. Good day!"

Stratford-upon-Avon

One could spend a lifetime in Stratford-upon-Avon, visiting or writing about it—and people have. But there's no need to. The formula is simple: TTA ÷ MS = TE. Total Time Available ÷ "Musts" to See = Time for

Each. But it does take planning and self-discipline. For, admittedly, Stratford is unique. Over five hundred thousand visitors from all over the world come there each year. A list of the writers alone who have come to pay homage to the greatest of them all would be well-nigh endless. It is hard indeed to think of Stratford as anything other than one unmitigated shrine to William Shakespeare.

But Shakespeare didn't grow up in a shrine. The Stratford he knew was a typical Warwickshire town.

And Stratford the typical Warwickshire town remains. By no means do all its twenty-three thousand people survive by catering to tourists. Small business men still ply their small businesses as they have since long before Shakespeare's father was a glover or wool dealer. On the outskirts, farmers still raise their produce and bring it to the weekly market, as they have ever since Richard I granted them the privilege in the twelfth century, four hundred years before Shakespeare's birth. The playwright's mother's family, the Ardens, were just such farmers.

Romans had occupied the place centuries before the Ardens, and Celts long before the Romans. The name of the town suggests why. It was the best spot for the "straet" (street) coming east from Bidford to ford the ever-wandering Avon River. By Shakespeare's day, Stratford's basic town plan, a medieval grid, was already established. John Leland, the antiquarian writer who died a dozen years before Shakespeare was born, wrote that it had "two or three very lardge streets, besyde bake lanes. The town is reasonably well buyldyd of tymbar." Moreover, according to Leland, it already had the handsome fourteen-arched bridge that now serves the A 34 as the entry to Stratford from Oxford, and that Shakespeare must have crossed many a time while growing up. It was the gift, interestingly enough, of Sir Hugh Clopton, builder of one of Stratford's finest houses, New Place, which Shakespeare was to buy and retire to in 1611 on the profits from such London stage hits as *Hamlet, Othello, Lear,* and *Macbeth.*

Clopton, who became Lord Mayor of London in 1491, was one of Stratford's most generous benefactors. In itemizing his bounty, Leland singles out the bridge: "He made also the great and sumptuous bridge upon Avon at the este end of the town. Before there was but a poore bridge of tymbar, and no causey [causeway] to come to it."

Coming in from Birmingham, the A 34 is also one of Stratford's two major entries from the north. The other is the A 46 from Coventry and Warwick. Both highways will take you within blocks of Shakespeare's birthplace as well as most of Stratford's major hotels. Whether you drive in for the day or plan to stay overnight or longer, you'll find the birthplace a sensible starting

STRATFORD-UPON-AVON

1. The Birthplace
2. Shakespeare Centre
3. Quiney's House
4. Harvard House
5. Nash's House
6. New Place
7. Theatre Picture Gallery and Museum
8. The Royal Shakespeare Theatre
9. Gower Memorial
10. Clopton Bridge
11. Guild Chapel
12. Stratford Grammar School
13. Mason Croft
14. Hall's Croft
15. Holy Trinity

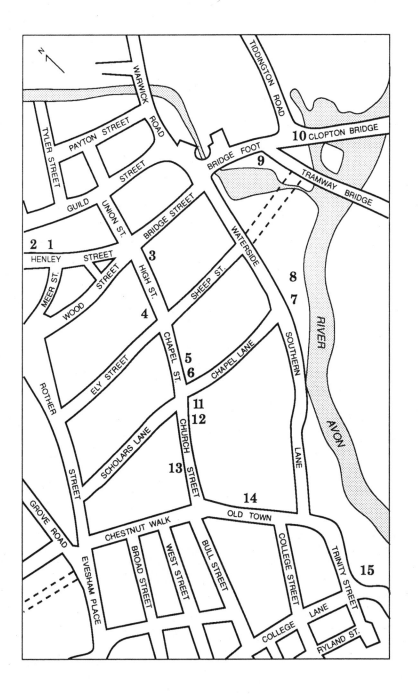

point for a tour of the town's highlights. By all means a walking tour! Parking a car anywhere near the various stops is out of the question. Besides, the route outlined below is easy walking and only about a mile and a half in all.

A Literary Tour of Stratford

1. Begin almost halfway down Henley Street at THE BIRTHPLACE. Here, in the half-timbered cottage on your left as you stroll towards Bridge Street and the river, William Shakespeare was born on or about April 23, 1564. What you see now was then two separate little buildings and the whole has been considerably restored since it was acquired for the nation in 1847. John Shakespeare used the building on the right for his shop; the family lived in the other. Its ground floor, their living room and kitchen, with what is believed to be the original broken stone floor, is now sparsely furnished with furniture of the sixteenth and seventeenth centuries such as the Shakespeares might be supposed to have used.

A narrow staircase leads to the tiny bedrooms, the one directly above the living room being the actual birth room. Most visitors react to its cramped dimensions much as Hawthorne did when he came in mid-nineteenth century: "we have to reconcile ourselves to the smallness of the space enclosed by these illustrious walls. . . . A few paces—perhaps seven or eight—take us from end to end of it. So low it is, that I could easily touch the ceiling, and might have done so without a tip-toe stretch, had it been a good deal higher." Hawthorne observes that "this humility of the chamber has tempted a vast multitude of people to write their names overhead in pencil. Every inch of the sidewalls, even the obscurest nooks and corners, is covered."

Even the most illustrious of visitors succumbed to such vanity. Among those who scrawled on the walls were Dickens, Thackeray, Browning, and Edmund Kean. Scratched on the window panes are the signatures of Sir Walter Scott, Isaac Watts, Thomas Carlyle, Alfred Tennyson, Henry Irving, and Ellen Terry.

The section of the house that was John Shakespeare's shop now serves as a museum, with documents, books, and a desk from the Stratford Grammar School said to have been Shakespeare's.

In the garden surrounding the cottage grow specimens of the various flowers, herbs, shrubs and trees mentioned in Shakespeare's plays and poems.

2. Flanking this garden is the SHAKESPEARE CENTRE completed in 1964,

containing the libraries of the Shakespeare Birthplace Trust and the Royal Shakespeare Theatre, and facilities for study.

3. Now continue to the end of Henley and turn right. On the corner (with Bridge Street) is QUINEY'S HOUSE, where Shakespeare's daughter Judith lived with her husband, Thomas Quiney, a wine merchant. You'll find it a useful stop. It's now the Tourist Information Centre.

4. At the end of this block, on the right, just before High crosses Sheep Street and becomes Chapel Street, is the HARVARD HOUSE. It was built in 1596 by Thomas Rogers, a butcher, who might well be called the grandfather of Harvard University. His daughter Katherine married a Robert Harvard of London, and their son John Harvard went off to Cambridge, Massachusetts, and in 1638 helped found what is now one of the greatest universities in the United States.

Continue on past the Town Hall down Chapel Street to where it intersects with what on your right is called Scholars Lane and on your left Chapel Lane. This area abounds with things to see. Nash's House, Guild Chapel and Almshouses, the Guildhall, Stratford Grammar School, New Place, the Theatre Picture Gallery, and Royal Shakespeare Theatre all lie within three hundred yards.

5. First comes NASH'S HOUSE at the south end of Chapel Street, almost at the corner it shares with Chapel Lane. Thomas Nash was the husband of Shakespeare's granddaughter, Elizabeth Hall, and his noteworthy timber-framed dwelling is now a museum depicting Stratford's history from prehistoric times, and giving you a good sense of the town that Shakespeare knew.

6. Immediately up Chapel Lane (ignoring for the moment Guild Chapel and the Guildhall) on your left as you proceed east is where NEW PLACE stood, the house that Sir Clopton built, that Shakespeare retired to in 1611, and died in on April 23, 1616, his fifty-second birthday. Today only the Great Garden and the building's foundations remain, but they indicate how impressive Shakespeare's final home must have been. (The adjoining Knott Garden, a beautiful replica of an enclosed Elizabethan garden, is well worth seeing, too.)

New Place, along with a celebrated mulberry tree said to have been planted by Shakespeare himself, was pulled down in 1759 by its crotchety owner, the Rev. Francis Gastrell, incensed over a tax assessment. But the town struck back. Gastrell, it is recorded, left town "amidst the rages and curses of the inhabitants" who passed a law that no one of that name should ever be allowed to live there again.

The outrage has never died. In July of 1853 during a visit to Stratford, a young Dante Gabriel Rossetti, only twenty-five and yet to win fame either as a poet or painter, was so worked up he dashed off a sonnet, "On the Site of a Mulberry Tree planted by Wm. Shakespeare; felled by the Rev. F. Gastrell." In it, Rossetti says that even such classic scoundrels as the notorious highwaymen, John Sheppard and Dick Turpin—both hanged for their sins, hence their black tongues—would lament that of all the great dastards of history, Gastrell stands out as the "supreme unhung."

> Lo! Sheppard, Turpin, pleading with black tongue
> This viler thief's unsuffocated breath!

The Poet Laureate John Masefield found the poem a "playful frolic."

7–8. Chapel Lane quickly ends at Waterside, between which and the river bank are the THEATRE PICTURE GALLERY AND MUSEUM and THE ROYAL SHAKESPEARE THEATRE. The Gallery and Museum has paintings by Sir Joshua Reynolds, George Romney, and others; and costumes and relics of noted Shakespearean figures, among them Sarah Siddons, David Garrick, Dame Ellen Terry, and Sir Henry Irving.

The theater, controversial in style when built in 1932 but quite accepted now, continues the tradition of high-quality productions of the whole range of Shakespeare's plays established by John Gielgud, Ralph Richardson, Michael Redgrave, Peggy Ashcroft, Laurence Oliver, Vivien Leigh, and others.

9. About two hundred yards further along the river bank—above the theatre and past the Bancroft Gardens—is the GOWER MEMORIAL, unveiled in 1888 with Oscar Wilde as one of the speakers. Beneath a towering seated figure of Shakespeare are four life-size characters from his plays: Hamlet, symbolizing philosophy; Lady Macbeth, tragedy; Falstaff, comedy, and Henry V, history.

10. Beyond the memorial to the right, CLOPTON BRIDGE spans the Avon with its fourteen arches of mellowed gray stone.

Retracing your steps down Chapel Lane now to its junction with Church Street (across from Nash's House) takes you to the Guild Chapel on the corner and the Almshouses bending around down Church. Just southwest of the Guild Chapel are the Grammar School and Guildhall.

11. The GUILD CHAPEL is another gift of Clopton, who paid for the fifteenth-century remodelling of the thirteenth-century original. Shakespeare would have attended morning services here as a schoolboy.

12. The STRATFORD GRAMMAR SCHOOL, two hundred and fifty years old when it was refounded by Edward VI eleven years before Shakespeare's birth, was (and is) on the upper floor of a two-storey building. Beneath the

room where Shakespeare would have been taught his "small Latin and less Greek"—in Ben Jonson's famous words—was the old Guild Hall. It was used in those days by companies of travelling actors, and may have provided the boy Shakespeare with his first intimation that "all the world's a stage."

13. Near the end of Church Street, on the right, is MASON CROFT, the eighteenth-century house where the novelist Marie Corelli (Mary Mackey) lived from 1899 until her death in 1924. Her books, overwrought and more than pretentious in style though they seem now, were vastly popular. Gladstone and Tennyson admired her, and she was the favorite author of Queen Victoria, who predicted her name would outlast those of George Eliot and Charles Dickens.

Mme. Corelli was hardly that adored by her Stratford neighbors, however. They laughed at her tooling up and down the Avon in a gondola called The Dream, and raged at her attempts to be manager-in-chief of all things Shakespearean. It was through her efforts, though, that Harvard House was bought and restored, and she charmed Mark Twain when she guided him through it.

14. From Church Street it is only a bend to the left and a few steps down Old Town to triple-gabled HALL'S CROFT, home of Shakespeare's daughter Susannah and her husband John Hall, an eminent Stratford physician. Today its dispensary and collection of flasks, jars, utensils and other paraphernalia of a Jacobean surgery offer a fascinating glimpse of seventeenth-century medicine. And think of what pride Shakespeare—he was only a playwright, after all, however successful—must have taken in introducing "my son-in-law, the doctor."

15. A short turn to the right down Trinity Street winds up the walking tour of Stratford proper at HOLY TRINITY, a lovely old riverside church dating back to the thirteenth century. Beneath the floor of the chancel is Shakespeare's tomb, guarded from the wall above by his life-size bust, carved in 1623 and presumed to be reasonably accurate. Also in the chancel is the broken fifteenth-century font in which he would have been baptized, and photos of the register entries of his baptism and burial.

Weary of all this sightseeing? Stratford has an abundance of good hotels and pubs to provide a refreshing drink, a reviving meal, or a restful night's sleep, a number of them with ties to Shakespeare.

Whoever in 1611 lived in what is now The Falcon (three-stars) in Chapel Street, for instance, would have been his neighbor. Then a private home, it became an inn in 1640, and in 1924 was the site of the founding of The Shakespeare Club. What's more, it has some of the panelling from New Place itself.

Shakespeare would have known the original section of what is now the four-star Shakespeare Hotel, too, also on Chapel Street. In the fifteenth century, it may have been a part of Sir Hugh Clopton's Great House. It wasn't until the eighteenth century that it became an inn, much patronized by actors who came to do Shakespeare.

The White Swan (three-star) in Rother Street, on the other hand, was already a hotel in Shakespeare's day, called The King's Head. Surely the creator of Falstaff, lover of inns and tap-rooms as he was, must have ambled over to it now and then from New Place to sample a tankard or two. The building still has some of the beams and panelling it had then, and in 1927 when the Jacobean walls of the living room were stripped, rare paintings from about 1560 were uncovered. Pictured is the Apocrypha's story of Tobias and the Angel—but the figures wear the Tudor clothes of Shakespeare's youth!

An interesting pub is The Black Swan in Waterside, fondly known as the "Dirty Duck." Just down the way from The Memorial Theatre, it has long been a favorite of actors. Like as not, if you go there for lunch you'll be bumping elbows with someone who will be Hamlet, Romeo, or maybe even Falstaff himself when you go to theatre that night.

One last word about both theatre and hotels, though: BOOK EARLY!

Shottery—Wilmcote—Charlecote Park— and Alveston

Three of the best-known places associated with Shakespeare are his mother's family home, the cottage where he wooed and won his wife, and the park where he allegedly poached deer. None of these, of course, is actually in Stratford. But Shottery, Wilmcote, and Charlecote, in that order, are all within walking distance (or so the hardy insist). Equally close is the hamlet of Alveston, which inspired yet another sonnet from D. G. Rossetti, in addition to "Mulberry Tree," during his stay in Stratford.

Shottery   Shottery is the easiest of these to walk to. It is only a mile to the northwest via the footpath off Evesham Place below Rother Street. But you can also take a bus, or drive there on Shottery Road (the A 422). At Shottery, in a sizeable timbered and thatched dwelling now called Anne Hathaway's Cottage, an eighteen-year-old William Shakespeare courted and won twenty-six-year-old Anne, daughter of a prosperous farmer.

It is a rewarding place to visit, for it was continuously owned and lived in by Hathaways until 1892, when the Birthplace Trust bought it. Wonderfully restored after a near-disastrous fire in 1969, it gives you a good feel of how folks lived in the playwright's day. There are some original pieces of Hathaway furniture, including their old oak four-poster bed, and the famous "courting settle" designed to keep over-passionate young lovers discreetly separated. Much good it did William and Anne. Their daughter Susannah was born scarcely six months after their wedding.

Among other treats are the stone-flagged kitchen with its bake oven and long-handled bread peel (shovel), and a Tudor candle and dining table of special interest to word-lovers. The candle is a small iron stand holding a "taper" (a fat-dipped weed about an inch wide) that could be lighted at one end and slowly drawn along through a slot as it was consumed. To give a brighter light, each end could be lighted simultaneously. But then, of course, you'd be burning your candle at both ends.

The table has a removable top, a board that slides out so either side can be used as needed: the elegant, shiny upper surface to show off to company, or the rough, burned and stained bottom side when the family got down to the actual business of eating. Turning the tables made good sense in those days.

Wilmcote   Another mile and a half northwest off the A 422 is Wilmcote (WILM-cut), the even more satisfying and much more rural site of the house where Mary Arden, Shakespeare's mother, grew up with her family, stout yeomen allied to the Ardens of Park Hall. Her handsome sixteenth-century home of timbered oak beams and native stone suggests all too clearly that Miss Arden did indeed marry beneath herself when in 1557 she married that John Shakespeare from nearby Snitterfield, just making a start as a Stratford tradesman.

By one good stroke of fortune, the place remained a working farm until well into the twentieth century, so its gabled brick barns, its stable, cider-mill, and square stone dovecote remain as they were in Mary's day, forming the nucleus of what's got to be a farming museum as fine as any in England. By another good stroke, following the death of Mary's father his possessions were fully inventoried, providing an invaluable blueprint of furnishings for the Birthplace Trust to consult when it acquired the place in 1930.

Charlecote Park   Four miles east of Stratford off the B 4088 is Charlecote (CHAR-li-cut) Park, one of the area's grand mansions and since medieval times the home of the Lucys. Here, according to eighteenth-century playwright Nicholas Rowe, twenty-one-year-old Shakespeare suffered "a Blem-

ish upon his good Manners" so severe "he was oblig'd to leave his Business and Family in Warwickshire for some time, and shelter himself in London."
    William, in short, was "engaged . . . more than once in robbing a Park [of deer] that belong'd to Sir Thomas Lucy of Cherlecot [sic]. For this he was prosecuted by that Gentleman." Ironically, so the story goes, it was Shakespeare's ensuing flight that led to his first involvement with the London stage.
    And so, Rowe continues cheerily, "it afterwards happily prov'd the occasion of exerting one of the greatest Genius's that ever was known in Dramatick Poetry." Moreover, says Rowe, Shakespeare took his revenge in *The Merry Wives of Windsor* by satirizing Lucy as the outlandish Justice Swallow.
    What a thrill it is to go to Charlecote Park yourself, and feed the descendants of the same animals that Shakespeare poached, as Hawthorne did in the visit he recorded in *Our Old Home* (1863): ". . . most probably, the stag that Shakespeare killed was one of the progenitors of this very herd . . . and it may have been his observation of the tamer characteristics in the Charlecote herd that suggested to Shakespeare the tender and pitiful description of a wounded stag in *As You Like It.*"
    The trouble is, facts keep getting in the way of such romantic speculation. The Lucys had no enclosed deer park in Shakespeare's day. And since whatever deer there were would have run wild, his sin at best would have been trespassing, hardly a prison offense. Moreover, the deer would have been a different breed, the red-skinned roe, not the yellow-hued fallow deer of today.
    And finally, Shakespeare harbored no grudge against the Lucys. On the contrary, in *Henry IV Part I,* he makes Sir William Lucy, a forebear of his supposed Charlecote prosecutor, a dauntless figure who demands that the French give back the bodies of valiant Lord Talbot and other English nobles killed at Boulogne. Says the French leader of Lucy,

> I think this upstart is old Talbot's ghost,
> He speaks with such a proud commanding spirit.
> For God's sake let him have 'em.

The French leader? No less than Joan of Arc herself.
    Legend or no, however, you can still go see Charlecote Park if you like. Open to the public most days of the week April to October, it's a pleasant enough mixture of original Tudor and unobjectionable Victorian, surrounded by the grounds so lovingly described by Henry James in *English Hours:* "innumerable acres, stretching away, in the early evening, to vaguely

seen Tudor Walls, lie there like the backward years receding to the age of Elizabeth."

Alveston   On your way to Charlecote Park, you'll pass a cluster of houses called Alveston. In the summer of 1853, Dante Gabriel Rossetti walked out there from Stratford, climbed a hill, and saw a glorious sunset. But as he trudged down again and the slopes darkened, he was overwhelmed by the sense that his life, too, was descending into darkness, though he was only twenty-five.

The result was his beautiful sonnet, "The Hill Summit," with its haunting final lines:

> And now that I have climbed and won this height
> I must tread downward through the sloping shade
> And travel the bewildered tracks till night,
> Yet for this hour I still may here be stayed
> And see the gold air and the silver fade
> And the last bird fly into the last light.

3. Rugby, Nuneaton, and Neighbors

Upper Warwickshire engulfs the eastern extremities of West Midlands on three sides, looking as if it would swallow poor Coventry whole at any moment. Crowding in upon that city are Nuneaton, a scant eight miles to the north, and Rugby, only twelve miles to the east. Both are easily reached from Coventry—Nuneaton by way of the A 444, and Rugby on the A 428.

Rugby   Almost everybody has heard of Rugby, where in the nineteenth century one glorious burst of boyish defiance contributed a unique element to the game now known the world over as football. A marble tablet at the local school proclaims . . . "the exploit of William Webb Ellis, who, with a fine disregard for the Rules of Football as played in his time, first took the ball in his arms and ran with it, thus originating the distinctive feature of the Rubgy Game. A. D. 1823"

Far more important than Rugby's contribution to sports, however, are its gifts to literature, especially since 1827, when an obscure young translator of Thucydides named Thomas Arnold took over what was then a badly run-down school for boys. Until he died fifteen years later, he governed the school—and according to Dean Arthur Stanley, of Westminster, a Rugbian who himself became a celebrated writer and historian—"precisely as he would have governed a great empire." In the process, he built what has become one of England's finest public schools, producer of a host of first-rate writers.

Earliest among these were his own son Matthew and Matthew's dearest friend Arthur Clough, who entered just two years after Dr. Arnold took over. Before his untimely death in 1861, Clough composed a number of excellent lyric poems, notably "Say not the struggle naught availeth." Matthew's tribute to Clough, *Thyrsis*, is one of the language's truly great elegies.

Matthew himself, who became Clough's fellow-student in 1836, must have proved a trial to his headmaster-parent. An idler and a dreamer, he went fishing when he should have been studying, and his constant pranks kept the classroom in an uproar. When, as was the custom, he was made to stand behind the headmaster's chair as punishment, he would peer over his unsuspecting father's shoulder and make faces at the other students. But one of Matthew Arnold's finest poems, surely, is his resounding tribute to that same father entitled "Rugby Chapel."

Walter Savage Landor attended Rugby long before Dr. Arnold got there, but among writers who came later were Thomas Hughes, Charles Lutwidge Dodgson (Lewis Carroll), P. Wyndham Lewis, and Rupert Brooke.

The title of Thomas Hughes's novel about Rugby, *Tom Brown's School Days* (1857) is far better known than his name is, and was vastly popular in its day. Hughes, a pupil from 1834 to 1841, embodies the muscular earnestness of Dr. Arnold, but leavens it with a good deal of zest for living: "Life isn't all beer and skittles; but beer and skittles, or something better of the same sort, must form a good part of every Englishman's education."

Rupert Brooke, whose father was a teacher there, was born in Rugby at No. 5 Hillmorton Road, and entered the school in 1901. He admirably combined the Arnoldian ideals of muscle and mind, playing both cricket and football for the school, and winning its poetry prize in 1905 for a piece called "The Bastille."

A visit to Rugby today is something of a disappointment. With over sixty thousand people, the town is a bit on the grim and grimy side, though the canal that wanders through it gives it a certain charm, and the little old villages that surround it are appealing. The present school buildings are unfortunately nineteenth century or later. Especially missing are the walls of the chapel—"cold, solemn, unlighted, austere"—immortalized in Matthew Arnold's poem. In the final chapter of Hughe's novel, Tom Brown comes there to pay tribute at the grave of Rugby's greatest headmaster.

Bilton—Dunchurch—Coombe Abbey

Bilton   Now a suburb on Rugby's southwestern edge, Bilton was the site of Bilton Hall, the country home that eighteenth-century essayist Joseph Addison bought in 1711. A late seventeenth-century mansion, it cost the then-considerable sum of £10,000, and Addison also spent much in laying out its gardens and avenues.

He was essentially an urbane city-dweller, but he loved to slip away from London a few months each year. An essay for *The Spectator* written shortly after he bought Bilton Hall reflects his special delight in sitting in his small summer house in the garden and watching his own little stream flow past: ". . . there is nothing that more enlivens a prospect than rivers, *jets d'eau*, or falls of waters, where the scene is perpetually shifting and entertaining the sight every moment with something that is new."

Dunchurch   Immediately adjacent to Bilton to the south, where the A 426 and the A 45 come together, are Dunchurch and the Dun Cow, a small hotel established in the sixteenth century and extensively rebuilt in the eighteenth. Its dozen or so rooms don't claim four-star elegance, but they're comfortable enough. And the main bar with its cozy inglenook fireplace is inviting in the winter, as is the pretty coach yard with tables spread about in summer.

Its lure for the literary, at least for Americans of a certain vintage whose teachers insisted that Henry Wadsworth Longfellow was a great poet, is that this English inn, and not some quaint New England hamlet, inspired him to write about the "Village Blacksmith," the fellow with large and sinewy hands who owed not any man.

Coombe Abbey   Between Rugby and Coventry on the A 427 is Coombe Abbey, where a Cistercian monastery was founded about 1150. Three centuries later, its monks accused a Warwickshire knight of "certeyn charges" and he was imprisoned. The charges were hardly petty: two counts of breaking into and plundering the abbey, plus extortion and rape.

His protestations of innocence futile, the man whiled away his sentence writing down a book that (his publisher said in 1485) he "dyde take out of certeyn bookes of frensshe and reduce it in to Englysshe." The book's been a literary gold mine ever since to prospectors, from the English poet laureate of *Idylls of the King* to the German composer of *Tristan und Isolde* and the Broadway producer of *Camelot*. The knight was Sir Thomas Malory. The book, *Morte d'Arthur.*

Nuneaton Neighbors—The Eliot Country: Nuneaton— Chilvers Coton—Griff House—Arbury Hall—and Meriden

The land encompassing Coventry, Nuneaton and the villages in between extends little more than ten miles in all. Yet few such limited areas have contributed so much in setting, characters, plot, and even moral fiber to a single author as this small stretch did to George Eliot.

Coventry has already been discussed. Of equal interest is Nuneaton itself and, clustered about it, Chilvers Coton, Griff House, Arbury (South) Farm, and Arbury Hall. Taken in chronological order, they figure thus: George Eliot was born—as Mary Ann Evans—on November 22, 1819, at Arbury (now South) Farm . . . christened in the Chilvers Coton parish church . . . taken by her parents in 1820 to Griff House, where she stayed until age twenty-two, during which time both Nuneaton and Arbury Hall were prominent in her life.

But for discussion and sightseeing alike, taking these places in geographical order is more practical, beginning with Nuneaton.

Nuneaton   The Benedictine nuns who came to this site on the River Anker (where the A 47 and the A 444 meet today) in the twelfth century also account for its name, Nun + "ea" (river + "tun" (farm or settlement). Nun's farm on the river: Nun-EE-t'n. Coal mining from the fourteenth century on, and railroads in the nineteenth, made it prosperous, but neither made it pretty. Elizabethan poet Michael Drayton had been born at Hartshill, three miles to the northwest; Robert Burton, author of *The Anatomy of Melancholy*, at Lindley Hall, two miles to the north. But the area hardly seemed likely to encourage literary genius. In her fiction, George Eliot described it as a "quiet, provincial place," but in private she conceded it was "more vicious."

Nuneaton is the "Milby" of Eliot's *Janet's Repentance*, whose impious citizens oppose the efforts of their new minister, the Rev. Edgar Tryan, to win them over. Leader of their resistance is the brutal, drunken lawyer Dempster.

Just about every place, character, and event in this book had real-life parallels in the Nuneaton George Eliot knew in the 1830s. Dempster and his grossly mistreated wife, Janet, for instance, were based on a real Mr. and Mrs. Buchanan, whose "Orchard Street" home can be seen on today's Church Street. Other points of interest in Nuneaton are the George Eliot collection in the library, the 1953 Memorial Gardens off Market Place, and the one-time workhouse (now Coton Lodge) where Amos Barton held services for the inmates.

Chilvers Coton   Now a Nuneaton suburb, but then a little village a mile to the south, Chilvers Coton (COAT'n) is the "Shepperton" whose clergymen are the heros of *The Sad Fortunes of the Rev. Amos Barton* and *Mr. Gilfil's Love Story*.[4] Both were close studies of actual men who had served there. The tactless, unloved Amos Barton who wins the sympathy of his parishioners only through the loss of his endearing wife Milly was drawn from the Rev. John Gwyther, and the death of his wife Emma suggested the novel's climax. Unknown to the author, Gwyther was still alive, poor man, when the book appeared, and was deeply hurt by the public baring of his story.

The original of Mr. Gilfil, undone by his love for Tina Sastri, was the Rev. Bernard G. Ebdell, the parson who christened George Eliot as Mary Anne Evans that November day in 1819. That was only the first of a gamut of names she was to run through before she invented the pen name by which the world knows her now.

The church register lists her as Mary Anne, but her father wrote it in his diary as Mary Ann, without the "e." Then came her girlish infatuation with things French, and it became Marianne. This phase past, she simplified it to Marian, which lasted to the end of her life. Even so, her nickname to intimates was Polly, the name used by George Lewes the years they lived together before they could marry.

It was Lewes who coaxed her into writing her first fiction, *Amos Barton*, published in book form (with *Mr. Gilfil* and *Janet's Repentance*) in 1858 as *Scenes of Clerical Life*. And there is more of Lewes, perhaps, than is generally recognized when she devised a pseudonym for that publication. The "George" was obviously and admittedly for him. But the "Eliot," she claimed, occurred to her only as a "good, mouth-filling, easily pronounced word." Maybe so. But if you say her friend's given name and the first letter of his last name together, you come mighty close to the whole thing: "George L—."

Don't expect to see the Chilvers Coton church as described in the

---

[4]Stockingford, the fictional "Paddiford," is also now a Nuneaton suburb.

opening chapter of *Amos Barton*. It had to be rebuilt after World War II bombing. But the churchyard still holds the graves of Emma Gwyther, and George Eliot's father and mother.

Griff House   Barely a mile down the A 444 is Griff House, George Eliot's home for all her formative years—from the time she went there as an infant in 1820 until 1841, when she went with her father to Coventry after he retired.

Now a separate entity across the road, it was then part of the extensive Arbury Hall estate that her father served as agent. The Griff House that George Eliot knew was a roomy, hospitable, even elegant red brick farmhouse, with a round pool and ample gardens of its own. The impressive drawing room boasted a bow window; a wide, handsome staircase swept up to the bedrooms above; and higher yet was a large attic, young Mary Anne's favorite hideaway. Years later she wrote: "I [still] seem to feel the air through the window of the attic, from which when a little girl, I often looked toward the distant view of the Coton College."

Memories of Griff House lurk in books like *Adam Bede* (Adam is in part based on her father) and *Mill on the Floss*. In *Mill on the Floss*, for instance, the author makes "Maggie's favourite retreat" much like the one she herself had known, where "Maggie fretted out all her ill-humours and talked aloud to the worm-eaten floors."

Mary Anne's childhood at Griff House was not a particularly happy one. She adored her brother Isaac, three years older than she, but they grew increasingly apart. Clashes over religion created a wide gap between her and her father, too. She was a lonely and altogether too serious child. Asked at a party at age nine if she were having a good time, she replied, "No. I don't like to play with children. I like to talk to grown up people."

Admittedly bright, she was just as admittedly homely. Her friend Herbert Spencer, the famous philosopher and writer, recalled her as the "most admirable woman—mentally." He even confessed that he had been in love with her, but added that her long nose had made her very difficult to kiss.

Life must have been almost impossible for Mary Anne when her mother died in 1836 and the girl had to abandon the studies she loved to become housekeeper to her father and family. Only with his retirement was she able at last to substitute Coventry for the confines of Griff House at last, and begin the long, earnest march to success as one of England's greatest novelists.

Griff House ultimately became a hotel, and later was taken over by a steak house chain. Now only the wing on the left retains the original wall.

Arbury Hall and Arbury (South) Farm   A sharp turn to the right (west) at
the traffic island in front of Griff House takes you into the Arbury estate,
since 1586 the seat of the Newdegates of Warwickshire.[5] Here in the middle
of the park is Arbury Hall itself, surrounded by giant oaks and beech, with
two pools that once were fishponds for a twelfth-century monastery.

Today's imposing edifice owes much to its eighteenth-century owner, Sir
Roger Newdigate (the family sometimes spelled it that way) who in 1750
rebuilt the huge hollow square of the original, and added the Gothic battlements, pinnacles, turrets, and oriel windows.

An ardent antiquarian, Sir Roger gave Arbury Hall a literary link that
endures to this day: he established Oxford's prestigous Newdigate Prize for
Poetry by undergraduates. Some of the young winners—Matthew Arnold,
for instance, John Ruskin, Oscar Wilde—went on to win a lasting place in
literature. Others—H. A. Milman, W. Garrod, Edwin Arnold—now bask in
oblivion.

In 1806, the first year the prize was given, Sir Roger died and the estate
went to a cousin, Francis Parker of Kirk Hallam, Derbyshire. Parker brought
with him to assist as agent, Robert Evans, and installed him, his wife and two
children in a modest cottage on the Arbury farm, now called South Farm.

Three years later Evans's wife Harriet died, and in 1813 he took as second
wife Christiana Pearson, daughter of substantial Astley people. It was in this
Arbury farm cottage that their daughter Mary Anne was born.

The girl grew up with easy access to the great hall and its library. Both
contributed to the novelist-to-be. With little attempt at disguise, George
Eliot made Arbury Hall the "castellated house of grey-tinted stone" she
called Cheverel Manor in *Mr. Gilfil's Love Story.*

Arbury Hall continues in the hands of the Newdigates, and they're happy
to welcome you as visitors (for a fee, sensibly) most afternoons except
Monday, from Easter to the end of September. On view in addition to the
various rooms described by George Eliot are the gardens and the seventeenth-century stables, where you can wind up your stay with tea.

Meriden   If you leave Arbury Hall by way of the Astley Lodge and have a
minute or two to spare—especially if you're going on to Coventry anyway—
you might well want to go by way of Meriden. It's right on the B 4102, only
about five miles down the road.

There's nothing much literary about the village, though its eleventh-

---

[5]The two main entries, however, are at the Round Towers of the North Lodge and the
Lodge at Astley, both off the B 4102. Follow the blue "Arbury Hall" markers.

century Church of St. Lawrence was supposedly founded by Lady Godiva. What Meriden does offer you, as you leave Nuneaton and Warwickshire, is the very heart of the heart of England. For Meriden is historically, geographically, indisputably the exact center of the country. There's a five hundred-year-old stone cross on the village green that says so.

Leicester, Northamptonshire, and Bedfordshire

Leicestershire, Northamptonshire, and Bedfordshire

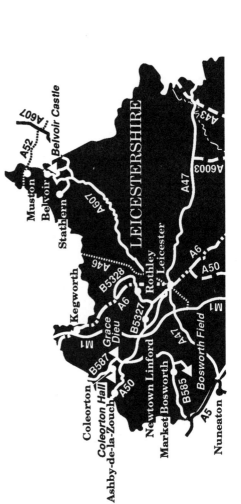

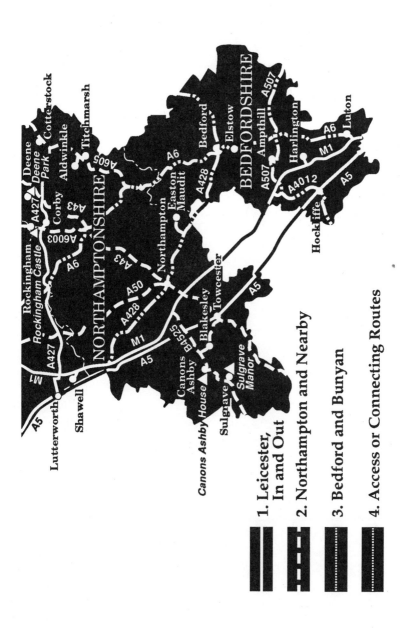

1. Leicester, In and Out
2. Northampton and Nearby
3. Bedford and Bunyan
4. Access or Connecting Routes

A horse! A horse! my kingdom for a horse!
> Richard III, about to die on a Leicestershire
> battlefield.
>
> (William Shakespeare, *Richard III*)

Poets love nature; like the calm of heaven,
Her gifts like heaven's love spread far and wide. . . .
Her flowers, like pleasures, have their season's birth,
And bloom through regions here below;
They are her very scriptures here on earth,
And teach us simple mirth where'er we go.
Even in prison they can solace me,
For where they bloom God is, and I am free.
> John Clare, locked in a Northamptonshire
> madhouse.
>
> ("Poets Love Nature")

The Giant, therefore, drove them before him, and put them into his castle, into a very dark dungeon, nasty and stinking to the spirits of these two men. Here, then, they lay from Wednesday morning till Saturday night, without one bit of bread or drop of drink, or light.
> John Bunyan, in a Bedfordshire gaol.
>
> (*Pilgrim's Progress*)

However, merit is not always unrewarded among us;
Our Gentry are very polite, and some of them very conversant with modern literature.
> Thomas Percy in a Northamptonshire rectory
> (letter to a friend, July 1, 1765)

Leicestershire, Northamptonshire, and Bedfordshire huddle together at the very center of Middle England, and in a sense seem hemmed in by the counties round about them. To the far west lie wilder, more picturesque Gloucestershire and Hereford-Worcester. Close in are industrial Birmingham and rebuilt Coventry to the northwest, the Derby-Sheffield-Nottingham complex to the north. To the south, urban proliferation runs through Hertford-shire and down to London. To the east, largely unsullied, is East Anglia. There's a touch of the defensive in Thomas Percy's letter about this part of England, as if there were more to it than strangers realized. Too often today, in fact, the seventy-five miles between Luton at the bottom of Bedfordshire and Kegworth at Leicestershire's top seem merely a stretch to be negotiated as rapidly as possible via the M 1.

To do so, however, is to miss much that is pleasant: the winding River Ouse and old brick-and-timber villages of Northern Bedfordshire, for in-stance . . . the medieval churches and still-remaining open fields of the fox-hunting gentry that once made Northamptonshire the land of "spires and squires . . . Charnwood Forest and Brandon Hill rising nine hundred feet and more in Leicestershire (LES-ter-sh're).

There are literary sites to see, too—not overwhelming, but a number of interest, and several of significance. Wordsworth loved Leicestershire's Coleorton. Northamptonshire was Dryden's homeland, and its Rockingham Castle gave Dickens many a happy day. Bedfordshire provided the best and worst of times for John Bunyan.

For each county, you'll find its county town the best base for explora-tion—beginning with Leicester and proceeding in turn to Northampton and Bedford if you're approaching from Warwickshire, Cambridgeshire, or the north; and reversing the order if you're coming from London or the south.

1. Leicester, In and Out

Leicester is served by a multitude of highways that come in from all direc-tions, in particular the M 1 from as far south as London and as far north as West Yorkshire and the Brontë country, and the A 47 running from Nuneaton and Warwickshire all the way east to Great Yarmouth and the Norfolk coast.

Lutterworth—Shawell—and Market Bosworth

Almost immediately out of Nuneaton—right after the A 47 crosses the county line into Leicestershire—are three points of interest. Lutterworth is nine miles southeast on the A 427, and Shawell three miles south of Lutter-worth on an unmarked road. Market Bosworth is on the B 585 about six miles north of the A 47.

Lutterworth   Rector of Lutterworth from 1374 until his death in 1384 was a man who affected the course of both the literature and religion of the English-speaking world: John Wycliffe. What Chaucer's *Canterbury Tales* did for English verse, Wycliffe's translation of various sections of the Bible into the vernacular helped do for English prose. Interestingly enough, Chaucer and Wycliffe were almost exact contemporaries, reaching their peak in the latter half of the fourteenth century. They even shared the same royal patron, John of Gaunt, he of the dreadful deathbed puns in Shakespeare's *Richard II.*

Unlike Chaucer, however, who seems to have managed to get along with just about everybody, Wycliffe was a rebel, who was lucky to escape with his life. His translation of the Bible, a good deal of it done after he came to Lutterworth, was part of an effort to win the laity's support for his increasingly bitter quarrel with the church. He wound up calling the pope himself an Anti-Christ and—probably the most unkindest cut of all—denouncing the clergy's vast property holdings by pointing out that Christ and his disciples owned nothing.

Wycliffe was denounced for heresy, but died in Lutterworth unpunished, and was buried there. Even so, the church struck back. Forty-four years later, under a papal directive, his remains were dug up and burned, and the ashes tossed into a nearby tributary of the Avon.

Ultimately, though it was Wycliffe who triumphed, as a popular verse had prophesied:

> The Avon to the Severn runs,
> The Severn to the sea,
> And Wycliffe's dust shall spread abroad
> Wide as the waters be.

Much of what the Reformation owed to Martin Luther, Luther owed to Wycliffe and his disciples.

Lutterworth has paid its respects to Wycliffe, too. St. Mary's Church has some relics supposed to be his, and a marble memorial of him preaching, and the town has an obelisk honoring his memory.

Shawell   The garden of the rectory at Shawell (now the Old Rectory) had special meaning for Alfred Tennyson. There he wrote many of the verses—"swallow flights of song," he called them—that he wove together into *In Memoriam* (1850), his elegy on the death of Arthur Hallam.

Tennyson came often to visit the rector, the Rev. Elmhirst, and his wife Sophie, for not only was Sophie like another sister to him—she had been his father's ward—but she and Mr. Elmhirst always did everything in their power to keep their guest happy.

The Elmhirsts even built Tennyson a little private hideaway in the garden. Mainly, of course, this was so that he could work at his poetry undisturbed. But Sophie had a secret reason of her own as well. Tennyson was rarely without a pipe in his mouth, sending up clouds of smoke. Sophie was more than happy to keep as much of this outside her house as possible.

Market Bosworth   Samuel Johnson's first job after poverty forced him to leave Oxford without graduating was as an usher (undermaster) at the Market Bosworth Grammar School. He arrived in March of 1732 after trudging afoot and through the mud the twenty-five miles from his home in Lichfield. But he felt fortunate. The school usually required a B. A. degree, and he had none. What followed, however, was utter disaster.

Sir Wolston Dixie, the chief trustee who'd hired him, proved coarse, ill-tempered, and a bully. He took particular pleasure in flaunting his power and defying rules, which is probably why Johnson got the job. Once while being served at dinner, for instance, Dixie was challenged for boasting he could name anyone he liked as his headmaster. So he appointed the butler on the spot.

In his *Life of Johnson*, Boswell reports Johnson said that his days at the school were ". . . unvaried as the note of the cuckow; and that he did not know whether it was more disagreeable for him to teach, or the boys to learn, the grammar rules." By July, Johnson could take no more. After a final bitter quarrel with Sir Wolston, he quit the position which, he told Boswell, "all his life afterwards he recollected with the strongest aversion, and even a degree of horror."

Market Bosworth's Grammar School is on the northwest side of the marketplace. Today's building dates from 1828, but is on the original site. Behind the school is Sir Wolston's Bosworth Hall. The inside has been drastically altered over the past one hundred years, but the seventeenth-century exterior remains much as Johnson would have known it.

Two miles south of Market Bosworth is Bosworth Field, where in 1385 Richard III, after calling vainly for that horse, yielded both throne and life to Henry Tudor. The site has become a major tourist attraction, open from the end of March through most of October, with all sorts of things to see and do if you have the time. Among these are an exhibition with models depicting the battle and medieval life, a variety of films, and battle trails through the countryside.

Dr. Johnson's Sir Wolston, incidentally, is tied to Bosworth Field in a tale beyond credulity, though the official historian of Market Bosworth Grammar School swore it was true. In one of his celebrated outbursts, goes the account, Sir Wolston tangled with a local squire and "battered him to insensibility." Years later, the story continues, he was introduced to His Majesty George II as "Sir Wolston Dixie of Bosworth Park."

"Oh, Bosworth," said the king, trying to be gracious. "Big battle at Bosworth, wasn't it?"

"Yes, Sire," said Sir Wolston. "But I thrashed him."

Leicester—Rothley—and Newtown Linford

In addition to being a hub for all those highways, Leicester is a good base for exploration because it is almost exactly in the center of its county— Nottinghamshire is fourteen miles to the north, Northamptonshire is sixteen miles to the south; Warwickshire is twenty miles to the west, Lincolnshire and Cambridgeshire twenty-six miles to the east.

On its doorstep are two attractive villages worth a quick look before you venture further afield: Rothley, six miles north on the B 5328, and Newtown Linford, six miles northwest on the B 5327.

Leicester   Richard came into Leicester on August 23, 1385, finally riding that horse he had vainly cried for at Bosworth Field. After Henry Tudor and his cohorts killed him there, they unceremoniously slung the king's body over a horse, head downward, and carted him back to the town he had left two days earlier leading fifteen thousand troops. Even more ignominiously, as the horse crossed the Soar River into Leicester, the monarch's dangling head smashed into the side of the bridge. In the watching crowd, an old woman muttered, "I told you so."

As you come in from the west on the A 47 today, a tablet on Bow Bridge marks the spot and tells her tale:

> UPON THIS BRIDGE,
> TRADITION HATH
> DELIVERED, STOOD A
> STONE OF SOME HEIGHT
> AGAINST WHICH KING
> RICHARD AS HE PASSED
> TOWARD BOSWORTH, BY
> CHANCE STRUCK HIS

SPUR. AND AGAINST THE
SAME STONE AS HE WAS
BROUGHT BACK HANGING
BY THE HORSE SIDE, HIS
HEAD WAS DASHED AND
BROKEN, AS A WISE WOMAN,
FORSOOTH, HAD FORETOLD.
WHO BEFORE RICHARD'S
GOING TO BATTLE, BEING
ASKED OF HIS SUCCESS,
SAID THAT WHERE HIS
SPUR STRUCK, HIS HEAD
SHOULD BE BROKEN.

Leicester is a major city now, large (three hundred thousand people or more) and industrial. But tokens of its long, long past remain. From the Romans and the early Christian era there's the Jewry Wall near St. Nicholas Circle. From the Saxons, there's St. Nicholas Church itself. And from the Normans, there's Leicester Castle, originally Saxon but rebuilt by William within two years of the Battle of Hastings. Some even say that King Lear and his daughters once lived in Leicester, but Bath, for one, claims the same thing.

More reliably connected with Leicester are Cardinal Wolsey. George Fox, and John Bunyan. Wolsey died at Leicester Abbey while on his way to London. He was probably lucky at that. An exile in York, stripped of high office, he was being taken back to London to stand trial for treason. Amid the ruins in what is now Abbey Park there's a slab marking the presumed site of his grave.

Leicester's prosperity for centuries depended upon the making of boots and shoes, and this remains an important industry. It was natural, then, that George Fox, born in 1624 in nearby Drayton, son of a weaver, should be apprenticed as a boy to a Leicester shoemaker. But at nineteen he left to embark on a spiritual quest that led him in 1650 to establish the Society of Friends, better known as Quakers. It says much about mankind that as a reward for preaching nonviolence, he should be brutally attacked by mobs, and eight times imprisoned.

As a writer, Fox is less than polished, and his grammar and spelling betray his lack of formal education. But his *Journal* especially has a simple, straightforward style and a vigor of narration that are highly effective. First published in 1694 with a preface by William Penn, it has been reprinted a number of times since.

Thomas Carlyle, powerfully moved by Fox, exalts him in *Sartor Resartus* (1833–4): "That Leicester shoe-shop, had men known it, was a holier place than any Vatican or Loretto-shrine." Carlyle then describes the young apprentice on his final day in that shop, fashioning himself a leather suit for his great mission: "[He] spreads-out his cutting-board for the last time, and cuts cowhides by unwonted patterns, and stitches them together," and concludes grandly: "Stitch away, thou noble Fox . . . greater than Diogenes himself."

For John Bunyan, too, Leicester was a place of emancipation. He came there in October 1672, to conduct one of his very first services as a man legally entitled to do so. Only five months earlier he had ended twelve years' imprisonment in Bedford Gaol for defying authorities and preaching without a license. Now, with the law's permission, "to teach as a congregational person," he gave his sermon and then made a holiday of it, walking about the town, viewing the Jewry Wall, admiring the great gates of the Castle, and staying overnight at a house near St. Nicholas Church.

Rothley   Rothley is a fascinating little place, with several houses built in a fashion that goes back to primitive times, a railroad station that is redolent of Queen Victoria, and a three-star hotel with a seven hundred-year-old history.

Rothley has a number of fine timber-framed houses, but most unusual are the one or two of an ancient construction called "cruck-built." Derived from the word crutch, this consists of joining three trunks together to form the chief framework.

Lovers of late Victorian novels will enjoy the Rothley station. Erected in the 1890s, it has been restored to its original state—gas lamps, enamelled advertisements, Victoria's portrait, and all.

The historic hotel is The Royal Court. Built as Rothley Temple in the thirteenth century by the Knights Templar, it was converted in the sixteenth century into a stately Elizabethan home, and served well into the nineteenth century as the seat of the Babington family.

William Wilberforce, author of the widely popular and politically influential *Practical View of the Religious System* (1797) was a visitor there in 1791, and the hotel has a memorial on the lawn indicating that it was here that he drafted his bill to abolish slavery.

Thomas Babington Macauley was born at the mansion in 1800, and the hotel has preserved the room pretty much as it looked then. Macauley's best-known works are his five-volume *History of England* (1848–61), which made him fabulously rich, and *The Lays of Ancient Rome* (1842). Most people still know "Then out spoke brave Horatius, / The Captain of the Gate" from their schooldays, even if they're a bit vague about exactly who wrote it.

Macauley was proud of his ties to old Rothley Temple. When he was raised to the peerage in 1857, he took the title Baron Macauley of Rothley.

Newtown Linford   At the north edge of the village of Newtown Linford lies Bradgate Park, 850 magnificent acres in the heart of Charnwood Forest. At the south edge are the dramatic ruins of Bradgate House, home of that pathetic figure, Lady Jane Grey.

The bare outlines of Lady Jane's life are, of course, heartbreaking: born in 1537, great-granddaughter of Henry VII . . . forced to marry in May 1553, at age sixteen . . . proclaimed queen against her will that same July, and imprisoned nine days later . . . executed for alleged treason in February 1554—age seventeen.

But her days before history caught and crushed her were appalling, too. In *The Scholemaster* (1570), Roger Ascham—her first teacher and later tutor to Elizabeth I—paints the picture. Were he talking about a grown young lady, it would be dreadful enough. But Jane was just thirteen at the time!

Ascham had made a special trip to see her, and found her all alone in her chamber, reading Plato. "Her parents, the Duke and Duchess [of Suffolk]," he explains, "with all the household, gentlemen and gentlewomen, were hunting in the park." Ascham continues:

> I asked her why she would lose such pastime in the park? Smiling, she answered me; "I wiss, all their sport in the park is but a shadow to that pleasure that I found in Plato. . . .
>
> "One of the greatest benefits that ever God gave me, is, that he sent me so sharp and severe parents, and so gentle a schoolmaster. For when I am in presence either of father or mother; whether I speak, keep silence, sit, stand, or go, eat, drink, be merry, or sad, be sewing, playing, dancing, or doing anything else; I must do it, as it were . . . even so perfectly as God made the world; or else I am so sharply taunted, so cruelly threatened, yea presently sometimes with pinches, hips, and bobs . . . that I think myself in hell, till time come that I go to Mr. Elmer."

Mr. Elmer is her current teacher, and he "teacheth me," Jane says, "so gently, so pleasantly, with such fair allurements to learning, that I think all the time nothing whilst I am with him. And when I am called from him, I fall on weeping, because whatsoever I do else but learning, is full of grief, trouble, fear, and whole misliking unto me."

Ascham ends this account on a haunting note: "I remember this talk gladly, both because it is so worthy of memory, and because also it was the last talk that ever I had, and the last time that ever I saw that noble and worthy lady."

Ashby-de-la-Zouch—Coleorton Hall—and Grace Dieu

There are no fewer than fourteen towns and villages in England called Ashby. To distinguish one from the other, most have added suffixes—some on the fancy side, like Ashby Parva and Ashby Puerorum. The most swash-buckling sounding, however, is Leicestershire's Ashby-de-la-Zouch, as is fitting. It as here that Sir Walter Scott staged the great tournament in *Ivanhoe*. The town is northwest of Leicester, seventeen miles straight up the A 50.

In the same neighborhood are Coleorton Hall and Grace Dieu, both associated with William Wordsworth. Coleorton Hall is only three miles to the northeast on the B 587, and Grace Dieu three miles east of Coleorton Hall.

Ashby-de-la-Zouch   Ashby-de-la-Zouch got its suffix in about 1160 when an Alan le Zouch (or Souche) acquired the Manor of Ashby and began building a modest sort of castle. In 1314, when a Shropshire family called Mortimer inherited the manor, they not only upgraded their name to Zouch, but went to work on the castle in earnest.

During the Wars of the Roses, it was a lively place indeed. The Earl of Ormonde, the owner then, was a Lancastrian, so when his group lost the Battle of Towson in 1461, the Yorkists cut off his head for picking the wrong side, and gave the castle to their Lord Hastings. But Hastings, as he puts it in Shakespeare's *Richard III*, soon finds he's about as secure as "a drunken sailor on a mast." After Richard gets through using him, he cuts off his head, too.

Scott goes all the way back to the 1190s for his use of Ashby-de-la-Zouch. Richard I (he of the lion heart) has secretly returned to England from the crusades, with Ivanhoe in tow, to thwart his brother John's plot to seize the throne. At a tournament that John sets up in a field near the castle, Ivanhoe routs every last one of John's knights, including the fierce Sir Brian de Bois-Guilbert and the odious Sir Reginald Front-de-Boeuf.

The impressive ruins of Ashby-de-la-Zouch Castle are open to the public, and can be viewed all year round. As Scott is careful to point out, they don't represent what existed in Ivanhoe's day. Mainly, in fact, they're what's left of massive construction undertaken by the unfortunate Lord Hastings.

Coleorton Hall   In 1806, William Wordsworth found his Dove Cottage in Grasmere beginning to get, as his sister Dorothy put it, "crammed edgefull" with his growing family. To help tide him over while he did something about larger quarters, Sir George Beaumont offered the use of Hall Farm, a comfortable cottage on his estate outside Ashby-de-la-Zouch, Coleorton (cole-OR-t'n) Hall. Wordsworth eagerly accepted, and arrived with his household the end of October 1806.

It was quite a company: the Wordsworths, their three children, their maid Molly, his sister Dorothy, and Mary Wordsworth's sister Sara, the wife of Samuel Taylor Coleridge. Beaumont, an admirer of Wordsworth's poetry, was a cultured and kindly man. His friend Sir Walter Scott called him "by far the most sensible and pleasing man I ever knew." And though they didn't know their guests all that well, the Beaumonts speedily made "all in order and comfort" for them, as Dorothy recorded in her journal.

Dorothy found Lady Beaumont's impulsive enthusiasm charming. Wordsworth and Sir George shared innumerable things: gardens, books, planting, painting, politics and poetry. Even more to Wordsworth's delight, Lady Beaumont loved to hear him read aloud. One evening he did the whole first book of *Paradise Lost* while she listened entranced.

The farmhouse, too, was a great pleasure. After Dove Cottage, its two bedrooms seemed spacious, its living room elegant, with a grand view of the setting sun.

After the Beaumonts left for the winter and the Wordsworths had the place to themselves, they found all sorts of things to do: walking about the estate, sightseeing in the neighboring villages, reading, playing with the children. Wordsworth's two special projects were planning and planting a winter garden for Lady Beaumont, and readying a new edition of poems for the press.

Now and then they had guests. Once William brought Sir Walter Scott back with him after a short trip to London, and in December Coleridge came to spend several months with his wife. With him he brought their son Hartley. Always a favorite of Wordsworth's, Hartley was the "six years Darling of pygmy size" of "Ode: Intimations of Immortality."

Both Coleridge and Wordsworth hoped to recapture the intimacy and mutual inspiration of the days together in Somerset that gave birth to *Lyrical Ballads* (1798), and at first the visit seemed to go well. Dorothy wrote in her journal that Coleridge even managed to curb his "craving for brandy, substituting ale"—albeit "at mid-morning, at dinner time, and at night."

One evening Wordsworth read aloud from what he was then calling "Poem to Coleridge," later published as *The Prelude*. Coleridge glowed at first, hearing himself praised lavishly. But even as the recitation went on, his mood changed to self-abasement. He was no longer either the man or the poet being described, and he knew it. Through weakness, especially the drugs and the alcohol, he had destroyed himself.

Before he slept that night, Coleridge wrote a poem of his own, entitled simply "To William Wordsworth." In it, he confesses how he had listened "with a heart forlorn." Starkly, he confronts these "poisons of self-harm," and tells of their terrible cost—the destruction

> . . . of past Youth, and Manhood come in vain
> And Genius given, and Knowledge won in vain.

When the Beaumonts returned in June, the Wordsworths went back to Grasmere. But Coleorton had produced a lasting memorial. In the new edition completed there, and published as *Poems in Two Volumes* the very month before they left, appeared some of Wordsworth's best work: "My Heart Leaps Up," for instance, "It Is a Beauteous Evening," "The World is too Much with Us," and the great "Ode: Intimations of Immortality."

Incredibly, the collection was attacked harshly by a critic or two, but Wordsworth shrugged this off as "pure, absolute, honest ignorance." He must have felt in his heart that Coleorton had provided one of the greatest creative periods of his life. And, as it turned out—though he was to live another forty years—the last.

Grace Dieu   One of the Wordsworths' Coleorton outings was a three-mile stroll to Grace Dieu and the ruins of an Augustinian priory built in 1240. For them, in addition to being picturesque, the place had special attraction. The ancestors of their host, Sir George Beaumont, had acquired the priory in 1539, at the Dissolution, and converted it into their family home. As such, therefore, it was also the birthplace of brother-poets of considerable talent, Sir John and Francis Beaumont.

Sir John, born in 1583, was the older by a year. Little survives of his verse save *Metamorphosis of Tabacco* (1602), published anonymously at age nineteen, and *Bosworth Field* (1629), published by his son. But Sir John deserves his reputation for helping to regularize seventeenth-century poetry and to prepare the heroic couplet for the poetic genius of Dryden and Pope.

Francis Beaumont is much better known. Both as collaborator with John

Fletcher on plays like *Knight of the Burning Pestle* (1609) and *Philaster* (1611), and as sole author of others like *The Woman Hater* (1607), he is a worthy heir to Shakespeare. Both Francis and Sir John are buried in Westminster Abbey, but Francis has the better spot—between Chaucer and Spenser.

Wordsworth remembers Grace Dieu in several poems, the best known being "For a Seat in the Groves of Coleorton." Composed for a resting place that Sir George Beaumont had built on his estate, the poem recalls rather successfully both the original priory, now

> The ivied Ruins of forlorn GRACE DIEU;
> Erst a religious House, which day and night
> With hymns resounded, and the chanted rite,

and the Beaumonts' ancestral home, where

> . . . on the margin of a streamlet wild,
> Did Francis Beaumont sport, an eager child.

Belvoir Castle—Stathern—Muston

George Crabbe, debunker of the kind of eighteenth-century it's-fun-to-starve-in-a-cottage nonsense exemplified by Goldsmith's *The Deserted Village* (1770), was preeminently an East Anglia man. For the first fifty years of his life he lived almost entirely in and about his native Suffolk, with three exceptions: Belvoir Castle, Stathern, and Muston. All three are at the northernmost tip of Leicestershire. Belvoir Castle is twenty-five miles northeast of Leicester, just off the A 607 . . . Stathern four miles southwest of Belvoir . . . Muston three miles north of it.

Belvoir Castle (pronounced BEE-ver, of all things) is tied to Ashby-de-la-Zouch in a curious way. When Edward IV gave Lord Hastings the Ashby-de-la-Zouch Castle, he gave him Belvoir Castle as well. And when Hastings decided to make the former a thing of beauty, he did so at the expense of Belvoir, tearing the place to pieces and carting most of the materials off for that massive reconstruction job at Ashby.

In 1528, however, the first Earl of Rutland took over Belvoir and began rebuilding it. In 1668, the eighth Earl decided castles were getting a bit passé, so he in turn made a big square mansion of it. This was the structure that George Crabbe came to in 1782 as chaplain to his patron, the castle's current Rutland, now a duke. In 1785, he was also made curate of Stathern. In 1789, he became rector of Muston.

Multiple benefices for a single clergyman were nothing unusual then, of course, nor was he necessarily obligated to live at any of them. Crabbe did live at each of his off and on. He had an apartment at Belvoir Castle and was there when *The Village* was published in 1783. He lived at the rectory at Stathern for a while and his three children were baptized in its church. In his early years as rector of Muston, he seems to have spent much of his time there, too. He was at Muston when his wife died in 1814, and she is buried in the church chancel. But in the middle years, 1792 to 1805, he spent most of his time in Suffolk.

In this he was only following a common practice, but one that he deplored, nevertheless. In *The Village*, Crabbe indicates sardonically that even a vicar who lived in his parish was often content to do no more for his flock than preach once a week, considering

> "his Sunday task
> As much as God or man can fairly ask."

The son of Crabbe's Duke of Rutland, finding towers and turrets all the rage once more, converted the mansion back into a castle, "medieval," of course. And that's what you'll see today if you go have a look. It's open April through September, daily except Friday.

2. Northampton and Nearby

Northampton

Northampton is thirty-two miles southwest of Leicester, straight down the A 50. A great fire in 1675 swept away most of its houses and much of its flavor. But the citizens got right to work and created what a few years later Daniel Defoe called the "handsomest and best built town in all this part of England."

While it's not quite that any more, it does have a tidy look about it for a city of 150,000 people. And the names of the streets radiating from its great Market Square conjure up the trades, at least, of the Northampton that was: Gold and Silver Streets, Woolmonger, the Draper, Sheep, Mercers, and Horsemarket.

More recent Northampton, as the antiquarian Fuller put it, "may be said to stand chiefly on other men's legs." Since the late eighteenth century particularly, shoe, boot, and leather manufacturing have been key industries. One of the sights to see in the Central Museum is the exhibit of footwear ranging from Roman sandals to Dame Margot Fonteyn's dancing shoes, and from Queen Victoria's wedding slippers to the boots made for an elephant used in a 1959 restaging of Hannibal's crossing the Alps.

Northampton has much else to see: one of three surviving Eleanor Crosses that Edward I erected to mark the route of the funeral procession for his wife from Nottinghamshire to London . . . one of the country's four remaining round churches . . . the manor house, now Abingdon Park Museum, where Shakespeare's last direct descendant, his granddaughter Lady Elizabeth Bernard, died in 1670 . . . and a borough roster containing the names of six hundred (that's right, six hundred!) former mayors, including Laurence Washington, ancestor of America's first president.

Northampton produced an American literary first, too, in Anne Bradstreet. Born in 1612 to a Northampton puritan, Thomas Dudley, she married Simon Bradstreet at sixteen, and two years later sailed off with him and her father to Massachusetts. Dudley and Bradstreet both went on to become governors of that state. Anne, with the printing of her *The Tenth Muse Lately Sprung Up in America* in 1650, became the New World's first published poet.

Except for the nineteenth-century poet, John Clare, however, Northampton's other literary ties are few. William Cowper used to come in now and then during his years at Olney in Buckinghamshire, ten miles away. Jerome K. Jerome died there in 1927 while on holiday. And Mary Mitford writes about her visit there in *Recollections of a Literary Life* (1852).

Actually, her account is more about John Clare than Northampton. She went to see him at the county lunatic asylum to which he had been committed in 1841 after simply walking away from similar confinement in Essex. Clare's fits of insanity brought remarkable delusions. At times he would claim to have written the works of Byron or Scott. At other times he was Lord Nelson; or he was Wellington—never Napoleon— and though he had won the Battle of Waterloo, he had had his head shot off there. (He never did explain how he managed to replace it).

Clare had lucid intervals, too, however, when he could "find solace," as he said, "even in prison," and write such poems as "Poets Love Nature" quoted in the introduction to this section, and the poignant "I Am":

> I long for scenes where man hath never trod,
> A place where woman never smiled or wept,
> There to abide with my Creator God,
> And sleep as I in childhood sweetly slept.

Corby—Rockingham Castle—and Deene Park

Corby, twenty miles from Northampton up the A 43, is much what you'd expect of a community of fifty thousand people built on the new town plan, with large shopping precinct and functional civic center, but with a two hundred-acre wooded park mitigating its built-up core. The two attractions that lure the literary traveler aren't in Corby really, but close by. Both are open to the public, and worth a stop.

Rockingham Castle, three miles to the north on the A 6003, was a favorite of Charles Dickens and, thinly disguised, is featured in *Bleak House*. The owner of Deene Park, four miles northeast of Corby off the A 43, gave rise to Tennyson's "Charge of the Light Brigade."

Rockingham Castle   The village of Rockingham would warrant a visit even without its castle and Dickens connections. It's a pretty little place, sitting amidst trees that climb the slope to its guardian fortress. Vintage thatched cottages, almost all of them built of the local ironstone, line the wide main street, with splendid vistas of the Welland Valley below.

Owners of the castle in Dickens's day were the Richard Watsons, whom Dickens had run into in Lausanne, Switzerland, while on a continental tour in 1846. They liked each other, and when his new friends insisted that the author must come see their castle one day, he promised that he would. He did so in 1849.

It was quite a castle he came to. In the sixteenth century, Queen Elizabeth I had granted it to Richard Watson's ancestor, Edward Watson. For five centuries before that it had been a royal stronghold. The gatehouse was Norman, the Great Hall, Tudor. The courtyard was enormous, the enclosing curtain wall set about with circular towers and numerous buttresses.

When Dickens arrived at the end of November 1849 for the pre-Christmas holidays, he was delighted. Gleefully he wrote his friend John Forster in a style burlesquing a wide-eyed Yankee tourist, inviting him to picture " . . . a large old castle, approached by an ancient keep, portcullis, &c, filled with company, waited on by six-and-twenty servants; the slops (and wine-glasses) continually being emptied; and my clothes (with myself in them) always being carried off to all sorts of places."

Dickens's high spirits continued. The Watsons pampered him shamelessly, laughing at his punning parody of Gray's "Elegy in a Country Churchyard," applauding his conjuring tricks, and holding country dances in the

Great Hall that went on until three in the morning. He flirted outrageously with their niece, a tiny blue-eyed miss named Mary Boyle two years older than he was, and she flirted right back. Together the two staged and starred in scenes from *Nicholas Nickleby* and Sheridan's *School for Scandal*, with Dickens as Sir Peter and Mary as Lady Teazle.

Little wonder, then, that Dickens faced the end of his visit reluctantly, but he had no choice. He wrote his novels in installments, and the first weeks of each month he was prisoner to a deadline. Right now, as he wrote Miss Boyle as soon as he was back home, he was the "slave of the Lamp called Copperfield."

But the visit had been one of the high spots of his life. He dedicated *David Copperfield* to the Watsons and promised to come again. He did return. In January of 1851 he put on several plays in their Long Gallery, with elaborate staging and sets of his own devising. And in 1855 he stopped by when one of his reading tours brought him to the area.

Dickens's next novel after *David Copperfield* was *Bleak House* (1852–53), in which he makes abundant use of Rockingham memories. Though he transplants the locale to Lincolnshire and changes the names, it is easy to recognize Rockingham (he calls it Chesney Wold), its Yew Walk, and the ancient little church in the park.

A hundred years or more after Dickens, another novelist felt equally at home at Rockingham Castle. Often in his later life, in the 1960s, E. M. Forster would come at Christmas time to stay with his good friends, Lady Faith Culme-Seymour and her husband. Even though he never quite lost his innate prejudice against things aristocratic, he enjoyed his visits and was amused by his hosts' mixture of grandeur and—unlike the days of Dickens—servantless domesticity.

Rockingham Castle, still owned by Watsons, is open from Easter Sunday to the end of September, with all sorts of goings on, including tours of various rooms with their fine furniture and paintings, twelve acres of gardens with four hundred-year-old yew hedges shaped like elephants, and a Civil War Exhibition.

Down in the village, you can enjoy a refreshing stop at the "Dedlock Arms" pub of *Bleak House.* In real life in Dickens's day, it was known as the Sondes Arms—and still is.

Deene Park   The medieval manor called Deene has been in the same family for nearly five hundred years, and since one or another of them found a need to add a bit here and there, it now amounts to quite a place. The first of this family was Sir Robert Brudenell, who acquired it in 1514.

Along with adding rooms, his descendants added titles, too, so by the time James Thomas Brudenell inherited Deene Park in the nineteenth century, he was the seventh Earl of Cardigan. He entered upon a military career in 1824 and speedily won another distinction—as the most unpopular officer in the entire army. Within two years he had ordered over 700 arrests and held 105 courts-martial. In 1854 England's joining the Crimean War against the Russians provided the earl with a chance not merely for fame, but for immortality, however unfortunately won.

He had been given command of a brigade of light cavalry. On October 25, 1854, word reached him at the Crimean village of Balaclava to attack the Russians. So off he charged. No matter that Lord Cardigan had to lead his 673 men against thousands and thousands through a narrow valley over a mile long, its sides bristling with enemy cannon and cavalry, with more of the same waiting at the end.

Tennyson's "Charge of the Light Brigade" tells the tale:

> Storm'd at with shot and shell,
> Boldly they rode and well,
> Into the jaws of Death,
> Into the mouth of Hell
>   Rode the six hundred.

And hell it proved, of course:

> Right thro' the line they broke;
> Cossack and Russian
> Reel'd from the sabre-stroke
>   Shatter'd and sunder'd
> Then they rode back, but not,
>   Not the six hundred.

In fact, nothing like six hundred. Fewer than two hundred of the men who had charged forth with Lord Cardigan returned with him just twenty minutes later. As *The London Times* reported tersely, "Some one had blundered." Yet Tennyson marvels:

> "Forward, the Light Brigade!"
> Was there a man dismay'd?
> Not tho' the soldier knew
>   Some one had blunder'd.

After all, says the poet,

> Theirs not to make reply
> Theirs not to reason why,
> Theirs but to do and die.

Maybe so. But one can't help thinking that a question or two, perhaps, might not have been all that much amiss. In the words of one French general, "C'est magnifique mais ce n'est pas la guerre." Magnificent, sure—but that's no way to run a war.

Historical records of this seventh Earl of Cardigan are among the displays that await you at Deene Park, along with the usual array of period furniture, paintings, and family portraits. At last report, it was open on Sundays from Easter to the end of August.

And, if you're wondering: yes, this was the earl of the Cardigan jacket.

Canons Ashby—Blakesley—Titchmarsh—Aldwinkle—and Cotterstock

On both sides of his family, John Dryden had roots that reached to most of Northamptonshire county. Closest tied to the poet on his father's side were Canons Ashby, fourteen miles southwest of Northampton on the B 4525, and Blakesley, three miles east of Canons Ashby. On his mother's side, the villages of chief interest are Titchmarsh and Aldwinkle (or Aldwincle), both about twenty miles northeast of Northampton, a couple of miles apart on either side of the A 605, and to a lesser extent, Cotterstock, six miles above Titchmarsh.[1]

Dryden was born at the Rectory in Aldwinkle in 1631. His parents, as listed in the registry record of their marriage, were Erasmus Dryden, "gentleman of Canons Ashby," and Mary Pickering, "a maiden of Aldwinkle." The Pickerings were a prominent family with extensive holdings in both Aldwinkle and Titchmarsh; and Mary's father, the Rev. Henry Pickering, was rector of Aldwinkle's All Saints Church, which explains the site of Dryden's birth.

As a boy, Dryden went to the Titchmarsh Grammar School, where he developed some decided opinions of his own. While writing about Edmund Spenser in later life, he was probably thinking of his own schooling as well when he said that the Roman education of a Plutarch was superior to that of

---

[1]Dryden had cousins at Cotterstock and visited them occasionally. He was there in the summer of both 1698 and 1699 and worked at his *Fables Ancient and Modern*, finished and published shortly before his death in 1700.

Spenser, "where the greatest part of our youth is spent on learning the words of dead languages." Dryden decries, too, the floggings so prevalent in the classrooms he had known. Students were not beaten in Plutarch's day: "Rods and ferulas [canes] were not used then as being properly the punishment of slaves, and not the correction of ingenuous free-born men."

Dryden attended the Titchmarsh church, too. Notable for its richly carved fifteenth-century tower, it still has the Pickering family pew and a monument pointing out that Dryden was "bred and had his first learning here."

In 1650, Dryden went off to Cambridge and received his B. A. degree in March 1654. But his plans for further study were abandoned when his father died four months later, and he had to assume the role of head of the family. It was a considerable role. Erasmus Dryden had left thirteen other children for John to keep an eye on, and extensive properties in both Canons Ashby, the Dryden's family seat since Tudor days, and nearby Blakesley.

The Drydens' Canons Ashby house was originally built about 1550 and considerably enlarged in the 1580s and again in the eighteenth century shortly after Dryden's death. One of its Elizabethan guests was Edmund Spenser, whose wife was a cousin of Dryden's great-grandfather, Sir Erasmus Dryden. Spenser is supposed to have written some of *The Faerie Queene* there in a room that now bears his name.

Dryden himself never lived in the mansion, but his son Erasmus did, and is buried in the local churchyard. The manor house is now owned by the National Trust and is open April through October, Wednesday to Sunday afternoons.

Sulgrave

Americans in the neighborhood of Canons Ashby may want to take a three-mile run down the B 4525 to Sulgrave Manor, once the home of Laurence Washington—the same Laurence Washington who was one of Northampton's six hundred mayors and ancestor (seven generations removed) of George Washington.

Laurence built the place in the 1550s, and the Washingtons lived there for over a hundred years. In 1657, Col. John Washington—great-grandfather of the man who became America's first president—emigrated to Virginia.

Sulgrave, a two-storey greystone mansion, has been restored and is now a George Washington Museum, thanks to a concerted effort by Englishmen and Americans alike that began in 1914.

Among its treasures are a number of historical furnishings, including a chair from Mount Vernon; a piece of Martha Washington's wedding gown; a snuff box with a likeness of George; and several portraits, one an original by Gilbert Stuart. Over the porch window is the Washington family coat-of-arms, two bars and a trio of mullets (stars), which may—the word is *may*—have inspired the original Stars and Stripes.

The museum is open daily except on Wednesday, the hour varying with the season.

Towcester

Towcester is at the junction of the A 43 and the A 5, eight miles southwest of Northampton. There's no need to go dashing down there, but it does have an old, old church, with parts of it going back to the thirteenth century and some interesting chained books. And if you're going to be thereabouts anyway, you might want to stop at the Saracen's Head.

In Dickens's *Pickwick Papers*, this is the inn where Sam Weller, dripping wet and shivering from the rain, persuades his master to put in for the night—for the horses' sake: "It's cruelty to animals, sir, to ask 'em to do it." Besides, Sam adds, "There's beds here, sir . . . everything clean and comfortable. Wery good little dinner, sir, they can get ready in half an hour—pair of fowls, sir, and a weal cutlet; French beans, 'taturs, tart, and tidiness."

Mr. Pickwick and his party are not disappointed. In ten minutes, "the fire was blazing brightly, and everything looked (as everything always does in all decent English inns) as if the travellers had been expected and their comfort prepared, for days beforehand."

You won't be disappointed, either. A special attraction is the bar on the left of the old coach entrance. This was formerly the kitchen where beside the cavernous fireplace, Mr. Pickwick winds up his evening serving as an involuntary buffer between those embattled journalists, Mr. Pott of the *Eatanswill Gazette* swinging his fire-shovel and Mr. Slurk of the *Eatanswill Independent* flailing away with his carpet bag . . . and Mr. Pickwick absorbing the blows of both.

3. Bedford and Bunyan

The A 428 runs directly southeast from Northampton to Bedford, twenty-one miles away. Just before you cross from Northamptonshire into Bedfordshire, you'll pass Easton Maudit.

Easton Maudit

If Thomas Percy, sitting in his Easton Maudit rectory writing his clergyman friend in Wales that "our Gentry are very polite, and some of them are very conversant with modern Literature" sounded unwontedly humble, he may well be excused. He was the Reverend Dr. Percy, Bishop of Dromore, true, and soon to publish the *Reliques of Ancient English Poetry*, a work that became a landmark in the study of early English and Scottish ballads. But in his library at that very moment was the eighteenth century's awesome arbiter of literature, Dr. Samuel Johnson, working on his long-awaited edition of Shakespeare.

Johnson arrived at Easton Maudit June 25, 1764, and stayed until August 18. With him he brought Miss Anna Williams, the blind old lady he had taken into his London home and befriended with infinite care. Johnson liked to pretend that the ballads that so preoccupied Percy were too simple a poetic form to be taken seriously, and had once dashed off an impromptu parody to prove it:

> I put my hat upon my head,
>   And walk'd into the Strand,
> And there I met another man
>   With his hat in his hand.

Actually Johnson had encouraged Percy to publish the collection of ballads in the first place, and was there to help him get it in final shape, so the visit went famously. Johnson helped his host compile a glossary for the book, and wrote the dedication. He indulged in what he confessed was a lifelong passion for old romances, rummaging daily through Percy's large collection. He and Miss Williams took drives through the countryside and sipped tea with those local gentry and their wives.

And best of all, Johnson at last found the impetus he needed to finish that edition of Shakespeare. It had been hanging over him now for seven years, the large sums he had collected from early subscriptions long since spent, the subscribers clamoring for something to show for their money. In October of 1765 it finally appeared, and triumphantly, thanks to the momentum born at Easton Maudit. It did, as T. S. Eliot was to say almost two centuries later, "what only Johnson could do."

Bedford and Elstow

Bedford   John Bunyan is known worldwide. His works, especially *Pilgrim's Progress* (1678) have been translated into most of the languages known to man. Yet in all the sixty years of his life, except for three of army service, he never wandered for long from a five-mile circle encompassing Bedford and Elstow. And even his military experience didn't take him far afield. He was stationed at Newport Pagnell, twelve miles west in Buckinghamshire.

Today Bedford, a town of seventy-five thousand, on the A 428 and the A 6 and Elstow, a village of perhaps eight hundred, on the A 6 are essentially one, though you can tell the difference if you drive a couple of miles south out of Bedford proper. When you reach a row or two of handsome cottages, overhung and half-timbered, that's Elstow.

Elstow   A stone in the fields outside Elstow on the lane leading to Harrowden indicates where, in November 1628, John Bunyan was born "of a low and inconsiderable generation," he said in *Grace Abounding*, "my father's house being of that rank that is meanest and most despised in the land." The register of Elstow's Abbey Church records his baptism: "John, the sonne of Thomas Bonnionn, Jun., the 30th of November."

Son of a tinker, a lowly trade, John was fortunate to go to the village school. He felt even luckier in 1644 when officers from Cromwell's Parliamentary army showed up ordering all able-bodied men between sixteen and sixty to report for duty. Bunyan wasn't quite sixteen, but he said he was, and went off to see what life was like outside Elstow.

He returned in 1647, became a tinker himself, soon married, and settled down at age twenty in a poor little cottage with a small attached lean-to for his forge. "This woman and I," says *Grace Abounding*, "came together as poor as poor might be, not having so much house-hold-stuff as a dish or spoon betwixt us both." She did bring a dowry of sorts, however—two little devotional books that were to shape his life. For as he and his wife read them together in the evening, John Bunyan got religion.

One day on the village green, playing a favorite game called tipcat, where you hit a bit of wood with a bat, he heard a voice thundering from heaven: "Wilt thou leave thy sins and go to Heaven? Or have thy sins, and go to Hell?" For a moment he wavered: "Wherefore, leaving my Cat upon the ground." But then "I resolved in my mind I would go on in sin, and I returned desperately to my sport again."

Soon, though, his sense of guilt overwhelmed him. He gave up his tipcat and his other favorite hobby, too, the ringing of the church bells. He even began to curb his prodigious capacity for swearing, apparently his one legacy from the army. In 1653, at twenty-five, he joined Bedford's nonconformist St. John's Congregation, and two years later moved into Bedford to be nearer to it. By 1657, he had been ordained a deacon by St. John's and began preaching in villages roundabout.

In 1660, disaster struck. At a farmhouse in the hamlet of Samsell near Harlington, just as he began his service, Bunyan was arrested. His crimes: not attending church (i.e., "the" church), not using the Book of Common Prayer, and preaching without permission. He spent the next twelve years in Bedford Gaol.

It was an odd confinement. Sometimes it was "the very dark dungeon, nasty and stinking," he describes in *Pilgrim's Progress*. But sometimes, too, the gaoler allowed him an occasional outing, even it seems, once or twice to attend St. John's. Now and then his wife came to visit him (a second wife, his first having died soon after their move to Bedford). Mainly, he occupied himself writing, nine books in all, the most important being *Grace Abounding* (1666), and perhaps some part of *Pilgrim's Progress*.

Finally in 1672 he was released, when Charles II issued a general pardon of religious prisoners, acknowledging that it was "evident by the sad experience of 12 yeares that there is little fruit of these forceable Courses."

Thereafter Bunyan spent his life as minister of St. John's (he had been given the post even before his release from prison) and in writing. In 1676 he was sent to prison once more, briefly, and there finished *Pilgrim's Progress*. The book was an enormous success. By Bunyan's death in 1688, it had gone through eleven editions and sold over one hundred thousand copies.

Bunyan died in London while visiting friends and is buried in the same Bunhill Fields cemetery there that holds the graves of Daniel Defoe, Isaac Watts, and William Blake. It was an ironic final resting place for a man so rarely far from his native heath.

There is much of Bunyan for today's visitor to Bedford and Elstow to see. At Elstow, the Abbey Church still has the carved octagonal font in which he was baptized, the bells which he gave up ringing, and two stained glass windows with a scene each from *Pilgrim's Progress* and *The Holy War*. In the sixteenth-century Moot Hall there is a museum with relics, furnishings, books, and documents of Bunyan and his period. Beside the road leading to Bedford there's a marker showing the location of the cottage he had lived in after his first marriage.

At Bedford, today's Bunyan Meeting in Mill Street, built in 1849 on the same site as Bunyan's chapel, has bronze doors with ten scenes from *Pilgrim's Progress* and a tablet on an outside wall with the legend:

JOHN BUNYAN
Author of "Pilgrim's Progress" used to come
Here for Talks with Rector John Gifford.
In 1653 he joined the St. John's Congregation.

> In 1657 he was ordained in St. John's
> For preaching (in the villages).
> This Place was the Interpreter's House of His Experience.

Under a roster of pastors in the vestibule of the Bunyan Meeting is the door from Bunyan's cell at Bedford Gaol.[2]

A small museum behind the chapel has such Bunyan mementoes as his iron fiddle, staff, table, and anvil. The Public Library has a Bunyan exhibit, too. And at the corner of High and Silver Streets, a pavement slab marks the spot where the old Bedford County Gaol stood.

Finally, on St. Peter's Green there's a bronze statue of Bunyan by Sir Joseph Boehm. Its dedication in 1874 drew people from all over the world, including a representative from *Punch* who was moved to verse. If his lines do little else, they prove there's nothing funnier than a comic magazine trying to be serious:

> The people are weary of vestment-vanities,
> Of litigation and inanities,
>
> And fain would listen, O Preacher and Peer,
> To a voice like that of the Tinker-Seer.

Ampthill

Eight miles south of Bedford on the A 509, the market town of Ampthill has tangential ties with Bunyan. On its northern edge the great Jacobean architect Inigo Jones built Houghton House for Sir Philip Sidney's sister Mary, the Countess of Pembroke, friend to Spenser, Jonson, Samuel Daniel and other poets.

Bunyan heard descriptions of the mansion from his father and apparently, like his father, had even plied his trade there on occasion. In any event, there is ample reason to believe that Houghton House was the original for his House Beautiful in *Pilgrim's Progress*, and that the hills about Ampthill were his "Delectable Mountains."

Only the ruins of Houghton House remain, but they are open to the public, and suggest how grand a place it must have been.

---

[2]The writer William Hale White, who used the pseudonym Mark Rutherford, was a Bedford native and attended the new chapel.

Hockliffe

The village of Hockliffe on the A 5 and the A 4102 is at the southern tip of Bedfordshire, fifteen miles south of Bedford and less than ten miles from the Hertfordshire border. In 1900, Arnold Bennett rented Trinity Hall Farm there. The place was pleasant enough, a large square house of yellow-grey brick with ample fields. But it was a brave venture on several accounts. At thirty-three, Bennett was scrapping his career as editor of the magazine *Woman*, and had an ailing father and mother and his sister Tertia to support. But he had come to detest the magazine—"a miserable female paper," he called it—and was eager to try his hand as a freelance writer.

The move proved unpropitious. The novel he wrote using the farm as background, *Teresa of Watling Street*, was admittedly bad. His father died in 1902, and when the lease ran out the following January, Bennett was happy to return to London. But *The Grand Babylon Hotel*, also written at the farm, was a work of merit, and an augury of the great success that lay ahead.

With Hockliffe, you're practically back in London, and ready for the third and final leg of your tour of Middle England—Essex and East Anglia, a region unto itself.

ESSEX AND
EAST ANGLIA

ESSEX

Essex

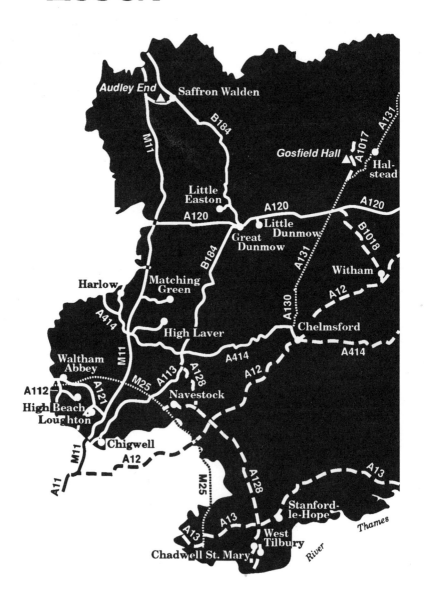

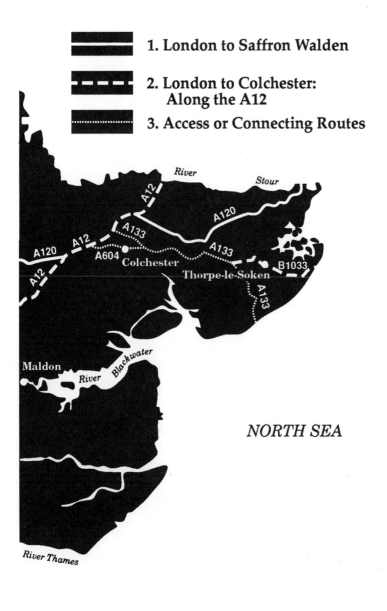

1. London to Saffron Walden

2. London to Colchester: Along the A12

3. Access or Connecting Routes

River *Stour*

A12

A120

A133

A120   A12

A133

A604   Colchester

A12

Thorpe-le-Soken

B1033

A133

Maldon

River *Blackwater*

NORTH SEA

River Thames

Essex is most fatte, fruiteful, and full of all profitable things.

> John Norden, *An Historical and Geographical*
> *Description of the County of Essex*

All the place names are from this part of Essex—which
I like more and more.

> Edward Thomas in a letter

There is much of Essex which is still fat and fruitful agriculturally, except for the southwest corner that Greater London has claimed all too voraciously for its own. Once away from this urban encroachment, it remains surprisingly open, rural, and unspoiled.

Essex is often listed as a "Home County," and sometimes included as a part of East Anglia, though purists frown on this. Its fifteen hundred or so square miles are pretty much bounded by water on three sides: the Thames and its estuary on the south, the North Sea on the east, and the Stour River and estuary on the north. To the west is Hertfordshire. The land undulates pleasantly, dotted by enticing villages with names of the sort that always attracted Edward Thomas—Wendens Ambo, Willingdale Doe, Matching Green.

But in a literary sense, "full of all things profitable" Essex is not. It provided the setting for one of the earliest English poems of merit, "The Battle of Maldon." And though its associations with writers have been neither numerous nor monumental, there are a number worth noting. These can be conveniently covered in two tours running out of London—one running north through eastern Essex, roughly paralleling the M 11; the other from the southwest to northeast following the A 12.

1. London To Saffron Walden: Off The M 11

The easiest way to the M 11 from Central London is to pick up the A 11 (Whitechapel Street) near London Bridge, follow it to where it runs into the A 12, then take the latter a mile and a quarter to the M-Way.

But unless you're absolutely wild about driving on superhighways, there's no need to get on the M 11 here, or for that matter, ever. None of the literary stops en route to Saffron Walden are on the M 11 itself.

Chigwell—Loughton—Waltham Abbey—and High Beach

Chigwell, off the A 113, Loughton, off the A 121, High Beach, off the A 112, and Waltham Abbey, on the A 121, are all within eight miles of where you'll first meet the M 11, for instance, but all are easily reachable on A-roads.

Chigwell   If the hour is right and you're hungry or thirsty, Chigwell's a grand place to begin your tour with a refreshing stop at its Ye Olde King's Head on the High Road.

With his tongue invading his cheek the slightest bit, perhaps, Charles Dickens called Chigwell the "greatest place in the world," and made the King's Head the "Maypole" of his *Barnaby Rudge* (1841). The real inn, built in the days of Henry VIII and much be-gabled, still looks as Dickens described it, "very old . . . perhaps as old as it claimed to be, and perhaps older," and still has the latticed bays above the ground floor that Mr. Chester noticed when innkeeper John Willet showed him to the Maypole's best apartment.

And you may still hear the same old legend that the Maypole's guests heard about King Henry's daughter, "not only that Queen Elizabeth had slept there one night while upon a hunting excursion . . . but that next morning, while standing on a mounting block before the door with one foot in the stirrup, the virgin monarch had then and there boxed and cuffed an unlucky page for some neglect of duty." Let "matter-of-fact and doubtful folks," scoff, even as they did in Dickens's day, if they will.

Loughton   The town of Loughton (LOW—as in "below") on the A 121 a mile and a half north of Chigwell, had a grand mansion in the seventeenth century, Loughton Hall. Here lived the Lady Mary Sidney Wroth, niece of Sir Philip Sidney. She tried her own hand at writing, an imitation of her uncle's *Arcadia* called *Urania*, and her beauty inspired poetic effusions from George Chapman and George Wither.

Two later writers who lived in Loughton for a time were Arthur Morrison and W. W. Jacobs, who had their heyday in the Edwardian era. Not widely remembered today, Morrison wrote with convincing realism in books like *To*

London Town (1899); and his *Cunning Murrell* (1900) merits particular mention here since it deals with pre-Victorian witchcraft in Essex. Jacobs wrote innumerable short stories, both comic and macabre, and one at least is surely a classic: "The Cat's Paw."

Waltham Abbey   Both John Foxe and Thomas Fuller lived in Waltham Abbey, a town on the A 121 four and a half miles northwest of Loughton. Foxe, who was there from 1565 until his death in 1587, is best known for his *Book of Martyrs* (1563), which is twice as long as Gibbon's *Decline and Fall*, and takes special relish in details of the martyrs' dying agonies.

Fuller was curate at the Abbey Church for nine years, beginning in 1648, during which time he worked away at *The Worthies of England*, published posthumously in 1662.

If you have the time, the Abbey Church that Fuller served is worth a look. It boasts the oldest Norman work in the country and—if you like such things—the very stocks and whipping post that helped make Fuller's parishioners behave.

Moreover, it has the tomb of King Harold. Immediately following his unfortunate meeting with William the Conqueror in 1066, Harold was unceremoniously buried under a cairn of stones on the beach near Hastings. But after the country settled down a bit, his body was recovered and given an internment in Waltham Abbey befitting the last Saxon king of Britain.

Harold did fight valiantly, if somewhat stupidly, at that Battle of Hastings, and literary works about him tend to be sympathetic. Among them are Charles Dickens's *Child's History of England* (1852–54); *Harold* (1848), a historical romance by Bulwer-Lytton; and the drama by Tennyson also called *Harold* (1876).

High Beach   High Beach lies at the edge of Epping Forest, off the A 11 and midway between Loughton and Waltham Abbey. Within the short span of eighty years, 1837 to 1915, three poets came there at crucial points in their lives.

When Alfred Tennyson arrived in 1837, he was a troubled man. Almost abnormally sensitive, he had been crushed by critics' assault on his *Poems* (1832), the collection containing such gems as "The Lotus Eaters" and "The Lady of Shalott." The following year his closest friend, Arthur Hallam— "more than my brothers are to me," Tennyson would write in *In Memoriam*— died suddenly in Vienna. And Tennyson was in High Beach at all only because his now-widowed mother had been forced to give up the house in which he had lived all his life, his father's rectory in Somersby, Lincs.

At High Beach, worse was to come. In 1838, the Rev. Henry Sellwood finally but reluctantly recognized Tennyson's engagement to his daughter Emily. His other daughter Louise had married Tennyson's brother Charles, and it wasn't working out. Besides, Alfred had neither money nor prospects, and his religious views were less than orthodox. In 1840, Mr. Sellwood forced Emily to break off the engagement and forbade her even to write to Alfred.

To top it all off, Tennyson proceeded to lose what little money he'd inherited, investing it in a wild scheme to carve wood by machinery. Perhaps he should have been warned in advance. The inventor of the machine, a Dr. Allen, was also owner of the High Beach lunatic asylum.

Quitting Somersby had been a double wrench for Tennyson. It also meant leaving the place where he and his sister, also named Emily, and Arthur Hallam had shared the happiest occasion of their lives. In 1832, Hallam had spent the Christmas holidays at the rectory, celebrating his coming of age, which brought the elder Tennyson's sanction to marry Emily.

In Memoriam, the poet's great tribute to Hallam, records the Tennysons' grim first Christmas in their new High Beach home. Abandoned were all the traditional family festivities they had shared with Hallam at Somersby— trimming the tree, singing carols, playing charades:

> Tonight ungather'd let us leave
> This laurel, let this holly stand;
> We live within the stranger's land,
> And strangely falls our Christmas-eve.

It would be 1850 before things began to come right. In that year *In Memoriam* was published with great success, Rev. Sellwood relented and let Tennyson marry Emily, and Queen Victoria made him poet laureate. But by then he had long departed High Beach, going first to Tunbridge Wells in Kent. His High Beach home, called Beach House, survives, but is much altered.

By the oddest of coincidences, the poet John Clare not only came to High Beach the same year that Tennyson did, but came under the care of none other than Tennyson's Dr. Allen. Known as the "Peasant Poet," Clare was a self-educated man, a farm hand from the age of twelve. In 1820, when he was twenty-seven, his *Poems Descriptive of Rural Life* won much attention, but the subsequent *Shepherd's Calendar* (1827) was a failure, and he went back to farm work.

When *The Rural Muse* appeared in 1835, only one critic bothered to notice it. Disappointment, worry, and overwork broke Clare down. Declared insane in 1837, he was committed to Dr. Allen's asylum. There he stayed for four years, until one day he simply wandered off and walked unattended back to his home in Northampton.[1] Clare deserved better. Not a poet of first rank, true, but a poet. Charles Lamb chided him for his "rustic cockneisms," but in the same breath acknowledged "your observation has astonished me."

To the third poet, Edward Thomas, High Beach initially brought happiness. A late-bloomer, he had turned seriously to writing poetry only in 1914, at age thirty-six, after being prodded by the American poet Robert Frost. He volunteered for military service almost immediately thereafter and was stationed at High Beach. As he confided in that letter to his daughter, "I like [Essex] more and more," and sent for his family to join him. All too soon, however, his company was shipped to France. In May 1917, he was killed in battle.

High Laver and Matching Green

Both High Laver and Matching Green are on minor roads off the M 11, to the east of Harlow and about a dozen miles northeast of High Beach.

John Locke, perhaps the most important figure in English philosophy and author of the great *Essay Concerning Human Understanding* (1690), came to High Laver in 1691 to live at Oates Manor, the county seat of his friends Sir Francis and Lady Masham. Though broken in health, he managed to write a number of controversial religious articles there, as well as his little classic called *Thoughts on Education* (1693). He died in 1704 and is buried in the village churchyard.

The showpiece of Matching Green in 1720 was Down-Hall. That was the year Matthew Prior bought it as triumphant proof that he had surmounted the political ruin the Whigs wrought upon him and other leading Tories following the death of Queen Anne.

Some of the purchase money came from subscriptions to Prior's *Poems on Several Occasions* (1719), vigorously promoted by fellow-authors Jonathan Swift, Alexander Pope, John Gay, and Dr. John Arbuthnot. But the bulk was a gift from Edward Harley, Earl of Oxford. This was the same Harley whose library furnished the vast collection now at the British Museum known as the Harleian manuscripts, which in turn led to the *Harleian Miscellany* edited by Dr. Johnson in 1744–46.[2]

---

[1]For the rest of Clare's story, see p. 245; for more about Thomas, pp. 156–57.
[2]As discussed on p. 172.

Prior said that his verse was only "the product of his leisure hours," and insisted that as a diplomat he had "business enough upon his hands and was a poet only by accident." Nevertheless, many of his poems are sprightly, witty and charming—among them one on Down-Hall itself, *Down-Hall, a Ballad* (1723).

The mansion Prior knew and landscaped so lovingly was replaced by another building in the 1870s that later became a girls' school and, later yet, a managerial college.

Great Dunmow—Little Easton—and Saffron Walden

Tucked into the northwest corner of Essex are Great Dunmow, Little Easton, and Saffron Walden, all strung out along the B 184 east of the M 11. Great Dunmow comes first, seven miles above Matching Green where the B 184 crosses the A 120. Next, about two miles northwest of Great Dunmow on a side road, is Little Easton, with another nine miles beyond that Saffron Walden.

Great Dunmow   The pleasant little market town of Great Dunmow boasts the pond where the first lifeboat was tested in 1785, and provided a setting for H. G. Wells's *Mr. Britling sees it through* (1916). But it shares a special fame with its sister village, Little Dunmow, for the award of the "Dunmow Flitch," a ceremony that goes back to medieval times before *Piers Plowman* (between 1360 and 1399) and *The Canterbury Tales* (about 1387), and is mentioned in both.

The flitch, a side of bacon, was given yearly to the married couple who could prove that they hadn't quarreled once during the past twelve months, or, as the rules quaintly put it, had "not repented them, sleeping or waking, of their marriage in a year and a day." Evidence was given, oaths taken, and the prize awarded at Dunmow Priory.

Chaucer's use of the custom in *The Canterbury Tales*, in the Wife of Bath's Prologue to her own tale, is delicious. Living in a male-dominated society and addressing a virtually all-male audience—after all, the Prioress is the only other woman in the group of thirty-one going to Canterbury—the doughty wife nonetheless proclaims that the real key to a successful marriage is for the woman, not the man, to be boss.

She ought to know, she continues. She'd had five husbands in all, and the best ones (well, for her, at least) were the first three. The last two, she admits, were "badde." But the "three were goode men, and riche and olde." And totally obedient to her; in fact, enslaved:

> I set them so a-working, glory be!
> That many a night they sang, "Ah, woe is me!"
> The bacon wasn't fetched for *them*, I trow,
> That some men had in Essex at Dunmow.[3]

The ceremony was abandoned in the eighteenth century, but was strikingly recalled by a Victorian novelist, William Harrison Ainsworth, in his *The Flitch of Bacon* (1854). As a result, the custom was revived in the Great Dunmow Town Hall the following year, with Ainsworth as honored guest.

The ruins of the Priory where all this began can still be seen, two and a half miles southeast of town, and the ceremony still takes place once every four years in the town park.

Little Easton   H. G. Wells got to know Great Dunmow when he gave up his London home in 1912 and moved to Little Easton, buying a commodious Georgian house called The Glebe, and staying until 1930. Works of this period, in addition to *Mr. Britling*, included *Bealby* (1915), *The Outline of History* (1920), *Short History of the World* (1922), *The World of William Clissold* (1926), and *The Open Conspiracy* (1928).

Among guests at Little Easton was Arnold Bennett, a close friend and warmhearted, but raucous at times and overly given to parading his wealth, success, and possessions. He amused himself by joining the Sunday afternoon hockey games and watching the stags rutting in Warwick Park.[4]

Bennett's words for The Glebe: "like a large cottage made comfortable by people rich but capricious."

Saffron Walden   Saffron Walden, named for the crocus whose commercial use in the Middle Ages made it prosperous, has rightly been called "a delightful town." The medieval houses on Church Street, their overhanging gables bedecked with plasterwork, are utterly beguiling. The church itself,

---

[3]I've modernized the language somewhat for those who don't know Middle English. Needless to say, Chaucer's exact words are more charming:

> I sette hem so a-werke, by my fey,
> That many a nyght they songen "Weilawey!"
> The bacon was nat fet for hem, I trowe,
> That som men han in Essex at Dunmowe.

[4]A wing of the Countess of Warwick's home, Easton Lodge, survives as Warwick House, whose extensive gardens and grounds are open on dates listed by the NGS.

St. Mary of the Virgin, is nearly two hundred feet long and one of the finest in Essex. Its turf maze, winding its bewildering way for nearly a mile, is England's largest.

But the sight to see isn't in Saffron Walden at all. It's a mansion a mile west of town called Audley End. Originally a priory, the site passed into private hands after the Dissolution. Its owner was Thomas Howard—a hero of the defeat of the Spanish Armada—when Sir Philip Sidney was a guest in 1578 while on a royal progress with Queen Elizabeth.

The visit turned out to be quite a literary occasion. Sidney was entertained by a deputation of dons from nearby Cambridge University. Their leader was Gabriel Harvey, mentor of Edmund Spenser and, like Sidney himself, a member of the distinguished poetical group known as the Areopagus.[5]

Thomas Howard was made Baron de Walden in 1597, and Earl of Suffolk in 1603, the year he began building the Audley End that still exists. When he was through, it was one of the grandest homes in England. Both of the seventeenth century's great diarists went to see it several times. On his first visit in 1645, John Evelyn was struck by its artful balance between antique and modern, and called it "without comparison one of the stateliest palaces of the Kingdome."

Samuel Pepys's praise on his initial visit in 1660 matched Evelyn's: "The housekeeper shewed us all the house, in which the stateliness of the ceilings, chimney-pieces, and form of the whole was exceedingly worth seeing. He took us into the cellar, where we drank most admirable drink. . . . Here I played on my flageolette, there being an excellent echo."

Audley End caught the eye of Charles II, also. Pepys's diary entry for March 7, 1666 records that "the King and Duke are to go tomorrow to Audley End, in order to the seeing and buying of it of my Lord Suffolke." The king did buy it, for £50,000. But neither he nor his successors managed to pay off the mortgage, and in 1701 the Suffolks got it back.

The Audley End you can visit today is still impressive, but considerably short of its original grandeur, thanks to another literary figure. Sir John Vanbrugh, author of *The Relapse* (1697) and *The Provok'd Wife* (1697). He combined the careers of playwright and architect, both with a heavy hand. In 1721 he hacked away at Audley End with appalling zeal and less than happy results, reducing its size and robbing it of the characteristic both Evelyn and Pepys had noted: "stateliness."

---

[5]Harvey was no stranger to Saffron Walden. He was born there about the year 1554, son of a rope-maker.

In season, Audley End is open to the public afternoons except on Monday.

2. London to Colchester: Along the A 12

To put it delicately, the A 12 is not always the best of roads. In summer it can be a trial, packed with refugees from London, white-skinned and weary, seeking respite and sunburn on the beaches of East Anglia. But if you want to see the eastern parts of Essex and Suffolk, and Norfolk, you take the A 12.

Navestock—Stanford-le-Hope and Chadwell St. Mary

Soon after it leaves Greater London and enters Essex, the A 12 cuts across the A 128, a road leading to three villages and three writers of note.

Navestock, with Charles Algernon Swinburne, is on a side road off the A 128, three miles above this junction . . . Stanford-le-Hope and Joseph Conrad ten miles below the junction, off the A 13 . . . and Chadwell St. Mary, with Daniel Defoe, three miles southwest of Stanford-le-Hope on the A 128.

Navestock   Swinburne was only in Navestock for a short while, but he never forgot its good if simple villagers—nor they him.

When wild behavior at Oxford made him fail his classics exam, he was sent to brush up with the Navestock vicar, the Rev. William Stubbs. The morning after his arrival, a Sunday, waking late and finding Stubbs already gone to his church next door, Swinburne wandered out to the vicarage garden, still in his nightclothes, to watch the natives pass by on their way to service. The parishioners came all right, but none passed by. For there, staring at them, was the Devil himself.

Of course it was only young Swinburne, but how were they to know? There stood the stranger, all five foot four inches of him, clad in his scarlet dressing gown, shod in his shining red slippers, his flaming red hair standing all a-bristle from his head.

Inside the church, the vicar, surveying the empty pews, summoned the sexton to ring the bells for a second and more urgent call to worship. With that, one villager bolder than the rest broke the spell, flying past the hedge, up the lane, and into the church, with the others in mad pursuit.

Watching them flee, Swinburne mused aloud: "How oddly the Essex yokel takes his Sunday service."

Stubbs got on well with his pupil, and it was his encouragement that produced Swinburne's first original poem, a piece entered in Oxford's annual poetry competition on the prescribed subject, "the heroic seaman Sir John Franklin." Somebody named Owen Alexander Vidal won the prize. But Swinburne did come in second.

If you want to see Mr. Stubbs's vicarage, by the way, it's on the village green, and now called Marley's.

Stanford-le-Hope   Conrad's arrival in Stanford-le-Hope in 1896 followed the complacent routine that marked all the many moves of his life. He had his wife Jessie single-handedly transfer their possessions to the new place, putting each item precisely where he had ordered and adhering to his rigid time schedule without so much as raising a little finger to help her. Then, and only then, would he move in, expressing usually some measure of content.

Soon thereafter, however, he would be roaring his displeasure—in this instance, justified. Their first quarters at Stanford-le-Hope were cramped: "a damned jerry-built rabbit hutch," he said. So they would move again; on this occasion it was to a sixteenth-century farmhouse called Ivy Walls. In between, as Jessie braced herself for whenever the next move might come, he would force himself to the always distressful business of writing.

It was at Stanford-le-Hope that Conrad decided he could make it as a writer, and gave up his career as an officer in the merchant marine. In 1895 he had published his first novel, *Almayer's Folly.* Based on his sea experiences, it had won him a small but devoted following. Now, during this Stanford-le-Hope period, came *An Outcast of the Islands* (1896) and *The Nigger of the Narcissus* (1898). Neither was much of a commercial success, but in later life he was to call *The Nigger of the Narcissus* the book "by which as a creative writer I stand or fall."

Literary friends came to see him: Stephen Crane, the young American novelist; Edward Garnett, essayist and dramatist, whose encouragement was timely; Ford Madox Hueffer, later to be known as Ford Madox Ford. And John Galsworthy, most welcome of all. They had first met in 1892, when Galsworthy was a passenger and Conrad the first mate of the clipper Torrens. It was Galsworthy more than anyone else who persuaded Conrad to become a writer.

Moving day for poor Jessie came again in 1898. By then Ivy Walls in its turn had grown intolerable. Her husband's words as he left Stanford-le-Hope for Postling in Kent and collaboration on a novel with Hueffer were classic Conrad: "This opportunity is a perfect Godsend to me. It preserves what's left of my piety and belief in a benevolent Providence and also probably my sanity."

Chadwell St. Mary   Often during his seventy-two years on earth, Daniel Defoe's exact whereabouts were hard to pin down, and with good reason.[6] He lived in slippery times. Controversies among Anglicans, Dissenters, and Roman Catholics, and between Whigs and Tories were bitter. Factions rose and fell as five monarchs with their varying backgrounds and prejudices came and went: Charles II, nominally, at least, head of the Church of England; James II, an avowed Catholic; William III, "foreigner" son of a Dutch prince; Anne, high church and English born; and George I, the German.

In such circumstances, choosing the wrong side could cost dearly. Defoe was a Dissenter, a supporter of the widely unpopular William III, and quite possibly a double-dealing agent who worked now for this side and now for that. So from time to time he found it convenient simply to disappear.

It seems fairly certain that he found himself in and about Chadwell St. Mary for two important periods of his life. The first was between 1694 and 1703, when he was part-owner of a tile business in nearby West Tilbury. Among his writings during these years, two were especially damaging. *The True-Born Englishman* (1701), a vigorous and satiric defense of King William, was provocative enough. But *The Shortest Way with the Dissenters* (1702) angered everyone.

At first taken in by its apparent support of their views, high churchmen were enraged when they realized that actually it was attacking them. And Defoe's fellow Dissidents feared they would bear the brunt of the inevitable reprisal. Though the pamphlet appeared anonymously, the author was soon detected, run down, pilloried, and imprisoned. There was one happy by-product: while in prison Defoe wrote *Hymn to the Pillory*, one of his best pieces in verse.

Evidence indicates that Defoe secretly returned to the area about 1718, either while hiding from the government, or working against it—or who knows, maybe both simultaneously.

Anyway, if so, he must have written part of his most famous book in

---

[6]He was born Daniel Foe, son of a London butcher, but came to use "Foe," "DeFoe," or "Defoe" almost interchangeably until finally settling on Defoe.

Chadwell St. Mary, for the first section of *Robinson Crusoe* appeared on April 25, 1719

Chelmsford—Maldon—and Witham

As the A 12 continues on its northeasterly way to Colchester, it runs right through Chelmsford and skirts Witham, the former eleven miles above the A 12–A 128 junction, and Witham another nine miles beyond Chelmsford on the B 1018. Maldon is ten miles due east of Chelmsford, on the A 414.

Chelmsford If you've come from London, have arrived in Chelmsford, and are on your way to Ipswich, you'll be duplicating the very route of Charles Dickens, who stayed at Chelmsford's Black Boy Inn on his way to East Anglia in 1834.

Dickens uses the Black Boy in *Pickwick Papers*. Mr. Weller, working a coach for a friend, almost by accident tells Mr. Pickwick about two passengers he has picked up there and taken to Ipswich recently, one "slim and tall, with long hair and the gift o' gab wery galloping," the other a "black-haired chap in mulberry livery, with a wery large head."

Mr. Pickwick, recognizing the pair at once as Mr. Jingle and Job Trotter, and remembering the wrongs he'd suffered at Jingle's hands, pounds the table.

"I'll follow him," vows Mr. Pickwick, "we may as well see Ipswich as any other place. I'll follow him."

If you do happen to be in Chelmsford, however, don't look for the Black Boy. It vanished in Dickens's day. But you can see on Hall Street the building, now marked by a blue plaque, where Guglielmo Marconi established the world's first radio station, and the place in New Street where in 1920 he began transmitting England's first radio programs two years before the BBC was born.

Maldon For all its fourteen thousand or so people, Maldon today retains something of the air of a village, perched on a hill above the Blackwater estuary where pleasure boats bob invitingly. It is hard to connect it now with the grim warfare of *The Battle of Maldon*, last of the great poems written in Anglo-Saxon.

The epic, incomplete in the only manuscript that survives, tells of the death in 991 of Byrhtnoth of Essex. Aged but gallant, Byrhtnoth stands on the riverbank beside the body of his slain leader and defies the invading Vikings:

> I am old in years. I will never yield.
> But here at the last beside my lord,
> By the leader I loved, I look to die.

And die he does, cut down by a poisoned spear.

Witham   Witham's two contributors to literature are a versatile pair: an early Jacobean poet-musician-doctor and a twentieth-century translator-playwright-detective story writer.

The Jacobean was Thomas Campion. Said by tradition to have been born in Witham in 1567, Campion leavened his duties as a physician by writing both words and music for several collections of lovely songs. "There is a garden in her face," for one, is exquisite.

The twentieth-century writer was Dorothy L. Sayers. She wrote first-rate translations of Dante's *Inferno* (1942) and *Purgatorio* (1955), and religious plays like *The Man Born to be King* (1942). But she is far better known, of course, for detective stories like *The Nine Tailors* (1934), starring the inimitable Lord Peter Wimsey.

The house on Newland Street (No. 24) where she lived from 1928 til her death in 1957 is now headquarters for the Dorothy L. Sayers Society, and is marked by a plaque.

Colchester—Gosfield Hall—and Thorpe-le-Soken

Colchester is in Essex's northeast corner, only five miles below where the A 12 crosses over into Suffolk, bound for Ipswich. Thirteen miles almost due west of Colchester is Gosfield Hall, off the A 1017; and nearly the same distance to the east is Thorpe-le-Soken, on the B 1033.

Colchester   For this part of England, Colchester with its eighty-four thousand or so inhabitants is a considerable town indeed. It is also the country's oldest recorded town. There was a settlement on the banks of its Colne River as early as 700 B. C. By the first century A. D., it was known as Camulodunon and served as capital for Cunobelin, king of southeast England. His name slightly changed, he is the central figure of Shakespeare's play, *Cymbeline*.

An even more legendary king was Coel, listed by Geoffrey of Monmouth in his *Historia Regum Brittanniae* (about 1139), and immortalized not only in the nursery rhyme "Old King Cole was a merry old soul," but also in the poem by John Masefield in *King Cole and Other Poems* (1923). Legendary or not, Colchester accepts him; there's a statue of his supposed daughter St. Helena atop the clock tower of the Town Hall.

From 43 A. D. when they invaded Britain until the fifth century when they withdrew, the Romans spasmodically controlled Colchester. Its modern name, bestowed by the Saxons who replaced them, reflects their presence—"Colne-ceaster," Roman Fortress ("ceaster") on the Colne.

In the eighteenth century, Colchester produced yet another of the world's best-known children's songs. There, between the years 1796 and 1811 lived two young ladies, the Misses Jane and Ann Taylor, who occupied themselves writing such children's books as *Original Poems for Infant Minds* (1804), and *Hymns for Infant Minds* (1810). Included in *Rhymes for the Nursery* (1806) was "Twinkle, twinkle little star." The Taylor house, identified by a plaque, is No. 11–12 on West Stockwell, which runs north off the High Street by the Town Hall.

Contemporary with the Taylors was Henry Crabbe Robinson, apprenticed to a Colchester lawyer in 1790. In 1807 he turned to journalism to become a foreign correspondent, one of the first such in England. But he is best remembered for his letters and the diaries—thirty-two volumes in all—containing priceless personal observations of the literary greats of his time. Wordsworth, Coleridge, Southey, Lamb, and Hazlitt were all his friends.

A third noteworthy resident of Colchester in the eighteenth century is fictional: Daniel Defoe's Moll Flanders. An abandoned waif, she flees the gipsies and is apprehended by the parish officers; she explains: "[and as] I was too young to do any work, being not above three years old, compassion moved the magistrates of the town to order some care to be taken of me." The Colchester people were kind: "It was my good hap to be put to nurse, as they call it, to a woman who was indeed poor but had been in better circumstances . . . a very sober, pious woman, very housewifely and clean, and very mannerly, and with good behavior."

Gosfield Hall   A mélange of Tudor and later architecture located a couple of miles southwest of Halstead, Gosfield Hall's one literary distinction is that in the nineteenth century it was owned by Robert Nugent, Lord Clare, poor Oliver Goldsmith's only patron.

Goldsmith won the attention of Clare with the publication of *The Traveller* in 1764, and visited at the Hall several times. Its staterooms, now open to the public two afternoons a week, give a fine picture of how the elegant lived in the days when Dr. Johnson and his circle, with Goldsmith as their beloved clown-in-residence, ruled the literary world.

Thorpe-le-Soken   Arnold Bennett bought Comarques, a mansion in the village of Thorpe-le-Soken, in 1912 and moved into it the following February. A charming Queen Anne house of red brick set off by gardens, it delighted the Bennetts. He wrote his friends: "We are going to install ourselves there definitely for everlasting; our deaths will one day cause a sensation in the village which we shall dominate, and the English villagers and landed gentry will wonder, as they stroll through the deserted house, why the madman had 3 bathrooms in a home so small; they will not know it was due solely to a visit in the U.S.A."

Actually, those English villagers weren't all that dominated. They looked askance at the new wife he had brought with him from France, and at the yacht he had purchased with the money pouring in from the sales of *Old Wives Tale* (1908) and the first two novels of the Clayhanger series, *Clayhanger* (1910) and *Hilda Lessways* (1911).

Even Bennett's friends recoiled at the way he flaunted his sudden wealth. Once, watching him roar past in his Rolls Royce, the novelist Hugh Walpole confided to his diary, "a guttersnipe." Still, the friends came to Comarques in droves: Hugh de Selincourt, the critic; Granville-Barker, dramatist and director; E. V. Lucas, essayist; Frank Swinnerton; the composer Maurice Ravel; and H. G. Wells.

During these years, Bennett finished *These Twain* (1916), last of the Clayhanger trilogy, and wrote *The Lion's Share* (1916), *The Roll Call* (1918), and others. But with the onset of World War I, things had begun to change. After 1915, when the military billeted forty horses in his yard, he lived more and more in his London flat. The charm of the country life was gone.

In 1921, the house went on the market, and Bennett left Comarques and Essex.

SUFFOLK
AND NORFOLK

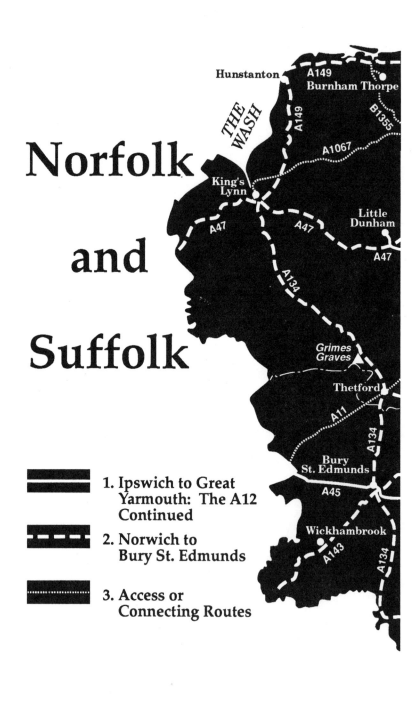

Norfolk and Suffolk

Hunstanton

A149
A149
Burnham Thorpe
B1355
THE WASH
A1067
King's Lynn
A47
A47
Little Dunham
A47
A134
Grimes Graves
Thetford
A11
A134
Bury St. Edmunds
A45
Wickhambrook
A143
A134

1. Ipswich to Great Yarmouth: The A12 Continued

2. Norwich to Bury St. Edmunds

3. Access or Connecting Routes

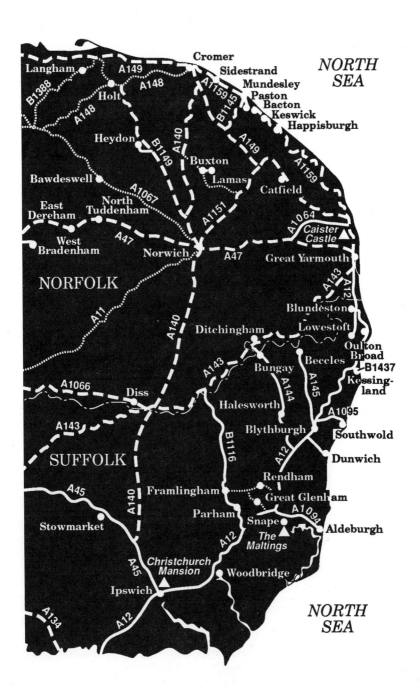

I was quite tired, and very glad, when we saw Yarmouth. It looked rather spongy and soppy, I thought, as I carried my eye over the great dull waste that lay across the river; and I could not help wondering, if the world were really as round as my geography book said, how any part of it came to be so flat. . . .

As we grew a little nearer, and saw the whole adjacent prospect lying a straight low line under the sky, I hinted to Peggotty that a mound or so might have improved it; and also that if the land had been a little more separated from the sea, and the town and the tide had not been quite so mixed up, like toast and water, it would have been nicer. But Peggotty said, with greater emphasis than usual, that we must take things as we found them, and that, for her part, she was proud to call herself a Yarmouth Bloater.

> David Copperfield in *David Copperfield* by Charles Dickens

. . . lonely and unprosperous by the bleak water-side, lay the lost little port of Slaughden, with its forlorn wharfs and warehouses of decaying wood, and its few scattered coastal-vessels deserted on the oozy river-shore.

> Wilkie Collins, *No Name*

1. Ipswich To Great Yarmouth: The A 12 Continued

They were not speaking of all of Norfolk or Suffolk by any means, but these two Victorian writers, Charles Dickens and Wilkie Collins—friends, fellow novelists, even collaborators—set forth what marks these counties: "Dull waste(s). . . spongy and soppy. . . flat. . . land and town and sea mixed up like toast and water," writes Dickens. "Lonely and unprosperous. . . bleak watersides . . . lost little port(s) . . . coastal-vessels deserted on the river-shore," adds Collins.

Noel Coward came to Norfolk and said, like David Copperfield, "Very flat." Not so, said a listener. Like Peggotty, he was a native, and proud of it. "I'd call it lumpy."

Swinburne found a lake-side and wood in Suffolk "so unutterably lonely that I thought instantly [of] Dante's wood of suicides."

And George Meredith described Aldeburgh (near Swinburne's lake and the Slaughden of Collins's novel) as "a place without charm," with "only grandeur of sea."

Clearly the sea—or more properly, water—dominates this great portion of East Anglia. The entire eastern boundary of both counties is the North Sea. So is all the northern boundary, in Norfolk. The southern boundary, in Suffolk, is chiefly water, too: the Stour River and its estuary.

Sea and rivers have shaped not only the contours but the very character of the land. In the south, the sea relentlessly invaded, eroding and devouring. In the north, conversely, it retreated, leaving in its wake great expanses of salt marshes and flats. Strange things have resulted. Today there are beaches you can't get to by land, and a few hard to reach by sea. There are one-time seaports now miles from the shore, and others that have disappeared beneath the waves.

Inland by the Cambridgeshire border there's a bit of the fens country, where water has to be pumped from the soil before it can be farmed, and old river beds sometimes lie high and dry above the land they once ran through. In places the earth is so "soppy," to use Dickens's word, that it is traversable neither afoot nor afloat. One has to wait for winter and hope for a hard freeze.

In fact, the people have their own word for very wet, "dreening." But they have their own words and pronunciations for so much else as well. If you're trying to get to Happisburgh in Norfolk, for instance, you'd better ask for "HAZE-boro"; and if Hunstanton, "HUN-ston." Our prosaic word *cuddle* can't begin to match their "cruddle"; nor our *busybody* their "blow-broth."

As for all the scholars' pother about what Hamlet really meant when he assured Rosencrantz and Guildenstern,

> I know a hawk from a hand-saw,

any East Anglian schoolboy could have set them straight in a jiffy. Hamlet didn't say handsaw at all, he said "harnser." A harnser's a heron, and everyone knows a hawk's not a heron.

The two counties have their other distinctions, of course. They are the easternmost in all England, and the most Teutonic in background. Together they cover a substantial area, a kind of square with rounded corners measuring roughly seventy by seventy miles. Yet there are no really big cities. The two largest, Norfolk's Norwich and Suffolk's Ipswich, have a lot of growing to do before they reach 150,000 people. Great Yarmouth, third in size, isn't much over 50,000.

What Norfolk and Suffolk do have is lovely old churches in surprising abundance. Rich in architectural detail and medieval woodcarving and art, many have the flintstone exterior and round towers characteristic of the region.

As those quotations from Dickens, Collins, Meredith, and Swinburne suggest, many of the two counties' points of literary interest are on or near the coast. These can be covered by continuing the northeasterly trek along the A 12 from Ipswich and the Orwell River to the highway's terminal at Great Yarmouth.

Points inland can be reached by taking the A 47 westward to Norwich, and then proceeding south through Diss to Bury St. Edmunds via the A 140 and the A 143, with side-excursions as needed.

Ipswich

Mr. Pickwick dismisses Ipswich almost offhand when he decides to go there in pursuit of Mr. Jingle: "We may as well see Ipswich as any other place." But then, Charles Dickens's enthusiasm for the town was easily contained.

Admittedly no Bury St. Edmunds, Ipswich is a no-frills county seat of about 125,000 that hides a past going back not just to the Romans, but to the Iron and even Stone Ages before them. The Anglo-Saxon original of its name, "Gippeswic," tells what the town was and is: the "wic" (port) on the Gipping, as the upper course of the Orwell River is called.

Safe and easy to navigate, the Orwell estuary for centuries has allowed seaborne ships their deepest penetration of inland Suffolk. No wonder that Chaucer's Merchant in *The Canterbury Tales* "wolde" (wished) that the sea be "kepe" (kept safe) "for any thing" (at any cost) to preserve his prosperous wool-trade between Holland's Middleborough and his home port on the Orwell:

> He wolde the see were kepe for any thing
> Betwixen Middleburgh and Orwelle.

In the early 1700s Daniel Defoe saw the harbor chock-a-block with "perhaps two hundred sail of ships" tied up there for the winter. And a hundred years later William Cobbett found the town "fine, populous, beautiful," helped no end by the exports of wheat.

The port still prospers. Over two and a half million tons of cargo keep the docks of Ipswich busy each year, thanks to the Orwell. The river came unbidden to Eric Blair's mind when he came to invent a pseudonym for his writing career: George Orwell. As a youth and young man, he had spent much of his time with his parents in Southwold, just up the coast.

Ipswich might have been a great university town, rivalling Oxford, if only Cardinal Wolsey had played his cards with Henry VIII more cannily. At least William Shakespeare seemed to think so. Thomas Wolsey, who rose to enormous power and wealth as Henry's Lord Chancellor, was an Ipswich boy, born there in 1475 of a butcher's wife. Wolsey Senior was also owner of a local inn, and got himself fined for having such disreputable clients as "friars and women of loose character."

Perhaps to refurbish the family name, Thomas Wolsey as chancellor started to build a college in his old hometown to equal the one, Cardinal College (now Christ Church), he had established at Oxford. Unfortunately, however, Wolsey fell from Henry's good graces, was sacked, and his Ipswich venture died aborning.

In his play *Henry VIII*, Shakespeare has Henry's Queen Katharine reminded of this when she, too, falls. Says Griffith, her gentleman usher:

> . . . . This Cardinal,
> Though from an humble stock, undoubtedly
> Was fashioned to much honor . . . .
> . . . . ever witness for him
> Those twins of learning that he raised in you,
> Ipswich and Oxford! one of which fell with him.

Today in College Street there stands all that remains of Wolsey's dream for Ipswich, a red brick gateway bearing his name, and marked, ironically, with the arms of Henry VIII. Henry even took up Wolsey's project. The school now in Henley Road was incorporated by him and ratified by Elizabeth I.

Jeremy Collier attended Ipswich school in the 1660s, and Rider Haggard in the 1860s. It was Collier who in 1698 attacked naughty playwrights like William Congreve and Sir John Vanbrugh in a piece whose title is almost an essay in itself: *A Short View of the Immorality and Profaneness of the English Stage*. Clara Reeves, author of the gothic novel *The Champion of Virtue* (1777), was born in Ipswich in 1729, and David Garrick made his stage debut there in 1741.

Charles Dickens visited Ipswich a number of times, first in 1835 as a twenty-three-year-old reporter, when he stayed at the Great White Horse Inn, and later on several of his reading tours. Dickens obviously never forgot that first visit, nor forgave those first lodgings.

In *Pickwick Papers*, Mr. Pickwick's encounter with The Great White Horse is not a happy one. He is startled by the inn's emblem, a stone statue "distantly resembling an insane cart-horse," and dismayed at the "labyrinths of uncarpeted passages" and "clusters of mouldy, badly lighted rooms." That night those same labyrinths do him in.

While undressing for bed, he wanders out to retrieve his misplaced watch, wanders back—and suddenly becomes aware of a "middle-aged lady in yellow curl papers, busily engaged in brushing what ladies call their 'back hair.'" Mr. Pickwick almost faints with horror.

"It is evident to me, ma'am," he says earnestly, "that I have mistaken this bedroom for my own."

"If this improbable story be really true, sir," says the lady, sobbing violently, "you will leave it instantly."

"I will, ma'am, with the greatest pleasure," replies Mr. Pickwick.

Edward FitzGerald lived practically all his life within ten miles of Ipswich, and was in and about the town often. On one visit he met E. B. Cowell, who was unwittingly to be responsible for FitzGerald's fame as a poet. Later a professor of Sanskrit at Cambridge, Cowell interested FitzGerald in oriental studies and sent him some verses by a Persian poet. FitzGerald was so enchanted he set about translating them into English quatrains. The poem was, of course, *The Rubáiyát of Omar Khayyám*.

Today's visitors to Ipswich's Christchurch Mansion, a rambling old museum in a large park at the north end of town, won't find much in its vaunted collection of "FitzGerald relics"—a cane chair, writing desk and book case, a walking stick, and a few other pieces of furniture.

Much more engrossing are the museum's mementoes of Margaret Catchpole, who caught the Victorians' fancy with her notorious ways. An almost illiterate Ipswich housemaid, she took up with smugglers and was twice sentenced to death, twice reprieved. Her erstwhile employer, the Rev. James Cobbold, wrote a novel about her, *Margaret Catchpole, a Suffolk Lass*, and made something of a name for himself.

Mr. Dickens's Great White Horse remains on Tavern Street as a two-star hotel. Its Dickens Wine Bar is dark and somewhat nondescript, but the Courtyard Lounge is large, light, and inviting. It actually *was* a courtyard that's been covered over. The two storeys of still-visible half-timber with their bullseye windows and flower boxes make you feel that you are indeed sitting outside—especially on a cool day with the windows flung wide to admit cold air all too real.

Way upstairs in the hotel is the Pickwick Room, a bedroom maintained in Dickens's style with antique furniture and four-poster beds. It's yours for the booking if some middle-aged lady in yellow curl papers hasn't beaten you to it.

One warning, though. You may remember that when he went after his watch, "the more stairs Mr. Pickwick went down, the more stairs there seemed to be to descend." Well, you'll have these same stairs to cope with, too, especially going UP! And there's no lift.

Woodbridge

Edward FitzGerald liked to complain about Woodbridge. Nothing ever happened there, he said, and the church bells rang out the same tune so incessantly that you finally wished to hang yourself. But he was only talking. Possessed of ample means, he clung to the center of town for fourteen years even though he had only two rooms over a shop, and even though for the last ten of those years he also owned a goodly house on its outskirts.

He had every reason to stay put. His apartment was smack in the middle of Market Hill. The Shire Hall, a striking red-brick Tudor building that still dominates the square, was only a few steps up the street to his right. Better yet, just a few feet down the street to his left was his favorite pub, The Bull. And below the hill was the beautiful Deben (DEE-ben) estuary. Anchored there among the others was his own little yacht, named, he said, for the town's leading product: The Scandal. How could a man want more whose idea of heaven was a life of flowers, books, music, and "knocking about" in that boat, bedecked in a top hat?

Besides, Woodbridge itself was charming. And so it remains—a winning little country town with a Georgian flavor on the A 12, eight miles north and east of Ipswich. It had been firmly established in 920 A. D., appropriately enough by a grant to the monks of Ely from a Saxon king called Edgar the Peaceable. By the time of Elizabeth I, it was a significant ship-building port supplying vessels to fight the Spanish Armada.

Her Majesty's Master of the Court Rolls, Thomas Seckford, was a Woodbridge man and its major benefactor. Lord Mayor of the town in 1550, Seckford built the distinctive almhouses that stand on Seckford Street, and left a generous sum to support the poor. The Shire Hall was his gift to the market place. Lexicographers credit the market for a contribution to our vocabulary hardly flattering. A major event each October was its St. Audrey's fair. As time went on and the name degenerated from "Saint Audrey" to "s'taudrey," so did the merchandise. St. Audrey's goods became—well, in a word, tawdry.

That Edward FitzGerald should settle in this placid little Suffolk town is not surprising. Without any prolonged hiatus, his whole life had centered on southern Suffolk. He was born in 1809 at Bredfield, only three miles north of Woodbridge. (Not as Edward FitzGerald, however, but as Edward Purcell. His father adopted his wife's family arms and name of FitzGerald in 1818.) When Edward was seven, the elder FitzGeralds went to France for almost six years, but he stayed pretty much where he was for his education, first at King Edward VI school in Bury St. Edmunds, then at Cambridge University, fifty miles away.

Between Cambridge and his coming to Woodbridge, FitzGerald continued to live in Boulge, the parish of his birthplace, until 1839 with his parents at Boulge Hall, and thereafter in a little thatched house called Boulge Cottage.[1] FitzGerald died while visiting Merton in Norfolk, but he is buried in St. Michael's churchyard in the grounds where Boulge Hall stood. On his grave grows a rose of Naishapur, brought there from the tomb of Omar Khayyám in 1893 by the Omar Khayyám Club.

During the Boulge Cottage years, FitzGerald took to walking over to Woodbridge to see Bernard Barton, a Quaker bank clerk who was something of a poet and a friend of Southey and Lamb. FitzGerald thought enough of Barton to write a "Life" for the collection of Barton's poems published in 1849, and to marry his daughter. That is, in 1860 Lucy Barton and Edward FitzGerald stood together before the vicar and said the requisite words, but nothing more romantic seems to have happened. Edward wasn't made for matrimony.

The Woodbridge house that FitzGerald bought in 1864 and moved into in 1874 was on the Pytches Road and called Little Grange. There, one September day in 1876, arrived, suddenly and totally without warning, Alfred Tennyson and his son Hallam. The warmest of friends while college mates at Cambridge, they had become estranged. But FitzGerald was delighted to see Tennyson. They took the river steamer down the Orwell and back and talked endlessly about the good old days, and FitzGerald felt that they had been apart for twenty days, not years.

There were jarring notes, however. FitzGerald put his visitors up at The Bull, as he did all his friends, and Tennyson fell afoul of the innkeeper, a redoubtable figure named John Grout. He was a world dealer in fine horses, and had played host to the King of Italy and the emissaries of the Kaiser and the Viceroy of India, who had come as purchasers for their royal stables. Grout was not about to be impressed at entertaining the poet laureate.

[1]His birthplace and Boulge Hall have been demolished, but the cottage, though altered, remains on the road to Debach.

"Well, he may be a fine poet," was Grout's assessment, "but he doesn't know a damn' thing about horses."

It didn't make Tennyson happier to discover that FitzGerald had left it for Tennyson to pay the bill. After the Tennysons returned home, FitzGerald tried to maintain the renewed friendship by correspondence. But all he ever got in return were replies from Hallam, and even that wasn't as filial as it sounds. Hallam doubled as his father's secretary.

Tennyson did try to make amends later. Shortly before FitzGerald died in 1883, Tennyson added a prologue to his poem "Tiresias" addressed as a birthday gift for "Old Fitz." Tennyson explains that "The Prologue describes Edward FitzGerald, as we had seen him at Woodbridge in 1876." The first lines share that reminiscence with FitzGerald himself:

> Whom yet I see as there you sit
> Beneath your sheltering garden tree,
> And watch your doves about you flit,
> And plant on shoulder, hand, and knee,
> Or on your head their rosy feet.

Then comes a most gracious tribute to the Rubáiyát:

> . . . Your golden Eastern lay,
> Than which I know no version done
> In English more divinely well.

For a small town, Woodbridge offers an interesting variety of lodgings for the overnight visitor. The two larger ones, both three-star and both ancient, are The Melton Grange and Seckford Hall. The Melton Grange, a country mansion set in its own woods and park, has parts that are eight hundred years old. And Seckford Hall was not only the stately home of Thomas Seckford when he was Lord Mayor of Woodbridge, but is said to have his Honor's ghost still parading about, resplendent in top hat, Elizabethan finery, and wand of office.

Two smaller inns are The Crown and The Bull, both two-star, both Tudor. The Crown, on Thorofare, is heart and soul of Woodbridge's shipping and ship-building past. In fact, a seventeenth-century owner was Peter Pett, Commissioner of the Admiralty, who acquired it by the simple process of marrying the innkeeper's daughter. Pett speedily made it the gathering place for the builders and sailors of ships alike, and established his own shipbuilding yard in the town.

Pett rates frequent and increasingly scathing mention in the famous diary of Samuel Pepys, no mean bureaucrat of the Royal Navy himself. Among Pett's sins, according to Pepys, are supplying the Navy with ships whose woodwork "do prove knotty and not fit for service" . . . "selling timber to the Navy under other names" . . . and allowing the Dutch enemy to seize a royal warship while at anchor. "What a knave Commissioner Pett hath been all along," Pepys concludes, "and [one who] deserves, therefore, to be hanged."

At The Bull, where the Omar Khayyám Club still meets once every ten years, there are two special treats if you look for them. One is a plaque on the bar wall, listing all the inn's landlords since 1734. Tennyson's John Grout, you'll find, held forth from 1861 to 1887.

The other treat is a framed poem half-hidden on the wall of the hall leading to "Toilets." Written by Victor Bridges, a visitor of the distant past (adding 1876 to the poem's "sixty years ago" suggests the year 1936), the ten stanzas are entitled "To Fitz." Bridges waxes lyrical over sighting FitzGerald's two-room apartment through The Bull's front windows, and muses about Tennyson's visit there. The piece begins:

> Through the oldfashioned window panes
> I looked across the Market Hill
> And saw the letters E.F.G.[2]
> Beneath your lodging's window sill.

and continues,

> Though sixty years have passed since,
> 'Tis little changed, this market square,
> You heard old Alfred's stately step
> Come tramping up your narrow stair.

There is, of course, one slight hitch to Mr. Bridges's rhapsody. Old Alfred could hardly have tramped up those narrow stairs on Market Hill. In 1876, FitzGerald happened to be living at Little Grange.

Framlingham

Framlingham (FROM-ling-'m), eight miles northwest of Woodbridge on the B 1116, is a quiet little town. Driving through it, the casual traveler would little guess its significance in both the history and the literature of England.

---

[2] They're still there.

Yet the great ruined castles on the hill once housed a family whose lives intimately touched every Tudor monarch from the first, Henry VII, who was crowned in 1485, to the last, Elizabeth I, who died in 1603. They were the Howards, buried now in Framlingham's Church of St. Michael. And among them lies a man without whom Shakespeare could hardly have written his plays and sonnets as we know them.

The story of the Howards is a roller coaster ride through 120 turbulent years of Tudor history. Thomas Howard, second Duke of Norfolk, who inherited the castle from his mother in 1476, set the pattern of precipitous ups and downs. During the final year of the Wars of the Roses, he plunged to the bottom by siding with the Yorks and being captured at the Battle of Bosworth Field in 1485. Freed in 1489, he then soared to the top, regaining the title of Earl of Surrey (but not Duke of Norfolk) and holding key positions under his Bosworth captor, now Henry VII.

With Howard's son, also a Thomas, the family fortunes at first rose even more. He won back the dukedom from Henry VIII, and as third Duke of Norfolk actually married Anne, sister of Henry VII's Queen Elizabeth. Now the most powerful noble in England, Thomas successfully opposed Cardinal Wolsey, supported Henry's divorce from Katharine of Aragon, and helped replace her as queen, in 1533, with of all people his own niece Anne Boleyn.

By then it seemed the Howards could scarcely go higher. Thomas had been named guardian of the king's illegitimate son, The Duke of Richmond. His own son Henry, who became Earl of Surrey at seven when Thomas was made Duke of Norfolk, was raised in the royal household as Richmond's companion. And while Henry VIII was courting her, Anne Boleyn had pushed young Surrey, still not quite twelve, as a suitable husband for the king's daughter, thirteen-year-old Mary, later to reign herself as history's "Bloody Mary." To top if off, Richmond married Thomas's daughter, another Mary. The Howards were all but royalty themselves.

Soon, however, the roller coaster ups-and-downs resumed.

First down: Anne Boleyn fell from favor and was executed in 1536, convicted of adultery in a trial conducted ironically by her Uncle Thomas in his position as Lord High Steward. Worse, Jane Seymour, of a family despised by the Howards, became Henry's third queen and produced the male heir he'd so desperately longed for.

Then up: Jane died soon after childbirth. Henry speedily married Anne of Cleves and just as speedily divorced her. Whom did he take in 1540 as his fifth queen? Catherine Howard, yet another of Thomas's nieces.

Then down again, twice—the second turn fatal to the young Earl of

Surrey and nearly so to his father Thomas. First, in 1542 Catherine was found guilty of adultery and executed.

Then in 1546 the Howards' enemies—and they were in generous supply, including the Seymours—made trumped-up charges of treason stick. Both father and son were sentenced to death. Even here, the roller coaster prevailed. Surrey's execution was set for January 19, 1547, his father's for January 29. Henry VIII died January 28. Surrey died. Thomas lived.

Thomas Howard remained in prison throughout the short reign of Henry's son, Edward VI. He emerged for a finale that went from down to up within the space of nine days. When the boy-king Edward died in 1553, Thomas's choice for a successor, Henry's daughter Mary, seemingly lost out; Lady Jane Grey, Henry's niece, was crowned. But Mary fled to Framlingham Castle, got herself proclaimed queen, and marched on London with three hundred men of Suffolk. Nine days later, Jane was in the Tower and Mary was Queen of England. Old Thomas Howard, aged eighty-one died in bed while yet she reigned.

But the Howards and the Tudors were not through with each other even yet. There was one more down to come. Surrey's son Thomas, who had succeeded his grandfather as fourth Duke of Norfolk, plotted to marry Mary Queen of Scots, rival of Queen Elizabeth, and oust Elizabeth in favor of Mary. But Elizabeth acted before he could. In 1572 he joined the other Howards in the sad procession from Tower to Executioner to a tomb in Framlingham's church. The space he had saved there for Mary between the tombs of his first two wives went unoccupied.

The literary Surrey of all this was the man to whom William Shakespeare owed so much, perhaps more than the playwright ever realized. For Henry Howard, Earl of Surrey, was a poet as well as a national figure. But most of his works circulated only in manuscript, the product of his idle hours. Some of those hours came unsought, brief sojourns in prison for youthful high jinks, such as roaming the midnight streets of London smashing windows with the son of his fellow poet, Sir Thomas Wyatt.

Nevertheless, it was Surrey's verse that established the particular form of sonnet now know as "Shakespearean" or "English." Even more important, Surrey's poetic translation of parts of *The Aeneid* provided the model for the blank verse that led to Christopher Marlowe's "mighty line" in plays like *Doctor Faustus* and *Edward II*, and in Shakespeare's hands became the vehicle for some of the greatest dramas of all time.

What survives of the Howards' castle on the Framlingham hill is mostly the outer shell, but suggests how extensive a structure it was. Dating back eight hundred years, there are thirteen towers in all, topped with attractive red-brick chimneys added by the Howards. Be forewarned, however. Only the chimneys on the eighth and ninth towers are real; the rest are dummies.

A spiral staircase in one of the towers takes you to a walk atop the walls, with a spectacular view of the town and countryside below. The castle is open to the public all year round, the hours varying with the season.

Framlingham's Church of St. Michael is worth a visit, too. There the Howards lie in their ornate tombs—dukes of Norfolk II, III, and IV . . . the latter's two wives with the empty niche between them . . . the Duke of Richmond and his wife Mary Howard . . . and her brother, the poet Surrey. Note his monument particularly. The Earl's coronet is carved lying *beside* the head on his effigy. It's hard to wear a coronet if you've been beheaded.

Aldeburgh

Aldeburgh, twelve miles southeast of Framlingham on the A 1094, is the town roundly damned by eighteenth and nineteenth-century writers: "a place without charm" (George Meredith) . . . "where Nature's niggard hand/ Gave a spare portion to the famished land" (George Crabbe). . . and "the sullen flow of the tidal river Alde ebbed noiselessly from the muddy banks" (Wilkie Collins).

This is neither the Aldeburgh of today, however, nor the Aldeburgh of the long, long ago.

In the sixteenth century, Aldeburgh was an important fishing and ship-building port. The Anglo-Saxons who had lived there one thousand years before that had called it, even then, Alde ("old") -burc ("Fort"). Benedictine monks ruled it for three hundred years before Henry VIII suppressed them. Aldeburgh men built and manned the "Greyhound" and the "Pelican," the ships with which Sir Francis Drake made history.

Then the sea took over. Silt made the Alde river impassable for larger vessels and destroyed the town's chief industries, though a bit of smuggling remained possible. Crabbe's *The Village* (1783) depicts the natives, "a wild amphibious race":

> . . . . Beneath yon cliff they stand,)
> To show the freighted pinnace where to land;
> To load the ready steed with guilty haste;
> To fly in terror o'er the pathless waste.

Much of the town was devoured by the waves. Its chief building, the Moot Hall, once in the central market square with two streets between it and the sea, found itself standing on the very edge of the water.

But Aldeburgh struck back.

Today it is an utterly charming little haven for holiday-goers and the retired, no longer marred by Collins's forlorn wharfs and decaying wood, yet untainted by modern industry or commercialism. To visit it, leave the A 12 ten miles above Woodbridge and follow the A 1094 eastward to the coast.

The truth is, the people of Aldeburgh have long been more than a wild amphibious race, if they ever were that. They can claim the first woman doctor in England and the first lady mayor of a borough. Elizabeth Garrett Anderson, who was both, was born in Aldeburgh in 1836.

And even in Meredith's own day, Aldeburgh was not without culture. The founder of both the Samuel Johnson Club and the Omar Khayyám Club was an Aldeburgh banker named Edward Clodd, and he and fellow members of the latter often sailed from Aldeburgh in his yacht to hold a meeting at The Bull in Woodbridge and visit Edward FitzGerald's grave. Among famous literary men who were guests of Clodd and passengers aboard his boat were Thomas Hardy; Anthony Hope (Sir Anthony Hope Hawkins), famous for *The Prisoner of Zenda* (1894); and Sir James George Frazer, author of the twelve-volume *Golden Bough* (1890–1915).

Aldeburgh's most important gift to literature, of course, was George Crabbe, master of realistic and often biting poetry. He was born there in 1754, son of a collector of salt taxes, and spent most of the next fifty years within thirty miles of it, as a quick chronology shows:

1765–66, (age eleven-twelve) schooling at Bungay and Stowmarket.

1768–70, apothecary apprentice at Wickhambrook.

1771–74, surgeon-apprenticeship at Woodbridge; meets Sarah Elmy, his future wife, at her uncle's in Parham.

1775–80, works as day laborer at Aldeburgh; open own surgery which fails.

1781, ordained a minister and made rector of Aldeburgh church.

1780–83, often in Beccles wooing Sarah, the "Mira" of his poems; marries her there in 1783.

1782–88, curate at Belvoir Castle, Leicestershire.

1785–89, curate at Stathern, too.

1789–1814, holds post of rector of Muston, also in Leicestershire, but is in Suffolk much of the time.

1792, in Parham as executor of Sarah's uncle's will.

1796–1801, lives at Great Glenham.
1801–05, lives at Rendham.

As noted, Belvoir Castle, Stathern, and Muston are in Leicestershire. But all the others are in Suffolk: Bungay and Beccles twenty miles or less northwest of Aldeburgh; Stowmarket about twenty-five miles due west; and Woodbridge, Parham, Great Glenham, and Rendham within a twelve mile arc from southwest to northwest. Wickhambrook is nine miles southwest of Bury St. Edmunds.

Crabbe's best writing is based on Aldeburgh, too. Chief among his works, in addition to *The Village*, are *The Parish Register* (1807), *The Borough* (1810), *Tales* (1812), and *Tales of the Hall* (1819). *The Village* was rather widely read and admired, but in the main Crabbe's success was critical rather than popular. Dr. Johnson helped revise *The Village* for publication, and William Wordsworth praised it. Sir Walter Scott dubbed Crabbe the "English Juvenal," and Byron called him "though Nature's sternest painter yet, yet the best." Edward FitzGerald, Cardinal Newman, and Thomas Hardy, too, all hailed his work.

In 1941, an article about George Crabbe and Aldeburgh led in the most haphazard fashion to the establishment of an internationally famous music and literary festival and the writing of two notable operas. Involved along the way were a bevy of now-famous names: W. H. Auden, Christopher Isherwood, E. M. Forster in literature; Benjamin Britten, Eric Crozier, Peter Pears in music.

The story begins in London in 1937. Christopher Isherwood, then thirty-three, and the thirty-year-old Auden had collaborated on a play, *The Ascent of F.6*, and asked Benjamin Britten—all of twenty-three—to write incidental music for it. E. M. Forster, friend of the playwrights, attended the dress rehearsal and wrote a highly flattering review after the play opened.

In 1939, Britten followed Auden to the United States. He even began to think now and then of becoming an American citizen, though he wavered. At just this moment, he idly picked up a magazine called *The Listener.* An article signed by his erstwhile acquaintance, E. M. Forster, caught his eye, and he began to read about George Crabbe and his absorption with Aldeburgh and the sea. The effect was electrifying. For Crabbe meant Suffolk, and Suffolk to Britten was home. He'd been raised in Lowestoft, just twenty-seven miles up the coast. Benjamin Britten went home.

He began to re-read George Crabbe, too. By 1948, he was working on a music festival for Aldeburgh with his friends Eric Crozier, the librettist, and Peter Pears, the singer. As centerpiece for their festival, Britten decided he would compose an opera. His subject seemed inevitable: the story of Peter Grimes from Crabbe's *The Borough*. Featured speaker and his topic for the inaugural ceremonies seemed inevitable, too: E. M. Forster lecturing on "George Crabbe and *Peter Grimes*."

Forster was delighted. He came to Aldeburgh a few days before the opening and stayed at Britten's Crag House overlooking the sea. Roaming about Crabbe country, he fell in love with the natives, "these sweetest of people."

Thereafter, Forster returned to Aldeburgh often. In March of 1949 he was back at Crag House for a whirlwind sixteen days collaborating on a libretto for *Billy Budd* based on Herman Melville's novel, which Britten planned as his next festival opera. Britten's music, however, was put off by a host of other projects. It wasn't until 1951 that Forster returned to work at Crag House. The stay was longer than he'd planned. While climbing the belfry of the parish church, he broke his ankle.

Britten nursed his guest with patience and unfailing good humor. As Forster improved, they worked hard at the opera. For recreation, they'd go sailing now and then with a young fisherman named Bill Burrell, who became a favorite of Forster's.

In later years, the novelist returned a number of times to stay with Burrell and his wife, though their quarters were odd to say the least. The front of the house was used by Mrs. Burrell for her hair-dressing shop. The back was used by fishermen in filthy oilskins. The smells from each end, Forster explained to a friend, sometimes met in the middle, and the effect was appalling. To compensate, however, there were "enormous intrusions of adorable fishermen."

Aldeburgh today has little to show of Crabbe's long association. His birthplace has disappeared beneath the sea. But there is a bust of him in the church, and an attractive little avenue called Crabbe Street opposite the Moot Hall on the beach. In the upstairs of the Hall is a small museum with old maps, chests, and pictures of the Aldeburgh Crabbe would have known, including a small engraving of his birthplace. There is also a full set of his works. *The Borough* is open at the first page of "Letter XXII," which contains the story of Peter Grimes. Moot Hall (moot means "meeting") has served variously as a Guild Hall, Council Chamber (they still meet there), court house, and jail. Britten's *Peter Grimes* opens with a trial there.

The festival that Britten began in 1948 remains Aldeburgh's biggest attraction, held every June. It's the largest such event in England, spread among The Maltings (a converted malt-house in the neighboring village of

Snape), Aldeburgh's fifteenth-century Church of St. Peter and St. Paul, and its Jubilee Hall.

But if you want to attend, plan (and book) well ahead. Tickets and accommodations have a way of vanishing early.

Dunwich—Southwold—and Kessingland

Twenty-seven miles of remote coast stretch upward from Aldeburgh to Lowestoft. First comes Dunwich, reached from the A 12 by an unnumbered road . . . then Southwold, via the A 1095 . . . and finally Kessingland on the B 1437.

Dunwich   Today's Dunwich (DUN-itch) has at best perhaps two hundred inhabitants, a single street that wanders off into the sand dunes, and no sign of the harbor that was. Daniel Defoe in the eighteenth century reported it was still exporting butter, cheese and corn. But you have to go back to the days before Chaucer for Dunwich in its heyday: a port teeming with up to a hundred great ships, twice the size of Ipswich, and with nine churches. Dunwich may be the most haunting of all testimony to the sea's powers of obliteration.

Swinburne came there in 1880 and was moved to some rather over-wrought verse:

> Waste endless and boundless and flowerless
> But of marsh-blossoms fruitless as free:
> Where earth lies exhausted, as powerless
> To strive with the sea.

Edward FitzGerald loved the village and often dropped by to visit friends—once bringing Thomas Carlyle along. Henry James was a visitor, too, as were Jerome K. Jerome and Edward Thomas.

Dunwich remains a place to see, with an eerie beauty all its own.

Southwold   When Swinburne went to Southwold in 1875, he was disap-pointed at first: "For four days I found [it] as dull as any place can be to me where I have the sea," he said in a letter. Only when he found those trees and the lonely lake that reminded him of Dante's wood of suicides did he perk up. The reason he felt let down may be that Southwold is no Dunwich or Aldeburgh, thanks to cliffs that rise above the beach.

The sea did hinder and change it, however. Its days as an important port and fishing center are long gone. Southwold began as an island, but in the thirteenth century silt filled the creek that had separated it from the mainland at Easton Bevants. And a pesky gravel bar still comes and goes, often blocking most of the harbor mouth.

The town had its moments in history. When Henry VIII supplanted the Church of Rome with one of his own, a by-product was widespread nonobservance of fast-days with disastrous consequences for the fishermen of Southwold. In 1659, a great fire raged through Southwold for over four hours, causing £40,000 in damage, and leaving four hundred families homeless. Those inviting little greens that dot the town are souvenirs of the fire, sites where buildings were never replaced.

In 1672, one of the bloodiest and most fruitless sea battles of the war between the British and the Dutch took place just off shore. When it was over, corpses littered Sole Bay. Thousands had been killed, commanders on both sides lay dead, both fleets were crippled—and nobody had won. The battle is commemorated on Southwold's town sign.

Up on Gun Cliff are six ancient cannon that provoked a moment of tension in World War I. George II had given the guns, antique relics of Elizabethan days even then, in response to the town's plea for additional defense. But after war broke out in 1914, the Germans claimed that this meant Southwold was "fortified" and lobbed a few shells into town. Heeding the hint, Southwold buried its cannon.

Three years after the war, a retired civil servant named Blair, who had served in India, moved to 40 Stradbroke Road in Southwold to be near Anglo-Indian friends. His son Eric, then eighteen, delayed only long enough to graduate from Eton before coming there, too. Following in his father's footsteps, Eric left within a year to serve with the Indian Imperial Police until 1928. But from 1930 to 1940, he was often back in Southwold at the house the family took in Queen Street (now the High Street), painfully working his way upward as a writer. His fame as George Orwell, author of *Animal Farm* and *Nineteen Eighty-Four,* was twenty years away.[3]

His letters from Southwold make good reading and provide an engaging picture of the town as it was sixty years ago. One letter, for instance, suggests that the townsfolk lived closer to nature than they might like: "The hedgehogs keep coming into the house, and last night we found in the bathroom a little tiny hedgehog no bigger than an orange. The only thing I

[3]For how he picked the pseudonym, see p. 20.

could think was that it was a baby of one of the others, though it was fully formed—I mean, it had its prickles."

Another letter indicates that even enjoying the beach could have its problems: "I nearly died of cold the other day when bathing, because I had walked out to Easton Broad not intending to bathe, & then the water looked so nice that I took off my clothes & went in, & then about 50 people came up & rooted themselves to the spot. I wouldn't have minded that, but among them was a coastguard who could have had me up for bathing naked, so I had to swim up and down for the best part of half an hour, pretending to like it."

And there was one memorable night after a wearing day of writing when, passing by the King's Head pub on the High Street, he was uplifted to hear the hilariously drunken singing of "Fo-or-*ee*'s a jorrigoo' fellow."

The Southwold years often sorely tested the would-be writer. When in 1931 the publishers rejected the manuscript of his maiden effort, he gamely rewrote it and indicated for the first time that if it ever was accepted, he would prefer to use a pseudonym. It was published in 1933: *Down and Out in Paris and London,* by "George Orwell." (One wonders what that last name might have been had he been at the time anywhere else but Southwold, so near to Ipswich and its River Orwell).

The struggle was in no way over, though. Two succeeding books, novels this time, brought their woe while he was at Southwold. In early 1934 Harper Brothers sent word that they wouldn't publish *Burmese Days* for fear of libel.[4] And that same year Orwell despaired of ever finishing *A Clergyman's Daughter.* "I am so miserable (he confided to a friend) struggling in the entrails of that dreadful book. . . . *Never* start writing novels, if you wish to preserve your happiness."

When he took rooms in London in 1936, and then leased a small place in Wallington, Herts., Orwell's Southwold days effectively ended. But the pen name he'd assumed there made certain that his little part of Suffolk would be remembered.

You'll like Southwold. It pretends to be nothing more than it is: a somewhat shabby-genteel little sea resort with a sprinkling here and there of better-sort homes, some modern, some Victorian or Georgian. Among things to see are the fifteenth-century church, George Orwell's house, and the pub that cheered him up that night in 1934.

Buried in the churchyard is Agnes Strickland, whose *Lives of the Queens of England* and *Lives of the Queens of Scotland* were great Victorian favorites.

[4]By the end of the year, though, they did publish it.

Dedicated to St. Edmund, martyr and last of the Anglian kings, the church is remarkable for a town of only two thousand people. The tower is all of a hundred feet high with a wondrous Jack in the north arch. The figure, a man-at-arms carved out of oak, strikes the bell with the axe in his right hand at the beginning of each service, or when a bride enters for her wedding.

If you've heard varying addresses for Orwell's house, don't be confused. Simply go down the High Street until you come to a fair-sized two-storey red brick building with a small brass plate on the door saying, "No. 36, Montague House." As you stand facing the door, look up at the wall to your right, and rest assured as you read:

THE AUTHOR
GEORGE ORWELL
(ERIC BLAIR)
1903–1950
RESIDED IN THIS HOUSE

While you're on the High Street, keep your eyes open for Orwell's The King's Head and stop in for a pint. It—and most of the pubs in town—serve what is possibly the best beer in England. It's Adnams' Beer, brewed right here in Southwold and still delivered by horse and dray.

Kessingland   At Kessingland, twelve miles up the coast from Southwold, the A 12 swings eastward almost to the shore. Rider Haggard came there to settle in 1900.

Another man with his background might have thought that he had come to the ends of the earth. After all, he had once played an imperial role for her Majesty in Transvaal, after Britain acquired that colony in 1877, first on the staff of the Special Commissioner, then as Master of the High Court.

Then he had thrust himself into the bustle of London in 1884, to live not one but two lives: as a practioner of law, and as a prolific writer. His novels, *King Solomon's Mines* (1886), *She* (1887), and others were wildly successful. Filled with fantastic adventure and exotic backgrounds like Zimbabwe ruins of Southern Rhodesia, they had made him the talk of London.

Now here he was, in an isolated little fishing village. His house, called The Grange and perched on a lonely cliff above the sea, was large but scarcely elegant. It had once been a coastguard station. But Haggard loved it all. He was back where he belonged.

The barrister and novelist that London society came to know had always been a country boy—and an East Anglian—at heart. Indeed, the knighthood bestowed on him in 1912 was a reward not for his romantic bestsellers, but for his serious consideration of England and rural problems in *Rural England* (1902), *The Poor and the Land* (1905), and *Rural Denmark and Its Lessons* (1911).

He had been born on his father's country estate, Bradenham Hall in Norfolk, twenty miles west of Norwich, and had gone to school in Ipswich. At Bradenham, he had carried on the family tradition of practical gardening and farming. When his wife inherited Ditchingham House, also in Norfolk, two miles north of Bungay, they lived there from 1889 until they moved on to Kessingland.

Haggard left Kessingland from time to time. He leased the house to Rudyard Kipling for the summer of 1914, and after World War I he spent his winters in Hastings, Sussex. He died in London in 1925. But to the end, he clung to The Grange and to his Norfolk-Suffolk roots.

Blythburgh—Halesworth—Bungay—and Beccles

There's an old Suffolk rhyme that goes:

> Beccles for a Puritan
> Bungay for the Poor
> Halesworth for a Drunkard,
> And Bliborough for a Whore.[5]

All four places are within fourteen miles of Southwold: "Bliborough" (today's Blythburgh), three and a half miles almost due west on the A 12 . . . Halesworth, four miles northwest of Blythburgh on the A 144 . . . Bungay, eight miles above Halesworth on the A 144 . . . and Beccles, eight miles northeast of Halesworth on the A 145. None is of any overpowering importance as a literary site, but a word about each can do no harm.

Blythburgh   Why Blythburgh was associated with whores no one who lives there now will say. In rebuttal, they're likely to point to their great church, nearly 130 feet long and called by many "one of the finest parish churches in Suffolk." But the same church contains a hint that there may be something to the rhyme after all. Inside are some marvelous effigies of the Deadly Sins—Pride, Gluttony, Avarice, and the rest. Someone has pretty well bashed in one of the figures: Lechery.

---

[5]I owe this rhyme, as well as several other charming details about the area, to John Seymour's highly readable *East Anglia*.

Halesworth   There doesn't seem to be any clear explanation for Halesworth's reputation for drunkards, either. The drinking to one side, however, during World War I the town did harbor some oddly-behaving strangers. Gossip had it that the couple weren't married . . . that the children were hers but not his . . . and that he and the younger man they had in tow had fled there to escape being conscripted into the army. And finally, that those peculiar people who came to see them belonged to a notorious group of writers and artists in London.

Gossip was right on all counts. The couple were Vanessa Bell and Duncan Grant, both painters. She was still firmly married to Clive Bell, art critic and writer, and the children were theirs. The younger man was David Garnett, later to write the little gem of a novel called *Lady into Fox* (1923). He and Duncan had indeed come to Halesworth to avoid conscription. They were conscientious objectors and hoped that the authorities would accept their working as farmers in lieu of military service.

They established themselves in a Victorian farmhouse called Wissett Lodge, and while the men tried to master the intricacies of fruit farming, Vanessa painted and the children ran happily wild about the countryside. Their appearance, as D. H. Lawrence and Virginia Woolf attest, would have made Vanessa and Duncan stand out anywhere, let alone so sedate a little village as Halesworth.

Lawrence used Grant as the model for the "Duncan Forbes" of *Lady Chatterley's Lover,* and calls him "a dark-skinned taciturn Hamlet of a fellow." The real Duncan wore paint-stained jackets, oversize waistcoats, and droopy trousers constantly in need of hitching up. Vanessa's get-up was equally bizarre. Virginia Woolf describes her sister striding along a street in Bath: "She had a gauze streamer red as blood flying over her shoulder, a purple scarf, a shooting cap, tweed skirt and great brown boots."

Gossip was right about those visitors who came up to Wissett Lodge from London, too. They were the core of the so-called Bloomsbury Group, famous for their outlandish views and ways: Lytton Strachey, Maynard Keynes, Roger Fry, and Leonard and Virginia Woolf. Virginia mocked their hosts' bucolic existence. Duncan, she said, picked bugs off the currant bushes eight hours a day, slept all night, and painted on Sunday.

In any event, this country saga soon came to an end. The authorities rejected Grant and Garnett's pleas that they were conscientious objectors. They might substitute farm work for army duty if they liked, but only if they found an employer and were supervised. They did, in Charleston in Sussex.

Bungay   The rhyme may have said "Bungay for the Poor" because at its peak the village was prosperous and hence generous to the needy. On the other hand, the reference may be to leaner days, when poverty was the word. The black oak pulpit in Holy Trinity Church, made in 1558, cost five shillings!

Bungay does have its literary associations. As noted earlier, George Crabbe went to school there, and Rider Haggard lived on his wife's estate at Ditchingham, two miles out of town. In 1794 the French writer Chateaubriand sought refuge there as a teacher after the French Revolution. He tumbled from his horse outside the rectory one day, was taken in by the rector and his wife, fell in love with their beautiful fifteen-year-old daughter, and was encouraged by the parents to marry her. Poor fellow—he had to confess he already had a wife.

In the nineteenth century, Bungay was a famous printing center, producing up to eighty thousand books a week. The owner of the press, J. R. Childs, was popular with writers, and George Borrow and Edward FitzGerald, among others, came often to dine with him. It was the Childs' company that printed the second edition of *Alice in Wonderland*. It's nice to know that the firm is still in business and still has the original wood blocks of those celebrated Tenniel illustrations.

Beccles   Beccles (rhymes with "freckles") did have its share of Puritans, but Suffolk had Dissenters of all kinds. It's an attractive town of about ten thousand people, with the distinct flavor of red-brick Georgian. Its literary ties can be handled with dispatch.

Chateaubriand lived there before he went to Bungay, working on ancient French manuscripts. George Crabbe was a frequent visitor while wooing Sarah Elmy, and married her in the parish church. And Sir John Suckling, gambler, wencher, profligate—and in between times a spry and witty poet—lived at Roos Hall when he wasn't adorning the court of Charles I. A gabled Tudor mansion, half a mile west of town, the Hall is open to the public several afternoons a week from May to September.

Lowestoft—Blundeston—Great Yarmouth—and Caister Castle

Lowestoft, Blundeston, and Great Yarmouth were the first three scenes of young David Copperfield's life. They lie along the final ten miles of the A 12. Lowestoft, five miles above Kessingland, is on the highway itself;

Blundeston, just off it to the west, is four miles above Lowestoft. At Great Yarmouth, six miles beyond Blundeston, the A 12, having crossed the border into Norfolk, comes to its end. Many a traveler who has followed the road all the way from London has been known to say, "Thank God!"

Lowestoft Two things happened in Lowestoft that led to all young David Copperfield's woes. Mr. Murdstone, who had taken the boy along on a seemingly innocent day's outing, signed papers there that paved the way for him to marry Mrs. Copperfield. And David hears her referred to as "bewitching" and "the pretty little widow." He repeats the words to his mother, she blushes, and the fateful marriage is all but inevitable.

There's not much you can say about Lowestoft, either past or present, except that it has built a lot of ships, especially trawlers; caught a lot of fish, especially herring and mackerel; and still makes some of the best real smoked kippers in the world.

It's the kind of seaside resort that makes you want to say "Oh dear!" Large, nondescript hotels and boarding houses front its long expanse of beach, jammed in summer with hordes of holidayers determined to be jolly. Behind them lies a town of over fifty-seven thousand people, the most easterly town, by the way, in England.

Lowestoft does offer some interesting literary footnotes. Thomas Nash was born there in 1567. Something of a scalawag but a lively writer of plays, pamphlets, and polemics of various sorts, Nash is credited by some as being the "grandfather" of the novel with his romance, *Jacke Wilton* (1594). Benjamin Britten, of course, was born in Lowestoft, too. It was his nostalgia, after all, for Lowestoft, aroused by E. M. Forster's article on Crabbe, Aldeburgh, and the Suffolk coast, that caused Britten to give up America and come back home for a career in England.[6]

Two Victorians fond of Lowestoft were the novelist George Borrow and the poet Edward FitzGerald. FitzGerald was there often, sometimes in one guise, sometimes in another. Now and again he would hove into the harbor as the gentleman skipper of his yacht, Scandal, on a leisurely cruise up from Woodbridge. Another time it might be as the sinewy silent partner of a young fisherman named Fletcher aboard their herring-trawler, the Meum and Tuum. (FitzGerald was "Meum.") Or happiest of all, especially when the growing fame of the *Rubáiyát* after 1859 made him uncomfortable, he'd take off for Lowestoft and hide himself among its beach bums, beachcombing with the best of them.

[6] Details on pp. 293–94.

George Borrow got snared by a local widow while passing through Lowestoft, though she had to chase him half over Europe to tie him down. Beginning in 1840, he lived off and on thereafter at her lakeside estate on Oulton Broad, two miles west of town. Here he wrote *The Bible in Spain* (1843) and *Lavengro* (1850); worked at *The Romany Rye* (1857); and, to the consternation of his wife and neighbors, entertained any gipsies who happened to wander by. In his great black hat and splendid Spanish cloak, many took him for a gipsy himself.

Another writer who featured Lowestoft and its gipsies was Theodore Watts-Dunton, friend of Rossetti and Swinburne, in his novel *Aylwin* (1898). This was no mere coincidence, however. Watts-Dunton had long known Borrow, and published editions of his *Lavengro* and *The Romany Rye* with recollections of their friendship.

In 1878 a young Polish seaman named Teodor Joseph Konrad Korzeniowski stepped ashore at Lowestoft for his first glimpse of England. He hardly knew a word of the language. His only reading of it had been an occasional English newspaper that had come his way, and "my first acquaintance by ear of it," he confessed later, "was in the speech of fishermen, shipwrights, and sailors of the East Coast."

He got a job aboard a coaster sailing the North Sea, worked hard to improve his English, and made up his mind to become a master in the British merchant service. By 1880 he had left Lowestoft and sailed as third mate aboard a clipper bound for Australia. His decision to quit the sea altogether and become a writer wouldn't come until 1894. But before he left Lowestoft he had made one decision for which students of English literature should be forever grateful: he decided to change his name. Joseph Conrad *is* a lot easier to spell.

Blundeston   Blundeston is the "Blunderstone" where David Copperfield is born in a snug little house called The Rookery. Why "The Rookery?" Because, David's mother explains to Aunt Betsey Trotwood when she unexpectedly drops by, Mr. Copperfield saw some nests, and liked to think there were rooks about. Where are the birds? demands Miss Betsey.

"We thought—Mr. Copperfield thought—it was quite a large rookery," poor Mrs. Copperfield stammers, "but the nests were very old ones, and the birds have deserted them a long while."

"David Copperfield all over!" cries Miss Betsey. "David Copperfield from head to foot! Calls a house a rookery when there's not a rook near it, and takes the birds on trust, because he sees the nests!"

Dickensians have tried in vain to identify this building or that in Blundeston as the author's model for the Copperfield house. And the natives are certain that theirs was the church with the high-backed Copperfield pew and the window through which Peggotty checks on their house during the morning service because, David explains, "she likes to make herself as sure as she can that it's not being robbed, or is not in flames." The Blundeston church's round Norman tower has even been restored and turned into a Dickens memorial.

Who cares if the author himself insisted that he chose "Blunderstone" as his hero's birthplace simply because he liked the sound of the name? Besides, the church does have an authentic literary connection. Its vicar in the late eighteenth century was the Rev. Norton Nicholls, a good friend of Thomas Gray, and Gray visited the rectory often.

Great Yarmouth   Charles Dickens couldn't have chosen a better symbol for Great Yarmouth than the dwelling to which Peggotty takes David Copperfield to meet her family. There it lies, high and dry on the ground but with water all about, the river on the one hand, the sea on the other. A house, but not a house. Rather, "iron funnel sticking out of it for a chimney and smoking very cozily . . . a black barge or some other superannuated boat." And as David notes with instant wonder, "a real boat, which had no doubt been upon the water hundreds of times."

That combination of sea and river has given Great Yarmouth two lives. Essentially, it is a spit of land three miles long. All its eastern boundary is the coast of the North Sea. All its western boundary is the river called the Yare—formed actually by the confluence of the Yare, Bure, and Waveney rivers just to the north. For their first thousand years and more, the people of Great Yarmouth made their living from the sea as shipbuilders, prodigious fishermen, prosperous traders. But they quite sensibly built their town facing the river and its always safe anchorage.

A trim little town it was, too, composed of a neat pattern of three chief north-and-south streets, gridded by 145 short east-and-west lanes called "Rows." Their alignment can still be seen, though much of the Rows succumbed to the savaging of two world wars.

Then in the nineteenth century, even as Dickens was reaching his zenith, the town he had known began to turn its back on the river and face the sea. For his fellow Victorians, like Dickens himself, had discovered the joys of bathing—or at least of huddling together en masse on some distant beach. The visitors came from all over England in ever increasing thousands all summer long, turning Great Yarmouth into what today seems, in season, one never-ending sea resort.

There are two piers, and pavilions and boating lakes, and sports and leisure centers, and amusement parks replete with gaudy light and futuristic rides. Yet somehow the holidayers here don't seem as depressing as those at Lowestoft. Maybe it's because they're less inhibited, less dogged about it all. Or in simple affirmative terms: more obviously having a good time.

Among Victorian visitors were those friends and lovers of gipsy lore, George Borrow and Theodore Watts-Dunton. In fact, they first met at the beach while bathing. Borrow stayed on for some years beginning in 1853, and was living at No. 169 King Street when he finished *The Romany Rye*. Other writers with one link or another to the town were Thomas Nash, John Cleveland, and Anna Sewell.

Nash took cover there for a while in 1597–98 when a satiric play he'd written with Ben Jonson, *The Isle of Dogs*, made London temporarily too hot for comfort. He amused himself in exile by writing *Lenten Stuffe*, with a lively tongue-in-cheek description of Great Yarmouth and a rhapsody of "resplendent laude and honour" on its most famous product, "the puissant red herring," known throughout Europe.

Even before the Normans, fishermen from The Cinque Ports of Sussex and South Kent would come annually to fill their boats with Yarrow herring and sell them both at home and abroad. Fittingly enough, Nash and his ally Robert Greene—writer, bon vivant, and a Norfolk man to boot—spent their last night together drinking and gorging themselves on the Yarrow delicacy. Greene died next day of a "surfeit of pickle herringe and Rennish wine."

John Cleveland was a poet who defended Charles I a bit too fiercely. During the Commonwealth he was reduced to wandering the country, living off handouts from Royalist friends, and in 1655 found himself spending three months in a Yarmouth jail. Only the intervention of Cromwell got him free. In his younger days Cleveland wrote a poem for the same volume of tributes to Edward King in which Milton's "Lycidas" first appeared. But any notion that he was another Milton is speedily dismissed by lines like

> I am no poet here; My pen's the spout
> Where the rain-water of mine eyes runs out.[7]

The appalling fact, though, is that in their own day, Cleveland was more esteemed than Milton.

By all odds the most famous literary work associated with Great Yarmouth is *Black Beauty* (1877). Although she was living with her mother in Norwich

---

[7] "On the Memory of Mr. Edward King, Drowned in the Irish Seas" (1638).

when she wrote it, Anna Sewell was born in Great Yarmouth in 1820, in Church Plain, and the seventeenth-century house is now a museum.

Caister Castle   Now officially a port of Great Yarmouth, Caister Castle is off the A 1064, four miles north of the main part of the town. Records show that a Sir John Fastolf was licensed to build it in 1432, and that when he died he left it to John Paston, whose family retained it well into the seventeenth century.

Both John Fastolf and the Pastons are of literary interest. Fastolf is supposed to have been the model for Shakespeare's Sir John Falstaff. The Pastons were writers of the famous "Paston Letters." Written by three generations of that family, they cover a period from Henry IV to Richard III, and provide a fascinating and unique record of nearly a hundred years of turbulent history. From 1787 on, portions of this correspondence were printed as various manuscripts came to light, and the first of several editions of the whole collection was published 1901–04.

Caister Castle is open to the public from mid-May to the end of September.

2. Norwich To Bury St. Edmunds

All of Norfolk and Suffolk lying outside the embrace of the A 12 can best be covered from two bases: Norwich for all the northern sector, Bury St. Edmunds for the southwest. Both towns are major highway junctions; both are of much interest in their own right.

Norwich is due west of Great Yarmouth via the A 47, which runs almost arrow-straight between the two. Bury St. Edmunds is forty miles southwest of Norwich.

Norwich

George Borrow, raised there 150 years ago, described Norwich in *Lavengro* as a "fine old city," the "genuine old English Town." [8] But standing today amid the skyscrapers and glass and concrete boxes, the clutter of modern

[8] Borrow's parents lived in Willow Lane in what's now called Borrow House.

industry, the carparks and the fast-food outlets imported from America, you may well ask: Where did it all go?

Don't despair. Even as you're surrounded by what one overzealous booster—one assumes he meant well—calls "the stark modernity of Anglia Square," simply face in the direction of Wensum Street and cast your eyes skyward. Soaring to majestic height, the tower of one of England's greatest cathedrals tells you at once: old Norwich lives on. High on the mound to the southwest of the Cathedral is the twelfth-century castle. At its feet is the ancient marketplace. On the narrow, steep-climbing streets are the houses of a Norwich of a far-distant past, some Tudor, some even medieval. Interwoven with it all—houses, castle, cathedral, narrow streets and market—are threads of literature.

The market has served without a break from 1066, when the town was among the nation's largest, to this very day. Norwich remains what it has always been, the major shopping center for towns and villages as much as forty miles away.

Frederick Marryat, nineteenth-century writer of sea tales, shopped there when he lived at Langham, twenty-five miles to the northwest. So did Rider Haggard when he lived at West Bradenham. As a teenager, the modern poet W. H. Auden on occasion slipped down from Gresham's School in Holt for boyish high jinks. And in the fourteenth century more than likely, Chaucer's Reeve, Oswald, would come in from Bawdeswell, a dozen miles northwest.

Some of those old houses in Norwich are old indeed. One in King Street now called the Music House may well be England's oldest private dwelling. When Sir John Paston, author of the first *Paston Letters* bought the house in 1487, it was already three hundred years old! Another building, mentioned by Paston in those same letters, is an inn that goes back to the thirteenth century. Then called The Molde Fish Tavern, it changed its name over the centuries, first to The Mayd's Head, and finally to today's The Maid's Head. It flourishes yet as a three-star hotel in Tombland Street. The "Tudor" timbers and gables that you see now are pseudo, but the old fireplace and stone ingle seats are real enough.

As for the Cathedral, those knowledgeable about such matters call it the most perfect example of the Norman style of church architecture now in existence. Its spire, rising to 315 feet above the ground, fills the viewer with an awe matched only by Salisbury's. The antiquity of its massive nave and transepts is felt rather than measured. The cornerstone was laid in 1096. That's almost one hundred years before Thomas à Becket was murdered at Canterbury, three hundred years before Chaucer dispatched those pilgrims to worship at Becket's tomb and tell tales along the way.

An odd pair associated with the Norwich Cathedral are George Crabbe, who was ordained there in 1782, and John Skelton. Both were poets, both were satirists, and both were clergymen—but hardly your run-of-the-mill clergymen. Especially Skelton, who was as merry, unrestrained, and bawdy as that eighteenth-century madcap, the Rev. Laurence Sterne.[9] Rector at Diss beginning about 1504, Skelton preached at the Cathedral during a visit to Norwich. This is the same visit when he ran into a young lady named Jane Scroupe. Discovering that her pet sparrow, Philip, had been killed by a cat, he proceeded to write a wild poetic saga about the tragedy, *The Boke of Phylyp Sparrowe*, including a lamentation in Jane's own words, a eulogy of her from Skelton, and a defense of the poem itself.

The entrance to the Cathedral from Tombland is through the elaborate Erpingham Gate, given in 1420 by that doughty old hero of the Battle of Agincourt and saluted in Shakespeare's *Henry V*. When King Henry suggests that the old man might wish himself safely back home in England:

> A good soft pillow for that good white head
> Were better than a churlish turf of France . . .

Erpingham replies:

> Not so, my liege, this lodging likes me better,
> Since I may say, "Now lie I like a king."

Inside the Erpingham Gate, to the northeast of the Cathedral, is King Edward VI School, founded in 1250 and re-established by young Edward in the sixteenth century. Three of its famous alumni are Robert Greene, born in Norwich about 1560; George Borrow; and Lord Nelson, who was born at Burnham Thorpe, some thirty miles to the northwest, in 1758. He didn't stay at school all that long—he entered the navy in 1770—but just the same, that is his statue standing there outside the school.

Up in the Market Place is another fine old church, St. Peter Mancroft, dating from 1430. The seventeenth-century writer, Sir Thomas Browne, who is buried there, has a statue outside, and not one, but two commemorative tablets inside. One of the tablets is the usual tribute you'd expect from any widow who was doing her duty. The other, however, was to make amends for some rather unseemly handling of the poor fellow's corpse.

Gravediggers in 1840, you see, dug up his skull, and it wound up being on display here and there as a medical showpiece. It wasn't until 1922 that it got reunited with the rest of him and Sir Thomas was given his second plaque.

---

[9]For a fuller treatment of Skelton, see p. 317.

Browne's *Religio Medici* had already been published, though without his permission, when he established a medical practice in Norwich in 1637. But his best book, *Urn Burial* (1658) was written there. A richly-styled meditation on death and burial practices of various times and peoples, the work was inspired when Browne went to take a look at some sepulchral urns workers had recently dug up by accident. Browne's knighthood came in 1671, when Charles II visited the city.

Several parts of Norfolk can lay claim to Anna Sewell. She was born in Great Yarmouth. Buxton, seven miles north of Norwich, furnished much of the background for *Black Beauty:* her love and knowledge of horses stemmed from her happy days there with her grandparents at Dudwick Farm, and the novel's Birtwick Park is based in part on her aunt and uncle's Dudwick House. She is buried at Lamas, a village only a little to the north of Buxton. But the book itself belongs to Norwich. She wrote it there in 1877 at 125 Spixworth Road, Old Catton, while living with her mother.

Norwich had other women writers, too, including the first ever to write in the English tongue, and the youngest ever to succeed professionally. The pioneer of female writers is known simply as "Juliana of Norwich," a fifteenth-century visionary who wrote *XVI Revelations of Divine Love.* The publishing prodigy was Daisy Ashford, who came to live in Norwich after her marriage. Her novel, *The Young Visiters*, the literary sensation of 1919, was written at the age of nine.

Other Norwich women authors were Anna Sewell's own mother, Mary Sewell, whose poems for children were popular, and Harriet Martineau, whose life was a chronicle of courage and indomitability.

A native of Norwich, born at Gurney Court in 1802, Harriet Martineau's early years were far from promising. As a child, she was sickly and deaf. The deafness persisted throughout life; the health, if anything, grew worse. When she was twenty, her father died, leaving the family penniless. She had no special training and no one to help her. Yet by the time she reached thirty, her books on economic reform had begun to make her something of a London celebrity.

She then went to America, managed somehow to survive three years there, and came home to write, at thirty-six, *Retrospect of Western Travel* (1838). Her novel the next year, *Deerbrook*, was followed by total physical collapse in Venice and medical advice that hereafter her invalidism would be permanent and well-nigh total.

Nevertheless, in 1840 she published the novel, *The Hour and the Man*, and in 1841 *The Playfellow*, a series of delightful adventure stories for young people. And, nothing daunted, she tried the popular Victorian form of hypnotism called mesmerism, which brought her an astonishing return to vigor. Off she gallivanted to Egypt, Syria, and Palestine, and in 1848 she published *Eastern Life*.

Not about to slow down, she then moved to Ambleside in the Lake District to be near the Wordsworths, producing, at age fifty-three, her *Complete Guide to the Lakes* (1855). Meanwhile she kept up a steady stream of articles for the *London Daily News* until well into her sixties. Even when she died in 1876 at age seventy-four, she wasn't through. Her *Autobiographical Memoir*, published posthumously, is a lively record of the notables she had known.

As the survival of old Norwich itself attests, they bred them tough in Norwich.

Norfolk and William Cowper: Catfield and North Tuddenham—Mundesley—Little Dunham—and East Dereham

Within a twenty-five mile radius from Norwich, William Cowper lived some of the early, and all of the final, days of his life. The first were among the happiest he was ever to know. The last were beyond doubt his most desperate.

The town and villages involved are Catfield and Mundesley, North Tuddenham, East Dereham and Little Dunham. The first two are reached via the A 1151 and the A 149; Mundesley is east of the A 149, on the B 1145 where it runs into the sea ten miles above Catfield.

The other three are strung out along the A 47—North Tuddenham twelve miles and East Dereham sixteen miles to the west of Norwich, and Little Dunham on an unmarked road seven miles beyond East Dereham.

Catfield As a boy and young man, Cowper often visited Catfield, where his uncle, Roger Donne, was rector. "Of all places in the earth I love Catfield," he wrote later, "where I passed some of the happiest days of my youth. He especially loved Harriet Rival Donne, "[my] good-tempered, cheerful cousin and playmate."

As he moved into manhood, he began to write poems addressed to another cousin, Theodora Cowper in London, whom he called "Delia." Judging from the lightness of his lyrics, it would have been a happy match:

> This ev'ning, Delia, you and I
> Have manag'd most delightfully,
> For with a frown we parted.

But, he continues archly, it was all a game:

> You knew, Dissembler! all the while
> How sweet it was to reconcile.

Theodora's father, however, refused his consent. In 1756, Cowper bid her farewell. They never met again, and neither ever married.

North Tuddenham   When Cowper came back to Norfolk in 1795, to the village of North Tuddenham, he was sixty-four and a broken man. With him came Mary Unwin. She and her husband, the Rev. Morley Unwin, had taken Cowper into their home in Huntingdon, Cambs. in 1765 and had helped him recover following his release from a mental institution. She was then forty-one, Cowper thirty-four.

Over the ensuing thirty years, she ministered to him similarly when bouts of depression or insanity reoccurred. After Morley Unwin died in 1767, she followed Cowper to Buckinghamshire, first to Olney—where he wrote his great hymns and major poems like *The Task* (1784)—then to Weston. But in 1791 she suffered a stroke. By 1795, at seventy-one she was in need of constant care herself, and anxiety for her reduced Cowper to near imbecility.[10]

To the rescue came the poet's devoted cousin, John Johnson, an amiable young clergyman known affectionately as "Johnny of Norfolk." Johnson housed his charges first in an untenanted parsonage in North Tuddenham, where his sister could keep an eye on them. Then after a month, when he judged they were up to it, he took them to his place in Mundesley on Norfolk's northwestern coast, hoping the sea air and bathing would be beneficial.

Mundesley   Mundesley (MUNZ-lee) is an unassuming little sea resort with a good sandy beach backed by cliffs. Tenderly cared for here in Johnson's house in the High Street (now called Cowper's house), the invalids improved a bit. Cowper was able to bathe and to make exploratory walks about the neighborhood. It was Johnson's plan to establish them more or less permanently in East Dereham, but from this time until Cowper died in 1800,

[10]For a more detailed account, see p. 58.

he was brought back to Mundesley now and again for a cheering change of scene.

Little Dunham   Between Mundesley, which they left in October of 1795, and East Dereham, Cowper and Mary spent nearly a year at Dunham Lodge in Little Dunham. Their quarters were more than comfortable, a sizeable eighteenth-century house in a pleasant park. But Mary was visibly deteriorating, and Cowper teetered on the edge of madness.

East Dereham   In October 1796, Cowper and Mary settled down in John Johnson's home in the East Dereham market place. The novelist George Borrow, who grew up there very shortly after Cowper's death, described it then as "the pattern of an English market town." Though now grown to a population of about eight thousand, East Dereham still has much of the charm that Borrow saw: "modest, pretty, quiet."

It's an old town, too. In 1954, by way of celebrating its thirteen hundredth anniversary, the townsfolk erected a wondrous "gallow" sign spanning the road by the market, within sight of where Cowper's red brick home had been, and where the Cowper Memorial Congregational Chapel stands now. Emblazoned on the sign are the dates: 654–1954.

In their day, East Dereham was what Borrow called it, "a beautiful little town," and Cowper and Mary should have enjoyed it. But in his final years, Cowper was beyond caring about much of anything, save for Mary. And Mary died in 1796. He never mentioned her name again.

He did manage to revise the translation of Homer he had published in 1791 and even wrote one final piece of original verse, the first-rate but melancholy "The Castaway" (1799). But death, when it came in 1800, was a welcome release.

Cowper is buried in the St. Edmund's Chapel of East Dereham's church. There's a memorial window and a monument with commemorative lines by his friend and biographer, William Hayley. But Hayley was a better friend than poet. More moving, more fitting is the tribute of George Borrow:

> England's sweetest and most pious bard.

Bacton—Paston—and Sidestrand

The B 1159 that goes through Mundesley as it follows the northwest coast of Norfolk from above Great Yarmouth to Cromer also runs through Bacton,

Paston, and Sidestrand. These three villages, almost within sight of each other, could furnish the stuff for a trilogy of merry little tales that might be called in order, "The Startled Wife" . . . "The Dauntless Dame" . . . and "The Outraged Cook."

Bacton   The startled woman appears in the Reeve's naughty story in Chaucer's *Canterbury Tales*. Two young students, Aleyn and John, have been put up for the night by a miller on a pallet in his own bedroom, where his daughter Molly has her bed as well. Incensed by the miller's cheating them of their grain, the students get the miller drunk and proceed to trick daughter and wife into making love, Aleyn in Molly's bed, her mother in John's.

Near daybreak, exhausted from a full night of highly satisfactory dalliance, the wife is still sleeping soundly alongside John when suddenly her husband trips in the dark and comes crashing down upon her. Startled into wakefulness, she cries upon the Lord to save her: "Help! holy cross of Bromeholm," she seyde.

What the miller's wife was really doing was appealing to the good monks of Bacton's Bromholm Priory. For they owned a piece of the very wood of the True Cross, made into a double crucifix and proven to work all manner of miracles like raising the dead, casting out dreams, and even restoring curdled milk to wholesomeness.

That "By the Holy Rood of Bromholm" was a truly potent medieval oath is verified by yet another major fourteenth-century work, the anonymous *Piers Plowman*. In it, no less than one of the Seven Deadly Sins, Avarice himself, repenting, insists:

> But I swear now, so may I thrive, to sin no longer,
> And never to weigh wickedly or use wily practice;
> But take the highway to Walsingham and my wife with me,
> And bid the rood of Bromeholm bring me from debt.

You can go take a look at the ruins of Bromholm Priory for yourself if you like. They're down there in a farm field along the road to Keswick.

Paston   The "dauntless dame" was Mistress Margaret Paston, wife of John Paston, head of the area's leading family. Margaret and John began the interchange of fascinating letters carried on by their descendants for nearly a hundred years, and published in the twentieth century as *The Paston Letters*.

A letter from Margaret to John, written about 1425 while he was away in

London, is typical of the vivid reflection of the period that makes this correspondence so readable.

The times were perilous, and marauding bands roamed the countryside. But even in John's absence, Dame Margaret would have none of it. While you're in London, she wrote him, get us some decent weapons to fight back. She knew exactly what she wanted, too. He was to make sure he got the short but powerful crossbow, which was held and fired horizontally. The longbow, at six feet and more in length and held vertically, was too tall to be used in the low-ceilinged cottages. Also, she warned, don't forget the windacs (strings) and quarrels (square-headed arrows or bolts) we'll need with them: "Right worshipful husband . . . Pray you to get some crossbows and windacs to bind them with, and quarrels; for your houses here be so low that there may be none man shoot out with no long bow, though we have never so much need." Margaret then adds a wifely P.S.—get me some cloth for a dress, but don't pay more than 44d the yard.

John Paston had a connection with that Bromholm Priory in Bacton, too. He was buried there in 1466, and *The Paston Letters* contain an account of both his burial and the funeral feast that followed. His tomb was later transferred to the Paston church, and the Paston monument that's there is supposed to be his. The old flint Paston Barn by the church, though, was built in the days of Queen Elizabeth.

Sidestrand The "outraged cook" lived at Sidestrand, a tiny village with a sandy beach below the cliffs. The gray tower of its ancient church still stands at the cliffs' edge, but its churchyard has dropped into the sea. The pair who so provoked the cook were Algernon Charles Swinburne and Theodore Watts-Dunton, that solicitor turned novelist and literary critic.

They came to Sidestrand in September of 1883, partly to celebrate the publication of Swinburne's *Tristram of Lyonesse* (1882), which some have called the poet's most flawless work, and lodged at a Mr. Jeremy's Mill House. They had a wonderful time, bathing and strolling at all hours of the day, talking at all hours of the evening.

The sea, said Swinburne, was much better than at Southwold. But their irregular meal hours increasingly annoyed the Mill House cook until she finally exploded, summing it all up in one magnificent outburst: "They never gave my puddings a chance!"

Heydon

Heydon is a most agreeable little village, twelve miles northwest of Norwich off the B 1149. But it wouldn't have rated so much as a nod in a literary guide if its Heydon Hall hadn't been, in 1803, the home of General William Bulwer. To him in that year was born a son who was to become a celebrated novelist, owner of a great estate in Hertfordshire called Kneb-worth, and possessor of a truly lordly name.

But that novelist might be known now as just Edward Bulwer of Heydon Hall, except that:

a) he was a fourth, not a first son;

b) and the general doted on the first son, and left him Heydon Hall;

c) and Edward's grandmother doted on the second son, and left *him* her estate;

d) and the third son died early;

e) so Edward's mother doted on Edward and left him Knebworth Hall, which she owned;

f) and since to spite her husband she had re-assumed her maiden name, becoming Elizabeth Bulwer-Lytton,

g) Edward took Bulwer-Lytton as his last name, too,

h) and in 1866, he was created a baron.

Thus it was that instead of being remembered today as plain Edward Bulwer of Heydon Hall, the author of *The Last Days of Pompeii* (1834), *Rienzi* (1835), and a string of other Victorian successes goes by the grandiose title of Edward Earl Lytton Bulwer-Lytton, 1st Baron Lytton.

King's Lynn

When you get to King's Lynn, forty-four miles west of Norwich, you're about to run out of Norfolk. Lincolnshire is within six miles, Cambridge-shire within nine. Descriptions of King's Lynn usually include adjectives like beautiful, romantic, even ravishing—and they're deserved. Wide, open squares called "Market Places" and named for days of the week, medieval stone alleys and great merchants' houses that doubled as warehouses, histor-ic buildings like the fifteenth-century St. George's Guildhall give the town a distinctive charm. Its charter goes back to 1202 and King John, hence "King's" Lynn—but you'll reveal yourself as an outsider if you call it anything but simply Lynn.

For all this, though, there's not all that much to discuss about its liter-ary past. Soon after 1400, a local girl named Margery Kempe, daughter of the mayor, produced *The Book of Margery Kempe*, a kind of travelog-autobiography-spiritual history that includes accounts of pilgrimages to Italy, Germany, and Jerusalem. What makes the work especially remarkable is that Margery was illiterate. (She dictated it.)

Far better known is another of King's Lynn's women—Fanny Burney. She was born there in 1752, though there is some dispute as to exactly where. Some say at No. 84 High Street, now rebuilt, or more likely at the still-standing St. Augustine's House in Chapel Street near the Tuesday Market. Her father, Dr. Charles Burney, was the organist at St. Margaret's. In 1760 he moved to London. There he became a close friend of Dr. Johnson, Edmund Burke, David Garrick, Sir Joshua Reynolds, and something of a writer himself. His four-volume *History of Music* was published between 1776 and 1789, and he wrote several accounts of travels through France, Germany, Italy, and the Low Countries.

Fanny, of course, went with the family to London to live, but she was frequently back in King's Lynn, staying with her father's friend, Mrs. Allen, whom he eventually married. As early as age ten, Fanny had begun writing, and faithfully kept a diary, a practice that covered over seventy-five years of her very long life and was to lead to two still-remarkable books. Her *Early Diary* of the years 1768–78 with bright little sketches of famous figures like Johnson and Garrick was published posthumously in 1889; the *Diary and Letters* of the years 1778–1840 appeared in 1842–46.

Her first novel, *Evelina*, had the old but sure plot of beautiful but poor girl discovers she's an heiress, and some appealing and droll writing. Published anonymously in 1777, it was an instant and wild success. When the author's identity was discovered, Fanny Burney became a celebrity. She was to write other novels, among them *Cecilia* (1782) and *Camilla* (1796), but none ever matched that first attempt.

On everyone's tongue in King's Lynn when Fanny was a girl was a fellow named Eugene Aram, who made his mark in literature, though unwillingly. For Mr. Aram was not only a master at the town's Grammar School, but managed a bit of murder on the side, for which he was arrested in 1758. Thomas Hood used the story in his rather good poem, *The Dream of Eugene Aram* (1829), and Bulwer-Lytton wrote a novel about it called *Eugene Aram* (1832).

Among Aram's pupils was Charles Burney, Fanny's younger brother, and maybe the final word on King's Lynn should be his. For though the things he wrote as a classical scholar go unnoticed today, he did leave a literary legacy of a sort: the largest collection of early English newspapers in existence.

Diss

Diss is twenty miles from Norwich, eighteen miles straight down the A 140, then a two-mile jog to the west on the A 1066. It has about forty-five hundred people, a fourteenth-century church, and a pretty little pond. Thanks to the pond, it got its name. The Anglo-Saxons called a small body of standing water "dice," akin to our own words dike and ditch. And thanks to his own irrepressible ways and biting pen, it got John Skelton as its rector in 1502.

Ordained in 1498, Skelton was undoubtedly one of the most learned men of his day, and had enjoyed the highest royal favor. The Countess of Richmond, Henry VII's mother, had been his patron, and he had tutored Henry's son, the future Henry VIII. He was named poet laureate by both Oxford and Cambridge. But he couldn't restrain a penchant for childish pranks and stinging satire. He even attacked the court itself in a poem called "The Bowge of Court."

Whether caused by the pranks, the satire, or both is not certain. But in 1502 he was imprisoned for a time, and by 1504 found it more than prudent to retire to Diss and its pulpit.[11] There he produced a torrent of boisterous and often gloriously coarse verse. Especially noteworthy were *Phylyp Sparrowe* (discussed in the earlier section on Norwich), and *The Tunning of Elynour Rumming*, an especially rollicking account of the alewife Eleanor and the "noppy ale" she brews for "travellers and tinkers, for sweters [those who sweat], and swynkers [those who toil], and all good drinkers."

But Skelton must have been at his best in the pulpit. Once he interrupted his sermon to ask the good people of Diss why they complained that he kept a "fair wench" in his rectory. To be sure, he did keep a fair wench. But she surpassed all the wives of the parish in beauty, and had given him a son.

In proof, he abruptly produced the child before their very eyes—naked. Brandishing it aloft, Skelton demanded:

> "How say you, neighbors all? Is not this child as fair as is the best of all of yours? It hath nose, eyes, hands, and feet, as well as any of yours. It is not like a pig, nor a calf, nor like no foul nor no monstrous beast. If I had brought forth this child without arms or legs, or that it was deformed being a monstrous thing, I would never have blamed you.
>
> But to complain without a cause! You be, and have been, and will be and shall be knaves to complain of me without a cause reasonable."

Thetford

The A 1066 runs almost directly west out of Diss, and ends after sixteen miles in Thetford. If you're curious about all the flint you've seen on

---

[11] Whether or not he had been born in Diss is also uncertain. Some accounts say it was Cumberland.

churches, houses, and buildings of every kind in Norfolk and Suffolk—where it comes from, how it's mined, and so on—Grimes Graves, seven miles northwest of Thetford, is the place to go, You can visit four thousand-year-old flint mines there, and a shaft is open for your inspection.

If you're curious about the man who first said "These are the times that try men's souls," go to Thetford itself. Thomas Paine, who wrote those words in *The American Crisis, No. 1* (1776) about the American Revolution, was born in Thetford January 29, 1737.

The son of a Quaker corsetmaker, he attended the Thetford Grammar School and at thirteen was apprenticed to his father's trade. At twenty he left Thetford, and in the next fifteen years somehow was able to squeeze in two failed marriages and an astounding series of failed occupations—as teacher, tobacconist, grocer, and exciseman among others—before writing *The Case of the Officers of Excise* (1771) and going bankrupt.

A chance acquaintanceship with Benjamin Franklin, whom the colonies had sent to represent them in England, persuaded him to start anew in America. His life thereafter was varied and usually hectic, including stays in England and France (where he was first made a French citizen, then later jailed as an Enemy Englishman), and finally back to America again.

Along the way he wrote such works as *The Rights of Man* (1791–92), in reply to Edmund Burke's *Reflections on the Revolution in France;* and *The Age of Reason*, a rather violent defense of Deism against Christianity and Atheism.

The reward for this lifetime of battling for freedom of thought and action was a bitter one, extending even beyond death. His final years were marked by ostracism, poverty, and ill health. When he died in 1809, interment in consecrated ground was refused, and he was buried on a farm in New Rochelle, New York. William Cobbett, the English reformer, tried to make amends in 1819 by bringing the remains back to England and proposing to erect a monument for them. But even that fell through. And as a final indignity, after Cobbett's death the bones of Paine were lost.

Paine is remembered in Thetford today, however. Opposite the three-star Bell Hotel on King's Street, a rambling combination of Tudor and modern, there's a gilded statue of Paine in front of the seventeenth-century King's House—gift of the Thomas Paine Society of The United States.

Though the house in which Paine was born is gone, on the site in White Hart Street is the garden of Grey Gables. White Hart Street also has the Ancient House Museum and the Thomas Paine Hotel. A timber-framed fifteenth-century building, Ancient House has some Thomas Paine material along with its local archeological exhibits. Finally, though the Thomas Paine is a small hotel, if you're in the mood you can have dinner by candlelight in "Tom's Pantry."

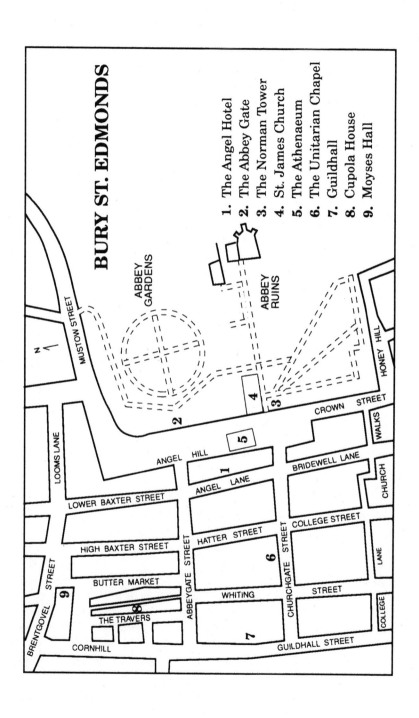

BURY ST. EDMONDS

1. The Angel Hotel
2. The Abbey Gate
3. The Norman Tower
4. St. James Church
5. The Athenaeum
6. The Unitarian Chapel
7. Guildhall
8. Cupola House
9. Moyses Hall

ABBEY GARDENS

ABBEY RUINS

MUSTOW STREET

HONEY HILL

LOOMS LANE

CROWN STREET

WALKS

ANGEL HILL

ANGEL LANE

BRIDEWELL LANE

CHURCH

LOWER BAXTER STREET

COLLEGE STREET

HATTER STREET

HIGH BAXTER STREET

ABBEYGATE STREET

CHURCHGATE STREET

LANE

BUTTER MARKET

WHITING

STREET

COLLEGE

BRENTGOVEL STREET

THE TRAVERS

CORNHILL

GUILDHALL STREET

Bury St. Edmunds

Bury St. Edmunds is only twelve miles from Thetford, straight south down the A 134. And any way you look at it, Bury St. Edmunds is a lovely town.

Admittedly, some ways of looking at it are better than others. You can't expect a town of over thirty thousand people to be all charm, and its more modern section up on the hill to the west does have a grubby part or two. So the best thing to do is turn from the hill toward the "prosperous brick town" that Thomas Carlyle discovered when he came there in 1840, "with its clean brick houses, ancient clean streets . . . the general grassy face of Suffolk; looking out right pleasantly from its hill-slope, toward the rising sun; and on the eastern edge of it, still runs long, black, and massive, a range of monastic ruins."

In *Pickwick Papers*, Mr. Pickwick and Sam Weller come upon the town in precisely the same way. Perched on the outside of their stagecoach with his master, Sam is talking his head off when suddenly he interrupts himself:

"Beg your pardon, sir," he asks. "Is this Bury St. Edmunds?"
"It is," replied Mr. Pickwick.
The coach rattled through the well-paved streets of a handsome little town, of thriving and cleanly appearance.

Bury St. Edmunds owes both its name and its crowning glory, the Abbey, to a ninth-century Anglian king who impetuously dashed out to fight some invading Danes and wound up being captured, tortured, and beheaded. All this entitled him to be a saint. The king's name was Edmund, the town's name was Bedericsworth, and the year was 870.

After the Danes were finished with Edmund, they threw his head and body into the woods. But a wolf led his followers to the spot. Wood-carvings of the wolf holding Edmund's head can be seen about town to this day, indicating that the citizens have remained duly grateful. Thirty-three years later, monks brought the poor king's bones back to the monastery.

By the time the Normans arrived to take over in the eleventh century, Edmund had become a saint; the town had become Bury St. Edmunds; and thanks to King Canute, in 1032 the monastery had become an abbey, eventually one of the noblest and wealthiest until destroyed by the Dissolution.

Dickens and Carlyle weren't the only literary figures drawn since then to Bury St. Edmunds and its abbey. In the fourteenth century the poet John

Lydgate was a student and later a monk there, and was buried in the Abbey Church. In the sixteenth century, John Leland, antiquarian and library-keeper to Henry VIII, came and raved about the Abbey.

Daniel Defoe, on a visit in 1704, reminded of a noble French city, called it the "Montpelier of England." Edward FitzGerald, who with the writer James Spedding was a pupil at the Bury St. Edmunds Grammar School from 1821 to 1826, confessed that he could spend hour after hour just gazing upon the Abbey ruins. Henry Crabb Robinson, friend and chronicler of Words-worth, Coleridge *et al,* and the novelist known simply as Ouida had special reason to love Bury St. Edmunds. Both were born there, Robinson in 1775, Ouida in 1839.

The major sites associated with these writers are in the area of Bury St. Edmunds near the Abbey, and you can tour them on foot in short order. For all sorts of reasons, start at the Angel Hotel (1) on Angel Hill. It's practically across the street from the Abbey, was Mr. Pickwick's destination, and FitzGerald's favorite vantage point. There's a big, open car park directly in front in which to rid yourself of your car. It has a number of interesting things to see in its own right. Best of all, when you return to it at the end of your tour, the Angel can offer anything from a meal and a night's lodging to simply a pleasant place to sit and enjoy a refreshing drink. Should you feel thirsty before you've finished your tour, incidentally, you'll pass two interesting pubs en route: the smallest pub in England, and a seventeenth-century place where Daniel Defoe stayed.

Letting an inspection of the Angel itself wait until you come back, begin the tour by walking down the hill and crossing the street to the great Abbey Gate (2) on your left, entry to the Abbey courtyard. The size of the gate suggests how enormous the rest of the Abbey must have been in its prime. Leland said about it in 1534 or so: "A man who saw the Abbey would say verily it was a city; so many gates there are in it, and some of brass; so many towers and a most stately church, upon which attend three other churches also standing gloriously in the same churchyard all of passing fine and curious workmanship."

So powerful and wealthy were the clergy then that the people sometimes rose up against them. So it had been with Bury St. Edmunds in the fourteenth century, when the citizens had stormed the Abbey, tearing down the gate. But a sign you can see under the archway today succinctly tells the result:

Destroyed by Townspeople 1327,
Rebuilt 1347.

Not only were the people forced to erect a new gate. Look at its west wall and you'll see that they also had to provide it with arrow slits so defenders could make sure it never happened again.

In the Abbey courtyard now are lovely gardens, aglow with flower beds, where the townspeople of today can stroll, picnic, or simply loll in the sun. Behind the gardens flows the River Lark, spanned by the handsomely-arched Abbot's Bridge, build in 1211.

The "massive range of monastic ruins" that Carlyle described lie to the south of the gardens. Carlyle's visit to the Abbey was in a sense a pilgrimage. In the 1830s he had grown increasingly skeptical of reformers who insisted that all England's millions of paupers needed was more liberty, meaning the right to vote. Then in quick succession in 1840 he visited a typical work-house (poor-house for adults) and read a history of the Abbey for the years 1173–1202 by one of its monks, Jocelyn de Brakeland. The contrast the two presented was shocking. The nineteenth-century pauper sat neglected and starving in a workhouse that provided no work. The twelfth-century serf, on the other hand, might be a slave with a brass collar around his neck—but he had work, and care, and food.

Carlyle went to see the Abbey for himself, and the ruins stirred him deeply. The nineteenth-century's answer would not do. "Liberty when it becomes the 'Liberty to die by starvation'" he decided, "is not so divine."

Putting aside the biography of Cromwell he'd been writing, he poured out *Past and Present* (1843) in two short months, depicting how much better off the serf—Gurth, he called him—was under his master Cedric: "Gurth, with the brass collar round his neck, tending Cedric's pigs in the glades of the wood, is not what I call an exemplar of human felicity." But, Carlyle went on, the serf-master roles of Gurth and Cedric were the way things should be, and were accepted by both: "Gurth's brass collar did not gall him; Cedric *deserved* to be his Master. The pigs were Cedric's, but Gurth too would get his parings of them."

For today's visitor, the spot among those ruins where the church's high altar stood has special meaning. There one day in November of 1214, the barons of England stood and took their oath to make King John yield them their lawful rights. Proof of their success, won at Runnymede the following year, is the document now known as Magna Carta.

The Abbey grounds are filled with points of interest, but if time is limited, go out in the street, this time via the south entrance gate—the twelfth-century Norman Tower (3) which later became the bell tower for St. James Church, (4) now the Cathedral.

As you begin going up Churchgate Street, you'll see on your right the

Athenaeum, (5) the eighteenth-century assembly hall where Charles Dickens gave readings on a number of occasions, staying of course at the Angel just behind it. Further along Churchgate on the right, after you cross Hatter Street, is the historic Unitarian Chapel (6) built in 1711, with its original three-decker pulpit and box pews (now moved to the gallery).

At the end of Churchgate you'll come to Guildhall Street. Turn right onto Guildhall, and almost immediately on your right you'll see the medieval Guildhall (7) itself. It was the meeting place of guildsmen who supplied the town's aldermen and mayor from the days of Lydgate to the end of 1966.

Next up Guildhall Street you come to Abbeygate Street again. Take a right onto Abbeygate, then immediately a left onto The Traverse. The big old house that you'll see on the right is Cupola House, (8) built for an apothecary in 1693. It was almost brand new when Defoe stayed there in 1704. And a few years earlier, it had hardly opened its doors when it was inspected by another writer who had no idea she *was* a writer.

She was Celia Fiennes, granddaughter of Viscount Saye, whose journal of her visits to every county in England had to wait until 1888 to be published, under the intriguing title of *Through England on a Side Saddle in the Time of William and Mary*. Though her spelling was inventive, her account of Cupola House shows that her ability as an observer was considerable. It was, she wrote, "at least 60 stepps up from the ground and gives a pleaseing prospect of the whole town, that is compack severall streets but no good buildings; except this, the rest are great old houses of timber and mostly in the forme of the country which are very long peaked roofs of tileing; this house is in the new mode of building, 4 rooms of a floor pretty sizeable and nigh . . ." and on and on she goes to describe it floor by floor from top to ground floor where the apothecary kept his shop.

Cupola House is now a pub, one of the two on the tour handy should thirst overpower you. The other is also right here on The Traverse. Called The Nutshell, it is supposed to be England's smallest, and holds only six people.

At the end of The Traverse, another right turn brings you in a step or two to Butter Market and Moyses Hall, (9) originally two twelfth-century dwellings but now converted into the Burough Museum. Alongside archeological exhibits and a thirteenth-century monk's chronicle, it has mementoes of home town novelist Ouida. The pen name came because as a child, "Ouida" was the closest that Marie Louise de la Ramée could come to pronouncing Louise. In all she wrote forty-five novels, but few are remembered now other than *Under Two Flags* (1867).

From Moyses Hall, it's no distance at all down Butter Market to where a left turn on to Abbeygate takes you back to Angel Hill and The Angel Hotel, where much awaits you.

Mr. Pickwick's coach, finished with its rattling through those well-paved streets, stops

> before a large inn, situated in a wide, open street, nearly facing the old abbey.
>
> "And this," said Mr. Pickwick, looking up, "is the Angel! We alight here, Sam."

Dickens himself stayed at The Angel often, from his earliest days in the 1830s as an unknown reporter coming up from London to cover the Suffolk elections to those readings at the Athenaeum as perhaps the most popular author in the whole world. Edward FitzGerald shared his enthusiasm for the place. His idea of heaven, FitzGerald once said, was "to look at the Abbey Gate—from the windows of The Angel Inn just opposite—with a Biscuit and a Pint of Sherry—as I have so often done."

A handsome ivy-covered structure, The Angel thrives still, full worthy of its three-star rating. Its origins date from 1452, when it was build as a hospice for the Abbey, and the medieval cellars with their arched vaultings survive.

Reminders of Dickens include a Pickwick Bar and, up one flight of stairs, his favorite bedroom when he stayed there. Attached to a wall en route is a framed check dated 1869 for £15 "to Mrs. Alfred Dickens—or bearer."[12] The bedroom, now called the Dickens Room, is No. 15, and has Dickens's own canopied bed and his dressing table.

There couldn't be a better place to end a trek through Norfolk and Suffolk than Bury St. Edmunds. What William Cobbett said of his own report of a similar tour of Suffolk may serve as well for both counties: "To conclude an account of Suffolk, and not to sing the praise of Bury St. Edmunds would offend every creature of Suffolk birth."

---

[12]Mrs. Alfred Dickens was Charles Dickens's sister-in-law.

CAMBRIDGESHIRE

Cambridgeshire

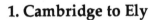 **1. Cambridge to Ely**

 **2. To Wisbech and the End**

3. Access or Connecting Routes

If you came this way,
Taking the route you would be likely to take
From the place you would be likely to come from,
If you come this way in May time, you would find the hedges
White again, in May, with voluptuary sweetness.

T. S. Eliot, "Little Gidding"

The whole place is very lovely with apple blossom now, later with roses. Will you come and stay here? I can promise you bathing and all manner of rustic delights, cheese and fruits, and expeditions into Cambridge to see the people and buildings there.

Rupert Brooke in a letter to a friend, 1910

But let my due feet never fail
To walk the studious Cloysters pale,
And love the high embowed Roof,
With antick Pillars massy proof,
And storied Windows richly dight,
Casting a dimm religious light.

John Milton, "Il Penseroso"

Cambridgeshire *is* Cambridge, of course, home of those "Cloysters pale" of Milton's poem, and producer of an unparalleled array of writers. But the quotations from T. S. Eliot and Rupert Brooke remind us that there is another Cambridgeshire, a Cambridgeshire of open countryside, flat and wet as befits an East Anglian county, crisscrossed by dykes and canals and fens. A Cambridgeshire, therefore, that produces those white hedges and roses and apple blossoms, too, and fruit in great abundance.

Aside from Cambridge, it is true, the county is not rich in literary spots. But in addition to Little Gidding and Cambridge, there are some: Huntingdon, with William Cowper and his first hymns, for instance . . . St. Ives, with Carlyle and *Past and Present* . . . Christchurch, with Dorothy Sayers and *The Nine Tailors* . . . and Grantchester, with Rupert Brooke and others who loved it dearly.

Cambridgeshire is not a large county—roughly forty miles by forty miles—and has only two cities of any size at all: Cambridge, with a little more than one hundred thousand people, and Peterborough with a little less. From London, Cambridge and the county are scarcely an hour away, fifty miles or so straight up the M 11. Suffolk is even closer—only ten miles or so via the A 45.

1. Cambridge to Ely

Cambridge

England's two great universities owe their locations and names to one simple fact: their sites were at a practical place to cross a stream. One, on the river Thames, was where oxen could ford: Oxen-ford. The other was where the river Granta could be bridged: Granta-brycge. When time softened the pronunciation to *Cam*bridge, the natives obligingly changed the name of the river to Cam, too, though Granta is still heard.

As benefits an East Anglian town, Cambridge is flat, and surrounded by wetlands. To the north lie the fens, to the south the swamps. Nowhere is the elevation more than fifty feet above sea level. Early British earthworks and Roman remains bespeak antiquity, but nothing much seems to have happened on the site before 1209, when riots shut down lectures at Oxford and a handful of students fled to a school of sorts existing at Cambridge.

By the end of the thirteenth century, things really began to pick up. The Bishop of Ely endowed Cambridge's first college, Peterhouse, in 1284, and by the end of the fifteenth century there were twelve colleges. When Erasmus, author of *The Praise of Folly* (1509) and Europe's leading scholar, came in 1510 to teach Greek, the school's status was assured.

Comparison of Oxford and Cambridge is inevitable. Cambridge seems smaller, though actually they are about of a size, with something over one hundred thousand people apiece. Cambridge doesn't seem quite so overrun, either. For one thing, it's a bit out of the way for split-second coach tours like "Blenheim-Oxford-Stratford-The Cotswolds-Bath-and-Wells . . . In Six Heavenly Days!!" For another it has no such great industrial works like car-maker William Morris established in Oxford in 1913.

But most of all, perhaps, it's because of the Backs, those green, secluded havens of peace and quiet that run from behind the Cambridge colleges to the banks of the gentle little Cam. You'll love the Backs as Henry James did, the "loveliest confusion," as he put it in *Portraits of Places* (1883), of "sun-chequered avenues and groves, of lawns and gardens and terraces, of single-arched bridges spanning the little stream."

The students of each school have always made their own comparisons of the two, of course—usually sharp, rarely impartial. Oxford's John Evelyn dispatched Cambridge, town and gown alike, in a single entry in his *Diary* for September, 1654: ". . . the whole Towne situated in a low dirty unpleasant place, the streets ill paved, the air thick, as infested by the fennes; nor are its Churches (of which St. Maries is the best) anything considerable in comparre to Oxford which is doubtless the noblest Universitie now in the whole World."

The sons of Cambridge could be equally Olympian. Nothing delighted Tennyson and his friends—Arthur Hallam, Edward FitzGerald, and other members of the elite group known as The Apostles—more than sitting around smoking their pipes, eating anchovy sandwiches and ridiculing those "cursed, idiotic oxford brutes." (Small "o" for Oxford, of course.)

Matthew Arnold's praise of his own alma mater in "Sweetness and Light" (1869) may have been striking a glancing blow at Cambridge when he says: "Yet we in Oxford, brought up amidst the beauty and sweetness of that beautiful place, have not failed to seize one truth—the truth that beauty and sweetness are essential characters of a complete human perfection."

A phrase in that same essay does suggest a major difference between the two schools, though Arnold was talking about the liberal religious leaders of his day, not about the universities. For "the Dissidence of Dissent" fits many a Cambridge man. Much more than those of Oxford, they have been a feisty and, often enough, rebellious lot.

In the sixteenth-century there are Spenser, Marlowe, and Ben Johnson defying the traditions and—Marlowe and Jonson at least—even the authorities of the Elizabethans. There is Milton in the seventeenth century, spokesman for the rebels of the Commonwealth and denouncer of the king himself. There are Wordsworth and Coleridge in *Lyrical Ballads* (1798) overturning the whole tenor of eighteenth-century poetry.

There are Byron, mocking everything the early nineteenth century held sacred, and Darwin, with *Origin of Species* (1859) threatening the core of Victorian belief. And finally in our own century, there is the Bloomsbury Group—born of Saturday night sessions in the Cambridge rooms of Virginia Woolf's brother Thoby Stephen, Leonard Woolf, Lytton Strachey, and Maynard Keynes—shattering the complacency of Edwardian society.

The other Cambridge, the tranquil one reflected in Milton's "studious Cloysters pale," is also recalled by E. M. Forster, Tennyson, and Coleridge. In *Longest Journey* (1906), Forster is thinking as much of himself as he is of his hero when he says Cambridge "soothed him, and warmed him, and laughed at him a little." In *In Memoriam* (1850), Tennyson yearns for the "revered walls/In which of old I wore the gown," and the days with Hallam and The Apostles:

> Where once we held debate, a band
> Of youthful friends, on mind and art,
> And labor, and the changing mart,
> And all the framework of the land.

In *Biographia Literaria* (1817) Coleridge sounds remarkably like Milton when he writes of "the friendly cloisters and the happy grove of quiet, ever honoured Jesus College." Yet Coleridge himself provides one of countless examples of just how lively—some would say rowdy—a place Cambridge could also be. Not only did Coleridge once drop out of school for a time to join the King's Light Dragoons and masquerade as "Pvt. Silas Tomkyn Comberbacke," but while at Jesus College he traced the revolutionary words "Liberty and Equality" in gunpowder on the lawn outside and set fire to them.

Similarly rollicking tales abound. Since Cambridge forbade pet dogs, Byron impudently found a substitute. Said he in a letter: "I have got a new friend, the finest in the world, a tame bear. When I brought him here, they asked me what I meant to do with him, and my reply was, he should sit for a fellowship."

After graduation from Cambridge, Thomas Gray returned to live at Peterhouse as a fellow, and fell victim to some high-spirited undergraduates. Knowing that he was so terrified of fire he kept a rope tied to his window as a means of escape, they had a student stand beneath his window and cry "Fire!", hoping to see the poet slide down the rope into their tub of water below. Legend says he did just that. Truth, alas, says he merely stuck his head outside the window, white nightcap and all—and went back to bed.[1]

Samuel Pepys, a student between 1651 and 1653, records in his *Diary* running into an old Cambridge acquaintance years later, hostess of an inn that friends took him to in Bishop's Stortford, Herts.—a Mrs. Aynsworth whom, Pepys reports slyly, "I knew better than they might think for." As well he might. She was, according to a footnote by Pepys's editor "a noted procuress at Cambridge, banished from that town by the university authorities for her evil courses."

---

[1]Gray also put protective iron bars across his window. If you're walking along Trumpington Street outside Peterhouse, look up and you can see them still.

As Pepys's party prepared to leave the inn the next morning, the account goes on, "their hostess refused to make any charge, saying that she was still indebted to the Vice-Chancellor, who, by driving her out of Cambridge, had made her fortune."

All this reflects a Cambridge lustiness that apparently goes back to its beginnings. After all, when Chaucer in *The Canterbury Tales* talks of Oxford, he depicts the sober-sided Clerk, who adorned his pillow with twenty books of Aristotle and his philosophy, and a psalm book, for: ". . . gladly wolde he lerne and gladly teche."

But Chaucer's Cambridge boys, Aleyn and John, were something else: "Testif [testy, spirited] they were, and lusty for to pley," and lived "oonly for hire [their] myrthe and revelrye." [2] It was Aleyn and John who, in the "Reeve's Tale," seduced both the miller's wife and daughter in a single night.

There is one respect in which the two universities are decidedly alike: writing about alma mater seems to bring out the worst in their poets. The sorriest effusions from Oxford can be matched, line by line, by the sons of Cambridge. Rupert Brooke shows they know better. He's obviously having fun in "The Old Vicarage, Grantchester," when he writes:

> And Cambridgeshire, of all England,
> The shire for Men who Understand.

But Abraham Cowley seems all too serious in "On the Death of Mr. William Harvey" with lines like:

> Ye fields of Cambridge, our dear Cambridge, say
> Have ye not seen us walking every day?

And Wordsworth, unfortunately, is even more so in *The Prelude* as he describes his college quarters with more detail than we really need:

> The Evangelist St. John my patron was:
> Three Gothic courts are his, and in the first
> Was my abiding-place, a nook obscure;
> Right underneath, the College kitchens made
> A humming sound. . . .

Then there's the Elizabethan Thomas Tusser's wonderful offering in "Stanzas" (1580):

---

[2] Their college, which Chaucer calls "Soler Halle," is said to be Clare College founded in 1326.

> In College best of all the rest,
> With thanks to thee, O Trinity!

Tusser's contemporary, Edmund Spenser, gets absolutely carried away in *The Faerie Queene* trying to describe the flow of the River Ouse, which after passing

> By many a city, and by many a towne
>
> ....
>
> Thence doth by Huntingdon and Cambridge flit,
> My mother Cambridge, whom as with a Crowne
> He doth adorne, and is adorn'd of it.

And finally in "Lines on Cambridge 1830," there's the great Tennyson himself recounting its glories:

> Your portals statued with old kings and queens,
> Your gardens, myriad-volumed libraries,
> Wax-lighted chapels, and rich-carven screens,
> Your doctors, and your proctors, and your deans. . . .

Remember, though it was the sons of Cambridge—some of them the same men—who also produced a list of truly great poems matched by no other university, not even Oxford: *The Faerie Queene*, *Paradise Lost*, *The Prelude*, *Don Juan*, and *In Memoriam*.

The advice given for visiting Oxford will serve equally well for touring Cambridge. First, do your homework. Make yourself familiar with the town's points of interest and their locations, select in order those you particularly want to see, and allot your available time accordingly. *Don't try to do too much.* Taking a short, overall guided tour, by bus or afoot, soon after you arrive can be a great help before you venture forth on your own.

When you are on your own, by all means go on foot, or you can spend your whole time fruitlessly looking for a place to park. If you're not staying at a hotel, leave your car in a car park even if the only one with available space isn't quite in the center of town.

And about those hotels: there's a nice variety to choose from—several truly elegant. But Cambridge is like Oxford in one more way—better come with reservations in hand.

Grantchester

Even more than the Cam and Cambridge, Grantchester and the river Granta are inseparable. The village name is practically unchanged from the original "Granta-ceaster" (camp or town on the Granta). So, too, are the meadowlands and great willow trees along its banks that have attracted lovers of quiet and beauty from the fourteenth century of Chaucer to the twentieth century of Rupert Brooke and Jeffrey Archer. By car, the village is only a two-mile drive (south off the A 10) from Cambridge, but the river is *the* way to get there if you have the time—either walking the footpath along its banks, or poling a punt upstream.

The site of Chaucer's mill in "The Reeve's Tale"—"at Trumpyngtoun ther stant a melle"—where young Aleyn and John enjoy that torrid night with the miller's spouse and daughter, was just above the pond known today as Byron's Pool. A powerful swimmer, Byron loved to come there while a student at Cambridge. Wordsworth visited Chaucer's mill, too; and Tennyson, like Byron a Trinity College man, had it in mind when he wrote "The Miller's Daughter." And a contemporary resident of Grantchester is Jeffrey Archer, author of such popular novels as *First Among Equals* and *Kane and Abel*.

This is the spot that Rupert Brooke yearned for while in Germany on school holiday in 1911, when he wrote in "The Old Vicarage, Grantchester":

> Oh, is the water sweet and cool
> Gentle and brown, above the pool!
> And laughs the immortal river still
> Under the mill, under the mill?

Brooke came up to Cambridge in 1906 and lived for several years at his college, King's. But in July of 1909 he moved to Grantchester, taking lodgings at The Orchard. He paid thirty shillings a week, and for this he got a sitting room looking out on the church across the way, a bedroom upstairs, free use of the river garden and the river itself to bathe in, and all his meals. No wonder he wrote ecstatically to friends asking, "Will you come and stay here?"

Lytton Strachey and E. M. Forster were among those who did so, and Virginia Woolf visited Brooke in Grantchester, too.

In 1910, he moved across the street to the Old Vicarage of his poem, still paying only thirty shillings a week, but now getting an extra room along with full board. His hosts, Mr. and Mrs. Neeve, were a warm-hearted pair. Mr. Neeve kept bees and Mrs. Neeve was a grand cook. Together they and the church next door provided the charming last two lines of that poem:

> Stands the Church clock at ten to three
> And is there honey still for tea?

There was honey still for tea when he got back. Mrs. Neeve had read the poem in his college's magazine.

The mill that stood on Chaucer's site burned down in 1928, but the grounds can be visited through the National Gardens Scheme, as can the gardens and grounds of the Old Vicarage, where Brooke wrote a number of his poems. In latter years The Orchard was converted into tea rooms, and at last report still awaits you. Don't count on the honey, though.

You can also, if you like, picnic in the riverside meadow by Byron's Pool. It's maintained as a recreational facility by the Cambridge City Council, and reached by a well-marked footpath. You'll find it particularly handy if instead of walking or punting to Grantchester, you drive over and want to do a bit of looking around. It has almost the only place there to park.

Wimpole Hall

Eight miles southwest of Cambridge, on the north side of the A 603 near New Wimpole is Wimpole Hall. Begun in 1632, in the eighteenth century it was the county seat of Robert Harley, Earl of Oxford, great collector of books and patron of literature.

Alexander Pope and John Dryden were among the many writers he entertained there. Another was that amusing poet Matthew Prior, a special recipient of his lordship's bounty and a frequent visitor. In fact, it was at Wimpole Hall that Prior died, while on a visit in 1721.

An example of Prior's wit is the epitaph he had written for himself years before, in the days of his poverty and political harassment. Defying his high-born adversaries, he impishly sets himself above even Louis XIV of the French royal house of Bourbon and England's King William III of the Dutch house of Nassau:

> Nobles and Heralds, by your leave,
>   Here lies what once was Matthew Prior;
> The son of Adam and Eve
>   Can Bourbon or Nassau claim higher?

Wimpole Hall remains one of the largest and finest mansions in Cambridgeshire. Its last private owner was the daughter of Rudyard Kipling, Mrs. George Bambridge. In 1976, she willed the estate, containing in all 2,443 acres with an approach through a double avenue of elms two and a half miles long and one hundred yards wide, to the National Trust.

Swaffham Prior—Ely—and Christchurch

Swaffham Prior and Ely lie outside Cambridge to the northeast—Swaffham Prior eight miles away on the B 1102, Ely fifteen miles on the A 10. To a man from each, separated by seven centuries, a debt is owed. One was the bishop who gave Cambridge its start as a university. The other gave those of us who can't speak German, Kafka.

Swaffham Prior   In 1956, following a year as the Charles Eliot Norton Professor at Harvard University, a Scotsman named Edwin Muir came to live at Swaffham (SWOFF-'m) Prior. At sixty-nine, he was in a sense beginning all over again. And though he loved Priory Cottage, the little house he moved into, and found the village charming, he had misgivings.

He had been a journalist, a book reviewer, a sometime poet, an occasional teacher of English literature. In 1937, he and his wife Willa had given Franz Kafka a new audience, beginning with their translation of *The Trial*. Now, Muir wrote his friend T. S. Eliot, "I confess that sometimes I have a slightly sinking feeling, knowing that . . . I have nothing to do but write, and must depend on it. But I feel it will be all right."

It was all right. His *Collected Poems*, published in 1960, the year after his death, proved that his place among significant poets of the twentieth century was secure. A tribute to his poem "The Horses," a poem Muir had published the year he came to Swaffham Prior, suggests why. T. S. Eliot says of "The Horses," ". . . that great, that terrifying poem of the 'atomic age,' celebrates the reconstitution of the human and the natural world after the destruction of our mechanized and inhuman 'civilization.'"

Ely   In 1870, Thomas Hardy, thirty years old and about to begin his career as a novelist with *Desperate Remedies*, came to Cambridge for the first time to visit his dear friend, Horace Mount and to see the sights. His diary records one memorable experience: "Next morning went with H. M. to King's Chapel early. M. opened the great West doors to show the interior vista; we got upon the roof where we could see Ely Cathedral gleaming in the distant sunlight. A never-to-be-forgotten morning."

One's first view of Ely Cathedral is indeed never to be forgotten. The area is called the "Isle of Ely" because until the fens were drained in the eighteenth century it was in fact an island, and the cathedral built on a mound rising from those flat lands can be seen for twenty miles or more. It is one of the largest of cathedrals, too. Its length of 537 feet and the great transepts spanning 190 feet surpass those of Canterbury. Its unique octagonal central tower, erected in 1322 to replace one that collapsed, has been called "perhaps the most beautiful design in all Gothic architecture."

The cathedral was begun in 1083 by the Abbot Simeon, whose abbey had been established on the site three centuries before that by St. Etheldreda.[3] Etheldreda's abbey was co-educational, and its monks supplied the more colorful of two explanations of how the town came to be called Ely. Both say the name comes from the Saxton "Eel-ig," meaning eel island, because the waters round about it teemed with eels. Bede's prosaic *Ecclesiastical History of the English People* (731 A. D.) lets it go at that.

But folklore's version tells us WHY all those eels. When St. Dunstan—a bear for celibacy if ever there was one—came to the abbey in the tenth century, you see, he was scandalized at the number of married monks, to say nothing about those who had never found time for a formal ceremony. So he changed every last offender into an eel.

Abbey and cathedral have had an interesting history and made their mark on literature. One of the last holdouts against William the Conquerer was Hereward the Wake, who headed an uprising against William in 1070. When things started going badly, Hereward fled to Ely Abbey for sanctuary, but was betrayed by the abbot himself. Much good it did the abbot. William replaced him with a Norman—Abbot Simeon. Charles Kingsley tells the story of Hereward in his novel *Hereward the Wake* (1865), making Hereward the son of Lady Godiva.

It was the thirteenth-century Bishop of Ely, Hugh (or Hugo) de Balsham, who in effect established Cambridge as a university—partly, it seems, out of pique at his king, Henry III. The monks of Ely elected Hugh their abbot in 1256, but Henry picked a fellow named John de Waleran for the post. When the Pope settled matters by backing de Balsham, Hugh took charge and cleaned house. Among other things, he got a charter in 1280 to sweep out the secular brothers who had been ensconced at St. John's Hospital in Cambridge, and replaced them with his own "studious scholars." Four years later he had this little band of scholars completely separated from the hospital brethren and set them up in an independent entity, endowing it and calling it Peterhouse, the university's first college.

Another Ely monk wrote a forerunner of Edmund Spenser's first important published work. He was a Benedictine called Alexander Barclay who, while serving at Ely, wrote his *Eclogues* between 1515 and 1521. These were the first English pastorals written, anticipating by sixty years and more those

[3]She was the saint whose name—shortened over time to St. Awdrey (or Audrey), then to 't-Audrey—came to describe shoddy goods sold at town fairs. See p. 285.

of Spenser's *Shepheard's Calendar* (1579). Barclay is also remembered for *The Ship of Fools* (1509).

Another of Ely's literary links is with the celebrated tenth-century Anglo-Saxon poem, *The Battle of Maldon*, about an event that took place around 991.[4] Its doughty old hero, Byrthnoth, had been a great benefactor of the Ely Abbey. Learning that their friend had been captured and beheaded at Maldon by the Danes, the abbot and his monks went out, found the headless corpse, and bore it back to their church. There they buried it honorably, placing a round lump of wax where the head should have been.

Centuries later, after the cathedral was built, the body was taken up and buried beneath an effigy of Byrthnoth in the Bishop's West Chantry—at least scholars said the bones were his. In 1769, however, somebody had his doubts. So the bones were dug up, examined, and a report duly sent to the Society of Antiquaries. It was a great day for scholars. No head was found, said the report, and "it was observed that the collar bone had been nearly cut through, as by a battle axe or two-handed sword."

Christchurch   Ten miles north of Ely, Christchurch lies just off the A 1101. Dorothy Sayers, who was born at Bluntisham outside St. Ives, used to spend vacations with her parents at the Christchurch rectory after they moved there in 1917. The fenlands all around Christchurch furnished her with settings for her mystery story about bell-ringing, *The Nine Tailors* (1934).

Fenchurch St. Paul, which housed the bells, was suggested by the church in Upwell. Upper Fen provided the overall locale, and Denver Ducis, the ancestral home of her charming detective Lord Peter Wimsey, was based on the real village of Denver.

2. To Wisbech and the End

Huntingdon—Brampton—and St. Ives

Huntingdon, Brampton, and St. Ives are a pleasant trio of towns seventeen to twenty miles northwest of Cambridge. Largest of the three, with about twenty thousand people, is Huntingdon on the A 604. Brampton is also on the A 604, two and a half miles west of Huntingdon. St. Ives, three miles east of Huntingdon, is on the A 123.

---

[4]For the story see pp. 273–74.

Huntingdon   For William Cowper, Huntingdon was the vital link between St. Albans and the mental asylum where he recovered his sanity and health, and Olney where he wrote *John Gilpin*, *The Task*, *Table Talk*, and the *Olney Hymns*.

Cowper's brother, John, a fellow at Corpus Christi College at Cambridge, had picked Huntingdon because it was near enough for him to check on William several times a week without having him as a daily burden. The poet arrived in June 1765, shepherded by a servant who had nursed him at St. Albans. Their first quarters were in a sixteenth-century house on the High Street down near the George Hotel. But five months later Cowper took lodgings in a much newer house up the High Street. It was a pivotal move.

The house belonged to the Rev. Morley Unwin and his wife Mary. Both were sufficiently older than their new boarder to feel paternal; Morley Unwin was sixty-one, Mary was forty-one. Cowper, thirty-four, quickly became a member of the family. Mr. Unwin, he wrote his friends, was "a Parson Adams in simplicity," and Mary Unwin "of a very uncommon, understanding, who had read much to excellent purpose, and was more polite than a duchess."

For the next nineteen months, nothing disturbed the pattern of their days, placid and infinitely pious. Following breakfast at eight, Cowper reported, came an hour each of reading scripture or sermons and the first of two daily services. From noon to three, he said, "we separate and amuse ourselves as we please." Cowper would read, garden, ride, or walk, often to the River Ouse: "It is a noble stream to bathe in, and I shall make that use of it three times a week."

Then if the weather permitted, they adjourned to the garden and "the pleasure of religious conversations until teatime," or sang hymns around Mrs. Unwin's harpsichord. After tea, he went on, "we sally forth to walk in good earnest . . . generally about four miles before we see home again." At day's end, the account concludes, after supper, "we commonly finish the evening either with hymns or a sermon; and last of all, the family are called to prayers."

It was, Cowper said, "a place of rest prepared for me by God's own hand," a feeling he repeated in his hymn:

> Far from the world, O LORD, I flee,
> From strife and tumult for. . . .

Suddenly the pattern shattered. Toward the end of June 1767, Mr. Unwin suffered a riding accident. On July 2 he died. On September 14, Cowper and Mary Unwin were on their way to Olney to live with the Rev. John Newton.[5]

[5]See p. 58.

Two other famous residents of Huntingdon were Oliver Cromwell and Samuel Pepys, whose histories intertwined in several curious ways. Both came of old local families, both attended Huntingdon Grammar School and Cambridge University, and both made their careers in London but returned to Huntingdon frequently. Most coincidentally of all, both had close ties to Huntingdon's grandest house, the mansion on the edge of town called Hinchinbrooke.

Cromwell was born in Huntingdon in 1599. His ancestors—related to Henry VIII's engineer of the Dissolution, Thomas Cromwell—had become wealthy and titled, and built Hinchinbrooke on the site of the priory that Thomas had received as part of his Dissolution booty. But extravagance undid them. Oliver's father was merely a middle-class farmer and brewer.

Cromwell attended Huntingdon's Grammar School and, briefly, Sidney Sussex College at Cambridge, but returned home to manage the family property after his father's death. Though he moved to St. Ives in 1631, he never lost touch with Huntingdon, once even setting up headquarters there during the revolution.

Samuel Pepys was born in London in 1633. His Uncle Robert, however, lived at Brampton, and it was under his aegis that Samuel went to Huntingdon's Grammar School and Magdalene College at Cambridge. Uncle Robert and Pepys's father provided the ties to Hinchinbrooke House. They were cousins of Lord Sandwich, son of the man who had bought it from the Cromwells. As a result, Pepys was in and about Hinchinbrooke much of his life, living there at one point serving Lord Sandwich.

You can still find reminders of Cowper, Cromwell, and Pepys in Huntingdon. The house Cowper shared with the Unwins survives on the High Street, marked with a plaque. All Saints Church has the register—rescued from the demolished church of St. John—recording Cromwell's birth and baptism and the notation, later excised by some kinder hand: "England's plague for 5 years." The school Cromwell and Pepys attended, also on the High Street, is now the Cromwell Museum, open most days of the week. Hinchinbrooke still stands, too, rebuilt after a great fire in 1830. It now serves as a school, and is frequently used to house antique fairs that are quite successful.

If you like, you can even dine or stay overnight in historic surroundings. The George, a three-star hotel on George Street with pre-Elizabethan origins and an open seventeenth-century gallery overlooking the court, was bought in 1574 by Henry Cromwell, Oliver's grandfather. Ironically enough, in 1645, it served as headquarters for Oliver's adversary, none other than His Majesty, Charles I.

Brampton   Not only while a student at Huntingdon's Grammar School and Cambridge's Magdalene College, but all his life, Samuel Pepys must have felt that his Uncle Robert's cottage in Brampton was home. First and foremost, even at the pinnacle of his career, he considered himself a Brampton man. His bookplates read: "Samuel Pepys of Brampton in Huntingdonshire,[6] Esq., Secretary of the Admiralty to his Maty King Charles the Second: Descended from ye antient family of Pepys of Cottenham in Cambridgeshire." His feelings were enhanced by knowing that the cottage would one day be his. Robert Pepys had promised to leave it to his younger brother John, Samuel's father.

John Pepys did inherit it and retired to it in 1661. In his *Diary* entry for October 10, 1667, Samuel records both his pleasure with the house and his bizarre reason for one particular visit:

> . . . come to Brampton at about noon, and [go] up and down to see the garden with my father, and the house, and do altogether find it pretty; especially the little parlour and the summer-houses in the garden, only the wall do want greens upon it; but that is only because of my coming from a house with higher ceilings. But altogether is very pretty; and I bless God that I am like to have such a pretty place to retire to.

But Pepys had more important things on his mind that day than retirement. In June he had given his gold to his wife and his father to bury for safekeeping temporarily, and they had done so, he later learned, "in open daylight, in the midst of the garden; where, for aught they knew, many eyes might see them." This news, he confessed, so angered him "that I fell out with my wife, that though new come to towne, I did not sup with her, nor speak to her tonight, but to bed and to sleep."

Now in October he was back to recover his gold. It makes a grand story:

> My father and I, with a dark lantern, it being now night, [go] into the garden with my wife, and there went about our great work to dig up my gold. But, Lord! What a tosse I was for some time in, that they could not justly tell where it was; that I begun heartily to sweat, and be angry, that they should not agree better upon the place. . . . God! to see how sillily they did it, not half a foot under ground, and in the sight of the world from a hundred places.

Worse was to come:

---

[6]Brampton was part of the county of Huntingdonshire before the reorganization of counties in 1974.

I was out of my wits, almost, and the more from that, upon my lifting up the earth with the spudd, I did discern that I had scattered the pieces of gold round about the ground among the grass and loose earth.

And worse—for after they'd picked up all the coins they could find, they were "short above a hundred pieces, which did make me mad." So Pepys returns to the garden at midnight with a trusted aide, and again at daybreak:

He and I, with pails and a sieve, did lock ourselves into the garden, and there gather all the earth about the place into pails, and then sift those pails in one of the summerhouses, just as they do for dyamonds in other parts of the world; and there, to our great content, did with much trouble by nine o'clock . . . make the last night's forty-five up to seventy-nine: so that we are come to about twenty or thirty of what I think the true number should be . . . so that I am pretty well satisfied that my loss is not great, and do bless God that it is so well.

There's an interesting P. S. to this tale. In 1842, while part of the old garden wall was being torn down, an iron pot full of silver coins was uncovered. For all his pains, apparently, poor Pepys still didn't get it all.

The cottage itself still stands, and when the owner is on hand, is open for an hour or two most weekdays. Better write for details, though, c/o Pepys House, Brampton.

St. Ives   The best-known literary association with St. Ives, perhaps, is that of Thomas Carlyle and *Past and Present* (1843). It was the site of the prototypical workhouse the book attacks so fiercely—the wretched Victorian style of poor-houses for adults, "pleasantly named" Carlyle said, because they provided no work.

Also connected with St. Ives are Oliver Cromwell, Laurence Sterne, and Theodore Watts-Dunton. Cromwell lived there from 1631 to 1636; his fourteenth-century tithe barn at Green End, north of town, is now known as Cromwell's Barn. That most improbable of clergymen, Laurence Sterne, author of *Tristram Shandy,* began his clerical career as assistant curate of All Saints Church following his graduation from Cambridge in 1737. And Theodore Watts-Dunton was born in St. Ives in 1832. As a boy he came to know the gipsies who lived round about, and depicts them in his novel *Aylwin* (1898).

Little Gidding—Barnack—and Wisbech

Cambridgeshire's last three literary sites—Little Gidding, Barnack, and Wisbech—can all be reached in one easy drive from Huntingdon by making Wisbech your destination and seeing the other two en route.

From Huntingdon, take the A 1 north for about seven miles and turn left when you come to the unnumbered road signposted Little Gidding. When you return to the A 1, continue on north to the outskirts of Peterborough. There turn east on to the A 47, which takes you straight into Wisbech. For a detour to Barnack, just out of Peterborough, take the A 15 north for about five miles, then go west on the B 1443. Even if you make both detours, the whole trip shouldn't be much more than sixty-five miles.

Little Gidding   In the "Little Gidding" section of his *Four Quartets*, after describing those white hedges with their voluptuary sweetness, T. S. Eliot tells what awaits you "if you come this way":

> . . . . you leave the rough road
> And turn behind the pig-sty to the dull facade
> And the tombstone.

The dull facade belongs to an unpretentious little seventeenth-century chapel built on a country lane by the man who lies beneath the tomb, Nicholas Ferrar. Man and chapel alike were humbleness itself. Yet they succoured a fallen king, preserved from flames the works of a poet whom else the world had never known, inspired a Victorian novel, and moved Eliot to write what he called his best poetry.

In 1625, at age thirty-three, Ferrar abandoned a promising parliamentary career to become a chaplain and take a small group to the manor of Little Gidding. Here they established an austere Anglican community dedicated to study and good works. After Ferrar's death in 1637, his followers tried to carry on. But in 1646 their quiet life of service came to a violent end. Puritan troups drove them away and despoiled their house and chapel. For a year earlier, the people had dared to harbor Charles I, the "broken king" of Eliot's poem, after his final defeat at Naseby, and his enemies had not forgotten.

The story of the community appeared in print twice in the last years of the nineteenth-century. A young woman member named Mary Collett had recorded the venture in five bound manuscript volumes, and part of these were published in 1899 as the *Little Gidding Story Books*. Before that in 1880 the Victorian writer Joseph Henry Shorthouse had written a novel called *John*

Inglesant in which he not only had his hero visit Little Gidding, but has him fall in love with the same Mary Collett.

More fascinating than any fiction, however, is the true story of how Nicholas Ferrar alone decided the fate of a poet and his works. Born in 1593 to a family of great power and wealth, this man, too, had renounced worldly success for a life of service and piety. Dying, he sent to Ferrar in 1633 the single manuscript containing all the poems he had written, asking his friend to make an awesome decision: consign them to the flames, or print them.

Fortunately, they were printed. For the man was George Herbert, considered by some to be second only to John Donne among metaphysical poets.

Nicholas Ferrar's little sanctuary was rebuilt in the ninteenth century. So today if you come this way, as Eliot might say, you will find chapel and tomb intact again, along with memorials to both its poets.

Barnack   Within two miles of the Lincolnshire county line, Barnack has a distinct air about it. Everything is built of stone from the local quarries— houses, inns, farm buildings, the church. The rectory was the home of those novel-writing brothers, Charles and Henry Kingsley, where their father was vicar from 1824 to 1830. Charles lived there from age five to age eleven; Henry was born there shortly before the family moved to Clovelly.

Charles's last novel, *Hereward the Wake* (1860) makes extensive use of the country all about Barnack: Bourne, Crowland Abbey, Peterborough, and Ely.[7]

While a boy at the rectory, Charles is supposed to have seen the ghost of an earlier vicar who had been doomed to haunt the place forever for cheating a widow. Apparently part of his punishment involved the wearing of a flowered dressing gown and a nightcap with a button on it. Anyway, the house still stands; the room in which the ghost makes his rounds is called The Button Room, and the building itself, not surprisingly, Kingsley House. Inside it's been divided into two private homes, but the exterior looks as Kingsley would have seen it. So, presumably, does the ghost.

Only two miles northeast of Barnack, is Burghley House, one of England's biggest and grandest mansions. Built by Elizabeth I's lord treasurer and chief minister, William Cecil Lord Burghley (or Burleigh), it provides several literary notes.

Burghley himself is lampooned in Richard Brinsley Sheridan's *The Critic* (1779). In the play, he comes on stage in Puff's burlesque tragedy, "The Spanish Armada," and when questioned can only shake his head, being far

---

[7]For details of the historical Hereward, see p. 337.

too occupied with matters of state to reply. Hence the expression, "Burgh-ley's nod."

In the seventeenth century, both Matthew Prior and John Dryden were at the mansion, Dryden as a guest in 1696, Prior as a tutor in 1688–89. In his "Epistle to Fleetwood Shepherd, Esq." Prior gives a typically light-hearted account of what he did when teaching chores got too much for him:

> Sometimes I climb my Mare, and kick her
> To bottled ale and neighb'ring vicar;
> Sometimes at STAMFORD take a quart. . . .

In 1809, John Clare worked at Burghley House, too, but at a much lower level—he was an apprentice gardener. But he didn't last long, thanks to "irregular habits." It's nice to know that after the publication of his *Poems* (1820), the master of Burghley House gave him a lifetime pension of £50 a year.

Also in the ninteenth century, no fewer than three writers retold the true-life story of Sarah Higgins, a local damsel of lowly birth who married above her station: Tennyson in "The Lord of Burleigh" (1833), Thomas Moore in *Irish Melodies* (1822), and William Hazlitt in *New Monthly Magazine*, also in 1822.

In season, Burghley House and its great collection of paintings, tapestries, and furnishings are on view most afternoons of the week.

Not far from Burghley House, on St. Martin Street in Stamford, is the three-star George Hotel, which despite its early origins is comfortable and well-equipped. It was built in 1597 for Lord Burghley, incorporating parts of a much older Norman hospice, and under its cocktail bar is a crypt that comes close to being a thousand years old. One of its guests was Sir Walter Scott, who stopped by on his way from London to Scotland.

Wisbech Wisbech (WIZ-beech) provides a most appropriate final look at Cambridgeshire and East Anglia, though not on literary grounds. These are hardly impressive and can be briefly told.

The town does have some priceless manuscripts and letters. John Clare was a resident as a youth when he came for a brief and abortive attempt to join a local law firm. And William Godwin, author of *Political Justice* (1793), was born there in 1756. He also wrote two novels, *Caleb Williams* (1794) and *St. Leon* (1799) and a *Life of Chaucer* (1803). But he is best remembered now for his daughter and stepdaughter. The daughter, Mary, married Shelley. The stepdaughter, Claire Clairmont, bore Byron an illegitimate child.

But Wisbech does merit attention as the last outpost of East Anglia.

Barely five miles away is Lincolnshire, where people not only sound different; they and their land look different. Wisbech eptomizes so many of the characteristics that set East Anglia apart—the part that retreats from the sea, the river that constantly shifts, the canals and their suggestion of the Dutch, and above all the fens.

Wishbech calls itself the Capital of the Fens, and with good reason. The repository of its relics of the past, and custodian of such literary treasurers as it does have, is called not The Wisbech Museum, but The Wisbech and *Fenland* Museum.

Tucked away just off an ancient churchyard bestrewn with leaning tombstones and yews, the museum has as incredible an assortment of odds and ends as you're likely to see under one small roof. Among the local memorabilia, paintings, letters, manuscripts, books, fossils, stuffed birds, and who knows what else, are a marble statue of some boy and his dog and a breakfast service captured from Napoleon's camp equipage.

Much of this was the gift of a wealthy landowner, Chauncey Hare Townshend, who packed it off to Wisbech in 1868 in two large covered wagons that required three horses apiece. And no wonder: there were fifty-one packages in all, weighing a total of fifteen tons. Of interest here is the fact that Townshend was a friend of a number of writers, among them Southey and Dickens, and amid the mélange he shipped off were letters of Robert Burns, Charles Lamb, John Clare, Swift, Goethe, Keats, and Byron. There are also first editions of Dickens's novels autographed by the author, and the manuscripts of his *Great Expectations* (1860–61) and Matthew Gregory Lewis's *The Monk* (1796). The manuscripts, however, are available only to serious scholars, who must qualify in advance—in writing—to see them.

As Wisbech provides the appropriate final look, so does that son of Cambridgeshire and ubiquitous traveler, Samuel Pepys, Esq., supply the fitting last words for what David Copperfield called this "spongey and soppy" land.

In a diary entry for September 17–18, 1663, Pepys describes a journey made "with much ado, through the fens, along dikes, where sometimes we were ready to have our horses sink to the belly." It is, he says, "a sad life which the people do live, sometimes rowing from one spot to another, and then wadeing." But these are independent people, too, these East Anglians, and determined. Like all good travelers, they get to where they are going. In Pepys's case, it was

> ". . . to Wisbeach, a pretty town."

INDEX

Key to the Index
1. AUTHORS: are in all capital letters
2. *Titles*: are in italics
3. Churches: are included if they are
   a. actual (not fictional)
   b. extant
   c. of enough literary interest to warrant a visit
4. Hotels—Inns—Restaurants—Pubs: are included only if they are
   a. actual (not fictional)
   b. of literary interest
   c. still serving the public.
A separate listing of such places also appears at the end of this index, arranged by cities with the page numbers where they are discussed.

Hotels, Inns, Restaurants and Pubs

A Note About the Author

At the time of his death, Robert M. Cooper had completed writing *The Literary Guide and Companion to Middle England*, second in a planned trilogy. His successful *Literary Guide and Companion to Southern England* was published by the Ohio University Press in 1985. Dr. Cooper was Professor Emeritus of English Literature at Rhodes College, Memphis, Tennessee.